A Guide to
DFW Private Schools

First printing 1991
Second printing 1993
Third printing 1996
Fourth printing 1999

ISBN
0-9627445-4-9

Printed in the United States of America

A Guide to DFW Private Schools

A handbook of everything you
need to know about the
Dallas-Fort Worth Metroplex
private schools

Lynn H. Magid
assisted by Cindy Perkins
and Shirin Khalili

Southwest Business Graphics
A Division of Southwest Forms
George Bryan, President
2414 Merrell Road
P.O. Box 29730
Dallas, Texas 75229
(972) 620-8700

Contents

CHAPTER 2

CHAPTER 3

CHAPTER 4

Acknowledgments

My sincere gratitude goes out to the fantastic staff that facilitated this publication. I always relish writing my Thank You list. The numerous changes in this 4th edition reflect the many obstacles that were necessary to overcome. This staff of very committed people has endured endless lists and more lists, and I am delighted with the format changes that enhance this 4th edition.

I would like to thank each and every participating school for sharing their information with the community members in a comparative format. You have been very informative to the readers, and each detail is greatly appreciated. Your contribution has facilitated our goal of meeting the needs of families, future educators, resource specialists, realtors and all those interested in private school education. The number of schools continues to increase in Dallas to accommodate the diverse needs of our children. We are fortunate to have numerous choices from various categories of schools. The Executive Directors of the accrediting organizations were instrumental in explaining to which guidelines the schools must adhere, and I thank them for their involvement.

Many thanks also to Cindy Perkins who managed the production of the book, web site, graduation, and wedding plans. I appointed myself her "spiritual Guidance counselor" and I hope to be always in your thoughts about work, marriage, and children. Your dedicated work is finally in print!

Next, the torch has been passed to Shirin Khalili. She worked hard to learn all the schools in a short time and tuned up all the categories. While working on the book, Shirin has moved homes, begun a new job, started her child in preschool, and coped with the technical elements of the web site. She remained calm and stable under these stressful circumstances, while I became frustrated with the wires, networking and phone tag!

Also, thanks to Debbie Wayne who was the elected calling master. She is as persistent as they come and always accurate with her information. Debbie had the task of re-interpreting my information when I went into "Lynn Psycho-Babble" mode. Thanks to her, the written presentations are more easily understood. I have watched her 4 year-old grow to become a young man and walk down the aisle in marriage. I know it is an exciting time, as she now accepts the role of a parent-hood graduate. Also, she has spread her wings and is in the classroom making a difference in children's lives. Best of luck, Deb. Remember all you've learned!

Gary Klingemann always said, "My job is to create the vision that you are trying to portray." Gary, as always I love your devotion to the guide and the fantastic design of the new book. The website, despite all the programming obstacles, is wonderful and I'm proud of our accomplishment. "Thank you" is never enough. I am grateful for your accuracy and the extraordinary graphic designs.

Bob Walton is a fantastic gentleman on the staff at Mapsco. I would not have been able to produce the precise map coverage without his expertise. Thank you for your endless commitment.

Sally Brown helped to coordinate all the pre-plotting, additions, and deletions, and served as a co-pilot in that very important chapter of the guide. She also developed a library room in our new office. Thanks for your dependability and precise eyes. You are really a genuine person.

Susan Rich is a wonderful mother whose 8th child is on the way. She was an asset in proofing the final manuscript. She also managed to find time to "school shop", select, and place her son in a new environment for the fall. I appreciate the night hours she spent reading the material. Thanks to her, the consistency of the book is wonderful.

Monica Spivey was the typesetter with whom it was wonderful to work. You always managed to be more organized and efficient than we ever were. Enjoy the brief vacation until the 5th edition!

George Bryan is my publisher with never-ending patience. I hope we can turn this book into an annual project. Congratulations on your daughter's acceptance into a premier school. As you nurture your daughters and their education, your values will be instilled in them.

Dennis Reed has been a very responsible, serious, thorough, and efficient office manager. I hope that one morning our conversation won't begin, "Lynn, let me tell you really seriously, you don't have the money." So, for the future, I have set my goals to hear the optimistic lecture, "There is sufficient money to pay all your bills." You managed to keep me in line and kept up with my constantly changing plans. I also appreciate all the extras you have done to assist me and accommodate my schedule.

Ruth Srulevitch has been a soft-spoken voice of wisdom, a gift which I have always admired. I appreciated your professional responses about school placement scenarios. You always kept me together and my projects organized. I value that. Thank you!

4

Anita Speier's sense of humor was always a bright spot in my days, as was the realism she brought to the office with her sage advice.

Joey Music Daniel's quick grasp of the project and great focus on details was greatly appreciated. I admire your enthusiasm and wish you the best of luck teaching!

Hilary Simon worked for me during the summers of 1998 and 1999. Her accomplishments are displayed in all four chapters. Hilary was there for the culmination of the publication and always smiled, despite changes that have been made along the way. The work ethic you displayed has convinced me that you will be a well-prepared adult. Thank you, Hilary, for sorting, checking, typing, and for spending part of your summer with me. My door is always open and I am glad you are now an accreditation expert.

Alyson Magid is my youngest niece and a person whom I truly miss. She was always aware of everything, and has oodles of talent. Once I unlocked her abilities, she became an indispensable asset. You have great memory skills, and I know the children will enjoy having you as their teacher.

Andrew Srulevitch your timing was perfect and we appreciate your editorial assistance!

Devon & Connor Youngblood were fantastic workers and very helpful. Thank you for all of your assistance.

Many wonderful thanks to my family:

My parents, Nancy & Ronnie Horowitz — you are always supportive and tolerant of my continuously chaotic lifestyle. To Mom — who wears the crown of Elle, Vogue, and Cosmo and annually informs me of the newest fashion for professionalism — Kelsey and Kirby are your next fashion statements. Dad, your advice has always been enlightening and wise. I am in your debt. You have made each edition possible. You are an inspiration for me always to do my best. This is why I feel the need to share my research. You are my models as strong, independent, and confident people. But you forgot to mention that child rearing was a full time joy!

AJ — I know how hard it was to have a working summer. Even though your spending habits reflect your mom's, you learned to earn. The help was invaluable.

Kelsey — I love your constant enthusiasm for life. Your ability to sort and to organize was always helpful. Have a great year in 3rd grade.

Kirby — I love how you enjoy collecting things and keep busy while I have to read, read, read. Your first grade marker is the end of my pre-school era. I' m a pre-school, kindergarten and primmer mom graduate.

To my husband Jeffrey, I appreciate all your patience and how you have grown accustomed to "the pile decor." House Beautiful will be out real soon to photo the essentials! You have always separated the unrealistic from the realistic and accepted how important it is to me to educate people about school choices. Despite my inability to cook and my hectic lifestyle, you have steadfastly supported me. I could not seesaw alone. We go up & down, but we go together.

My reason for the highlighted extra tidbits about these people is that, despite having different personalities, we managed to cooperate and make things happen. All of us were overcoming problems and trying to find a balance. However, I think going with the unexpected is the real key to it all. On my way to board a plane to Atlanta last weekend, I got in the car with my father. He asked why I had two suitcases for an overnight trip, one filled with clothes and the other with the manuscript. I said, "Simplicity and Communication is my new credo." He turned his head, smiled, and replied, "I think that is much easier said than done."

Friendship:

It involves many things, but above all, the power of going out of one's self and seeing and appreciating whatever is noble and loving in another.
— Thomas Hughes

Shanaz Amin — For weekly maintenance on my nails. She always listens and offers opinions on hair, fashion, child rearing and headaches.

Charlotte Hazel — For weekly tune-ups and constant concern for my well being. "YOU ARE TOO STRESSED OUT" is her mantra. She acts like my second mother and is so proud of all my accomplishments. I thank her for sharing in my happiness.

Lynn Nolan — I know I am on the eraser end of your pencil as we continue to try to stretch out this stressed out body. But, hey, at least I'm consistent and show commitment. Your encouragement and physical guidance is appreciated, as I am at my all-time high.

Pam Burger— "Oh, G-d, Lynn" seems to be your favorite expression to start our conversations. I am so glad you are back to town, since I need to remain friends. You will volunteer for the millennium 5th edition, or else!

Cris Watson— You are always ready to discuss any important topic, without losing the element of fun. I always appreciate your feedback on the book and parenting suggestions.

Dianne Eyles— I hope one day the shoe will be on the other foot in our friendship, so I can laugh at your day! Thanks for helping me cope.

Lesley Armstrong — 007 remains alive and all waiters take note — she always changes the recipe.

Rebecca Siegel— Dinner & make-up always does the trick! I look forward to those enlightening experiences.

Carolyn Cheatum— Our monthly dinners are always a real treat for me. You have always remained a true friend in every sense of the word.

During the past three years I have had the pleasure of assisting many special students to acquire the skills for academic success. To each and every one that I have had the pleasure of knowing, I want to say that you all have a special strength and talent that will guide you in your educational endeavors. I'm glad to have shared a sliver of it with you. My thanks to you for keeping me informed about schools from your perspective and for sharing your thoughts about education.

To all the parents: I know that you will plan a strategy and your child will help you find your way.

Without the endless support of those listed above, this fourth edition would not have been possible.

This edition is dedicated
in loving memory of my grandmother,
Mrs. Fannie S. Herman.

A Perspective
from the Author...

All parents want quality education for their children, but often they confuse "the best school" with "the right school". A school that is appropriate for one child may not be right for another. In my opinion, the right school is one in which your child enjoys the curriculum, has good peer relationships and is a facility that you can support as a family. If the child is happy at his or her school and you are satisfied with the academic aspects, I recommend re-enrolling your child. However, sometimes it is necessary to explore other options and re-assess what feels appropriate both for your child and for you.

My first piece of advice is to take advantage of school open house question-and-answer discussions. They are an excellent way to get a sense of the school environment. After visiting several schools, you should begin to research independently each school that might provide a comfortable match for your child. If you discover the programs that you are pursuing are right for your child, then the schools will provide you with admittance policies and procedures. My experiences with each child have confirmed my belief in two educational principles: first and foremost, you should always trust your instincts; and secondly, you need to be objective and honest about your child's ability and the schools' expectations.

Sometimes research alone is not sufficient. As an education strategist, I have had the opportunity to meet with families to discuss complex issues concerning their educational choices. Common issues are:

1. A child is asked to relocate to a more appropriate school after learning differences are discovered.
2. The family is new to the DFW area.
3. The parents want an additional and independent opinion when choosing between schools to which their child has been accepted.
4. Parents seek additional advice about school evaluation criteria.
5. Parents are overwhelmed by the entire admissions and selection process and want to discuss their options , and understand the procedure.

As a parent of three, I have personally experienced many unexpected school changes. I have learned from my own experiences and those of my consultation families that finding the right school for your child takes time and patience. I hope this guide and the companion Web site, www.dfwprivateschools.com, will enhance your school selection process.

Education is what survives when what has been learned has been forgotten.
— B.F. Skinner

Procedural Suggestions for Selecting a School

_____Conduct first-round research on schools of potential interest. Attempt to begin 12 months before the "first day of school."

_____Set up appointments to tour the schools or attend open houses.

_____Conduct second-round research on candidate schools.

_____Complete the necessary paperwork for each school in which you have an interest.

_____Set up an appointment for an admissions assessment.

_____Grades 5 and above require scores from the ISEE test. Ask the school for forms to register for the test.

_____Check on the final notification procedure (e.g. personal call or letter).

_____Schedule and attend your child's follow-up evaluation conference with admissions. Be sure to attend whether your child is accepted or declined.

If your current plan does not work out as you expected, do not despair. You will always be able to develop a new educational plan. I have never seen a child left "school-less." Dallas and Fort Worth are filled with a variety of educational possibilities, including home schooling, public school, private and alternative schools.

The more faithfully you listen to the voices within you,
the better you will hear what is sounding outside.
— Dag Hammarskjold

Preface

I planned this 4th publication to inform readers, who are interested in learning about the variety of educational choices. As a parent, my role expanded when faced with placing my own children in proper school environments. During this process in 1991, many problems presented themselves in selecting a school. In discussions with other parents, I found that a common concern is knowing what school options are available. While reputation and "word-of-mouth" are always excellent sources of information, I decided that a factual resource book about Dallas-Fort Worth area private schools would help parents decide which educational facilities would be suitable for their children.

This handbook was compiled as an informative reference for parents with concise summaries of schools admission policies, curricula, philosophies and other pertinent information. All of the schools listed were invited to submit detailed information about themselves. A nominal fee was charged for that information to be included in the guide in order to help finance the publication. Even schools that declined to participate are included in the alphabetical listing in Chapter 4 for you to pursue independently. Each school was responsible for providing the factual information for this publication. While the author compiled this material, no representation or guarantee is made by the author for its accuracy.

Any parent interested in a particular school should visit the educational institution and follow procedures designed by that school for application and admission.

I also decided that a Web site would be a good companion to the book format (as strongly suggested by a father and a previous family consultation). The Web site would be an advantageous way to share the schools' information worldwide. With the assistance of many talented individuals, we designed a large database on the schools and amassed a wealth of information. The Web site, www.dfwprivateschools.com, has been visited by people both inside the United States and beyond. Many families are re-locating to the Dallas-Fort Worth Metroplex. They plan their school options first and then locate their home. These facts are all gathered in this book to assist you, as a parent, to decide which school will adhere to your needs.

If you are interested in learning more about sponsoring a school for future publications or for the Web site, please contact us at (972) 702-9133 or e-mail us at info@dfwprivateschools.com. We will be expanding the features of the site and adding schools throughout the year. Together we can keep the DFW Metroplex informed and aware of what our private school sector has to offer. Please visit us at www.dfwprivateschools.com and keep us bookmarked.

As long as one keeps searching, the answers come.

— Joan Baez

Glossary of Terms

Accreditation: A voluntary process that schools may choose to pursue. The various accrediting organizations have specific requirements, standards and guidelines to which each school must adhere. Upon completion, the participating schools receive credentials which maintain the standards for their institution.

ACCS: Association of Classical Christian Schools

ACSI: Association of Christian Schools International

ACST: Association of Christian Schools of Texas

ACTABS: Accreditation Commission of the Texas Association of Baptist Schools

Additional Schools: An educational facility that is currently not licensed or accredited. Accreditation is NOT MANDATORY in Texas. It is a voluntary process.

Affiliation/Organization: A variety of educational associations which are available to schools and individuals by voluntary membership to enhance their professional development.

Alternative Schools: An educational facility that implements an individualized or alternative curriculum to meet the specific needs of its students.

AMI: American Montessori International

AMITOT: Association of Montessori International Teachers of Texas

AMS: American Montessori Society

ASESA: Association for Specialized Elementary School Accreditation

Blue Ribbon Schools: Schools with strong leadership, high-quality teaching, a challenging curriculum, a commitment to parental involvement, and evidence that the school helps all students achieve high standards. The U.S. Department of Education awards this honor to schools that have demonstrated a strong commitment to educational excellence.

CASE: Council for the Advancement and Support of Education

CCMS: Child Care Management Services

COPSES: Council of Private Specialized Education Services

Curriculum Alternative: An educational facility that implements a specialized curriculum which is unique to that school.

DAEYC: Dallas Association for the Education of Young Children

ICAA: International Christian Accrediting Association

ISAS: Independent School Association of the Southwest

LSAC: Lutheran Schools Accreditation Commission

MACTE: Montessori Accreditation Council for Teachers in Education

MDO: Mother's Day Out

Montessori: An educational facility that implements Maria Montessori's philosophy of early childhood education.

NAEYC: National Association for the Education of Young Children

NAIS: National Association of Independent Schools

NCACS: North Central Association of Colleges and Schools

NCSA: National Christian Schools Association of America

Non-public/private school: An institution that educates students independently according to its own curriculum. Schools operate under a profit or non-profit status.

NLSA: National Lutheran School Association

ORUEF: Oral Roberts University Educational Fellowship

Public School: A school or educational institution supported by taxation from local or state sources.

SACS: Southern Association of Colleges and Schools

SAES: Southwestern Association of Episcopal Schools

SAILS: Schools with Alternative and Independent Learning Strategies

SECA: Southern Early Childhood Association

TAAPS: Texas Alliance of Accredited Private Schools

TACLD: Texas Association of Children with Learning Disabilities

TAEYC: Texas Association for the Education of Young Children

TANS: Texas Association of Non-Public Schools

TAPS: Texas Association of Private Schools

TCCED: Texas Catholic Conference Education Department

TDPRS: Texas Department of Protective and Regulatory Services requires child care programs to meet minimum standards and guidelines in order to be licensed.

TEA: Texas Education Agency

TEPSAC: Texas Private School Accreditation Commission

TSDA: Texas Seventh Day Adventist School System

Chapter I
TEPSAC
Overview of the Texas Private School Accreditation Commission

ACCREDITATION INFORMATION

The Texas Private School Accreditation Commission (TEPSAC) helps ensure quality in private schools by monitoring and approving organizations that accredit the various non-public elementary and secondary educational institutions in Texas.

TEPSAC, which began operating in 1986, is NOT an accrediting organization. It is instead a confederation of accrediting associations whose primary purpose is to maintain standards of accreditation among its membership. Individual schools may seek accreditation from a TEPSAC associate member. Accrediting organizations monitor the quality of the accredited schools through on-site visits at least once every five years.

The following organizations have been recognized by TEPSAC and the Commissioner of Education:

Association of Christian Schools International (ACSI) South-Central Region
4300 Alpha Road, Suite 205
Dallas, Texas 75244
John Schimmer, Ed.D.
(972) 991-2822 Fax: (972) 991-5303
www.acsi.org E-mail: John Schimmer@acsi.org

Accreditation Commission of the Texas Association of Baptist Schools (ACTABS)
P.O. Box 97215
Waco, Texas 76798
Randy Woods, Executive Director
(254) 710-2410

International Christian Accrediting Association (ICAA)
7777 South Lewis Avenue - LRC 310
Tulsa, OK 74171
David Hand, Director
(918) 495-7054 Fax: (918) 495-6191
www.icaa1.org E-mail: icaa@oru.edu

Independent Schools Association of the Southwest (ISAS)
4700 Bryant Irvin Court, Suite 204
Fort Worth, Texas 76104
Geoffrey C. Butler, Executive Director
(817) 569-9200 Fax: (817) 569-9103
www.isasw.org E-mail: gbutlerisas@worldnet.att.net

The Texas District, The Lutheran Church- Missouri Synod (LSAC)
7900 E. Highway 290
Austin, Texas 78724-2499
(512) 926-4272 Fax: (512) 926-1006
www.txdistlcms.org E-mail:WVHinz@aol.com

National Christian Schools Association of America
P.O. Box 28295
Dallas, Texas 75228-0295
(214) 270-5495

National Association for the Education of Young Children (NAEYC)
1509 16th Street N.W.
Washington, D.C. 20036-1426
Dr. Sue Bredekamp
1(800) 424-2460 ext. 360
www.naeyc.org E-mail: naeyc@naeyc.org
(NAEYC, a nationally recognized organization, is not an accrediting body of TEPSAC.)

Southern Association of Colleges and Schools (SACS)
The University of Texas at Austin
P.O. Box 7307
Austin, Texas 78713-7307
(512) 471-6660 Fax: (512) 471-5987
www.sacs.org

Southwestern Association of Episcopal Schools (SAES)
5952 Royal Lane, Suite 204
Dallas, Texas 75230
William P. Scheel, Ed.D, Executive Director
(214) 692-9872 Fax: (214) 692-9874
www.swaes.org E-mail: saes@flash.net

Texas Alliance of Accredited Private Schools (TAAPS)
137 Calhoun Plaza
Port Lavaca, Texas 77979
(361) 552-5757 Fax: (361) 552-1900

Texas Catholic Conference Education Department (TCCED)
3725 Blackburn Street
P.O. Box 190507
Dallas, Texas 75219
(214) 528-2360 Fax: (214) 522-1753
www.cathdal.org E-mail: dvasquez@cathdal.org

Texas Conference Seventh-Day Adventists School System (TSDA)
P.O. Box 800
Alvarado, Texas 76009-0800
(817) 783-2223

Additional Recognized Organizations:

Montessori Educator International, Inc.
P.O. Box 143
Cordova, Tennessee 38018
Jane Dutcher
(Montessori schools do not currently have an accrediting organization.)

Texas Department of Protective and Regulatory Services (TDPRS)
Mail Code E-554
P.O. Box 149030
Austin, Texas 78714-9030
www.tdprs.state.tx.us

DIRECTORY OF SCHOOLS

School Name	Phone	Accreditation	Grades	Page(s)
Academic Achievement Associates	(972) 490-6399	Additional Schools	K - Adult	234-236
Akiba Academy	(972) 239-7248	NAEYC/ SACS	18 mos. - 8th	139-141
Alexander School, The	(972) 690-9210	SACS	8th - 12th	142-144
Alpha Academy	(972) 272-2173	ICAA/ NCSA	2 years - 12th	52-54
Anderson Private School for the Gifted and Talented, The	(817) 448-8484	TDPRS	K - 12th	392-395
Andrew Austin Montessori School	(214) 350-3371	Montessori	3 years - 9th	332-334
Arbor Acre Preparatory School	(972) 224-0511	Alternative/ SACS/ TACLD	4 years - 8th	250-252
Ashbury Academy- Montessori AMI	(972) 780-4700	Montessori	18 mos. - 6th	335-337
Ashleys Private School	(972) 291-1313	TDPRS	4 years - 4th	396-398
Bending Oaks High School	(972) 669-0000	SACS/ Alternative	9th - 12th	253-255
Bent Tree Child Development Center	(972) 931-0868	NAEYC	3 years - K	102-104
Bent Tree Episcopal School	(972) 248-6505	TDPRS	2 years - K	399-401
Beth Torah Preschool & Kindergarten	(972) 234-1549	TDPRS	3 years - K	402-404
Bishop Dunne Catholic High School	(214) 339-6561 ext. 292	TCCED	7th - 12th	196-199
Bishop Lynch High School, Inc.	(214) 324-3607	SACS/ TCCED	9th - 12th	200-202
Bridgeway School	(214) 770-0845	SACS/ Alternative	7th - 12th	256-259

School Name	Phone	Accreditation	Grades	Page(s)
Buckingham North Christian School	(972) 495-0851	TACLD	6 mos. - K	260-262
Buckingham Private School	(972) 272-2173	ICAA/NCSA	18 mos. - 12th	52-54
Cambridge Square Private School of DeSoto	(972) 224-5596	TAAPS pending/ TDPRS	3 years - 8th	405-407
Canterbury Episcopal School, The	(972) 572-7200	SAES	K - 8th	169-171
Carlisle School, The	(214) 351-1833	Additional Schools	2 years - K	237-239
Carrollton Christian Academy	(972) 242-6688	SACS	3 years - 12th	145-147
Children's Workshop, The	(972) 424-1932	NAEYC	3 years - 5th	105-107
Christ The King School	(214) 365-1234	TCCED	K - 8th	203-205
Clariden School, The	(817) 481-7597	Montessori/ TAAPS pending	3 years - 12th	185-187
Coughs and Cuddles for Mildly Ill Children	(972) 608-8585	Additional Schools	6 wks - 16 years	240-242
Country Day Montessori School	(972) 771-6680	Montessori	3 years - K	228-340
Covenant Classical School	(817) 731-6447	Curriculum Alternative	K - 5th	314-316
Creative Preschool Co-op	(972) 234-4791	NAEYC	2 years - 4 years	108-110
Creative School, The - Walnut Hill United Methodist Church	(214) 352-0732	NAEYC	Preschool - K	111-113
Cross of Christ Lutheran School	(972) 223-9586	LSAC	3 years - 6th	85-87
daVinci School, The	(214) 373-9504	TDPRS	18 mos. - K - Primer	408-410
Dallas Academy	(214) 324-1481	Alternative	7th - 12th	263-265

19

School Name	Phone	Accreditation	Grades	Page(s)
Dallas Christian School	(972) 270-5495	NCSA/ SACS	4 years - 12th	134-136
Dallas Learning Center	(972) 231-3723	Alternative	9th - 12th	266-268
Dallas Montessori Academy	(214) 388-0091	Montessori	3 years - 8th	341-343
DeSoto Private School	(972) 223-6450	TDPRS	3 years - 6th	411-413
Eastlake Christian School	(214) 349-4547	ACSI	4 years - 6th	28-30
Epiphany Day School	(972) 690-0275	NAEYC/ SAES	16 mos. - K	172-174
Fairhill School and Diagnostic Assessment Center	(972) 233-1026	SACS/ Alternative	1st - 12th	269-271
First Baptist Academy	(214) 969-2488	ACSI/ ACTABS/ SACS	K - 12th	31-33
First Christian Elementary and Preschool	(972) 937-1952	TDPRS	K - 5th	414-416
First United Methodist Church Day School	(972) 494-3096	NAEYC	3 years - K, MDO	114-117
Fulton Academy of Rockwall, The	(972) 772-4445	TDPRS	1st - 8th	417-419
Glen Lakes Academy	(972) 517-7498	SACS pending/ Alternative	2nd - 9th	272-274
Glen Oaks School	(972) 231-3135	NAEYC	2 years - 4th	118-120
Glenwood Day School	(972) 530-4460	NAEYC	18 mos. - K	121-123
Good Shepherd Catholic School	(972) 272-6533	TCCED	3 years - 8th	206-208
Good Shepherd Episcopal School	(214) 357-1610 ext. 215	ISAS/ SAES	4 years - 8th	60-63
Grace Academy of Dallas	(214) 696-5648	ACSI	3 years - 6th	34-36
Happy Hill Farm Academy/Home	(254) 897-4822	SACS/ Alternative	K - 12th	275-277

School Name	Phone	Accreditation	Grades	Page(s)
Highland Academy	(972) 238-7567	ASESA/ Alternative	K-8th	278-280
Highland Meadow Montessori Academy	(817) 488-2138	Montessori	2 years - 6th	344-346
Highland Park Presbyterian Day School	(214) 559-5353	TAAPS	3 years - 4th	188-190
Highlander-Carden School, The	(214) 348-3220	Curriculum Alternative	3 years - 6th	317-319
Highlands School, The	(972) 554-1980	TCCED	3 years - 12th	209-212
Hillcrest Academy, The	(972) 788-0292	SACS pending	3 years - 8th	148-151
Hillier School of Highland Park Presbyterian Church	(214) 559-5363	TAAPS/ Alternative	1st - 8th	281-283
Holy Cross Lutheran School	(214) 358-4396	LSAC	3 years - 6th	88-90
Holy Trinity Catholic School	(214) 526-5113	TCCED	3 years - 8th	213-215
Holy Trinity Episcopal School	(972) 772-6919	SAES	3 years - 3rd	175-177
J. Erik Jonsson Community School	(214) 915-1890	SACS pending/ TAAPS	4 years - 6th	191-193
Keystone Academy	(972) 250-4455	ACSI/ SACS/ Alternative	K - 8th	284-286
Lakehill Preparatory School	(214) 826-2931	ISAS/ SACS	K - 12th	64-66
Lakemont Academy	(214) 351-6404	ACSI/ SACS/ Montessori	18 mos. - 8th	152-154
Legacy Christian Academy	(972) 712-5777	seeking ACSI/ SACS	K - 9th	37-39
Logos Academy	(214) 357-2995	ACCS pending/ Additional Schools	7th - 12th	243-245

School Name	Phone	Accreditation	Grades	Page(s)
Lovers Lane United Methodist Church	(214) 691-4721	NAEYC	6 mos. - 1st	124-126
Lutheran High School	(214) 349-8912	LSAC	7th - 12th	91-93
Meadowbrook School	(214) 369-4981	Montessori	3 years - K	347-349
Meadowview School	(972) 289-1831	ASESA/ COPSES/ Alternative	1st - 8th	287-289
Montessori Children's House and School	(214) 348-6276	Montessori	3 years - K	350-353
Montessori School of Las Colinas	(972) 717-0417	Montessori	6wks. - 1st	354-356
Montessori School of North Dallas	(972) 985-8844	Montessori	2 years - 1st	357-359
Montessori School of Westchester	(972) 262-1053	Montessori	18 mos. - K	360-362
Northbrook School	(214) 369-8330	NAEYC	2 years - 4th	127-129
NorthPark Presbyterian Day School	(214) 361-8024	TDPRS	1 year - K	420-422
Notre Dame of Dallas Schools, The	(214) 720-3911	TCCED/ Curriculum Alternative	3 years - 21 yrs.	320-322
Oak Hill Academy	(214) 368-0664	ASESA/ COPSES/ Alternative	4 years - 8th	290-292
Oakridge School, The	(817) 451-4994	ISAS/ SACS	3 years - 12th	67-69
Our Redeemer Lutheran School	(214) 368-1465	LSAC	3 years - 6th, MDO	94-96
Parish Day School, The	(972) 239-8011	ISAS/ SAES/ NAEYC	3 years - 6th	70-72
Preston Hollow Presbyterian School	(214) 368-3886	ASESA/ Alternative	1st - 6th	293-295
Preston Meadows Montessori	(972) 596-7094	Montessori	3 years - K	363-365

School Name	Phone	Accreditation	Grades	Page(s)
Prestonwood Christian Academy	(972) 404-9796	TDPRS	4 years - 10th	423-425
Providence Christian School of Texas	(214) 691-1030	TDPRS	1st - 9th	426-428
Redeemer Montessori School	(972) 257-3517	Montessori	2 1/2 years - 5th	366-368
Richardson Adventist School	(972) 238-1183	TSDA	K - 10th	230-232
Rise School of Dallas, The	(214) 373-4666	Curriculum Alternative	Preschool	323-325
Rosemeade Baptist Christian School	(972) 492-4253	TDPRS	K - 5th	429-431
St. Alcuin Montessori	(972) 239-1745	Montessori	18 mos. - 8th	369-371
St. Andrew's Episcopal School	(972) 262-3817	SAES pending	3 years - 5th	178-180
St. Bernard of Clairvaux	(214) 321-2897	TCCED	K - 8th	216-219
St. Christopher Montessori	(214) 363-9391	Montessori	2 years - 3rd	372-374
St. James Episcopal Montessori	(214) 348-1349	SAES/ Montessori	2 years - 6th	375-377
St. Mark's School of Texas	(214) 363-6491 ext. 172	ISAS	1st - 12th	73
St. Mary's Catholic School	(903) 893-2127	TCCED	3 years - 6th	220-222
St. Monica Catholic School	(214) 351-5688	TCCED	K - 8th	223-225
St. Paul the Apostle	(972) 235-3263	TCCED	K - 8th	226-228
St. Therese Academy	(972) 252-3000	NAPCIS pending/ Additional Schools	4 years - 12th	246-248
St. Vincent's Episcopal School	(817) 354-7979	SAES	3 years - 6th	181-183

School Name	Phone	Accreditation	Grades	Page(s)
Scofield Christian School	(214) 349-6843	ACSI	3 years - 6th	40-42
Selwyn School	(940) 382-6771	ISAS	13 mos. - 8th	74-76
Shelton School and Evaluation Center	(972) 774-1772	SACS/ Alternative	3 years - 12th	296-298
Solomon Schechter Academy of Dallas	(972) 248-3032	SACS	18 mos. - 8th	155-157
Southwest Academy	(972) 359-6646	SACS/ TAAPS/ Alternative	3 years - 8th	299-302
Star Bright Academy.	(972) 517-6730	Curriculum Alternative	1st - 12th	326-328
Texas Christian Academy	(817) 274-5201	ACSI	4 years - 12th	43-45
Trinity Christian Academy	(972) 931-8325	ACSI/ SACS	K - 12th	158-160
Trinity Christian School	(972) 291-2501	ICAA	3 years - 12th	55-57
Trinity Lyceum	(817) 469-6895	ACSI	4 years - 12th	46-48
Trinity Valley School	(817) 321-0100	ISAS	K - 12th	77-79
Ursuline Academy of Dallas	(214) 363-6551	ISAS/ TCCED/ SACS	9th - 12th	80-82
Vanguard Preparatory School	(972) 404-1616	SACS/ Alternative	4 years - 12th	303-305
Walden Preparatory School	(972) 233-6883	SACS/ Alternative	9th - 12th	306-308
West Plano Montessori School	(972) 618-8844	Montessori	2 years - 1st	378-380
Westminster Presbyterian	(214) 350-6155	NAEYC	2 years - K, MDO	130-132
Westwood Montessori School	(972) 239-8598	Montessori	3 years - 8th	381-386
White Rock Montessori School	(214) 324-5580	Montessori	3 years - 8th	384-386

School Name	Phone	Accreditation	Grades	Page(s)
White Rock North School	(214) 348-7410	SACS/ Montessori	2 1/2 years - 8th	161-163
Windsong Montessori School	(972) 620-2466	Montessori	2 1/2 years - 5th	387-389
Winston School, The	(214) 691-6950	ISAS/ Alternative	1st - 12th	309-312
Wise Academy, The	(972) 789-1800	SACS pending	1st - 4th	164-166
Zion Lutheran School	(214) 363-1630	LSAC	3 years - 8th, MDO	97-99

ACSI
Association of Christian Schools International

South-Central Region
4300 Alpha Road, Suite 205
Dallas, Texas 75244
(972) 991-2822
(972) 991-5303 FAX
E-MAIL: John Shimmer@asci.org
Web Site: www. asci.org

John Schimmer, Ed.D.
Director, South-Central Region

The Association of Christian Schools International is a service organization serving Protestant evangelical Christian schools across the United States and around the world. Each member school or college retains its individual distinctions and operating independence. Member schools must annually sign a doctrinal statement and confirm their policy of non-discrimination in enrollment and hiring. Services are provided through a network of regional offices. The South-Central Region's headquarters are in Dallas, Texas.

ACSI offers a national elementary and secondary school accreditation program. ACSI accreditation is recognized in Texas through TEPSAC (Texas Private School Accreditation Commission). The association published its standards for accreditation in a manual entitled *School Accreditation Manual*.

A school must be in existence for a minimum of three years before applying for candidacy status. Once candidacy is granted, a consultant is assigned to guide the school through the self-study process. The school is expected to spend a minimum of one year in the process of preparing for the accreditation visit. The final decision regarding accreditation rests with the Accreditation Commission. The commission is comprised of eight members elected by member-accredited schools.

Bethany Christian School (see Ch. 4)
Canyon Creek Academy (see Ch. 4)

ChristWay Academy (see Ch. 4))
Covenant Christian Academy (see Ch. 4)
Eastlake Christian School
Evangel Temple Christian School (see Ch. 4)
First Baptist Academy
Garland Christian Academy (see Ch. 4)
Glenview Christian School (see Ch. 4)
Gospel Lighthouse Christian Academy (see Ch. 4)
Grace Academy of Dallas
Keystone Academy (see Alternative)
Lakemont Academy (see SACS)
Legacy Christian Academy
Metropolitan Christian School (see Ch. 4)
Scofield Christian School
Shady Grove Christian Academy (see Ch. 4)
Texas Christian Academy
Trinity Christian Academy (see SACS)
Trinity Lyceum

EASTLAKE CHRISTIAN SCHOOL

721 Easton
Dallas, TX 75218
Contact: **Dr. Larry W. Wilson**
(214) 349-4547
(214) 341-6238 FAX

Office Hours: 8:00 a.m. - 4:00 p.m.
E-MAIL: info@ecsptf.org
Web Site: www.ecsptf.org
MAPSCO: 38A

PHILOSOPHY OF SCHOOL

Conservative Evangelical Christian

CREDENTIALS

Accreditations: (see glossary) ACSI, ACTS
Awards and special recognition: (see glossary) N/A
Qualification of administrator: Graduate degree
Qualification of faculty: College degrees, certification
Other: Affiliated with Assembly of God

GENERAL

Alternative: No
College preparatory: No
Montessori: No
Nondenominational: Yes
Church affiliated: Yes
Denomination: Christian
Jewish: N/A
Other denominations: Eastlake Christian School is an outreach ministry of Dallas First Assembly of God Church.
Student type: Co-ed
Grade category (for details see specific grades offered below): Elementary
Infants: Yes
Preschool: Half Day
Kindergarten: Full Day
Primary / Transition: No
Elementary: Yes
Secondary or Middle School: 7th and 8th

Specific grades offered: 5 year-olds to 8th grade

Other: Eastlake Christian Day Care provides child care for students from 3 months through age 12. We provide after school care for students from Victor H. Hexter and Martha Turner Reilly Elementary Schools.

Student teacher ratio average: 15:1

Classes offered per grade: N/A

Average class size: 15

Total enrollment: 180

Recommended grades to apply: 1-8

School hours: 8:20 a.m. - 3:30 p.m.

Calendar school year: August - May

Uniforms required: Yes

Parental involvement opportunities and requirements: Required

Average SAT scores: N/A

Visitation procedures: Parents are welcome to visit at any time.

Personal appointments for touring the facility: Offered

Group tour dates: N/A

Open house dates: February

Classroom visits: N/A

Profit or non-profit: Non-profit

ADMISSIONS

Application form required: Yes

Forms required: Application

Application deadline: Early enrollment begins in February

Application fee: $275 for new students; Returning students $250

Contact: Dr. Larry W. Wilson

Phone: (214) 349-4547

Student interview required: Yes

Parent interview required: Yes

Entrance test required: Yes

Specific tests administered: Kindergarten: Entrance exam, 1st - 4th Grade: Entrance exam, Fifth and above: Entrance exam

Accept test scores from other schools: Yes

Testing fee: Included in registration

Time of year testing is administered: Spring and Summer

Test dates offered: As needed

Out of state applicants: N/A

Notification by phone: Yes

Notification by mail: Yes

FINANCIAL

Preschool tuition: N/A

Elementary tuition: K5: $3150, 1st - 6th: $3250, 7th - 8th: $3450

Secondary tuition: N/A

Other tuition: Curriculum fee (K4/K5) $60, (1-6) $160

Cash discounts: Yes **Description:** 10%

Personal check: Yes

Automatic bank draw: N/A

Credit cards: MasterCard, Visa

Monthly: Yes, 10 equal payments

Per semester: N/A

Annually: Yes, 10% discounts for prepayment

Financial assistance offered: Yes

Cancellation insurance: N/A

Sibling discount: Yes, 10%

Application acceptance deposit required: N/A

SERVICES

Before school care offered: Yes

After school care offered: Yes, 3:30 p.m. - 6:00 p.m.; afternoon snack

Transportation provided: N/A

Lunch/snack program: No lunches provided

Other: Computer lab, library, enrichment curriculum & extra curricular activities offered.

FIRST BAPTIST ACADEMY

Box 868
Dallas, TX 75221
Contact: Admissions Office
(214) 969-2488
(214) 969-7797 FAX

Office Hours: 8:00 a.m. - 4:30 p.m.
E-MAIL: info@dallasprivateschools.com
Web Site: www.fbacademy.com
MAPSCO: 45K and 38H

PHILOSOPHY OF SCHOOL

FBA emphasizes the historic, theistic Christian view of life as presented in the Bible, along with academic excellence and extracurricular activities to develop the student's spiritual, academic, social and physical growth. Through the Academy's rigorous, college-preparatory curriculum and emphasis on developing Christian character, students are prepared for success in college and to serve as responsible, God-honoring citizens in their community.

CREDENTIALS

Accreditations: (see glossary) ACSI, ACTABS, SACS

Awards and special recognition: (see glossary) Downtown lower school is a Reading Renaisance Model School.

Qualification of administrator: Mr. Mike Beidel, headmaster, is a member of TANS, ACSI, NCTM, and PAIDEIA, Inc.; and for eight years an AP Calculus Reader.

Qualification of faculty: State teaching certificate, plus six hours Bible credit; additional advanced degree/professional growth credit each year

GENERAL

Alternative: No
College preparatory: Yes
Montessori: No
Nondenominational: Yes
Church affiliated: Yes
Denomination: Baptist
Jewish: N/A
Other denominations: FBA has two locations for grades K-6: downtown and Casa View. FBA accepts students of all Christian denominations. 99% of seniors enter college.
Student type: Co-ed
Grade category (for details see specific grades offered below): Preschool - 12th
Infants: No

Preschool: Half Day (3 or 5 days per week)

Kindergarten: Full Day

Primary / Transition: No

Elementary: Yes

Secondary or Middle School: Yes

Specific grades offered: 5-yr-old kindergarten - 12th. See below for preschool and infants which are in DLC. A Pre-K program is offered on the east campus.

Other: Preschool (for 6 weeks through 4 years) is offered in the Child Development Center. Call (214) 969-2428 for information.

Student teacher ratio average: 18:1

Classes offered per grade: 2 or 3 - downtown campus & 1 or 2 - east campus

Average class size: 14-23, varies by grade.

Total enrollment: 890

Recommended grades to apply: Kindergarten, 1st grade, 7th grade, 9th grade

School hours: 8:20 a.m. - 3:30 p.m.

Calendar school year: August-May

Uniforms required: Yes

Parental involvement opportunites and requirements: Parents are invited to play an active role in their child's education at FBA as volunteers, as PTF members and officers and many other activities.

Average SAT scores: 1130 for the class of 1999 All seniors are included.

Visitation procedures: Call admissions office for a tour or to arrange a visit. Open houses are held in October, November and February.

Personal appointments for touring the facility: Call the admissions office.

Group tour dates: November 1999 for downtown kindergarten, October for east campus kindergarten, November for Middle School.

Open house dates: See above. Call for February, 1999 dates.

Classroom visits: Arranged through the office of the appropriate school head after the application is received in admissions office.

Profit or non-profit: Non-profit

Other: Entrance testing and a family interview with the school head is required as part of the admissions process.

ADMISSIONS

Application form required: Yes

Forms required: Application forms and other forms available by calling (214) 969-2488 or www.fbacademy.com - $50 fee. Immunization records, birth certificate required.

Application deadline: March 15

Application fee: $50

Contact: Director of Admissions

Phone: (214) 969-2488
Student interview required: Yes
Parent interview required: Yes
Entrance test required: Yes
Specific tests administered: Kindergarten: A developmental readiness evaluation is given at the time of the family interview., 1st - 8th grade: parts of the Stanford Achievement Test, Secondary: Stanford or PSAT
Accept test scores from other schools: Yes, if they meet criteria.
Testing fee: Included in application fee of $50
Time of year testing is administered: February and March
Test dates offered: See admissions packet
Out of state applicants: Same as above or scores from current school
Notification by phone: Yes, parents are notified if the grade is full.
Notification by mail: Yes, at the end of the application process

FINANCIAL

Preschool tuition: Varies $1525 - $2025
Elementary tuition: Varies $3800-$5000
Secondary tuition: Varies $5500-$5900
Other tuition: A one-time matriculation fee of $275
Cash discounts: Yes. Description: 4% off for cash
Personal check: N/A
Automatic bank draw: Yes
Credit cards: N/A
Monthly: Yes
Per semester: Yes
Annually: Yes
Financial assistance offered: Yes, based on need.
Cancellation insurance: N/A
Sibling discount: Yes, $100
Application acceptance deposit required: Yes, $275
Other: The Director of Admissions is happy to answer questions by phone or in person. Tours of the school are available.

SERVICES

Before school care offered: Yes, 7:30 a.m.
After school care offered: Yes, for grades K - 6
Transportation provided: N/A
Lunch/snack program: Varies by grade
Other: Uniforms are required.

GRACE ACADEMY
OF DALLAS

11306 A Inwood Road
Dallas, TX 75229
Contact: **Letitia Brittain**
(214) 696-5648
(214) 696-8713 FAX

Office Hours: 7:45 a.m. - 4:00 p.m.
E-MAIL: N/A
Web Site: N/A
MAPSCO: 24D

PHILOSOPHY OF SCHOOL

 The mission of Christian education at Grace Academy of Dallas is to prepare students to live successful Godly lives in an ungodly world. It is our objective to assist parents to fulfill their God-given commission by teaching the children entrusted to us that each person : 1) is made in God's own image, unique in personality; 2) is endowed with special gifts of genius which he/she can discover; 3) can achieve, with excellence, God's purpose in his/her life.

CREDENTIALS

Accreditations: (see glossary) ACSI
Awards and special recognition: (see glossary) N/A
Qualification of administrator: Master's degree with 28 years experience in
    education, 14 years experience in administration
Qualification of faculty: Degrees and certification by state of Texas and ACSI

GENERAL

Alternative: No
College preparatory: No
Montessori: No
Nondenominational: No
Church affiliated: No
Denomination: Christian
Jewish: N/A
Other denominations: N/A
Student type: Co-ed
Grade category (for details see specific grades offered below): Elementary
Infants: N/A
Preschool: Yes, 3 and 4 years old
Kindergarten: Full Day

Primary / Transition: No
Elementary: Yes
Secondary or Middle School: N/A
Specific grades offered: K3 - grade 6
Student teacher ratio average: 14:1
Classes offered per grade: N/A
Average class size: 14
Total enrollment: 170
Recommended grades to apply: Preschool
School hours: 8:30 a.m. - 3:00 p.m.
Calendar school year: Late August - May
Uniforms required: Yes, K5 - 6th
Parental involvement opportunities and requirements: Encouraged
Average SAT scores: N/A
Visitation procedures: N/A
Personal appointments for touring the facility: Yes
Group tour dates: N/A
Open house dates: November 14, 1999 and January 27, 2000 at 9:30 a.m.
Classroom visits: N/A
Profit or non-profit: Non-profit

ADMISSIONS

Application form required: Yes
Forms required: Enrollment form & parent interview form
Application deadline: January
Application fee: 1 time new family fee $250 and registration fee of $470
Contact: Letitia Brittain
Phone: (214) 696-5648
Student interview required: Yes, 3rd - 6th grade
Parent interview required: Yes
Entrance test required: Yes, K5 - 6th grade
Specific tests administered: OLSAT, SAT
Accept test scores from other schools: Yes, OLSAT or SAT
Testing fee: $50.00
Time of year testing is administered: All Year
Test dates offered: N/A
Out of state applicants: N/A
Notification by phone: Yes
Notification by mail: Yes
Other: Enrichment classes in art, music, Spanish, computer, science and physical
education

FINANCIAL

Preschool tuition: $4,700
Elementary tuition: $4,700
Secondary tuition: N/A
Other tuition: N/A
Cash discounts: N/A
Personal check: Yes
Automatic bank draw: N/A
Credit cards: N/A
Monthly: Yes (Surcharge)
Per semester: Yes "Semi-annually" (Surcharge)
Annually: Yes
Financial assistance offered: Yes
Cancellation insurance: Yes, Tuition Refund Plan
Sibling discount: Yes
Application acceptance deposit required: Yes
Other: Sibling discount for K5 - Grade 6

SERVICES

Before school care offered: Yes
After school care offered: N/A
Transportation provided: N/A
Lunch/snack program: Snacks brought from home for preschool - K5. hot
    lunch program K5 - 6th
Other: Computerized 5000 volume library

LEGACY CHRISTIAN ACADEMY

7185 Main Street, Suite 201*   **Office Hours:** 8:00 a.m. - 4:00 p.m.
Frisco, TX   75034   **E-MAIL:** legacychra@aol.com
Contact: **Jody Capehart, Head of School**   **Web Site:** N/A
(972) 712-5777   **MAPSCO:** 36C
972-712-8222 FAX
*We are moving to a new campus and until the city names the street, we can say it is near "Preston and El Dorado" in Frisco.

PHILOSOPHY OF SCHOOL

We believe that spiritual development and academic excellence go hand in hand. With God as the source of all truth, education becomes an exciting adventure. By challenging our students to excellence in all areas of their live: spiritually, mentally, socially and physically, we are preparing strong leaders with Biblical convictions for tomorrow.

CREDENTIALS

Accreditations: (see glossary) Seeking ACSI and SACS
Awards and special recognition: (see glossary) New school to open in fall of 1999
Qualification of administrator: 30 years experience getting EdD
Qualification of faculty: Degreed, certified

GENERAL

Alternative: No
College preparatory: Yes
Montessori: No
Nondenominational: Yes
Church affiliated: Yes
Denomination: Non-denomination, but in a Bible church
Jewish: N/A
Other denominations: N/A
Student type: Co-ed
Grade category (for details see specific grades offered below): N/A
Infants: N/A
Preschool: N/A

Kindergarten: Yes
Primary / Transition: Bridge class between Kindergarten and 1st grade
Elementary: Yes
Secondary or Middle School: Yes
Specific grades offered: Kindergarten - 9th grade
Student teacher ratio average: 15:1
Classes offered per grade: 1-2 for fall of 1999, 2-3 for 2000-2001
Average class size: 15
Total enrollment: 180 (fall 1999)
Recommended grades to apply: K - 9th
School hours: 8:30 a.m. - 3:30 p.m.
Calendar school year: August 16 - June 2 for 1999-2000
Uniforms required: Yes
Parental involvement opportunities and requirements: Yes
Average SAT scores: (School opens in 1999-2000)
Visitation procedures: Yes
Personal appointments for touring the facility: Yes
Group tour dates: TBA
Open house dates: Call school
Classroom visits: Yes
Profit or non-profit: Non-profit

ADMISSIONS

Application form required: Yes
Forms required: Yes
Application deadline: New school
Application fee: Yes, $100
Contact: Tammy Schlorholtz
Phone: (972) 712-5777
Student interview required: Yes
Parent interview required: Yes
Entrance test required: Yes
Specific tests administered: Woodcock-Johnson, Santa Clara, Reading Style Inventory, Berry Developmental Test of Visual-Motor Integration, Auditory discrimination check, Sequencing tasks, Dictation tasks, Wechsler Intelligence Scale, Reading Style Inventory to determine learning style.
Accept test scores from other schools: Yes
Testing fee: Yes, $100
Time of year testing is administered: Spring
Test dates offered: To be announced
Out of state applicants: Yes

Notification by phone: Yes
Notification by mail: Yes

FINANCIAL

Preschool tuition: N/A
Elementary tuition: $1850 Kindergarten; $3750 1st - 4th; $4000 5th - 9th
Secondary tuition: $4000 5th - 9th
Other tuition: N/A
Cash discounts: No
Personal check: Yes
Automatic bank draw: N/A
Credit cards: N/A
Monthly: Option available: March - December
Per semester: Option available
Annually: Yes, 5% discount
Financial assistance offered: Yes
Cancellation insurance: No
Sibling discount: Yes
Application acceptance deposit required: Yes

SERVICES

Before school care offered: Yes
After school care offered: No
Transportation provided: No
Lunch/snack program: Yes
Other: Athletics, band, orchestra, choral, cheerleading, drama, art, speech

SCOFIELD CHRISTIAN SCHOOL

7730 Abrams Road
Dallas, TX 75231
Contact: **Ray Klodzinski, Principal**
(214) 349-6843
(214) 342-2061 FAX

Office Hours: 8:00 a.m. - 4:00 p.m.
E-MAIL: SCSCH@Scofield.org
Web Site: www.scofield.org
MAPSCO: 27J

PHILOSOPHY OF SCHOOL

The mission of Scofield Christian School is to provide children with an education based on Biblical precepts incorporated into the curriculum that will prepare each child academically, spiritually, and morally to lead a life that honors God. We believe it is desirable for the student body to contain a cross-section of society racially, socially, and economically, and that it be limited in size so that a sense of community can be established and maintained. We further believe the school can be of special service to the children of parents who share our concern for each person's relationship to God. We believe our curriculum should be governed largely by the word "excellence." Consequently, we have chosen to be accredited by the Association of Christian Schools International and comply with its standards for curriculum, student assessment, and promotion. ACSI is recognized by the Texas Education Agency.

CREDENTIALS

Accreditations: (see glossary) ACSI
Awards and special recognition: (see glossary) N/A
Qualification of administrator: Christian; master's degree
Qualification of faculty: Christian; bachelor's degree, certification
Other: Ministry of Scofield Church

GENERAL

Alternative: No
College preparatory: Yes
Montessori: No
Nondenominational: Yes
Church affiliated: Yes
Denomination: Christian
Jewish: N/A

Other denominations: N/A

Student type: Co-ed

Grade category (for details see specific grades offered below): Elementary

Infants: N/A

Preschool: Full Day

Kindergarten: Full Day

Primary / Transition: No

Elementary: Yes

Secondary or Middle School: N/A

Specific grades offered: 3K, 4K, 5K, Grades 1-6

Other: Half day Preschool and Kindergarten also available

Student teacher ratio average: 20:1 approximately

Classes offered per grade: Art/Music/Computer/PE/Library/Spanish/Latin

Average class size: 17

Total enrollment: 390

Recommended grades to apply: Open

School hours: 3,4,5 K: 8:15 a.m. - 11:30 a.m.; 12:15 p.m. - 3:30 p.m./
1st - 6th: 8:15 a.m. - 3:30 p.m.

Calendar school year: Middle of August - end of May

Uniforms required: Yes

Parental involvement opportunities and requirements: Parent-Teacher
Fellowship (PTF)

Average SAT scores: N/A

Visitation procedures: Call for an appointment

Personal appointments for touring the facility: Yes

Group tour dates: Open

Open house dates: January

Classroom visits: Open

Profit or non-profit: Non-profit

Other: After school care until 6:00 p.m.

ADMISSIONS

Application form required: Yes

Forms required: Application, immunization records, proof of medical insurance,
copy of birth certificate, signed doctrinal statement, signed philosophy
statement

Application deadline: Open

Application fee: All students pay $300 annual registration fee.

Contact: Gloria Brinkman, Administrative Assistant

Phone: (214) 349-6843

Student interview required: Yes

Parent interview required: Yes

Entrance test required: Yes

Specific tests administered: Preschool: None, Kindergarten: Readiness, 1st - 4th Grade: Achievement tests, Fifth and above: Achievement tests

Accept test scores from other schools: No

Testing fee: $35

Time of year testing is administered: Open

Test dates offered: Open

Out of state applicants: Yes

Notification by phone: N/A

Notification by mail: Yes, letter sent if the child is accepted or rejected; notification sent if the child is on the waiting list.

FINANCIAL

Preschool tuition: 3K $1800; 4K $2520; 5K $3260

Elementary tuition: Grades 1 - 6 $4000; study skills $35 (grades 3-6)

Secondary tuition: N/A

Other tuition: Extended day program; field trips $28; uniform $150-$220 annually

Cash discounts: N/A

Personal check: Yes

Automatic bank draw: N/A

Credit cards: Yes

Monthly: Yes, 10 payments (August-May)

Per semester: Yes

Annually: Yes

Financial assistance offered: Yes

Cancellation insurance: N/A

Sibling discount: Yes, 10% 2nd child; 15% 3rd; 20% 4th

Application acceptance deposit required: $150.00

SERVICES

Before school care offered: N/A

After school care offered: Yes, until 6:00 p.m.

Transportation provided: N/A

Lunch/snack program: Lunch fee is $3.50 per day (optional); snacks for preschool and extended-day students.

Other: Transportation provided by parents and local daycare. Computer lab and library weekly on site; enrichment curriculum and extracurricular activities offered.

TEXAS CHRISTIAN ACADEMY

915 WEB
Arlington, TX 76011
Contact: **Tim Vanderveer**
(817) 274-5201
(817) 265-5329 FAX

Office Hours: 8:00 a.m. - 4:30 p.m.
E-MAIL: TCA@Cyperramp.com
Web Site: N/A
MAPSCO: 83B

PHILOSOPHY OF SCHOOL

Our philosophy is based upon a Christian world view holding that God is the Creator and Sustainer of the universe, the ultimate reality, and the source and essence of all goodness and truth. We believe the Bible is the inerrant Word of God and the final authority. Effective education can best be accomplished in an environment which recognizes that all truth is God's Truth. The Bible clearly teaches that parents are responsible for the education and discipline of their children. Teachers and administrators assist the parents, helping them fulfill their God-given responsibilities. Together, the home, the school, and the church should prepare the student for a life of fellowship with God and service to man.

CREDENTIALS

Accreditations: (see glossary) ACSI
Awards and special recognition: (see glossary) N/A
Qualification of administrator: M.A. School Administration
Qualification of faculty: College degree
Other: Certified by the Association of Christian Schools International, affiliated with Texas Association of Private and Parochial Schools and Texas Christian Athletic League

GENERAL

Alternative: No
College preparatory: Yes
Montessori: No
Nondenominational: No
Church affiliated: Yes
Denomination: Baptist
Jewish: N/A
Other denominations: N/A

Student type: Co-ed
Grade category (for details see specific grades offered below): Preschool - 12th
Infants: N/A
Preschool: Half Day (K4 only)
Kindergarten: Full Day
Primary / Transition: No
Elementary: Yes
Secondary or Middle School: Yes
Specific grades offered: PK (age 4) - grade 12
Student teacher ratio average: 15:1
Classes offered per grade: Varies by grade
Average class size: See other
Total enrollment: 370 (1998-1999)
Recommended grades to apply: All
School hours: 8:10 a.m. - 3:00 p.m.
Calendar school year: August - May
Uniforms required: Yes
Parental involvement opportunities and requirements: Parents' Day at School, Grandparents' Day at School, two conferences per year; School welcomes volunteer work.
Average SAT scores: 1060
Visitation procedures: Contact principal for on-campus visits.
Personal appointments for touring the facility: Individual interviews
Group tour dates: Any time
Open house dates: N/A
Classroom visits: Contact principal
Profit or non-profit: Non-profit
Other: Maximum Class Size: K4=16, K5=16, Grades 1-3=22, 4-6=24, 7-12=25

ADMISSIONS

Application form required: Yes
Forms required: School records, any testing, immunization records, medical background, recommendations from previous teacher
Application deadline: Open until classes are full
Application fee: None
Contact: Angela Arthur - Elementary, Tim Vanderveer - Secondary
Phone: (817) 274-5201
Student interview required: Yes
Parent interview required: Yes
Entrance test required: Yes
Specific tests administered: Preschool: No testing, Kindergarten: Missouri KIDS

Test, 1st - 4th Grade: Teacher developed, Fifth and above: 5-6th grade teacher developed, Secondary: Stanford Ach. Test for grade 7-12

Accept test scores from other schools: Yes, if applicable

Testing fee: $25

Time of year testing is administered: TBA

Test dates offered: TBA

Out of state applicants: N/A

Notification by phone: Yes, within 5 days

Notification by mail: Yes

FINANCIAL

Preschool tuition: K4, Half-day K $1975/year, K5 Full Day $2975/year

Elementary tuition: Grades 1-6 $2975/year

Secondary tuition: Grades 7-12 $3570/year

Other tuition: Registration fee:$150-$200

Cash discounts: Yes, 5% year- Tuition only

Personal check: Yes

Automatic bank draw: N/A

Credit cards: N/A

Monthly: Yes, 10 or 12 payments

Per semester: Yes, 3%

Annually: Yes, 5% discount if paid before 1st school day

Financial assistance offered: See administration

Cancellation insurance: N/A

Sibling discount: Yes

Application acceptance deposit required: N/A

Other: Uniforms can be purchased from Merl Uniform Store in Ft. Worth. Program Fee: $175.00 - $275.00. Cash discounts:.03% semester-Tuition only

SERVICES

Before school care offered: N/A

After school care offered: Yes, ext care K4 from 12:00 p.m. - 3:00 p.m., K4-5 from 3:00 p.m. - 6:00 p.m.

Transportation provided: N/A

Lunch/snack program: Lunch fee: $2.75 per day for full lunch

Other: Computer lab, library, fine arts (choral, drama, band) sports (FB, VB, BB, baseball, softball, track, golf, cheerleading)

TRINITY LYCEUM

Temporary Address while remodeling:
2315 Crown Colony Drive   *Office Hours:* 8:15 a.m. - 4:30 p.m.
Arlington, TX 76011   *E-MAIL:* N/A
Permanent Address: *Web Site:* N/A
305 S. West   *MAPSCO:* N/A
Arlington, TX 76010
Contact: **Bernice Reid**
(817) 469-6895
(817) 261-0925 FAX

PHILOSOPHY OF SCHOOL

To prepare students for service and leadership for any field of endeavor in an environment with a biblical foundation.

CREDENTIALS

Accreditations: (see glossary) Membership

Awards and special recognition: (see glossary) 30th percentile above national norms of 50th percentile. Students place in the 80th percentile on standardized tests. This is an average.

Qualification of administrator: Ph.D.

Qualification of faculty: Bachelors and Masters Degrees

Other: School is a member of ACSI. Faculty also consists of teaching assistants.

GENERAL

Alternative: No
College preparatory: Yes
Montessori: No
Nondenominational: Yes
Church affiliated: No
Denomination: N/A
Jewish: N/A
Other denominations: N/A
Student type: Co-ed
Grade category (for details see specific grades offered below): N/A
Infants: N/A
Preschool: Half Day

Kindergarten: Full Day

Primary / Transition: N/A

Elementary: Yes

Secondary or Middle School: Yes

Specific grades offered: N/A

Other: Plans in the future will include after school care. Students may take advanced placement courses.

Student teacher ratio average: 3 teachers at least for each student

Classes offered per grade: Since program offers individualized instruction for the core subjects, the curriculum is not by class. Foreign languages, art and music are taught in traditional classroom settings.

Average class size: 10

Total enrollment: 30

Recommended grades to apply: All grades since program is individualized.

School hours: 8:30 a.m. - 3:45 p.m.

Calendar school year: August - May

Uniforms required: Yes

Parental involvement opportunities and requirements: Parents pledge to support school and its programs.

Average SAT scores: N/A

Visitation procedures: Arranged through administration.

Personal appointments for touring the facility: Arranged

Group tour dates: N/A

Open house dates: October and February

Classroom visits: Upon arrangement

Profit or non-profit: Non-profit (501 C8)

ADMISSIONS

Application form required: Yes

Forms required: N/A

Application deadline: N/A

Application fee: $200.00

Contact: Bernice D. Strand Reid

Phone: (817) 469-6895

Student interview required: Yes

Parent interview required: Yes

Entrance test required: Yes

Specific tests administered: Preschool: Preschool Reading Readiness; Kindergarten: ABC's with Ace & Christi; Primer: Selected reading materials tied to curriculum.

Accept test scores from other schools: Yes, if diagnostic tests are same.

Testing fee: $160-$200

Time of year testing is administered: During spring, summer and upon entry.

Test dates offered: TBA

Out of state applicants: N/A

Notification by phone: Yes

Notification by mail: Yes

Other: Final Interview

FINANCIAL

Preschool tuition: $250 - $350 (2,3,4 day programs)

Elementary tuition: $300 per month

Secondary tuition: N/A

Other tuition: N/A

Cash discounts: Yes, see below

Personal check: Yes

Automatic bank draw: Yes

Credit cards: Visa, MasterCard, Discover, American Express

Monthly: Yes, 10 month August - May

Per semester: Yes, 5% discount

Annually: Yes, 10% discount

Financial assistance offered: When available

Cancellation insurance: No

Sibling discount: $50 monthly for 1st child, $100 monthly for 2nd child, $150 discount for 3rd child, $200 discount for 4th child

Application acceptance deposit required: After interviews with parents and students

SERVICES

Before school care offered: N/A

After school care offered: N/A

Transportation provided: N/A

Lunch/snack program: N/A

ACTABS
Accreditation Commission of the Texas Association of Baptist Schools

P.O. 97215
Waco, TX 76798
(254) 710-2410

Randy Woods
Executive Director

Constitution

Article I. Description and Membership
The Accreditation Commission of the Texas Association of Baptist Schools (ACTABS) is an approved unit of the Texas Association of Baptist Schools (TABS). It is made up of schools that voluntarily meet the following criteria:

A. are affiliated with churches cooperation as members of local associations of churches of the Southern Baptist Conventions (or the school may be affiliated with the Baptist General Convention of Texas or a local Texas Southern Baptist Association)

B. are members of the Texas Association of Baptist Schools

C. are certified by ACTABS as having met (and are continuously meeting) the standards of accreditation prescribed by ACTABS

Thus, ACTABS is an association of schools sponsored by TABS and authorized to accredit Southern Baptist schools operating in Texas.

Christian schools not meeting the criteria above may become affiliate members by meeting the criteria stated in Section 1.B. of the Standards for Accreditation.

Article II. Purpose

ACTABS has two (2) primary purposes:

A. to promote high standards in academic, physical, and spiritual programs among Southern Baptist schools of Texas and to honor by accreditation those schools that demonstrate such standards are being maintained;

B. to maintain recognition of ACTABS as an approved accreditation commission by any Texas non-public school umbrella approved to grant such recognition by the Texas State Board of Education (e.g., the Texas Private School Accreditation Commission of the Texas Association of Non-Public Schools).

STANDARDS FOR ACCREDITATION
A SCHOOL OR SYSTEM OF SCHOOLS

I. Eligibility for Membership and Affiliate Membership

A. Any Texas preschool, elementary, middle or high school, or system of schools is eligible to seek accreditation by ACTABS. The combination of grades offered must be contiguous and reasonable for the philosophy of the school.

B. The school seeking accreditation and membership must be affiliated with a church that is a member of a local association of Southern Baptist churches. (The school may be affiliated directly with the Baptist General Convention of Texas or a local association).

C. The school seeking accreditation must be a member of the Texas Association of Baptist Schools. If not a member, it may seek accreditation as an affiliate school.

D. The entire school, consisting of all grades currently offered (K-12 with preschool optional), must be evaluated for accreditation initially, and all grades must have been operated successfully for at lease one (1) year prior to the site visit. If an accredited school adds grades, the new grades must operate successfully for a minimum of one (1) year. The new grades will remain unaccredited until a request is made for a team visit and approval by a majority vote of ACTABS.

First Baptist Academy (see ACSI)
Liberty Christian High School (see Ch. 4)

ICAA
The International Christian
Accrediting Association

7777 South Lewis Avenue - LRC 310
Tulsa, OK 74171
(918) 495-7054
(918) 495-6191 FAX
E-MAIL: icaa@oru.edu
Web Site: www.icaa1.org

David Hand
Director

The International Christian Accrediting Association, an affiliate of Oral Roberts University Educational Fellowship, is an accrediting agency dedicated to the recognition and support of excellence in Christian education.

With an ever-growing number of schools participating in its accreditation process nationwide and overseas, ICAA is meeting the needs of Christian schools and post secondary institutions by establishing a credible and reliable witness to their performance, integrity, and quality.

Alpha Academy
Buckingham Private School
Trinity Christian School

ALPHA ACADEMY & BUCKINGHAM PRIVATE SCHOOL

Alpha Academy Campus:
701 State Street
Garland, TX 75040
Buckingham Private School Campus:
3170 W. Buckingham
Garland, TX 75040
Contact: **Charles or Wilma York**
(972) 272-2173 or (972) 272-4638 B.P.S.
(972) 295-3263 FAX

Office Hours: 8:00 a.m. - 6:00 p.m.
E-MAIL: alphaacademy.org
Web Site: N/A
MAPSCO: N/A

PHILOSOPHY OF SCHOOL

Alpha Academy is a private K - 12th, Christ-centered school dedicated to providing the highest quality education possible. At Alpha Academy our staff are degreed, certified, involved and caring. We provide academic excellence, spiritual growth, and physical development to help each student reach their full potential.

CREDENTIALS

Accreditations: (see glossary) ICAA, NCSA, Non-public/private schools, TAAPS, TEPSAC, ORUEF
Awards and special recognition: (see glossary) Graduations observed K - 1st, 4th - 5th, 5th - 6th, and 12th; perfect attendance awards given
Qualification of administrator: 23 years with the school; doctorate degree
Qualification of faculty: All degreed teachers

GENERAL

Alternative: No
College preparatory: Yes
Montessori: No
Nondenominational: Yes
Church affiliated: No
Denomination: N/A
Jewish: N/A

Other denominations: N/A

Student type: Co-ed

Grade category (for details see specific grades offered below): N/A

Infants: Yes

Preschool: Full Day

Kindergarten: Full Day

Primary / Transition: N/A

Elementary: Yes

Secondary or Middle School: Yes

Specific grades offered: Infants - 12th grade

Other: Preschool and kindergarten offered at Buckingham Private School. 1st - 12th offered at Alpha Academy.

Student teacher ratio average: 16:1

Classes offered per grade: 2-3

Average class size: 16-18

Total enrollment: 325

Recommended grades to apply: All grades

School hours: 8:30 a.m. - 3:30 p.m.

Calendar school year: We follow the GISD calendar.

Uniforms required: Yes, at Alpha Academy and Buckingham Private School Kindergarten only

Parental involvement opportunities and requirements: Volunteers are definitely welcome to help in fundraising, reading to children, field trips, plays, etc. We have an open door policy for parents.

Average SAT scores: N/A CAT testing

Visitation procedures: Please call for an appointment to tour school.

Personal appointments for touring the facility: N/A

Group tour dates: N/A

Open house dates: Each progress statements day is Parent-Teacher Day.

Classroom visits: Open door policy

Profit or non-profit: Non-profit

Other: Sports teams and physical education

ADMISSIONS

Application form required: Yes

Forms required: Forms provided by school.

Application deadline: Open enrollment year round.

Application fee: $100

Contact: Dr. Charles York

Phone: (972) 272-2173

Student interview required: Yes

Parent interview required: Yes
Entrance test required: No
Specific tests administered: N/A
Accept test scores from other schools: Yes
Testing fee: N/A
Time of year testing is administered: April
Test dates offered: N/A
Out of state applicants: Yes
Notification by phone: Yes
Notification by mail: Yes

FINANCIAL

Preschool tuition: Call for rates
Elementary tuition: $2343 *Alpha Academy*
Secondary tuition: $2609 *Alpha Academy*
Other tuition: Book fees: K5: $80; 1st : $155; 5th - 12th: $240; After school care: $50/week
Cash discounts: Yes, 2% by first, 10% annually
Personal check: Yes
Automatic bank draw: Yes
Credit cards: Visa, MasterCard, American Express
Monthly: Yes. 10, 11, or 12 months
Per semester: N/A
Annually: Yes
Financial assistance offered: We accept grants and C.E.O. program. Scholarship programs available for graduates going to ORU.
Cancellation insurance: One month's tuition
Sibling discount: Yes, check with headmaster
Application acceptance deposit required: N/A

SERVICES

Before school care offered: Yes, 6:30 a.m. - school starts at Buckingham for Alpha.
After school care offered: Yes, 3:30 p.m. - 6:30 p.m. at Buckingham for Alpha.
Transportation provided: Yes
Lunch/snack program: Hot lunches available daily, average cost $3.00. We also accept USDA food program national school.
Other: Please check with office about additional learning center. Summer camp program, call for details. New at Alpha Academy, interested students can visit with the class for a day before enrolling. Please call for other Alpha Academy Child Development Centers near you at (972) 272-2173, ask for Paul.

TRINITY CHRISTIAN SCHOOL

1231 E. Pleasant Run Road
Cedar Hill, TX 75104
Contact: **Chet Steele, Headmaster**
(972) 291-2501
(972) 291-4739 FAX

Office Hours: 7:30 a.m. - 4:30 p.m.
E-MAIL: N/A

Web Site: www.trinityministries.org
MAPSCO: 72X

PHILOSOPHY OF SCHOOL

It is the mission of Trinity Christian School to glorify God by introducing, embracing, guiding and training students to develop an eternal relationship with Christ.

CREDENTIALS

Accreditations: (see glossary) ICAA, ACTS
Awards and special recognition: (see glossary) N/A
Qualification of administrator: College degree; certified
Qualification of faculty: College degree; certified
Other: Affiliated with Assembly of God, Accreditation: ACTS

GENERAL

Alternative: No
College preparatory: No
Montessori: No
Nondenominational: No
Church affiliated: Yes
Denomination: Christian
Jewish: N/A
Other denominations: N/A
Student type: Co-ed
Grade category (for details see specific grades offered below): Preschool - 12th
Infants: N/A
Preschool: Full Day
Kindergarten: Full Day
Primary / Transition: No
Elementary: Yes
Secondary or Middle School: Yes

Specific grades offered: PK3 - 12
Student teacher ratio average: 22:1
Classes offered per grade: N/A
Average class size: 22
Total enrollment: 646
Recommended grades to apply: N/A
School hours: 8:00 a.m. - 3:00 p.m.
Calendar school year: August 17 - May 19
Uniforms required: Yes
Parental involvement opportunities and requirements: Parent-teacher
conferences, Parent Intercessory Prayer, Band Booster, Athletic Booster, PRO
Average SAT scores: 1075
Visitation procedures: N/A
Personal appointments for touring the facility: Offered
Group tour dates: N/A
Open house dates: N/A
Classroom visits: N/A
Profit or non-profit: Non-profit

ADMISSIONS

Application form required: Yes
Forms required: Transcript, birth certificate, immunization records
Application deadline: Apply mid-January for next year
Application fee: Yes
Contact: Patty Nielsen, Admissions Secretary
Phone: (972) 291-2501
Student interview required: Yes
Parent interview required: Yes
Entrance test required: Yes
Specific tests administered: N/A
Accept test scores from other schools: No
Testing fee: Yes
Time of year testing is administered: Upon application
Test dates offered: N/A
Out of state applicants: N/A
Notification by phone: N/A
Notification by mail: Yes

FINANCIAL

Preschool tuition: PK3&4 $3600 w/o Extended Care; w/ Extended Care $3800
Elementary tuition: K5 - 5th $3250

Secondary tuition: 6th - 8th $3590; 9th - 11th $3900; 12th $4400

Other tuition: N/A

Cash discounts: N/A

Personal check: Yes

Automatic bank draw: N/A

Credit cards: Visa, MasterCard, American Express

Monthly: Yes, 10 or 12 payments

Per semester: N/A

Annually: N/A

Financial assistance offered: Yes

Cancellation insurance: N/A

Sibling discount: Yes, 2nd child, 3rd, 4th, 5th FREE

Application acceptance deposit required: Pre-school $100 ; K5-12th $200

Other: New students fee $35

SERVICES

Before school care offered: Yes, begins 6:00 a.m.

After school care offered: Yes, 3:00 p.m. - 6:00 p.m.

Transportation provided: N/A

Lunch/snack program: Lunch fee $2.50/meal elementary; $3.25/meal secondary; Students bring their own snacks; snack bar open to secondary students during lunch

Other: Computer lab, library; enrichment and extracurricular activities available

ISAS
Independent Schools
Association of the Southwest

4700 Bryant Irvin Ct., Suite 204
Fort Worth, Texas 76104
(817) 569-9200
(817) 569-9103 FAX
E-MAIL: gbutlerisas@worldnet.att.net
Web Site: www.isasw.org

Geoffrey C. Butler
Executive Director

The Independent Schools Association of the Southwest, a non-profit, tax-exempt, voluntary accreditation organization, serves 73 independent elementary and secondary schools in Texas, Arizona, New Mexico, Louisiana, Oklahoma, Kansas, and Mexico.

ISAS welcomes variety and diversity in its membership. Schools range in size from 100 to over 1200 students. They include boarding schools and day schools; single-sex and coeducational schools; elementary schools, secondary schools, and various combinations of the two; nonsectarian schools, church schools, and church-related schools; which serve students with clearly defined college ambitions, as well as students with learning differences.

The Association was a leader in the creation of the Texas Private School Accreditation Commission.

Schools voluntarily seek membership in ISAS. A school must meet the Association's Standards; must conduct a thorough self-study; and must be visited by an ISAS Evaluation Committee before it will be considered for membership. After accreditation and membership are granted, the school is required to participate in a rigorous and continuous evaluation program.

The Independent Schools Association of the Southwest also conducts seminars, conferences, and institutes for school heads, teachers, trustees, first-year teachers, business managers, and middle-management administrators.

ISAS sponsors on athletic league for its students and conducts an annual Fine Arts Festival in which over 2000 students participated.

The Independent Schools Association of the Southwest is a member of the College Board, the Educational Records Bureau, and the National Association of Independent Schools.

Cistercian Preparatory School (see Ch. 4)
Episcopal School of Dallas, The (see Ch. 4)
Fort Worth Country Day School (see Ch. 4)
Good Shepherd Episcopal School
Greenhill School (see Ch. 4)
Hockaday School, The (see Ch. 4)
Lakehill Preparatory School
Lamplighter School, The (see Ch. 4)
Oakridge School, The
Parish Day School, The
St. Alcuin Montessori (see Montessori)
St. John's Episcopal School (see Ch. 4)
St. Mark's School of Texas
St. Philip's School (see Ch. 4)
Selwyn School
Trinity Valley School
Ursuline Academy of Dallas
 Winston School, The (see Alternative)

GOOD SHEPHERD EPISCOPAL SCHOOL

11122 Midway
Dallas, TX 75229
Contact: **Nancy Lawrence, Director of Admissions**
(214) 357-1610 ext 215
(214) 357-4105

Office Hours: 8:00 a.m. - 4:00 p.m., M-F
E-MAIL: NLawrence@GSES.org

Web Site: www.gseschooldallas.org
FAX MAPSCO: 24F

PHILOSOPHY OF SCHOOL

Good Shepherd Episcopal School's mission is to uplift and honor the students of the community by equipping them with Christian principles, a love of learning, a creative mind, and a giving spirit.

CREDENTIALS

Accreditations: (see glossary) CASE, ISAS, NAIS, Non Public Private Schools, SAES

Awards and special recognition: (see glossary) Member NAES; One of the first schools recognized as a U.S.Department of Education "Blue Ribbon School of Excellence"

Qualification of administrator: J.Robert Kohler, Headmaster: B.A. Austin College; M.A. Southern Methodist University; 26 years in education; 3 years as Headmaster of Good Shepherd Episcopal School; 23 years at St. Mark's School of Texas as Spanish teacher, Head of Middle School, and one year as Interim Headmaster

Qualification of faculty: Bachelor's Degree required and Teacher Certification; 43% have advanced degrees

GENERAL

Alternative: No
College preparatory: No
Montessori: No
Nondenominational: No
Church affiliated: Yes
Denomination: Episcopal
Jewish: N/A
Other denominations: N/A
Student type: Coed

Grade category (for details see specific grades offered below): Elementary

Infants: N/A

Preschool: Half Day

Kindergarten: Full Day

Primary / Transition: Yes

Elementary: Yes

Secondary or Middle School: Yes

Specific grades offered: Grades four-year-olds through eighth grade.

Other: Kindergarten is half-day Monday and Friday, and full-day Tuesday, Wednesday, Thursday.

Student teacher ratio average: 12:1

Classes offered per grade: 3 sections per grade

Average class size: 20 (1st through 8th)

Total enrollment: 560

Recommended grades to apply: Prekindergarten, 1st, 6th, 7th

School hours: 8:00a.m. - 3:25p.m.

Calendar school year: August 26, 1999 - June 2, 2000

Uniforms required: Yes

Parental involvement opportunites and requirements: The Parents' Organization provides active, on-going support for the school; creates, promotes, and conducts social and fundraising events; and aids the school with such non-teaching activities as needed.

Average SAT scores: N/A

Visitation procedures: Full-day student visitation required as part of the admission process for grades 2nd through 8th. Visitation may be scheduled after application is submitted.

Personal appointments for touring the facility: The Admission Office schedules Prospective Parent Orientation Meetings and Tours on selected Thursday mornings from October through January. Please call if you would like to attend one of the meetings and tours.

Group tour dates: October 19, November 2, November 16, November 30, December 14, January 11, February 22, April 11. Please call to reserve space.

Open house dates: Admission Open House Sunday, November 7, 1999 2:00 p.m. - 3:30 p.m.

Classroom visits: N/A

Profit or nonprofit: Non-profit

ADMISSIONS

Application form required: Yes

Forms required: Please call to receive admission packet.

Application deadline: January 7, 2000

Application fee: $75
Contact: Mrs. Nancy Lawrence
Phone: (214) 357-1610 ext 215
Student interview required: Yes
Parent interview required: No
Entrance test required: Yes
Specific tests administered: Preschool: Small group evaluation, Kindergarten: Small group evaluation, Primer: Small group evaluation, 1st - 4th Grade: 1st: Small group evaluation 2nd-4th: ERB standardized test , Fifth and above: 5th: ERB standardized test 6th-8th: ISEE standardized test
Accept test scores from other schools: Yes, please call to verify type of test is consistent with our testing.
Testing fee: 6th - 8th grades: $59 ISEE fee
Time of year testing is administered: January and February
Test dates offered: Specific dates by grade level.
Out of state applicants: Please call to arrange testing.
Notification by phone: N/A
Notification by mail: Yes

FINANCIAL

Preschool tuition: $4804 - $5838 annually
Elementary tuition: $6524 annually
Secondary tuition: 6th-8th: $6524 annually
Other tuition: N/A
Cash discounts: N/A
Personal check: Yes
Automatic bank draw: N/A
Credit cards: N/A
Monthly: Yes, ten monthly payments
Per semester: Yes
Annually: Yes
Financial assistance offered: Limited assistance is available. SSS applications are available from the Business Office--applications must be submitted to the School and Student Service Financial Aid Program by February 2000.
Cancellation insurance: Yes, Dewar's Tution Insurance is optional.
Sibling discount: N/A
Application acceptance deposit required: Enrollment Fee and Deposit with contract.

SERVICES

Before school care offered: Yes, 7:00 a.m. - 7:50 a.m.

After school care offered: Yes, 12:00 noon - 3:00 p.m.; 3:00 p.m. - 6:00 p.m.

Transportation provided: N/A

Lunch/snack program: Snacks provided for prek.& kinder. Lunch available for purchase for primer - 8th grade.

LAKEHILL PREPARATORY SCHOOL

2720 Hillside Drive
Dallas, TX 75214
Contact: Fran Holley
(214) 826-2931
(214) 826-4623 FAX

Office Hours: 7:45 a.m. - 4:30 p.m.
E-MAIL: N/A
Web Site: N/A
MAPSCO: 36V

PHILOSOPHY OF SCHOOL

Traditional college-preparatory accelerated curriculum offered in a nurturing, supportive learning environment designed to optimize individual potential.

CREDENTIALS

Accreditations: (see glossary) ISAS, SACS
Awards and special recognition: (see glossary) N/A
Qualification of administrator: Advanced degree required; experience required.
Qualification of faculty: College degree required; experience preferred.
Other: Affiliated with the National Association of Secondary School Principals, Texas Association of Secondary School Principals, National Middle School Association, Associates for Research in Private Education, Independent School Management; many subject-area and curriculum-related affiliations; Association for Supervision and Curriculum Development, ISAS Admissions Group, Dallas Area Association of Admissions Directors

GENERAL

Alternative: No
College preparatory: Yes
Montessori: No
Nondenominational: Yes
Church affiliated: No
Denomination: N/A
Jewish: N/A
Other denominations: N/A
Student type: Co-ed
Grade category (for details see specific grades offered below): 1st - 12th
Infants: No
Preschool: No

Kindergarten: Full Day
Primary / Transition: No
Elementary: Yes
Secondary or Middle School: Yes
Specific grades offered: Kindergarten - Grade 12
Student teacher ratio average: 11:1
Classes offered per grade: 1 - 2
Average class size: K:16; grades 1-4:19; mid/high school: 23
Total enrollment: 275
Recommended grades to apply: All levels
School hours: 8:15 a.m. - 3:15 p.m., after school care available.
Calendar school year: Fourth week in August to last week in May
Uniforms required: No
Parental involvement opportunities and requirements: Parent-Faculty Club, Room Parents, field trip chaperones, annual auction, carnival, scout sponsors, coaches, annual fund drive, capital fund drive. We expect, encourage and enjoy our parents' involvement.
Average SAT scores: 1140
Visitation procedures: Call for individual appointment.
Personal appointments for touring the facility: Tours and information by appointment
Group tour dates: Individualized tours
Open house dates: N/A
Classroom visits: By appointment
Profit or non-profit: Non-profit

ADMISSIONS

Application form required: Yes
Forms required: Applications, student questionnaires, essays, recommendations, school records, interview
Application deadline: Apply: Sept. - Dec. for next fall; rolling admissions
Application fee: $100
Contact: Fran Holley
Phone: (214) 826-2931
Student interview required: No
Parent interview required: No
Entrance test required: Yes
Specific tests administered: Kindergarten: Morning session for group & individual assessment, 1st - 12th Grade: Standardized testing session with small groups
Accept test scores from other schools: Yes, ISEE, Stanford, CPT III

Testing fee: Included in application fee
Time of year testing is administered: Begins in January
Test dates offered: N/A
Out of state applicants: Yes
Notification by phone: Yes
Notification by mail: Yes

FINANCIAL

Preschool tuition: N/A
Elementary tuition: $6770 - $7090
Secondary tuition: $8240 - $9190
Other tuition: No
Cash discounts: N/A
Personal check: Yes
Automatic bank draw: N/A
Credit cards: N/A
Monthly: Yes, with interest
Per semester: N/A
Annually: Yes
Financial assistance offered: Need-based financial assistance available.
Cancellation insurance: N/A
Sibling discount: Yes, 5%
Application acceptance deposit required: Yes

SERVICES

Before school care offered: No
After school care offered: Yes
Transportation provided: No
Lunch/snack program: Lunch may be purchased daily or brought from home; kindergarten & first grade students have daily snacks of wholesome foods. Other grades have snacks at various times.
Other: Computer lab, library, enrichment curriculum and extracurricular activities offered.

THE OAKRIDGE SCHOOL

5900 W. Pioneer Parkway   *Office Hours:* 8:00 am - 4:00 p.m.
Arlington, TX 76013   *E-MAIL:* admiss@oakridge.pvt.k12.tx.us
Contact: **Andy Broadus, Headmaster**   *Web Site:*
(817) 451-4994   www.oakridge.pvt.k12.tx.us
(817) 457-6681 FAX   *MAPSCO:* 81T

PHILOSOPHY OF SCHOOL

We believe the role of Oakridge School is to provide a challenging educational program that emphasizes the total development of each child, encompassing basic skills as well as cultural, emotional, and physical development which prepares students for higher education and life. We believe an environment that employs a variety of teaching techniques and learning activities best enables each student to achieve as an individual and as a member of a group. We believe an orderly environment stressing personal and academic self-discipline provides an atmosphere most conducive to success. We believe in academic excellence, in high moral and ethical standards, in honor, in the respect of the opinions and the rights of others, in the realization and acceptance of the consequences of an individual's actions, and in the pursuit of knowledge as a lifelong experience. We believe the graduates of The Oakridge School should be men and women of good character who have developed a healthy respect for self, an awareness of the privileges and obligations of citizenship, and a keen sense of empathy for, and responsibility to, fellow human beings.

CREDENTIALS

Accreditations: (see glossary) ISAS, SACS
Awards and special recognition: (see glossary) N/A
Qualification of administrator: E-mail us to have a school brochure sent to you.
Qualification of faculty: E-mail us to have a school brochure sent to you.
Other: Affiliated with the National Association of Independent Schools, Texas
Association of Non-Public Schools, and Texas Independent School
Consortium

GENERAL

Alternative: No
College preparatory: Yes
Montessori: No
Nondenominational: Yes
Church affiliated: No

Denomination: N/A
Jewish: N/A
Other denominations: N/A
Student type: Co-ed
Grade category (for details see specific grades offered below): Preschool - 12th
Infants: N/A
Preschool: Half Day
Kindergarten: Full Day
Primary / Transition: Yes
Elementary: Yes
Secondary or Middle School: Yes
Specific grades offered: PK3 - Grade 12
Student teacher ratio average: N/A
Classes offered per grade: N/A
Average class size: Varies by division.
Total enrollment: 805
Recommended grades to apply: N/A
School hours: 8:00 a.m. - 3:30 p.m.
Calendar school year: August - May
Uniforms required: Yes
Parental involvement opportunities and requirements: Yes
Average SAT scores: 1100 - 1150
Visitation procedures: Call/e-mail for information.
Personal appointments for touring the facility: Offered
Group tour dates: Call/e-mail for information.
Open house dates: Call/e-mail for information.
Classroom visits: Call/e-mail for information.
Profit or non-profit: Non-profit

ADMISSIONS

Application form required: Yes
Forms required: Application, official transcript from prior schools, teacher recommendations
Application deadline: Based on availability.
Application fee: $50
Contact: Linda Broadus or Carol Wilson
Phone: (817) 451-4994 ext 704
Student interview required: Yes
Parent interview required: Yes
Entrance test required: Yes

Specific tests administered: 1st - 12th Grade: Otis-Lennon School Ability Test, Stanford Achievement Test.

Accept test scores from other schools: Yes

Testing fee: $75

Time of year testing is administered: Winter and Spring

Test dates offered: Call/e-mail for more information.

Out of state applicants: Yes

Notification by phone: Yes

Notification by mail: Yes

FINANCIAL

Preschool tuition: $2,310 - $7,200

Elementary tuition: $7,644

Secondary tuition: $8,142 - $8,700

Other tuition: Books-grades 5-12; uniform $100 or less (cost varies)

Cash discounts: N/A

Personal check: Yes

Automatic bank draw: N/A

Credit cards: N/A

Monthly: Yes, 10 and 12 month payment plans

Per semester: N/A

Annually: Yes

Financial assistance offered: Yes, based on financial needs

Cancellation insurance: Yes

Sibling discount: N/A

Application acceptance deposit required: $500

SERVICES

Before school care offered: Yes, 7:15 a.m. - 6:00 p.m.

After school care offered: Yes, 7:15 a.m. - 6:00 p.m.

Transportation provided: Yes

Lunch/snack program: Lunch fee is optional; snacks for preschool children.

Other: Transportation: carpool, individually contracted bus service; computer lab, library, and extracurricular activities

THE PARISH DAY SCHOOL

14115 Hillcrest Road
Dallas, TX 75240
Contact: **Marci McLean, Director of Admission**
(972) 239-8011; (800) 909-9081
(972) 991-1237 FAX

Office Hours: 8:00 a.m. - 4:00 p.m.
E-MAIL: mmclean@mail.parishday.org
Web Site: www.parishday.org
MAPSCO: 15G

PHILOSOPHY OF SCHOOL

The Parish Day School of the Episcopal Church of the Transfiguration provides a learning environment, within a Christian framework, in which each student is encouraged to excel academically, spiritually, emotionally, and physically.

CREDENTIALS

Accreditations: (see glossary) ISAS, NAEYC, SAES
Awards and special recognition: (see glossary) Blue Ribbon School of Excellence 1993-94
Qualification of administrator: University of Texas (Austin), B.A. 1959; Southern Methodist University, M.L.A. 1976
Qualification of faculty: N/A

GENERAL

Alternative: No
College preparatory: No
Montessori: No
Nondenominational: No
Church affiliated: Yes
Denomination: Episcopal
Jewish: N/A
Other denominations: N/A
Student type: Co-ed
Grade category (for details see specific grades offered below): Elementary
Infants: N/A
Preschool: Half Day
Kindergarten: Full Day
Primary / Transition: No
Elementary: Yes
Secondary or Middle School: N/A
Specific grades offered: Pre-kindergarten - 6th grade

Student teacher ratio average: Range from 8:1 to 20:1
Classes offered per grade: 2-4 classes per grade
Average class size: 14-20
Total enrollment: 430
Recommended grades to apply: N/A
School hours: 8:00 a.m. - 3:30 p.m.
Calendar school year: 1999-2000: August 30 - June 2
Uniforms required: Yes
Parental involvement opportunities and requirements: The Parish Day School Parents' Club
Average SAT scores: N/A
Visitation procedures: Call Admissions Office in October - January for appointment.
Personal appointments for touring the facility: Call Admissions Office in October - January for appointment.
Group tour dates: October - January
Open house dates: N/A
Classroom visits: January-March
Profit or non-profit: Non-profit

ADMISSIONS

Application form required: Yes
Forms required: Parish Day School application form
Application deadline: January 28, 2000 for 2000-2001 school year
Application fee: $75 per child
Contact: Marci McLean
Phone: (972) 239-8011 ext. 122
Student interview required: Yes
Parent interview required: No
Entrance test required: Yes
Specific tests administered: Preschool: In-house test; Kindergarten: ERB Kids Test; 1st - 4th Grade: CTP or Stanford/Otis Lennon; Fifth and above: ISEE
Accept test scores from other schools: Yes. Scores from ISAS schools will be accepted.
Testing fee: $75 per child
Time of year testing is administered: November - February
Test dates offered: Not set for 2000-2001 school year
Out of state applicants: As necessary
Notification by phone: Yes
Notification by mail: Yes

FINANCIAL

Preschool tuition: $2820-4670; $310-515 enrollment fee

Elementary tuition: $6735; $600 enrollment fee

Secondary tuition: N/A

Other tuition: One-time new student fee: $500

Cash discounts: N/A

Personal check: Yes

Automatic bank draw: N/A

Credit cards: N/A

Monthly: Yes

Per semester: Yes

Annually: Yes

Financial assistance offered: Yes, contact Marci McLean for information.

Cancellation insurance: Yes, A.W.G. Dewar

Sibling discount: N/A

Application acceptance deposit required: Due by January 28, 2000 for 2000-2001 school year

SERVICES

Before school care offered: Yes, 7:50 a.m.

After school care offered: Yes, until 6:00 p.m.

Transportation provided: N/A

Lunch/snack program: Daily hot lunch available for purchase for Grades K-6. Snacks for all children in pre-kindergarten and kindergarten.

ST. MARK'S SCHOOL
OF TEXAS

10600 Preston Road
Dallas, TX 75230-4000
Contact: **Director of Admission**
(214) 346-8700
(214) 346-8701 FAX

Office Hours: 8:00 a.m. - 4:30 p.m.
E-MAIL: admission@smtexas.org
Web Site: www.smtexas.org
MAPSCO: 25K

For more information, please contact the Director of Admission.

SELWYN SCHOOL

3333 University Drive West
Denton, TX 76207
Contact: Director of Admission
(940) 382-6771
(940) 383-0704 FAX

Office Hours: 8:00 a.m. - 5:00 p.m.
E-MAIL: selwyn@iglobal.net
Web Site: N/A
MAPSCO: Denton

PHILOSOPHY OF SCHOOL

The primary purpose of The Selwyn School is to prepare students to become responsible and effective citizens in an increasingly interdependent world. The school encourages an atmosphere of caring, mutual respect, and service to others so that students may develop self-confidence, a respect for truth, and commitment to community.

CREDENTIALS

Accreditations: (see glossary) ISAS
Awards and special recognition: (see glossary) N/A
Qualification of administrator: Advanced degree
Qualification of faculty: College degree required; experience preferred; 30% of faculty have master's degree and higher
Other: Affiliated with NAIS

GENERAL

Alternative: No
College preparatory: Yes, grades 4th - 8th
Montessori: Yes, 3 years - 3rd grade
Nondenominational: Yes
Church affiliated: No
Denomination: N/A
Jewish: N/A
Other denominations: N/A
Student type: Above average ability; co-ed
Grade category (for details see specific grades offered below): Elementary/
    Middle School
Infants: N/A
Preschool: Full Day
Kindergarten: Full Day
Primary / Transition: N/A

74

Elementary: N/A

Secondary or Middle School: Yes

Specific grades offered: Preschool (13 months) - grade 8th

Student teacher ratio average: Varies with level, 5:1 - 12:1

Classes offered per grade: N/A

Average class size: Varies with level

Total enrollment: 240

Recommended grades to apply: N/A

School hours: Preschool: 9:00 a.m. - 3:00 p.m.; Lower school: 8:00 a.m. - 3 p.m.;
3 years - K and 1st - 5th: 8:00 a.m. - 3:15 p.m.;
Middle school: 8:00 a.m. - 3:30 p.m.

Calendar school year: August - May

Uniforms required: Preschool - no; Lower school - yes; Middle school - dress
code

Parental involvement opportunities and requirements: Yes, many opportunities
for parents to donate their time and talents

Average SAT scores: N/A

Visitation procedures: By appointment

Personal appointments for touring the facility: Scheduled through the Admission Office

Group tour dates: N/A

Open house dates: N/A

Classroom visits: Offered October - April, by appointment

Profit or non-profit: Non-profit

Other: Goals for students: Selwyn challenges students to take intellectual risks.
Through all levels of the school, our goal is to provide students with the tools
for lifelong success and to encourage a love of learning.

ADMISSIONS

Application form required: Yes

Forms required: Application, teacher recommendations, transcripts including
current grades and standardized test scores

Application deadline: Rolling admissions

Application fee: Yes

Contact: Maribelle Robbins

Phone: (940) 382-6771

Student interview required: Informal meeting

Parent interview required: Informal meeting

Entrance test required: Yes

Specific tests administered: Faculty designed evaluation

Accept test scores from other schools: No

Testing fee: Yes
Time of year testing is administered: Year-round by appointment
Test dates offered: N/A
Out of state applicants: N/A
Notification by phone: Letter and/or phone call
Notification by mail: Letter and/or phone call

FINANCIAL

Preschool tuition: Based on number of days enrolled, $110-431 per month
Elementary tuition: $4855 - $6065 per year
Secondary tuition: Middle school $6140 per year
Other tuition: N/A
Cash discounts: N/A
Personal check: N/A
Automatic bank draw: N/A
Credit cards: N/A
Monthly: Yes
Per semester: Yes
Annually: Yes
Financial assistance offered: Yes, need-based
Cancellation insurance: Yes
Sibling discount: Yes
Application acceptance deposit required: Yes, amount varies with level
Other: Annual fund drive

SERVICES

Before school care offered: Yes, 7:30 a.m. to the start of school
After school care offered: Yes, dismissal until 6:00 p.m.
Transportation provided: None provided by the school
Lunch/snack program: Snacks provided for students K and younger; optional lunch offered 1 day per week.
Other: Computer lab, library, pool; extracurricular activities offered; sports: competitive team sports (grades 4th - 8th) in soccer, softball, basketball, and volleyball; enrichment curriculum; instrumental music program (grades 4th - 8th)

TRINITY VALLEY SCHOOL

7500 Dutch Branch Road
Ft. Worth, TX 76132
Contact: **Judith Kinser**
(817) 321-0100
(817) 321-0105 FAX

Office Hours: 8:00 a.m. - 4:00 p.m.
E-MAIL:
tvs@ns.trinityvalleyschool.org
Web Site: www.trinityvalleyschool.org
MAPSCO: 88X

PHILOSOPHY OF SCHOOL

To provide for above-average to superior students - from kindergarten through grade 12 - an education of the highest quality.

CREDENTIALS

Accreditations: (see glossary) ISAS
Awards and special recognition: (see glossary) N/A
Qualification of administrator: Headmaster Walter W. Kesler -
    B.S., U.S. Naval Academy; M. Div., Virginia Theological Seminary
Qualification of faculty: Bachelor's degree and teacher certification are
    minimum requirements in K - 7; more than half have graduate degrees.
Other: Affiliated with NAIS, NACAC, ERB, SSS (Financial Aid), & TISC (Texas
    Independent School Consortium)

GENERAL

Alternative: No
College preparatory: Yes
Montessori: No
Nondenominational: Yes
Church affiliated: No
Denomination: N/A
Jewish: N/A
Other denominations: N/A
Student type: Co-ed
Grade category (for details see specific grades offered below): 1st - 12th
Infants: N/A
Preschool: N/A
Kindergarten: Full Day
Primary / Transition: No
Elementary: Yes
Secondary or Middle School: Yes

Specific grades offered: Kindergarten - 12
Other: Kindergarten hours: 8:30 a.m. - 2:45 p.m.
Student teacher ratio average: 12:1
Classes offered per grade: 3-4
Average class size: 20
Total enrollment: Approximately 880
Recommended grades to apply: K, 5
School hours: 8:30 a.m. - 3:30 p.m.
Calendar school year: August - May
Uniforms required: Yes
Parental involvement opportunities and requirements: Parents' Club includes groups to support athletics, fine arts, outdoor program, as well as fundraisers and individual opportunities.
Average SAT scores: 1272 (1999)
Visitation procedures: N/A
Personal appointments for touring the facility: Call to schedule
Group tour dates: N/A
Open house dates: November & January
Classroom visits: Call to schedule
Profit or non-profit: Non-profit

ADMISSIONS

Application form required: Yes
Forms required: Application, 3 or 4 recommendations, transcript for grades 1 - 12
Application deadline: K: Feb. 4; grades 1-4: Mar 20; grades 5-12: Mar 4
Application fee: $75; re-application fee $25
Contact: Judith Kinser or Richard Brennan
Phone: (817) 321-0100
Student interview required: No
Parent interview required: No
Entrance test required: Yes
Specific tests administered: Kindergarten: Individual testing, January and February; 1st - 8th: Testing end of March; 9th - 12th: Testing in January, February and March
Accept test scores from other schools: Yes, with consortium
Testing fee: N/A
Time of year testing is administered: January, February, March
Test dates offered: N/A
Out of state applicants: Handled individually, testing may be administered off-site.
Notification by phone: N/A

Notification by mail: Yes, by letter with contract; parents have 2 weeks to pay deposit.

Other: Student interviews are strongly recommended and may be required. Parent interviews are also strongly recommended.

FINANCIAL

Preschool tuition: N/A

Elementary tuition: K - 6 $8275

Secondary tuition: 7 - 8 $8575; 9 - 12 $8775

Other tuition: N/A

Cash discounts: N/A

Personal check: Yes

Automatic bank draw: N/A

Credit cards: Yes

Monthly: Yes, through bank.

Per semester: N/A

Annually: Yes

Financial assistance offered: Approximately 125 students receiving approximately $632,000 in 1999-00

Cancellation insurance: Yes

Sibling discount: N/A

Application acceptance deposit required: No

Other: $750 deposit, 60% by July 1 & 40% by Jan 15; 100% in advance or loan through school's bank

SERVICES

Before school care offered: Yes, Clayton Child Care on site, 7:00 a.m. - 8:30 a.m.

After school care offered: Yes, Clayton Child Care on site, until 6:00 p.m.

Transportation provided: N/A

Lunch/snack program: Can buy or bring lunch, no requirement to buy; Cafeteria provides snacks for additional fee in K only.

Other: One computer lab for Upper School elective courses in computer science, three for subject-based instruction at all grade levels; enrichment curriculum & extracurricular activities offered.

URSULINE ACADEMY OF DALLAS

4900 Walnut Hill Lane
Dallas, TX 75229
Contact: **Tim Host**
(214) 363-6551
(214) 363-5524 FAX

Office Hours: 10:00 a.m. - 4:00 p.m.
E-MAIL: thost@ursuline.pvt.k12.tx.us
Web Site: N/A
MAPSCO: 24R

PHILOSOPHY OF SCHOOL

Founded in 1874, the Ursuline Academy of Dallas, under the sponsorship of the Ursuline Sisters of Dallas, Texas, is a private Catholic college preparatory high school for young women. The Academy encourages each student to develop her individual talents, interests, and potential through programs focused on academic excellence, spiritual formation, physical development, leadership, community-building and service in a caring and challenging environment of students, parents and educators. Ursuline Academy, with its valued traditions, prepares young women to think critically and act responsibly in global society.

CREDENTIALS

Accreditations: (see glossary) ISAS, TCCED
Awards and special recognition: (see glossary) 1. Blue Ribbon School of Excellence 2. ComputerWorld Smithsonian Award for Information Technology 3. Selected Program for Improving Catholic Education through Technology (S.P.I.C.E.)
Qualification of administrator: Master's degree
Qualification of faculty: Bachelors degree in his/her teaching field
Other: Masters degree or higher preferred

GENERAL

Alternative: No
College preparatory: Yes
Montessori: No
Nondenominational: No
Church affiliated: Yes
Denomination: Catholic
Jewish: N/A
Other denominations: N/A

Student type: All girls
Grade category (for details see specific grades offered below): Secondary
Infants: N/A
Preschool: N/A
Kindergarten: N/A
Primary / Transition: No
Elementary: N/A
Secondary or Middle School: Yes
Specific grades offered: 9th - 12th grade
Student teacher ratio average: 11:1
Classes offered per grade: N/A
Average class size: 17
Total enrollment: 800
Recommended grades to apply: 9th grade begins first semester of 8th grade year
School hours: 7:30 a.m. - 3:25 p.m.
Calendar school year: 1999-2000 August 30, 1999 to June 6, 2000
Uniforms required: Yes
Parental involvement opportunities and requirements: 1. Parents' Association Board 2. Parent Class Representatives 3. Mothers' Club 4. Dads' Club 5. Mardi Gras Ball 6. Ursuline Parents' Association 7. Parents' Newsletter 8. Parent/Faculty Liaison 9. Bear Necessities (Book Store) 10. Teacher Wish List Coordinator
Average SAT scores: 1150
Visitation procedures: Call Admissions Office to schedule meeting.
Personal appointments for touring the facility: Call Admissions Office for appointments.
Group tour dates: October and November
Open house dates: October 17, 1999
Classroom visits: Call Admissions Office
Profit or non-profit: Non-profit

ADMISSIONS

Application form required: Yes
Forms required:
Application deadline: January 28, 2000
Application fee: Yes
Contact: Tim Host
Phone: (214) 363-6551
Student interview required: No
Parent interview required: No
Entrance test required: Yes

Specific tests administered: Secondary: ISEE
Accept test scores from other schools: Yes
Testing fee: N/A
Time of year testing is administered: January
Test dates offered: January 15 and January 22, 2000
Out of state applicants: Yes
Notification by phone: N/A
Notification by mail: Yes

FINANCIAL

Preschool tuition: N/A
Elementary tuition: N/A
Secondary tuition: $7300
Other tuition: Laptop computers required.
Cash discounts: N/A
Personal check: Yes
Automatic bank draw: Yes
Credit cards: N/A
Monthly: Yes, $730 for 10 months
Per semester: Yes, $3650
Annually: Yes, $7300
Financial assistance offered: Yes, renewable annually
Cancellation insurance: N/A
Sibling discount: N/A
Application acceptance deposit required: $500 registration fee (nonrefundable)

SERVICES

Before school care offered: N/A
After school care offered: N/A
Transportation provided: N/A
Lunch/snack program: A hot and cold lunch available. The average cost is $3.50.
Other: Summer Schools is available. Please call the office for more details.

LSAC
Texas District of
The Lutheran Church -
Missouri Synod

7900 E. Highway 290
Austin, TX 78724-2499
(512) 926-4272
(512) 926-1006 FAX
E-MAIL: WVHinz@aol.com
Web Site: www.txdistlcms.org

The Lutheran School Accreditation Commission (LSAC) of the Texas District is one of the recognized accrediting agencies for non-public schools in Texas. LSAC is an accrediting association recognized by the Commissioner of Education of the State of Texas. LSAC also has a working agreement with the Southern Association of Colleges and Schools (SACS) for joint accreditation. Accreditation is a process of evaluation to help schools improve the quality of their programs. A team of outside, objective educators visit the school for several days and submit a written report with their recommendations to the District Commission before a certificate of accreditation is awarded. It is a completely voluntary process which is available for every school sponsored by one or more congregations of the Texas District of The Lutheran Church - Missouri Synod. LSAC is a rigorous district accreditation process that can also lead to a recommendation for National Lutheran School Accreditation (NLSA). The accrediting process is designed to evaluate schools on the basis of their unique purposes as Lutheran schools. As a result, the Standards, process, and awards reflect not only the quality of the academic nature of the school, but also especially the school's spiritual dimension. The standards and report forms are based on other regional accrediting agencies both secular and religious. Commissions supervise both district and national accreditation. The process has been authorized and approved by both the Board of Directors of the Texas District and the National Accreditation Commission of The Lutheran Church - Missouri Synod. Accreditation is granted for a seven-year period with annual reporting required. The entire process must be repeated to renew accreditation for an additional seven years.

Prince of Peace Christian School (see Ch. 4)
Christ Our Savior Lutheran School (see Ch. 4)

Cross of Christ Lutheran School
Faith Lutheran School (see Ch. 4)
Holy Cross Lutheran School
Lutheran High School
Our Redeemer Lutheran School
Redeemer Lutheran School (see Ch. 4)
St. Paul Lutheran (see Ch. 4)
Zion Lutheran School

CROSS OF CHRIST LUTHERAN SCHOOL

512 N. Cockrell Hill
DeSoto, TX 75115
Contact: **Dennis Boldt, Principal**
(972) 223-9586
(972) 223-8432 FAX

Office Hours: 8:15 a.m. - 3:15 p.m.
E-MAIL: dennisbl@airmail.net
Web Site: N/A
MAPSCO: 82H

PHILOSOPHY OF SCHOOL

The Cross of Christ Lutheran Church was established in 1988 to teach the good news of free forgiveness and eternal life in Jesus Christ and to provide a program that values each student as a loved, redeemed, unique creation of God. We are committed to providing the best education possible to help your child become a loving Christian, a good citizen, and a purposeful adult.

CREDENTIALS

Accreditations: (see glossary) LSAC, NLSA
Awards and special recognition: (see glossary) N/A
Qualification of administrator: Master's degree in administration
Qualification of faculty: College degree & certification; dedicated Christians
Other: Affiliated with the Lutheran Church, Lutheran Education Association

GENERAL

Alternative: No
College preparatory: Yes
Montessori: No
Nondenominational: No
Church affiliated: Yes
Denomination: Lutheran
Jewish: N/A
Other denominations: N/A
Student type: Co-ed
Grade category (for details see specific grades offered below): Elementary
Infants: N/A
Preschool: Full Day
Kindergarten: Full Day
Primary / Transition: No

Elementary: Yes

Secondary or Middle School: N/A

Specific grades offered: 3 year olds - grade 6

Student teacher ratio average: 20:1

Classes offered per grade: Preschool 3's - (1); Preschool 4's - (2); Kindergarten - (2); Grade 1 - (2); Grade 2-6 - (1)

Average class size: 16

Total enrollment: 210

Recommended grades to apply: N/A

School hours: 8:15 a.m. - 3:15 p.m.

Calendar school year: August - May

Uniforms required: Uniforms required for grade 1-6.

Parental involvement opportunities and requirements: Active parent-teacher organization

Average SAT scores: N/A

Visitation procedures: N/A

Personal appointments for touring the facility: Offered

Group tour dates: Offered

Open house dates: N/A

Classroom visits: N/A

Profit or non-profit: Non-profit

ADMISSIONS

Application form required: Yes

Forms required: Student academic, immunization, and health records

Application deadline: Enrollment begins February 1

Application fee: $50 due at time of enrollment

Contact: Dennis Boldt

Phone: (972) 223-9586

Student interview required: Yes

Parent interview required: Yes

Entrance test required: Yes*

Specific tests administered: N/A

Accept test scores from other schools: No

Testing fee: N/A

Time of year testing is administered: N/A

Test dates offered: N/A

Out of state applicants: N/A

Notification by phone: N/A

Notification by mail: N/A

Other: *Entrance test required for grade 2-6

FINANCIAL

Preschool tuition: Non member $3000; New $2,700; Member $2,200
Elementary tuition: Non member $3000; New $2,700; Member $2,200
Secondary tuition: N/A
Other tuition: N/A
Cash discounts: N/A
Personal check: N/A
Automatic bank draw: Yes
Credit cards: Yes
Monthly: N/A
Per semester: N/A
Annually: Yes, 4% discount if paid in full by first day of school
Financial assistance offered: Yes
Cancellation insurance: N/A
Sibling discount: Yes
Application acceptance deposit required: N/A
Other: Method of Payment: FACTS Tuition Management

SERVICES

Before school care offered: Yes, 7:00 a.m. - 8:00 a.m.
After school care offered: Yes, 3:15 p.m. - 6:15 p.m.
Transportation provided: N/A
Lunch/snack program: Yes

HOLY CROSS LUTHERAN SCHOOL

11425 Marsh Lane
Dallas, TX 75229
Contact: **Larry Hoffschneider, Principal**
(214) 358-4396
(214) 358-4393 FAX

Office Hours: 8:15 a.m. - 4:45 p.m.
E-MAIL: N/A
Web Site: N/A
MAPSCO: 23M

PHILOSOPHY OF SCHOOL

Holy Cross Lutheran School, a ministry of the church for students and their families, provides a Christian, spiritually based education and environment for meeting the needs of the whole person.

CREDENTIALS

Accreditations: (see glossary) LSAC, NLSA, TEPSAC
Awards and special recognition: (see glossary) N/A
Qualification of administrator: Master's degree, Lutheran teacher's diploma
Qualification of faculty: Bachelor's degree, Lutheran teacher's diploma

GENERAL

Alternative: No
College preparatory: No
Montessori: No
Nondenominational: No
Church affiliated: Yes
Denomination: Lutheran
Jewish: N/A
Other denominations: N/A
Student type: Coed
Grade category (for details see specific grades offered below): Elementary
Infants: N/A
Preschool: Half Day
Kindergarten: Full Day
Primary / Transition: No
Elementary: Yes
Secondary or Middle School: N/A
Specific grades offered: Preschool (3- and 4-year-olds) - grade 6

Student teacher ratio average: 13:1, 22:1

Classes offered per grade: N/A

Average class size: 16

Total enrollment: 140

Recommended grades to apply: N/A

School hours: K-6 8:30 a.m. - 3:30 p.m.; 4's M-F 8:30 a.m. - 11:30 a.m.;
3's M/W/F 8:30 a.m. - 11:30 a.m.

Calendar school year: August - May

Uniforms required: Yes, for grades K-6.

Parental involvement opportunities and requirements: Yes (field trips, room mothers, special events, playground monitors, lunch duty, library)

Average SAT scores: N/A

Visitation procedures: N/A

Personal appointments for touring the facility: Offered

Group tour dates: N/A

Open house dates: N/A

Classroom visits: N/A

Profit or nonprofit: Non-profit

ADMISSIONS

Application form required: Yes

Forms required: Application, health form

Application deadline: Apply any time

Application fee: 3's $175; 4's $250; K-6 $375

Contact: Church-school office

Phone: (214) 358-4396

Student interview required: No

Parent interview required: Yes

Entrance test required: Yes

Specific tests administered: 1st - 4th Grade: Grade K-1 Gesell Developmental; Grades 2-4 ITBS achievement testing , Fifth and above: ITBS achievement testing

Accept test scores from other schools: Yes

Testing fee: $32.50, Gesell

Time of year testing is administered: N/A

Test dates offered: N/A

Out of state applicants: N/A

Notification by phone: Yes, conference by phone with principal.

Notification by mail: N/A

FINANCIAL

Preschool tuition: 3's $1600; 4's $2350
Elementary tuition: Kindergarten - grade 6 $3750
Secondary tuition: N/A
Other tuition: N/A
Cash discounts: N/A
Personal check: N/A
Automatic bank draw: N/A
Credit cards: N/A
Monthly: Yes, 10 payments, August - May
Per semester: N/A
Annually: 5% discount if paid in advance
Financial assistance offered: Yes, based on need
Cancellation insurance: N/A
Sibling discount: Yes, 10% 2nd & 3rd child
Application acceptance deposit required: N/A
Other: N/A

SERVICES

Before school care offered: Yes, supervision begins at 7:00 a.m.
After school care offered: Yes, 3:30 p.m. - 5:45 p.m.
Transportation provided: N/A
Lunch/snack program: Lunch fee $2.50 for optional catered lunch, children bring their own snacks
Other: Computer lab, library, enrichment curriculum (Spanish, Band) and extra curricular sports activities offered

LUTHERAN HIGH SCHOOL

8494 Stults Road
Dallas, TX 75243
Contact: **Patricia Klekamp, Principal**
(214) 349-8912
(214) 340-3095 FAX

Office Hours: 8:00 a.m. - 4:00 p.m.
E-MAIL: donnafrieling@usa.net
Web Site:
www.lhsdfw.com
MAPSCO: 26C

PHILOSOPHY OF SCHOOL

Lutheran High School offers a Christ centered education to students in grades 7th - 12th with an emphasis upon a strong academic program in a Christian caring environment.

CREDENTIALS

Accreditations: (see glossary) TAAPS, TAPS, TEPSAC
Awards and special recognition: (see glossary) Christian Award (LCMS)
Qualification of administrator: Master's degree in education with special experience in secondary education. Member LCMS
Qualification of faculty: Certified by TEA. Working on or have advanced degree.

GENERAL

Alternative: No
College preparatory: Yes
Montessori: No
Nondenominational: No
Church affiliated: Yes
Denomination: Lutheran
Jewish: N/A
Other denominations: N/A
Student type: Co-ed
Grade category (for details see specific grades offered below): Secondary
Infants: N/A
Preschool: N/A
Kindergarten: N/A
Primary / Transition: No
Elementary: N/A
Secondary or Middle School: Yes
Specific grades offered: 7th grade - 12th grade
Student teacher ratio average: 17:1

Classes offered per grade: N/A
Average class size: 25
Total enrollment: 285
Recommended grades to apply: 6th grade and up
School hours: 8:00 a.m. - 3:30 p.m.
Calendar school year: 8/16/99 through 5/26/00
Uniforms required: Yes
Parental involvement opportunities and requirements: PTL
Average SAT scores: 1160
Visitation procedures: Contact the admissions office for an appointment.
Personal appointments for touring the facility: Contact the admissions office for a tour.
Group tour dates: N/A
Open house dates: 10/21/99 and 1/8/00
Classroom visits: N/A
Profit or non-profit: Non-profit

ADMISSIONS

Application form required: Yes
Forms required: Application, Teacher analysis, Student analysis, Records and Testing
Application deadline: Open - Rolling
Application fee: $350.00
Contact: N/A
Phone: (214) 349-8912
Student interview required: Yes
Parent interview required: Yes
Entrance test required: Yes
Specific tests administered: Secondary: 7th & 8th Gates MacGinitie, 9th - 12th Nelson Denny
Accept test scores from other schools: Yes, will also test.
Testing fee: $25.00
Time of year testing is administered: Will test students individually.
Test dates offered: 1/8/00
Out of state applicants: N/A
Notification by phone: N/A
Notification by mail: N/A

FINANCIAL

Preschool tuition: N/A
Elementary tuition: N/A
Secondary tuition: 7th & 8th $5120, 9th-12th $6950
Other tuition: N/A
Cash discounts: N/A
Personal check: Yes
Automatic bank draw: N/A
Credit cards: N/A
Monthly: Yes
Per semester: Yes
Annually: Yes
Financial assistance offered: Yes, need based.
Cancellation insurance: N/A
Sibling discount: N/A
Application acceptance deposit required: No
Other: N/A

SERVICES

Before school care offered: N/A
After school care offered: N/A
Transportation provided: N/A
Lunch/snack program: Lunch program

OUR REDEEMER LUTHERAN SCHOOL

7611 Park Lane
Dallas, TX 75225
Contact: **Dr. John R. Troutman**
(214) 368-1465
(214) 368-1473 FAX

Office Hours: 8:00 a.m. - 5:00 p.m.
E-MAIL: cforc.com//cms/tx/dallas/our_redeemer
Web Site: N/A
MAPSCO: 26S

PHILOSOPHY OF SCHOOL

Our Redeemer Lutheran School of Dallas exists to share the good news of Jesus Christ by disciplining young people towards reaching their full potential; enabling the child to grow in Love and Commitment to God, Love and Commitment toward their families, and Love and Commitment toward their community; and empowering young people to integrate knowledge. This process is modeled by a staff of caring, nurturing, qualified Christian educators, who are committed to excellence, and by example, enrich and encourage self- respect as a gifted Child of God, in whom the Light of the Lord will shine.

CREDENTIALS

Accreditations: (see glossary) NLSA, TEPSAC
Awards and special recognition: (see glossary) N/A
Qualification of administrator: Master's degree
Qualification of faculty: Bachelor's degrees or higher

GENERAL

Alternative: No
College preparatory: No
Montessori: No
Nondenominational: No
Church affiliated: Yes
Denomination: Lutheran
Jewish: N/A
Other denominations: N/A
Student type: Co-ed
Grade category (for details see specific grades offered below): Elementary
Infants: N/A
Preschool: Half Day

Kindergarten: Full Day
Primary / Transition: No
Elementary: Yes
Secondary or Middle School: N/A
Specific grades offered: Preschool (3 years) - grade 6
Other: Infants: 1yr-3yr, Parents Day Out. Preschool: 3K-4K, Extended Care Available.
Student teacher ratio average: 18:1
Classes offered per grade: Kindergarten: 2 sections; All other: 1 section
Average class size: 18
Total enrollment: 170
Recommended grades to apply: PreK, Kindergarten, 1st grade
School hours: 8:30 a.m. - 3:30 p.m. (hours of operation, 7:00 a.m. - 6:00 p.m.)
Calendar school year: August 16, 1999 - May 25, 2000
Uniforms required: Yes
Parental involvement opportunities and requirements: Parent Teacher League provides active ongoing support for the school; promotes and conducts social fundraising events.
Average SAT scores: N/A
Visitation procedures: Contact the school office. Families are encouraged to tour campus and monitor classes.
Personal appointments for touring the facility: Offered
Group tour dates: During open house
Open house dates: November 14, 1999
Classroom visits: Available on request
Profit or non-profit: Non-profit

ADMISSIONS

Application form required: Yes
Forms required: Achievement Test Scores, copy of most recent report card, Student Referral Form
Application deadline: February 1
Application fee: $100
Contact: School office
Phone: (214) 368-1465
Student interview required: Yes
Parent interview required: Yes
Entrance test required: Yes
Specific tests administered: Kindergarten: Gessell Developmental Readiness Test, 1st - 6th Grade: Use student's Achievement Test Scores in Reading and Math from within the last year.

Accept test scores from other schools: Yes
Testing fee: N/A
Time of year testing is administered: N/A
Test dates offered: N/A
Out of state applicants: N/A
Notification by phone: N/A
Notification by mail: Yes
Other: Entrance test required if transcripts not available.

FINANCIAL

Preschool tuition: $1800 - $2500
Elementary tuition: $3900
Secondary tuition: N/A
Other tuition: $400 comprehensive fee
Cash discounts: No
Personal check: Yes
Automatic bank draw: No
Credit cards: Yes
Monthly: Yes, 10 payments
Per semester: Yes
Annually: Yes
Financial assistance offered: Yes, limited
Cancellation insurance: No
Sibling discount: Yes, 10%
Application acceptance deposit required: No

SERVICES

Before school care offered: Yes, 7:00 a.m. - 8:10 a.m.
After school care offered: Yes, 3:30 p.m. - 6:00 p.m.
Transportation provided: N/A
Lunch/snack program: Lunch fee is $2.50 per day. Snacks are provided for kindergarten and preschool students.
Other: Computer lab, library, and extracurricular activities offered

ZION LUTHERAN SCHOOL

6121 East Lovers Lane
Dallas, TX 75214
Contact: **Douglas C. Molin, Principal**
(214) 363-1630
(214) 361-2049 FAX

Office Hours: 8:00 a.m. - 5:00 p.m.
E-MAIL: dmolin@ziondallas.org
Web Site: N/A
MAPSCO: 36C

PHILOSOPHY OF SCHOOL

The purpose of Zion Lutheran School is to provide Christian education in partner-ship with parents so that children may be provided with a comprehensive program of education; children may be nurtured in the Word of God; children may in faith learn to know Jesus Christ; children, by God's grace, may experience a full Christian life; children may learn to recognize themselves as person's of worth; children may learn to understand and appreciate their talents and gifts.

CREDENTIALS

Accreditations: (see glossary) LSAC, NLSA, TANS, TEA
Awards and special recognition: (see glossary) N/A
Qualification of administrator: Minimum degree: M.Ed. (preferred); certified by the Lutheran Church (Missouri Synod); same as below
Qualification of faculty: Minimum degree: B.A.; state-issued teaching certificate; member of the Lutheran Church (Missouri Synod); preferred credential: certification by the Lutheran Church (Missouri Synod)
Other: Accreditations: Texas District of the Lutheran Church - Missouri Synod

GENERAL

Alternative: No
College preparatory: No
Montessori: No
Nondenominational: No
Church affiliated: Yes
Denomination: Lutheran
Jewish: N/A
Other denominations: Denomination:LCMS (Lutheran Church Missouri Synod)
Student type: Co-ed
Grade category (for details see specific grades offered below): Elementary
Infants: N/A
Preschool: Half Day and Full Day

Kindergarten: Full Day
Primary / Transition: No
Elementary: Yes
Secondary or Middle School: N/A
Specific grades offered: N/A
Other: Parents day out: grade 8, Infants: Parents day out
Student teacher ratio average: 15:1
Classes offered per grade: One class per grade
Average class size: 18
Total enrollment: 252
Recommended grades to apply: N/A
School hours: 7:00 a.m. - 6:00 p.m.
Calendar school year: August 17, 1999 - May 26, 2000
Uniforms required: Yes
Parental involvement opportunities and requirements: Yes, in a variety of volunteer opportunities
Average SAT scores: N/A
Visitation procedures: Call the school office for an appointment and tour. (214) 363-1630
Personal appointments for touring the facility: Individual interview by appointment
Group tour dates: N/A
Open house dates: N/A
Classroom visits: See above in Visitation Procedures
Profit or non-profit: No

ADMISSIONS

Application form required: Yes
Forms required: Grade transcripts & current achievement transcripts, immunization records and birth certificate
Application deadline: New applications accepted after January 15
Application fee: $120-$300
Contact: Douglas C. Molin
Phone: (214) 363-1630
Student interview required: No
Parent interview required: Yes
Entrance test required: No
Specific tests administered: N/A
Accept test scores from other schools: No
Testing fee: N/A
Time of year testing is administered: N/A

Test dates offered: N/A
Out of state applicants: N/A
Notification by phone: Yes
Notification by mail: Yes
Other: Student interview is not required for Preschool 3 - grade 6. It is required
for grades 7-8.

FINANCIAL

Preschool tuition: $1145-$3800
Elementary tuition: $2000-$4200
Secondary tuition: N/A
Other tuition: Uniform - $200 (average cost)
Cash discounts: Yes, available for full prepaid tuition
Personal check: Yes
Automatic bank draw: Yes
Credit cards: N/A
Monthly: Yes
Per semester: N/A
Annually: Yes, see above for discounts
Financial assistance offered: Yes
Cancellation insurance: N/A
Sibling discount: N/A
Application acceptance deposit required: N/A

SERVICES

Before school care offered: Yes, 7:00 a.m. - 8:00 a.m.
After school care offered: Yes, 3:30 p.m. - 6:00 p.m.
Transportation provided: N/A
Lunch/snack program: Snacks provided to preschoolers. Hot lunch available to
Kindergarten through grade 8.

NAEYC
National Association for the Education of Young Children

1509 16th Street N.W.
Washington, D.C. 20036-1426
1 (800) 424-2460 ext. 360
E-MAIL: naeyc@naeyc.org
Web Site: www. naeyc.org

Dr. Sue Bredekamp

The National Association for the Education of Young Children (NAEYC), the nation's oldest and largest organization of early childhood educators, is a non-profit, professional organization comprised of educators, parents, pediatricians, students, directors, and other individuals who are concerned with and involved in the development of children ages birth through eight. The National Academy of Early Childhood Programs administers a national, voluntary accreditation system for all types of preschools, kindergartens, child care centers, and school-age child care programs. Accreditation is a three-step process which involves a self-study, validation visit, and a commission decision. The accreditation process improves the quality of programs by evaluating curriculum, administration, staff qualifications and development, physical environment, health and safety, interactions among staff and children, and parental involvement. Accreditation from NAEYC is valid for a three-year period. At the end of the term, programs must re-apply for accreditation. You may request a list of accredited programs by writing NAEYC.

> **Akiba Academy (see SACS)**
> **Bent Tree Child Development Center**
> **Callier Child Development Preschool (see Ch. 4)**
> **Children's Workshop, The**
> **Creative Preschool Co-op, The**
> **Creative School, The - Walnut Hill United Methodist Church**
> **Early Learning Center at First Christian Church (see Ch. 4)**
> **East Dallas Community School (see Ch. 4)**
> **Epiphany Day School (see SAES)**
> **First United Methodist Church Day School**
> **Glen Oaks School**
> **Glenwood Day School**

Highland Park United Methodist Church Child Development Program
    (see Ch. 4)
Jewish Community Center of Dallas (see Ch. 4)
Lakewood United Methodist Development Learning Center (see Ch. 4)
Lovers Lane United Methodist Church
North Dallas Day School (see Ch. 4)
Northaven Co-operative Preschool & Kindergarten (see Ch. 4)
Northbrook School (see TDPRS)
Parish Day, The (see ISAS)
Preston-Royal Preschool (see Ch. 4)
Rainbow Connection Preschool & Kindergarten (see Ch. 4)
Schreiber Methodist Preschool (see Ch. 4)
Temple Emanu-El Preschool (see Ch. 4)
Westminister Presbyterian Preschool & Kindergarten

BENT TREE CHILD DEVELOPMENT CENTER

17275 Addison Road
Addison, TX 75001
Contact: Charlotte Buchanan
(972) 931-0868
(972) 931-2103 FAX

Office Hours: 7:00 a.m - 6:30 p.m. M-F
E-MAIL: CBuchanan@BentTreecdc.com
Web Site: N/A
MAPSCO: 4U

PHILOSOPHY OF SCHOOL

Developmental enrichment program designed to foster children's individual interests and abilities through a center based learning environment.

CREDENTIALS

Accreditations: (see glossary) DAEYC, NAEYC, SECA, TAEYC
Awards and special recognition: (see glossary) N/A
Qualification of administrator: Bachelor of Science Degree Family & Child Development, Early Childhood Education, 25 years experience
Qualification of faculty: 2 - 4 year degrees/master's in Early Childhood or related field.
Other: Staff sign yearly contracts.

GENERAL

Alternative: No
College preparatory: No
Montessori: No
Nondenominational: Yes
Church affiliated: No
Denomination: N/A
Jewish: N/A
Other denominations: N/A
Student type: Co-ed
Grade category (for details see specific grades offered below): Preschool
Infants: N/A
Preschool: Full Day
Kindergarten: Full Day
Primary / Transition: No
Elementary: N/A

Secondary or Middle School: N/A

Specific grades offered: Toddler thru Kindergarten program

Other: After school program.

Student teacher ratio average: NAEYC standards set for low teacher/child ratios.

Classes offered per grade:N/A

Average class size: N/A

Total enrollment: 250

Recommended grades to apply: 18 mos. - Kindergarten

School hours: 9:00 a.m. - 3:00 p.m./ Extended 7:00 a.m. - 6:30 p.m.

Calendar school year: Year round

Uniforms required: No

Parental involvement opportunites and requirements: Numerous parental involvement opportunities and special events.

Average SAT scores: K ITBS Test:Read Math 99% Natl. Rating

Visitation procedures: Classrooms have an observation window. Parents are welcome anytime.

Personal appointments for touring the facility: Stop by anytime.

Group tour dates: N/A

Open house dates: First Saturday in December

Classroom visits: Parent Conferences: Fall and Spring.

Profit or nonprofit: Profit

ADMISSIONS

Application form required: Yes

Forms required: Can be mailed or picked up at the front office.

Application deadline: Classes form yearly in late August. Ongoing

Application fee: None

Contact: N/A

Phone: (972) 931-0868

Student interview required: Yes

Parent interview required: Yes

Entrance test required: Yes

Specific tests administered: Preschool: Gesell Developmental Evaluation, Kindergarten: Gesell Developmental Evaluation plus school criteria

Accept test scores from other schools: No

Testing fee: $ 60.00

Time of year testing is administered: June, July and August

Test dates offered: Daily

Out of state applicants: Yes

Notification by phone: Yes

Notification by mail: N/A

FINANCIAL

Preschool tuition: Level II $180/wk. Levels lll & IV $155/wk.

Elementary tuition: Kindergarten $160/wk. Extended 1/2 day $130/wk.

Secondary tuition: N/A

Other tuition: Toddler $ 200/wk.; after school $ 90/wk.

Cash discounts: N/A

Personal check: Yes

Automatic bank draw: N/A

Credit cards: N/A

Monthly: Yes

Per semester: Yes

Annually: Yes, required weekly.

Financial assistance offered: No

Cancellation insurance: N/A

Sibling discount: N/A

Application acceptance deposit required: Registration fee $130, final week tuition fee - one week's rate of tuition

SERVICES

Before school care offered: N/A

After school care offered: Yes, 3:00 p.m. - 6:30p.m.

Transportation provided: Yes

Lunch/snack program: Yes

Other: Security System requires passcode to enter the locked front door. Extra curricular activities 3:00 p.m. - 6:00 p.m. daily. Computers in all Level III preschool classes and above.

THE CHILDREN'S WORKSHOP

1409 14th Street
Plano, TX 75074
Contact: **Jo M. Howser, Director**
(972) 424-1932
(972) 424-8315 FAX

Office Hours: 8:30 a.m. - 4:30 p.m.
E-MAIL: N/A
Web Site: N/A
MAPSCO: 659Z

PHILOSOPHY OF SCHOOL

We build on the strengths of each child. We believe children are born wanting to discover, learn, grow, and be loved and accepted by others. Our school fosters the individual child's strengths while giving help in those areas in which the child has difficulty. Children and teachers alike are learning in an atmosphere that fosters discovery, critical thinking, language development, and respect for the genius in each of us.

CREDENTIALS

Accreditations: (see glossary) NAEYC
Awards and special recognition: (see glossary) N/A
Qualification of administrator: Teaching certificate, UN London; 30 years ongoing experience learning, teaching, and administering
Qualification of faculty: Minimum: bachelor's degree and teaching/parenting experience

GENERAL

Alternative: No
College preparatory: No
Montessori: No
Nondenominational: No
Church affiliated: No
Denomination: N/A
Jewish: N/A
Other denominations: N/A
Student type: Co-ed
Grade category (for details see specific grades offered below): Elementary
Infants: N/A
Preschool: Half Day

Kindergarten: Full Day
Primary / Transition: Yes
Elementary: Yes
Secondary or Middle School: N/A
Specific grades offered: Preschool (3 years) - grade 5
Other: Half day Kindergarten also available
Student teacher ratio average: 10:1, 7:1
Classes offered per grade: N/A
Average class size: N/A
Total enrollment: 140
Recommended grades to apply: N/A
School hours: 8:30 a.m. - 3:15 p.m.
Calendar school year: P.I.S.D. calendar
Uniforms required: No
Parental involvement opportunities and requirements: Lots
Average SAT scores: N/A
Visitation procedures: Set up meeting with director
Personal appointments for touring the facility: Yes
Group tour dates: N/A
Open house dates: N/A
Classroom visits: At time of visit with director
Profit or non-profit: No

ADMISSIONS

Application form required: Yes
Forms required: Necessary medical verification
Application deadline: N/A
Application fee: Registration
Contact: Jo Howser, Neva Smith
Phone: (214) 424-1932
Student interview required: Yes
Parent interview required: Yes
Entrance test required: No
Specific tests administered: N/A
Accept test scores from other schools: No
Testing fee: N/A
Time of year testing is administered: N/A
Test dates offered: N/A
Out of state applicants: N/A
Notification by phone: N/A
Notification by mail: Yes

FINANCIAL

Preschool tuition: $1,200 - $2,550
Elementary tuition: $4,300
Secondary tuition: N/A
Other tuition: N/A
Cash discounts: N/A
Personal check: Yes
Automatic bank draw: N/A
Credit cards: N/A
Monthly: Yes
Per semester: N/A
Annually: N/A
Financial assistance offered: N/A
Cancellation insurance: N/A
Sibling discount: N/A
Application acceptance deposit required: Yes

SERVICES

Before school care offered: N/A
After school care offered: N/A
Transportation provided: N/A
Lunch/snack program: Yes, snack

CREATIVE PRESCHOOL CO-OP

1210 W. Beltline Road
Richardson, TX 75080
Contact: Kristie Carruthers, Director
(972) 234-4791
N/A FAX

Office Hours: 8:30 a.m. - 12:30 p.m.
E-MAIL: N/A
Web Site: N/A
MAPSCO: 16C

PHILOSOPHY OF SCHOOL

The Creative Preschool Co-op seeks to develop in each child high self-esteem and a love of learning; facilitate positive social development, foster the child's imagination & creativity; and support parents and help them develop their parenting skills to their highest potential.

CREDENTIALS

Accreditations: (see glossary) NAEYC
Awards and special recognition: (see glossary) Discovery Science for Preschool Grant recipient
Qualification of administrator: College degree
Qualification of faculty: College degree

GENERAL

Alternative: No
College preparatory: No
Montessori: No
Nondenominational: Yes
Church affiliated: No
Denomination: N/A
Jewish: N/A
Other denominations: N/A
Student type: Co-ed
Grade category (for details see specific grades offered below): Preschool
Infants: N/A
Preschool: Half Day
Kindergarten: N/A
Primary / Transition: No
Elementary: N/A

Secondary or Middle School: N/A
Specific grades offered: Two year olds - four year olds
Student teacher ratio average: 2's 6:1; 3 & 4's 7:1
Classes offered per grade: N/A
Average class size: 12
Total enrollment: 88
Recommended grades to apply: N/A
School hours: 9:00 a.m. - 12:00 p.m.
Calendar school year: August - May
Uniforms required: No
Parental involvement opportunities and requirements: Assist teacher in classroom on a rotation schedule; help administer school
Average SAT scores: N/A
Visitation procedures: Call the school to arrange a visit.
Personal appointments for touring the facility: N/A
Group tour dates: N/A
Open house dates: N/A
Classroom visits: N/A
Profit or non-profit: Non-profit

ADMISSIONS

Application form required: Yes
Forms required: Up-to-date vaccination history and medical history signed by doctor; filled out Creative Preschool Co-op enrollment forms
Application deadline: Apply anytime
Application fee: $100
Contact: Kristie Carruthers
Phone: (972) 234-4791
Student interview required: No
Parent interview required: No
Entrance test required: No
Specific tests administered: N/A
Accept test scores from other schools: No
Testing fee: N/A
Time of year testing is administered: N/A
Test dates offered: N/A
Out of state applicants: N/A
Notification by phone: Yes
Notification by mail: N/A
Other: Or notified at time of visit

FINANCIAL

Preschool tuition: $100/mo. (PDO); $155/mo. 2-day class
Elementary tuition: N/A
Secondary tuition: N/A
Other tuition: $175/mo. 3-day class, $200/mo. 4-day class
Cash discounts: N/A
Personal check: Yes
Automatic bank draw: N/A
Credit cards: N/A
Monthly: Yes
Per semester: N/A
Annually: N/A
Financial assistance offered: None
Cancellation insurance: Yes, registration fee and supply fee non-refundable; prepaid. May tuition refundable for students who withdraw before January.
Sibling discount: Yes, monthly tuition $15 off
Application acceptance deposit required: N/A

SERVICES

Before school care offered: N/A
After school care offered: Yes, extended-day program on Tues., Wed. and Thurs. until 2:30 p.m.
Transportation provided: N/A
Lunch/snack program: Extended-day students bring their own lunch; tuition $25 per month. The co-op parent provides a nutritious snack and drink for entire class.
Other: Computer and library; extracurricular and enrichment activities available.

THE CREATIVE SCHOOL - WALNUT HILL UNITED METHODIST CHURCH

10066 Marsh Lane
Dallas, TX 75229
Contact: **Pam Douce, Director**
(214) 352-0732
(214) 357-3753 FAX

Office Hours: 8:30 a.m. - 2:00 p.m.
E-MAIL: Creative@whumc.com
Web Site: www.whumc.com
MAPSCO: 23M

PHILOSOPHY OF SCHOOL

The Creative School is dedicated to the education and nurturing of the preschool child in a loving, caring environment. Development of the whole child, emotionally, socially, physically, intellectually, and spiritually.

CREDENTIALS

Accreditations: (see glossary) DAEYC, NAEYC
Awards and special recognition: (see glossary) Discovery Science for Pre-School grant recipient
Qualification of administrator: Master of Education, Early Childhood Education, Director's Certificate
Qualification of faculty: All teachers are degreed.

GENERAL

Alternative: No
College preparatory: No
Montessori: No
Nondenominational: No
Church affiliated: Yes
Denomination: Methodist
Jewish: N/A
Other denominations: N/A
Student type: Co-ed
Grade category (for details see specific grades offered below): Kindergarten
Infants: N/A
Preschool: Half Day

Kindergarten: Half Day
Primary / Transition: No
Elementary: N/A
Secondary or Middle School: N/A
Specific grades offered: Preschool: 9 a.m. - 12 noon;
  Kindergarten: 9 a.m. - 2 p.m.
Student teacher ratio average: 10:1
Classes offered per grade: N/A
Average class size: 10 - 12
Total enrollment: 115
Recommended grades to apply: N/A
School hours: PK: 9:00 a.m. - 12 noon; K: 9:00 a.m. - 2:00 p.m.
Calendar school year: August - May
Uniforms required: No
Parental involvement opportunities and requirements: Parent Council, Dad's
  Club
Average SAT scores: N/A
Visitation procedures: Visitors welcome, call office for appointment
Personal appointments for touring the facility: Yes
Group tour dates: N/A
Open house dates: N/A
Classroom visits: By appointment
Profit or non-profit: Non-profit

ADMISSIONS

Application form required: Yes
Forms required: Creative School Application Form
Application deadline: None - registration begins in February
Application fee: PK: $110; Kindergarten: $135
Contact: Debbie Blades
Phone: (214) 352-0732
Student interview required: No
Parent interview required: No
Entrance test required: No
Specific tests administered: N/A
Accept test scores from other schools: No
Testing fee: N/A
Time of year testing is administered: N/A
Test dates offered: N/A
Out of state applicants: N/A
Notification by phone: N/A

Notification by mail: N/A

FINANCIAL

Preschool tuition: Varies by age group
Elementary tuition: N/A
Secondary tuition: N/A
Other tuition: N/A
Cash discounts: Yes, 10% discount - church members
Personal check: Yes
Automatic bank draw: N/A
Credit cards: N/A
Monthly: Yes
Per semester: Yes
Annually: Yes
Financial assistance offered: Some scholarships are available.
Cancellation insurance: N/A
Sibling discount: N/A
Application acceptance deposit required: N/A

SERVICES

Before school care offered: N/A
After school care offered: Yes, Preschool Extended Day; Lunch Bunch Extended 12:00 p.m. - 2 p.m.
Transportation provided: N/A
Lunch/snack program: Lunch Bunch offered daily: 12 noon - 2 p.m. for PK, additional fee

FIRST UNITED METHODIST CHURCH DAY SCHOOL

801 W. Ave. B at Glenbrook
Garland, TX 75040
Contact: **Grace Ashley, Director**
(972) 494-3096 or (972) 272-3471
(972) 272-3473 FAX

Office Hours: 8:30 a.m. - 4:30 p.m.
E-MAIL: fumcgar@airmail.net
Web Site: www.shr.net/fumc
MAPSCO: 19Y

PHILOSOPHY OF SCHOOL

To provide learning experiences for children of the church membership and the community in an environment which encourages the child to ask questions, explore and experiment, develop a new security and independence in the world outside the home, make friends and learn to get along with children and adults, and find that he/she is a person to be valued for his/her own unique being-a child of God. Our school is Christian oriented but not denominationally sectarian. We stress those elements of the faith common to all Christians. We plan for our enrollment to include a cross-section of races, nationalities, and economic backgrounds. Under the leadership of quality teachers, the classes include a balance of guided play activities, creative art work, music, outdoor play, conversation, storytime, dramatic play, and group activities. Each child is helped to grow in independence, social development, and to develop his/her own unique talents and abilities.

CREDENTIALS

Accreditations: (see glossary) NAEYC, TDPRS
Awards and special recognition: (see glossary) N/A
Qualification of administrator: B.S. in Elementary Education, M.Ed. in Early Childhood Education, Certified Director of Christian Education, United Methodist Church, Diaconal Minister, United Methodist Church, teacher and administrator, 29 years
Qualification of faculty: College degree and experience
Other: Also accredited by the National Academy of Early Childhood Program. Affiliated with Association for Childhood Education International, DAEYC, SACUS, Kindergarten Teachers of Texas, Dallas Methodist Nursery Kindergarten Association, Ecumenical Childcare Network

GENERAL

Alternative: No

College preparatory: No

Montessori: No

Nondenominational: No

Church affiliated: Yes

Denomination: United Methodist

Jewish: N/A

Other denominations: N/A

Student type: Co-ed

Grade category (for details see specific grades offered below): Preschool

Infants: Mother's Day Out Tuesday & Wednesday

Preschool: Half Day, 9:00 a.m. - Noon (Extended Day Noon - 2:00 p.m.)

Kindergarten: Half Day, 9:00 a.m. - Noon (Extended Day Noon - 2:00 p.m.)

Primary / Transition: No

Elementary: N/A

Secondary or Middle School: N/A

Other: Mother's Day Out: Tuesday & Wednesday, age 3 months +,
9:00 a.m. - 2 p.m.

Specific grades offered: Preschool (ages 3 and 4) and Kindergarten

Student teacher ratio average: 8-10:2 - 10-12:2

Classes offered per grade: Multiple

Average class size: 8-12

Total enrollment: 115

Recommended grades to apply: N/A

School hours: Monday - Friday 9:00 a.m. - 12:00 p.m.; extended day Mon- Thurs
until 2:00 p.m.

Calendar school year: Late August - mid May

Uniforms required: No

Parental involvement opportunities and requirements: Volunteers, parenting
programs, class activities

Average SAT scores: N/A

Visitation procedures: Always welcome

Personal appointments for touring the facility: Offered anytime

Group tour dates: Offered anytime

Open house dates: August 29, 1999 and Spring 2000

Classroom visits: By appointment

Profit or non-profit: Non-profit

ADMISSIONS

Application form required: Yes
Forms required: N/A
Application deadline: Apply anytime
Application fee: $75 - $95
Contact: Grace Ashley, Director
Phone: (972) 494-3096 or (972) 272-3471
Student interview required: No
Parent interview required: No
Entrance test required: No
Specific tests administered: N/A
Accept test scores from other schools: No
Testing fee: N/A
Time of year testing is administered: N/A
Test dates offered: N/A
Out of state applicants: N/A
Notification by phone: N/A
Notification by mail: Yes

FINANCIAL

Preschool tuition: 1999-2000 Tuition Schedule

	Enrollment Fee	Monthly Tuition
3 Year Olds: 2 Day	$75	$115
3 Year Olds: 3 Day	$85	$135
4 Year Olds: 2 Day	$75	$115
4 Year Olds: 3 Day	$85	$135
4 Year Olds: 5 Day	$95	$160
Kindergarten	$95	$190

Elementary tuition: N/A
Secondary tuition: N/A
Other tuition: Extended Day - $6 per day
Cash discounts: N/A
Personal check: Yes
Automatic bank draw: N/A
Credit cards: N/A
Monthly: Yes
Per semester: N/A
Annually: N/A
Financial assistance offered: No
Cancellation insurance: N/A

Sibling discount: N/A
Application acceptance deposit required: N/A

SERVICES

Before school care offered: N/A
After school care offered: Yes, Monday - Thursday until 2:00 p.m.
Transportation provided: N/A
Lunch/snack program: Snacks available
Other: Library and enrichment curriculum offered. Spanish, music, large shaded playground

GLEN OAKS SCHOOL

12105 Plano Road
Dallas, TX 75243
Contact: **Ashley Hutto, Director**
(972) 231-3135
(972) 644-6373 FAX

Office Hours: 6:30 a.m. - 6:15 p.m.
E-MAIL: glenoaks@flash.net
Web Site: N/A
MAPSCO: 18W

PHILOSOPHY OF SCHOOL

Mission Statement: The mission of Glen Oaks School is to provide a nurturing environment where children, parents, and staff work together to empower each child to reach his/her fullest potential. Goals of the school: For children: To enable students to develop their full potential for life. (The social, emotional, cognitive, and physical development of each child is viewed as a whole, and each child is given the opportunity to develop at his/her own individual pace.) For parents: To be a resource in the areas of child development and appropriate parenting methods. To encourage parents to interact with the staff and their child in the developmental process at Glen Oaks School. For the Community: To support community efforts to improve the condition for the care and education of children through teacher training workshops, parent seminars, and advocacy efforts.

CREDENTIALS

Accreditations: (see glossary) CCMS, NAEYC, TDPRS
Awards and special recognition: (see glossary) CCMS four-star status
Qualification of administrator: Same as faculty's plus at least three years' experience.
Qualification of faculty: Primary grades - bachelor's degree; early childhood-child development degree, certificate or experience
Other: Also accredited by NSACCA

GENERAL

Alternative: No
College preparatory: No
Montessori: No
Nondenominational: Yes
Church affiliated: No
Denomination: N/A
Jewish: N/A
Other denominations: N/A

Student type: Co-ed

Grade category (for details see specific grades offered below): Elementary

Infants: N/A

Preschool: Full Day

Kindergarten: Full Day

Primary / Transition: No

Elementary: Yes

Secondary or Middle School: N/A

Specific grades offered: Primary grades (K-4); early childhood
   (24 months - 5 years)

Student teacher ratio average: Primary grades 17:1, early childhood 11:1 to 13:1

Classes offered per grade: N/A

Average class size: 15

Total enrollment: 260

Recommended grades to apply: N/A

School hours: 8:30 a.m. - 3:00 p.m.

Calendar school year: Mid-August - May; extended care year-round

Uniforms required: No

Parental involvement opportunities and requirements: Strongly encouraged.
   We have a parent-support group that meets monthly. Each class has a potluck
   dinner to get to know other families, parent-education seminars, class parties,
   open house, and end-of-the-year celebrations.

Average SAT scores: N/A

Visitation procedures: Open-door policy

Personal appointments for touring the facility: Available upon request

Group tour dates: Available upon request

Open house dates: Call for information

Classroom visits: Available upon request

Profit or non-profit: Profit

Other: Uniforms are under consideration.

ADMISSIONS

Application form required: Yes

Forms required: Enrollment, medical, field-trip, swimming, and emergency
   forms

Application deadline: February - full enrollment

Application fee: N/A

Contact: Ashley Hutto

Phone: (972) 231-3135

Student interview required: No

Parent interview required: No

Entrance test required: No
Specific tests administered: N/A
Accept test scores from other schools: No
Testing fee: N/A
Time of year testing is administered: N/A
Test dates offered: N/A
Out of state applicants: Yes
Notification by phone: Yes
Notification by mail: Yes
Other: Two weeks notice to disenroll.

FINANCIAL

Preschool tuition: PS: $450/mo. or $114 wk.; PK: $436/mo. or $111/wk.
Elementary tuition: K: $446/mo.; 1st-4th: $462/mo. Both costs include
   extended care.
Secondary tuition: N/A
Other tuition: Supply fees cover all school supplies & field trips. PS/PK $55
   (Aug & May); K $90 (Aug); 1st-4th: $150 (Aug); K-SA Summer $75 (May)
Cash discounts: N/A
Personal check: Yes
Automatic bank draw: N/A
Credit cards: N/A
Monthly: Yes
Per semester: Yes
Annually: Yes
Financial assistance offered: CCMS
Cancellation insurance: N/A
Sibling discount: N/A
Application acceptance deposit required: 1/2 mo. tuition refund w/14 day
   notice to disenroll

SERVICES

Before school care offered: Yes
After school care offered: Yes, 3:15 p.m. - 6:30 p.m.
Transportation provided: Yes
Lunch/snack program: Snacks given in the morning and afternoon. Hot lunch
   served homestyle each day, included in supply fee/tuition.
Other: Extracurricular activities and enrichment curriculum offered including
   computer learning, physical education, art, music, and Spanish; transportation
   provided to area schools.

GLENWOOD DAY SCHOOL

2446 Apollo
Garland, TX 75044
Contact: **Rhonda Corn-Kidd**
(972) 530-4460

Office Hours: 7:30 a.m. - 5:30 p.m.
E-MAIL: glenwood@flash.net
Web Site: N/A
MAPSCO: 19A

PHILOSOPHY OF SCHOOL

The mission of Glenwood Day School is to provide a nurturing environment where children, parents, and staff work together to empower each child to reach his/her fullest potential.

CREDENTIALS

Accreditations: (see glossary) NAEYC; four-star vendor of Child Care Management Services (CCMS)
Awards and special recognition: (see glossary) N/A
Qualification of administrator: Bachelor's degree in elementary education; master's degree in early childhood development
Qualification of faculty: (Kindergarten) bachelor's degree in education

GENERAL

Alternative: No
College preparatory: No
Montessori: No
Nondenominational: No
Church affiliated: No
Denomination: N/A
Jewish: N/A
Other denominations: N/A
Student type: Co-ed
Grade category (for details see specific grades offered below): Preschool
Infants: N/A
Preschool: Yes
Kindergarten: Yes
Primary / Transition: N/A
Elementary: N/A
Secondary or Middle School: N/A
Specific grades offered: Pre-K (18 months) - kindergarten; before-and-after school programs

Student teacher ratio average: Varies (NAEYC accreditation ratios); kindergarten - 15:1

Classes offered per grade: N/A

Average class size: 12-26

Total enrollment: 199

Recommended grades to apply: N/A

School hours: 6:30 a.m. - 6:00 p.m.

Calendar school year: August - May; open year round

Uniforms required: No

Parental involvement opportunities and requirements: Parent committees, P.T.C.

Average SAT scores: N/A

Visitation procedures: N/A

Personal appointments for touring the facility: N/A

Group tour dates: N/A

Open house dates: N/A

Classroom visits: N/A

Profit or non-profit: Profit

ADMISSIONS

Application form required: Yes

Forms required: Enrollment forms from Glenwood, shot records

Application deadline: Year round

Application fee: $35

Contact: Rhonda Corn-Kidd

Phone: (972) 530-4460

Student interview required: N/A

Parent interview required: N/A

Entrance test required: N/A

Specific tests administered: N/A

Accept test scores from other schools: N/A

Testing fee: N/A

Time of year testing is administered: N/A

Test dates offered: N/A

Out of state applicants: N/A

Notification by phone: Yes

Notification by mail: N/A

FINANCIAL

Preschool tuition: $460 per month or $117 per week
Elementary tuition: N/A
Secondary tuition: N/A
Other tuition: Technology fee $20 annually, supply fee $30/$35
Cash discounts: N/A
Personal check: N/A
Automatic bank draw: N/A
Credit cards: N/A
Monthly: Yes
Per semester: N/A
Annually: N/A
Financial assistance offered: CCMS
Cancellation insurance: None
Sibling discount: None
Application acceptance deposit required: N/A
Other: Parents may pay tuition weekly also. Enrollment deposit one-half of monthly tuition.

SERVICES

Before school care offered: Yes, 6:30 a.m. - 7:15 a.m.
After school care offered: Yes, 3:00 p.m. - 6:00 p.m.
Transportation provided: No
Lunch/snack program: Morning, afternoon snacks and lunch in classroom with teachers.
Other: Computer lab, toots classroom and up, library, science, Spanish and music classes available depending on age.

LOVERS LANE UNITED METHODIST CHURCH

9200 Inwood Road
Dallas, TX   75220
Contact: **Karla Perry**
(214) 691-4721
(214) 692-0803 FAX

Office Hours: 8:30 a.m. - 2:00 p.m.
E-MAIL: linda@llumc.org
Web Site: N/A
MAPSCO: 24R

PHILOSOPHY OF SCHOOL

Our program offers developmentally appropriate activities for each child. These activities encourage growth in the whole child by focusing on social skills, physical skills, and academics. We want each child to have a positive self-concept and to know he or she is unique.

CREDENTIALS

Accreditations: (see glossary) Affiliated with DAEYC, TAEYC; accredited by the state
Awards and special recognition: (see glossary) N/A
Qualification of administrator: Bachelor of science
Qualification of faculty: College degree
Other: Affiliated with MNKA

GENERAL

Alternative: No
College preparatory: No
Montessori: No
Nondenominational: No
Church affiliated: Yes
Denomination: Methodist
Jewish: N/A
Other denominations: N/A
Student type: Coed
Grade category (for details see specific grades offered below): Preschool - 1st
Infants: Yes
Preschool: Half Day

Kindergarten: Half Day
Primary / Transition: No
Elementary: Yes
Secondary or Middle School: N/A
Specific grades offered: 6 months to 1st
Other: Adding 2nd grade in Fall 2000. Preschool and Kindergarten Extended
Option available.
Student teacher ratio average: Depends on age of child
Classes offered per grade: Varies with each age level
Average class size: Depends on age of child
Total enrollment: 300
Recommended grades to apply: N/A
School hours: 9:00 a.m. - 2:00 p.m.; 1st : 8:30 a.m. - 2:30 p.m.
Calendar school year: Labor Day - Memorial Day
Uniforms required: Yes, 1st grade only
Parental involvement opportunities and requirements: Yes
Average SAT scores: N/A
Visitation procedures: Call for appointment.
Personal appointments for touring the facility: Any time
Group tour dates: Any time
Open house dates: N/A
Classroom visits: Arranged with teacher
Profit or nonprofit: Non-profit
Other: Uniforms required for 1st grade.

ADMISSIONS

Application form required: Yes
Forms required: Health card, application card, signed notarized form for medical
emergencies.
Application deadline: Main registration in February.
Application fee: $ 15 (church members exempted)
Contact: Weekday office - 8:30 a.m. - 2:30 p.m.
Phone: (214) 691-4721
Student interview required: Yes
Parent interview required: No
Entrance test required: No
Specific tests administered: N/A
Accept test scores from other schools: Yes
Testing fee: N/A
Time of year testing is administered: N/A
Test dates offered: N/A

Out of state applicants: N/A
Notification by phone: Yes
Notification by mail: Yes
Other: Verbal or written; Student interview required for 1st grade.

FINANCIAL

Preschool tuition: $135 - $190 per month
Elementary tuition: $1825 Kindergarten, $4280 Elementary
Secondary tuition: N/A
Other tuition: Mother's Day Out $70 per month
Cash discounts: N/A
Personal check: N/A
Automatic bank draw: N/A
Credit cards: N/A
Monthly: Yes, Kindergarten, PK, MDO
Per semester: N/A
Annually: Yes, Kindergarten & 1st grade
Financial assistance offered: Some scholarships are available.
Cancellation insurance: N/A
Sibling discount: N/A
Application acceptance deposit required: N/A

SERVICES

Before school care offered: Yes, limited.
After school care offered: Yes, limited.
Transportation provided: N/A
Lunch/snack program: Parents and school provide snacks.
Other: Computers in Kindergarten & 1st grade, church library, enrichment
activities offered - music, Spanish, manners, tumbling and chapel.

NORTHBROOK SCHOOL

5608 Northaven Road
Dallas, TX 75230
Director: **Larry Goldman, Director**
(214) 369-8330
(214) 369-8592 FAX

Office Hours: 6:45 a.m. - 6:00 p.m.
E-MAIL: LGOLD5608@aol.com
Web Site: N/A
MAPSCO: 25C

PHILOSOPHY OF SCHOOL

Each child is unique, and individual differences must be respected & encouraged. Instruction is based on the child's level and learning style. The school is concerned with the development of the whole child. Thus, being concerned with the child's intellectual growth, the school helps to foster the child's creativity, as well as emotional, social, and physical growth.

CREDENTIALS

Accreditations: (see glossary) NAEYC, TDPRS
Awards and special recognition: (see glossary) N/A
Qualification of administrator: B.S or M.S. degree, previous administrative & teaching experience, continuing education, participation in professional seminars, organizations, & director credentials
Qualification of faculty: B.S or M.S. degrees, previous teaching experience, continuing education

GENERAL

Alternative: No
College preparatory: No
Montessori: No
Nondenominational: Yes
Church affiliated: No
Denomination: N/A
Jewish: N/A
Other denominations: N/A
Student type: Co-ed
Grade category (for details see specific grades offered below): Elementary
Infants: N/A
Preschool: Half Day
Kindergarten: Full Day
Primary / Transition: No

Elementary: Yes
Secondary or Middle School: N/A
Specific grades offered: Preschool (2 years) - grade 4
Student teacher ratio average: 1:12
Classes offered per grade: N/A
Average class size: 12
Total enrollment: 110
Recommended grades to apply: N/A
School hours: PK 8:30 a.m. - 11:30 a.m., K 8:30 a.m. - 3:00 p.m.,
    Elem 8:30 a.m. - 3:30 p.m.
Calendar school year: Mid-August - May, summer camp
Uniforms required: No
Parental involvement opportunities and requirements: Yes
Average SAT scores: N/A
Visitation procedures: Call for appointment
Personal appointments for touring the facility: Individual
Group tour dates: N/A
Open house dates: N/A
Classroom visits: N/A
Profit or non-profit: Profit

ADMISSIONS

Application form required: Yes
Forms required: Health & school records
Application deadline: Spring
Application fee: N/A
Contact: Director
Phone: (214) 369-8330
Student interview required: No
Parent interview required: No
Entrance test required: No
Specific tests administered: N/A
Accept test scores from other schools: Yes
Testing fee: N/A
Time of year testing is administered: In summer for placement only
Test dates offered: N/A
Out of state applicants: N/A
Notification by phone: N/A
Notification by mail: N/A
Other: Depends on space availability

FINANCIAL

Preschool tuition: $1462 - $4512

Elementary tuition: $4693

Secondary tuition: N/A

Other tuition: Registration & Supply Fees

Cash discounts: N/A

Personal check: N/A

Automatic bank draw: N/A

Credit cards: N/A

Monthly: Yes. Bi-monthly also.

Per semester: Yes

Annually: Yes

Financial assistance offered: Pre-payment discounts available

Cancellation insurance: Yes

Sibling discount: N/A

Application acceptance deposit required: $150 - $300

SERVICES

Before school care offered: Yes, from 6:50 a.m.

After school care offered: Yes, until 6:00 p.m.

Transportation provided: Yes

Lunch/snack program: Snacks provided by school twice a day.

Other: Before and after school care provided at no additional cost.

WESTMINSTER PRESBYTERIAN PRESCHOOL & KINDERGARTEN

8200 Devonshire Drive
Dallas, TX   75209
Contact: **Cristine L. Watson, M.S.**
(214) 350-6155
(214) 351-0145 FAX

Office Hours: 8:30 a.m. - 1:00 p.m.
(ext. hrs. TWTH - 2:30 p.m.)

E-MAIL: info@dfwprivateschools.com
Web Site: N/A
MAPSCO: 35A

PHILOSOPHY OF SCHOOL

Our learning environment focuses on the total development of each child; cognitive, social, emotional, physical, aesthetic and spiritual. Children experience success through age-appropriate, hands-on learning activities.

CREDENTIALS

Accreditations: (see glossary) NAEYC
Awards and special recognition: (see glossary) Not at this time
Qualification of administrator: BS Child Development MS Child Development Adjunct Faculty Early Childhood Trainer
Qualification of faculty: Degreed in Early Childhood, Child Development, Elementary Education along with numerous years of experience.
Other: Individual resource teachers for Music, Art, Motor Skills and Library/ Language.

GENERAL

Alternative: No
College preparatory: No
Montessori: No
Nondenominational: No
Church affiliated: Yes
Denomination: Christian
Jewish: N/A
Other denominations: N/A
Student type: Coed

Grade category (for details see specific grades offered below): N/A

Infants: N/A

Preschool: Half Day

Kindergarten: 3/4 Day

Primary / Transition: No

Elementary: N/A

Secondary or Middle School: N/A

Specific grades offered: Kindergarten requires three extended afternoons until 2:00 p.m.

Student teacher ratio average: Varies by ages; 12:3, 10:2 - 16:2

Classes offered per grade: 2-4 classes per age level

Average class size: Ranges from 10-16

Total enrollment: 206

Recommended grades to apply: One year prior to desired enrollment

School hours: 9:00 a.m. - 12:00 p.m. daily with some extended days

Calendar school year: September - May

Uniforms required: No

Parental involvement opportunities and requirements: Many opportunities available in the preschool and Kindergarten levels.

Average SAT scores: N/A

Visitation procedures: Call school office to schedule appointment.

Personal appointments for touring the facility: Available by scheduling through school office.

Group tour dates: N/A

Open house dates: N/A

Classroom visits: Scheduled through school office.

Profit or nonprofit: Non-profit

ADMISSIONS

Application form required: No

Forms required: Wait list accepted year round

Application deadline: N/A

Application fee: N/A

Contact: Cristine L. Watson

Phone: (214) 350-6155

Student interview required: No

Parent interview required: Yes

Entrance test required: No

Specific tests administered: N/A

Accept test scores from other schools: No

Testing fee: N/A

Time of year testing is administered: N/A

Test dates offered: N/A

Out of state applicants: Yes

Notification by phone: Yes, wait listed families receive phone calls after completion of registration in late February.

Notification by mail: N/A

FINANCIAL

Preschool tuition: MONTHLY - $75.00 - $260.00

Elementary tuition: Kindergarten - Monthly $400.00

Secondary tuition: N/A

Other tuition: N/A

Cash discounts: No

Personal check: Yes

Automatic bank draw: Yes

Credit cards: No

Monthly: Yes

Per semester: Yes

Annually: Yes

Financial assistance offered: Scholarships available. Inquire in school office.

Cancellation insurance: N/A

Sibling discount: No

Application acceptance deposit required: Registration Fees $95 - $350

Other: Church members receive a 10% discount on monthly tuition.

SERVICES

Before school care offered: No

After school care offered: No

Transportation provided: No

Lunch/snack program: School provides daily snack and parents provide juice and a Friday Fresh snack. Children bring lunch on extended days.

NCSA
National Christian Schools Association of America

P.O. Box 28295
Dallas, TX 75228-0295
(214) 270-5495

Definition:

Christian professionals from different schools work together to improve efforts in molding children in the image of Christ.

Eligibility for NCSA accreditation:

1. A school must be a member of NCSA or a state affiliate of NCSA.
2. The school must pay annual membership fees.
3. The school's board must be composed of members of churches of Christ.
4. The school must not discriminate on the basis of race, color, national, or ethnic origin.
5. A school must offer four or more consecutive grades with at least 60 students and four full-time faculty members.
6. A school will be accredited for a period of five years.

(TEPSAC) Texas Private School Accreditation Commission

In order to be accredited as a private school with Texas Education Agency, schools must meet accreditation requirements through a recognized organization. The National Christian Schools Association is one that they recognize.

There is a large book of accreditation requirements that the commission uses to accredit schools.

Alpha Academy (see ICAA)
Buckingham Private School (see ICAA)
Dallas Christian School
Fort Worth Christian School (see Ch. 4)

DALLAS CHRISTIAN SCHOOL

1515 Republic Parkway
Mesquite, TX 75150
Contact: **Elem: Ken Farris; Upper: Steve Woods**
(972) 270-5495
(972) 270-7581 FAX

Office Hours: 8:00 a.m. - 4:00 p.m.
E-MAIL: N/A
Web Site: www.dallaschristian.com
MAPSCO: 39A-N

PHILOSOPHY OF SCHOOL

The mission of Dallas Christian School is to provide a thoughtful, nurturing, educational environment and working partnership that will develop intelligent, courteous, skillful servants prepared to carry out God's will confidently in a global marketplace.

CREDENTIALS

Accreditations: (see glossary) SACS, NCSA, and TEA
Awards and special recognition: (see glossary) N/A
Qualification of administrator: M.A.; meets minimum qualifications required by the Southern Association of Colleges and Schools
Qualification of faculty: Teaching certificate

GENERAL

Alternative: No
College preparatory: Yes
Montessori: No
Nondenominational: No
Church affiliated: Yes
Denomination: Church of Christ
Jewish: N/A
Other denominations: N/A
Student type: Co-ed
Grade category (for details see specific grades offered below): K4 - 12th
Infants: No
Preschool: Yes
Kindergarten: Yes
Primary / Transition: Yes
Elementary: Yes

Secondary or Middle School: Yes

Specific grades offered: K4 - 12th

Student teacher ratio average: 15:1

Classes offered per grade: Varies

Average class size: 25

Total enrollment: 885

Recommended grades to apply: N/A

School hours: 8:30 a.m. - 3:30 p.m. (Elem); 8:15 a.m. - 3:30 p.m. (junior high); 8:05 a.m. - 3:20 p.m. (high school)

Calendar school year: August - May (178 days)

Uniforms required: 1st - 5th graders have uniforms; upper grades have a dress code

Parental involvement opportunities and requirements: Yes, volunteers

Average SAT scores: N/A

Visitation procedures: By appointment

Personal appointments for touring the facility: Offered

Group tour dates: N/A

Open house dates: N/A

Classroom visits: N/A

Profit or non-profit: Non-profit

ADMISSIONS

Application form required: Yes

Forms required: Transcript, application, reference forms, immunization record.

Application deadline: Open enrollment February 7, 2000

Application fee: N/A

Contact: Elementary school: Ken Farris; Secondary school: Steve Woods

Phone: (972) 270-5495

Student interview required: Yes

Parent interview required: Yes

Entrance test required: Yes

Specific tests administered: N/A

Accept test scores from other schools: No

Testing fee: $125, K5 - 12th

Time of year testing is administered: By appointment

Test dates offered: By appointment

Out of state applicants: By appointment

Notification by phone: No

Notification by mail: Yes

FINANCIAL

Preschool tuition: 2 day program: $1663 one payment
Elementary tuition: (1st - 5th) $4815
Secondary tuition: 6th - 8th: $5878; 9th - 12th: $6351
Other tuition: High school art fee, $25 per semester.
Cash discounts: Early payment discount.
Personal check: Yes
Automatic bank draw: Yes
Credit cards: No
Monthly: Yes
Per semester: Yes
Annually: Yes
Financial assistance offered: Yes, limited
Cancellation insurance: Yes
Sibling discount: After third sibling
Application acceptance deposit required: Yes, $200 non-refundable.

SERVICES

Before school care offered: Yes, 7:00 a.m.
After school care offered: Yes. 6:00 p.m.
Transportation provided: No
Lunch/snack program: Lunch menu offered or students may bring lunch; school provides snacks for those in after-school care program.

SACS
Southern Association of Colleges and Schools

Southern Association of Colleges and Schools
The University of Texas at Austin
P.O. Box 7307
Austin, TX 78713-7307
(512) 471-6660
(512) 471-5987 FAX
Web Site: www.sacs.org

The Southern Association of Colleges and Schools, established in 1895, is governed by a 27-member board of trustees including an elected president. The purpose of the Southern Association is to improve education. The Association is voluntary, non-profit, and non-governmental.

Membership is open to public and private institutions in 11 southern states and Latin America. Currently, there are more that 11,000 members enrolling nearly 10 million students. The Southern Association is composed of:
  universities
  senior colleges
  two-year colleges
  vocational-technical schools
  high schools
  junior high schools
  middle schools
  elementary schools
  early childhood centers and kindergartens

Accreditation is a process of helping institutions improve through a systemic program of evaluation and the application of educational standards or criteria. Accreditation means not only that minimum standards are met, but also that the school community is committed to raising the quality of its program.

Regional accreditation is comprehensive: it covers the total school, not just certain programs. Member schools must undertake exhaustive self-studies involving teachers, administrators, students, and those on governing bodies. Then there is an evaluation by a visiting committee of peers—professional educators who, serving as volunteers, give an objective and candid reaction to the self-study and make recommendations based on their assessment of the institution.

Accreditation is not a permanent status. Continuing membership in the Southern Association depends on continuing improvement demonstrated through a regular cycle of annual reports, interim reviews, and periodic re-evaluations with a self-study and visiting team. Member institutions form three commissions:

Commission of Elementary and Middle Schools
Commission on Secondary and Middle Schools
Commission of Colleges

Each member institution has one vote in the delegate assembly of its commission and each assembly sets the standards or criteria for its members.

Akiba Academy
Alexander School, The
Arbor Acre Preparatory School (see Alternative)
Bending Oaks High School (see Alternative)
Bishop Lynch High School (see TCCED)
Bridgeway School (see Alternative)
Carrollton Christian Academy
Country Day School of Arlington (see Ch. 4)
Dallas Academy (see Alternative)
Dallas Christian School (see NCSA)
Fairhill School and Diagnostic Assessment Center (see Alternative)
First Baptist Academy (see ACSI)
Happy Hill Farm Academy/Home (see Alternative)
Hillcrest Academy (pending)
J. Erik Jonsson Community School (see TAAPS)
Keystone Academy (see Alternative)
Lakehill Preparatory School (see ISAS)
Lakemont Academy
Liberty Christian School (see Ch. 4)
Oakridge School, The (see ISAS)
Shelton School and Evaluation Center, The (see Alternative)
Solomon Schechter Academy of Dallas
Southern Methodist University Study Skills Classes (see Ch. 4)
Southwest Academy (see Alternative)
Trinity Christian Academy
Tyler Street Christian Academy (see Ch. 4)
Ursuline Academy of Dallas, The (see ISAS)
Vanguard Preparatory School (see Alternative)
Walden Preparatory School (see Alternative)
White Lake School, The (see Ch. 4)
White Rock North School
Wise Academy, The (pending)

AKIBA ACADEMY

6210 Churchill Way
Dallas, TX 75230
Contact: **Hanna Lambert**
(972) 239-7248
(972) 239-6818 FAX

Office Hours: 7:45 a.m. - 5:30 p.m.
E-MAIL: Headmaster@akiba.dallas.tx.us
Web Site: N/A
MAPSCO: 15U

PHILOSOPHY OF SCHOOL

Akiba Academy is committed to preparing the Jewish child to successfully integrate into a complex, diverse society while at the same time developing a strong personal commitment to our American-Jewish heritage. Akiba's philosophy facilitates the emotional, intellectual, and spiritual growth of each student, guiding and motivating each child to become a responsible, informed citizen.

CREDENTIALS

Accreditations: (see glossary) NAEYC, SACS
Awards and special recognition: (see glossary) Recipient of U.S. Department of Education Award of Excellence, 1986
Qualification of administrator: Master's degree or equivalent
Qualification of faculty: Bachelor's degree or teacher's license

GENERAL

Alternative: No
College preparatory: Yes
Montessori: No
Nondenominational: No
Church affiliated: No
Denomination: N/A
Jewish: Orthodox
Other denominations: N/A
Student type: Co-ed
Grade category (for details see specific grades offered below): Preschool, Elementary, Middle School
Infants: Yes
Preschool: Yes
Kindergarten: Full Day
Primary / Transition: No
Elementary: Yes

139

Secondary or Middle School: Middle school only
Specific grades offered: Grades: 18 months - 8th grade
Student teacher ratio average: 6:1 (pre-school)
Classes offered per grade: N/A
Average class size: 15
Total enrollment: 400
Recommended grades to apply: N/A
School hours: 8:30 a.m. - 12:00 p.m. PK, 8:00 a.m. - 2:00 p.m. K,
    8:00 a.m. - 3:30 p.m. Grades 1-4, 8:00 a.m. - 4:15 p.m. Grades 5-8
Calendar school year: August - May
Uniforms required: Yes, grades 1st - 8th
Parental involvement opportunities and requirements: Total
Average SAT scores: N/A
Visitation procedures: Contact school office
Personal appointments for touring the facility: Individual
Group tour dates: N/A
Open house dates: January
Classroom visits: By appointment
Profit or non-profit: Non-profit

ADMISSIONS

Application form required: Yes
Forms required: After acceptance
Application deadline: N/A
Application fee: $200
Contact: Hanna Lambert
Phone: (972) 239-7248
Student interview required: Yes
Parent interview required: Yes
Entrance test required: Yes
Specific tests administered: Preschool: Interview only, Kindergarten: Interview
    and Testing, 1st - 4th Grade: Testing, Fifth and above: Testing
Accept test scores from other schools: No
Testing fee: N/A
Time of year testing is administered: Spring
Test dates offered: By appointment
Out of state applicants: N/A
Notification by phone: Yes, in Spring.
Notification by mail: Yes, in Spring.

FINANCIAL

Preschool tuition: $2375 - $4150
Elementary tuition: $5825 - $7400
Secondary tuition: N/A
Other tuition: books, uniform
Cash discounts: Yes, if paid in full.
Personal check: Yes
Automatic bank draw: Yes
Credit cards: Credit cards accepted if paid in full.
Monthly: Yes
Per semester: Yes
Annually: Yes, semi-annually also.
Financial assistance offered: Yes, K-8 only.
Cancellation insurance: Yes
Sibling discount: Yes, 10% for second child, 15% for 3rd child in grades K-8.
Application acceptance deposit required: $250.00 Registration fee

SERVICES

Before school care offered: Yes, extra fee
After school care offered: Yes, extra fee
Transportation provided: Parents carpool
Lunch/snack program: Preschool snacks distributed morning & afternoon.
Other: Preschool afternoon enrichment, Camp Kulanu Preschool Summer Camp, after school activities, interscholastic sports.

THE ALEXANDER SCHOOL

409 International Parkway
Richardson, TX 75081
Contact: **David Bowlin, Director**
(972) 690-9210
(972) 690-9284 FAX

Office Hours: 8:15 a.m. - 4:30 p.m.
Mon.-Thurs., 9:00 a.m. - 1:00 p.m. Fri.
E-MAIL: tas1@airmail.net
Web Site: www.alexanderschool.com
MAPSCO: 17D

PHILOSOPHY OF SCHOOL

The Alexander School is dedicated to promoting academic excellence, personal growth, and good citizenship in its students, in a relaxed, safe, comfortable environment that is most conducive to learning and preparation for a higher or continued education. Alexander believes that "only by making the individual responsible can responsibility be learned." True learning and growth occur by giving each student information, guidelines, alternatives, and choices. The school recognizes that individual students learn in individual ways, and, therefore, must be provided with the best opportunity to accomplish this.

CREDENTIALS

Accreditations: (see glossary) Non-public/private schools, SACS, TEA
Awards and special recognition: (see glossary) N/A
Qualification of administrator: B.S., education; M.Ed., school administration
Qualification of faculty: Degreed and/or certified (70% advanced degrees); average 13 years of teaching experience

GENERAL

Alternative: Yes
College preparatory: Yes
Montessori: No
Nondenominational: Yes
Church affiliated: No
Denomination: N/A
Jewish: N/A
Other denominations: N/A
Student type: Coed
Grade category (for details see specific grades offered below): Secondary
Infants: N/A
Preschool: N/A
Kindergarten: N/A
Primary / Transition: No

Elementary: N/A

Secondary or Middle School: Yes

Specific grades offered: Grades 8 - 12

Student teacher ratio average: 4:1

Classes offered per grade: English, Math, Social Studies, Science, + 2-4 electives

Average class size: 7:1 or 1:1

Total enrollment: 65

Recommended grades to apply: 8th - 12th

School hours: 8:15 a.m. - 4:30 p.m. Monday - Thursday, 9:00 a.m. - 1:00 p.m. Friday

Calendar school year: Mid August - early June

Uniforms required: No

Parental involvement opportunities and requirements: Parent participation encouraged and appreciated.

Average SAT scores: 1150 (Range 800 - 1570)

Visitation procedures: Parents and students are welcome to visit the school during school hours, to observe the school in action and meet with an administrator for an initial conference and evaluation.

Personal appointments for touring the facility: Please call the school office for an appointment at (972) 690-9210.

Group tour dates: N/A

Open house dates: Mid semester Fall and Spring

Classroom visits: Brief classroom visits on the day of the scheduled interview may be available.

Profit or nonprofit: Profit

Other: Uniforms are not required . A moderate dress code is strictly enforced.

ADMISSIONS

Application form required: Yes

Forms required: Information form (provided by school), transcripts, standardized test records, & health form

Application deadline: rolling

Application fee: none

Contact: David B. Bowlin

Phone: (972) 690-9210

Student interview required: Yes

Parent interview required: Yes

Entrance test required: Yes

Specific tests administered: Secondary: California Achievement Test

Accept test scores from other schools: Yes, if current (within past 6 months). Students must score a minimum of 50% on standardized testing to enroll in core curriculum group classes. Students scoring below 50% in any subject area will be required to take that subject as a one-to-one class.

Testing fee: $100.00 (covered by tuition if enrolling)

Time of year testing is administered: Upon enrollment

Test dates offered: (see above)

Out of state applicants: (see above)

Notification by phone: Yes

Notification by mail: N/A

FINANCIAL

Preschool tuition: N/A

Elementary tuition: N/A

Secondary tuition: $12,000 per year; $6,500 for one semester

Other tuition: 1 - 1 classes $750 per subject/semester

Cash discounts: Yes, when paid in full before school year begins.

Personal check: Yes

Automatic bank draw: N/A

Credit cards: N/A

Monthly: N/A

Per semester: Yes

Annually: Yes

Financial assistance offered: $500.00 per semester scholarship is given to students with ALL A's for the semester.

Cancellation insurance: N/A

Sibling discount: Yes, 5 % of each sibling's tuition. This does not apply to book and lab fees.

Application acceptance deposit required: Yes

SERVICES

Before school care offered: N/A

After school care offered: N/A

Transportation provided: N/A

Lunch/snack program: Seniors passing all courses, juniors with a minimum of all B's, and sophomores with all A's are allowed to leave the campus for the 45 minute lunch period. Two refrigerators, three microwave ovens, and a student lounge with lunch tables and snack machines are available for students who bring lunch to school.

CARROLLTON CHRISTIAN ACADEMY

1820 Pearl Street
Carrollton, TX 75006
Contact: **Jan Foster**
(972) 242-6688
(972) 245 - 0321 FAX

Office Hours: 7:30 a.m. - 4:00 p.m.
E-MAIL: jfoster@ccasaints.org
Web Site: N/A
MAPSCO: 12D

PHILOSOPHY OF SCHOOL

Carrollton Christian Academy is more than a "private school." It is uniquely a Christian school which strives to equip each student enrolled in K-12 academically, socially, emotionally, and spiritually, at a reasonable cost. The administration, faculty, and staff are committed to integrating Biblical principles into all facets of school life, curricular and extracurricular, and to help students determine God's will for their lives. We hold precious our role in preparing students who may be called into full-time ministry and work diligently to provide a gentle balance of guidance, encouragement, instruction, and example. Our continual purpose is to glorify God by offering Him our best. Our missions statement is developing future leaders through Christ-centered academics, art, and athletics who choose character before career, wisdom beyond scholarship, service before self and participation as a way of life.

CREDENTIALS

Accreditations: (see glossary) SACS
Awards and special recognition: (see glossary) N/A
Qualification of administrator: Administrative certificate
Qualification of faculty: Certified teachers
Other: Currently working toward ACSI accreditation.

GENERAL

Alternative: No
College preparatory: Yes
Montessori: No
Nondenominational: Yes
Church affiliated: Yes
Denomination: Methodist
Jewish: N/A

Other denominations: N/A
Student type: Co-ed
Grade category (for details see specific grades offered below): Preschool - 12th
Infants: N/A
Preschool: Half Day
Kindergarten: Full Day
Primary / Transition: No
Elementary: Yes
Secondary or Middle School: Yes
Specific grades offered: Age 3 - grade 12
Student teacher ratio average: 1:20 or 1:25
Classes offered per grade: 7-8
Average class size: 22
Total enrollment: 825
Recommended grades to apply: 3's -12th
School hours: 7:50 a.m. - 3:30 p.m.
Calendar school year: August - May
Uniforms required: Yes
Parental involvement opportunities and requirements: Parent-teacher
    fellowship
Average SAT scores: 1060
Visitation procedures: Check in at school office
Personal appointments for touring the facility: Offered through the admissions
    office
Group tour dates: Possibility of group appointments.
Open house dates: January 23, 2000
Classroom visits: By appointment only
Profit or non-profit: Non-profit

ADMISSIONS

Application form required: Yes
Forms required: Enrollment application
Application deadline: February-August (date to apply)
Application fee: $75
Contact: Jan Foster
Phone: (214) 242-6688 ext 104
Student interview required: Yes
Parent interview required: Yes
Entrance test required: Yes
Specific tests administered: Kindergarten: Missouri Kindergarten of
    Developmental Skills (KIDS), 1st - 4th Grade: Stanford Abbreviated Test,

Fifth and above: Stanford Abbreviated Test, Secondary: Stanford Abbreviated Test

Accept test scores from other schools: Yes, schools with either the Stanford Test or Iowa Basic Skills Test. TAAS test is not accepted.

Testing fee: Included in the $75 application fee.

Time of year testing is administered: Group testing in February and March

Test dates offered: February 19, 2000 and March 25, 2000

Out of state applicants: On individual basis

Notification by phone: Yes, follow-up and questions.

Notification by mail: Yes, letter

FINANCIAL

Preschool tuition: 3's $1400, 4's $1,600, pre-k $1850

Elementary tuition: K $2450, 1-5 $4000

Secondary tuition: 6-8 $4400, 9-12 $4700

Other tuition: books $210-250, $2.50 daily lunch fee, activity fees for preschool - $45-$130; student campus fee grades 1-12: $225

Cash discounts: N/A

Personal check: Yes

Automatic bank draw: N/A

Credit cards: N/A

Monthly: Yes, 10 payments

Per semester: Yes

Annually: Yes, no discount

Financial assistance offered: Yes

Cancellation insurance: N/A

Sibling discount: Yes, 10% on additional children

Application acceptance deposit required: no

SERVICES

Before school care offered: Yes, 7:00 a.m.

After school care offered: Yes, until 6:00 p.m.

Transportation provided: N/A

Lunch/snack program: Cafeteria with hot lunches along with a la carte menu

Other: Computer lab, library, music room, band, orchestra rooms, art room and all sports available in secondary school.

THE HILLCREST ACADEMY

12302 Park Central Drive   *Office Hours:*
Dallas, TX   75251   8:00 a.m. - 5:00 p.m. Mon. - Fri.
Contact: **Carrie Madden, Director of Admission**
(972) 788-0292   *E-MAIL:* HCAcad1@aol.com
(972) 788-1392 FAX   *Web Site:* www.HILLCRESTACADEMY.org
MAPSCO: 16W

PHILOSOPHY OF SCHOOL

The Hillcrest Academy offers a spectrum of children the opportunity for achievement of the highest academic excellence based on consistent and competitive standards, as well as an environment which nurtures personal integrity, self-esteem, individual artistic and imaginative expression, responsibility for one's own actions, and respect for others and the educational process.

CREDENTIALS

Accreditations: (see glossary) SACS pending, TDPRS

Awards and special recognition: (see glossary) N/A

Qualification of administrator: Bob Hess has been with Hillcrest Academy for 18 years of its 22 year history. He holds a Bachelor of Arts Degree *summa cum laude* from the University of Kentucky, and a Master's of Fine Arts Degree *summa cum laude* from Trinity University. He took over the Headmaster position in the fall of 1996, after having been chairman of the English Department for the preceeding ten years. Bob was recently recognized by Who's Who Among America's Teachers.

Qualification of faculty: All instructors must have at least earned their Bachelor's Degrees. In the Lower School, that degree must be in the field of education or child development. At the Middle School level, teacher degrees may be in their particular area of focus, such as music, art or mathematics. 75% of our teachers have completed some postgraduate work. 33% of our teachers have earned their Master's Degrees.

GENERAL

Alternative: No
College preparatory: Yes
Montessori: No
Nondenominational: Yes
Church affiliated: No

Denomination: N/A

Jewish: N/A

Other denominations: N/A

Student type: Coed

Grade category (for details see specific grades offered below) : Preschool - 12th

Infants: N/A

Preschool: Full Day

Kindergarten: Full Day

Primary / Transition: No

Elementary: Yes

Secondary or Middle School: Yes

Specific grades offered: Preschool - 8th grade

Other: Begin at age 3 by September 1 (must be potty trained).

Student teacher ratio average: 15:1

Classes offered per grade: 2

Average class size: 15

Total enrollment: 275

Recommended grades to apply: Preschool, Pre-K, Kindergarten, First Grade

School hours: 8:00 a.m. - 3:00 p.m. (varies depending on grade)

Calendar school year: August 30,1999 - June 2, 2000

Uniforms required: Yes

Parental involvement opportunities and requirements: At Hillcrest, students are encouraged to invite their parents to be a part of our program in some way. Our Parents' Association (HAPA) is an integral part of the Hillcrest community, and we of the faculty and staff truly appreciate the relentless dedication and support this group offers. It allows us to function as a team and to meet the many needs of our school.

Average SAT scores: N/A

Visitation procedures: As a part of the application process, students are required to do a full-day visitation (half-day for preschool and kindergarten) once the application has been made.

Personal appointments for touring the facility: Parents are encouraged to find out more about Hillcrest through our Open House, The Dallas Private School Preview, and our website (www.HillcrestAcademy.org). Parents may make an appointment for an individual meeting with the Director of Admission and a tour of the facility by calling the office.

Group tour dates: N/A

Open house dates: November 7, 1999, 1:00 p.m. - 3:00 p.m.

Classroom visits: Classroom visits are scheduled on an individual basis through the Director of Admission.

Profit or nonprofit: Non-profit

149

ADMISSIONS

Application form required: Yes

Forms required: Full application packet including application, parent questionnaire, student statement, request for release of records, and teacher recommendations can be obtained through the Office of Admission

Application deadline: February 25, 2000

Application fee: $50

Contact: Carrie Madden, Director of Admission

Phone: (972) 788-0292

Student interview required: Yes

Parent interview required: Yes

Entrance test required: Yes

Specific tests administered: Preschool: Individual Development Observation, Kindergarten: Individual Diagnostic Testing, 1st - 4th Grade: Parents may submit any previous standardized or diagnostic testing less than one year old. We may request additional testing., Fifth and above: Students applying for 5th- 8th grade must take the ISEE.

Accept test scores from other schools: Yes

Testing fee: Diagnostic Evaluation $125. Preschool $50

Time of year testing is administered: Throughout the year

Test dates offered: See ISEE Schedule for 1999-00

Out of state applicants: Yes, on an individual basis. Contact the Office of Admission for details.

Notification by phone: N/A

Notification by mail: Yes, a decision of acceptance, wait pool acceptance or non-acceptance will be mailed only after the admission packet is complete. We cannot make a decision if items are missing. Letters will be mailed on March 17, 2000.

FINANCIAL

Preschool tuition: Preschool $6060/Kindergarten $6350 (1999-2000)

Elementary tuition: Lower School, Grades 1-4 $7450/Middle School, Grades 5-8 $8025 (1999-2000)

Secondary tuition: N/A

Other tuition: N/A

Cash discounts: N/A

Personal check: Yes

Automatic bank draw: N/A

Credit cards: N/A

Monthly: Yes, all student accounts must be paid in full by December. A finance charge applies.

Per semester: N/A
Annually: Yes
Financial assistance offered: On an individual basis
Cancellation insurance: N/A
Sibling discount: N/A
Application acceptance deposit required: $500.00 Non-refundable

SERVICES

Before school care offered: Yes, beginning at 7:00 a.m. - 7:45 a.m.

After school care offered: Yes, end of school day - 6:00 p.m.

Transportation provided: N/A

Lunch/snack program: A hot lunch is available on days of choice. Paid in advance monthly. The average cost is $3.50 per meal.

Other: Summer Camp Program is available. Please call office for more details.

LAKEMONT ACADEMY

3993 West Northwest Highway   *Office Hours:* 8:00 a.m. - 6:00 p.m.
Dallas, TX   75220   *E-MAIL:* N/A
Contact: **Edward Fidellow, Headmaster**   *Web Site:* N/A
(214) 351-6404   *MAPSCO:* 24W
(214) 358-4510 FAX

PHILOSOPHY OF SCHOOL

A Christian Montessori Entrepreneurial School built on Biblical principles, parent involvement and teaching the success tools of life - a work ethic, taking responsibility, goal setting, risk taking, people, time and money management.

CREDENTIALS

Accreditations: (see glossary) ACSI, Montessori, SACS, TANS
Awards and special recognition: (see glossary) N/A
Qualification of administrator: Founder of the school MFA, Montessori trained
Qualification of faculty: Degreed and Montessori certified

GENERAL

Alternative: No
College preparatory: Yes
Montessori: Yes
Nondenominational: Yes
Church affiliated: No
Denomination: Christian
Jewish: N/A
Other denominations: N/A
Student type: Co-ed
Grade category (for details see specific grades offered below): Preschool - 12th
Infants: N/A
Preschool: Full Day
Kindergarten: Full Day
Primary / Transition: Yes
Elementary: Yes
Secondary or Middle School: Yes
Specific grades offered: 18 months - grade 8th offered
Other: The program starts at 18 months.
Student teacher ratio average: 15:1

Classes offered per grade: 1

Average class size: N/A

Total enrollment: 90

Recommended grades to apply: N/A

School hours: 8:15 a.m. - 3:30 p.m.

Calendar school year: August - May + Summer

Uniforms required: Yes

Parental involvement opportunites and requirements: Parenting classes, educational programs, classroom observations, lunch invitations

Average SAT scores: N/A

Visitation procedures: Call for appointment

Personal appointments for touring the facility: Mutually convenient times

Group tour dates: N/A

Open house dates: Announced periodically

Classroom visits: Mutually convenient times

Profit or non-profit: Non-profit

ADMISSIONS

Application form required: Yes

Forms required: School forms

Application deadline: Open

Application fee: $50 for Kindergarten up

Contact: Barbara Fidellow

Phone: (214) 351-6404

Student interview required: Yes

Parent interview required: Yes

Entrance test required: Yes

Specific tests administered: Kindergarten: WRAT, Primer: WRAT, 1st - 4th Grade: WRAT, Fifth and above: WRAT

Accept test scores from other schools: No

Testing fee: $50

Time of year testing is administered: On going

Test dates offered: Open

Out of state applicants: N/A

Notification by phone: Yes

Notification by mail: N/A

FINANCIAL

Preschool tuition: $8700 - 12 months

Elementary tuition: $7400-8425 - 10 months

Secondary tuition: N/A

Other tuition: N/A
Cash discounts: Yes
Personal check: Yes
Automatic bank draw: Yes
Credit cards: N/A
Monthly: Yes, $ 764-883
Per semester: Yes, $ 3783-4467
Annually: Yes, $ 7400-8700
Financial assistance offered: Yes
Cancellation insurance: Yes
Sibling discount: Yes, on individual basis
Application acceptance deposit required: N/A

SERVICES

Before school care offered: Yes, 7:30 a.m. - 8:15 a.m.
After school care offered: Yes, 3:30 p.m. - 6:00 p.m.
Transportation provided: N/A
Lunch/snack program: Hot Lunch - formal dinning room: table cloths, napkins, china, crystal
Other: Summer camp program for elementary students

SOLOMON SCHECHTER ACADEMY OF DALLAS

18011 Hillcrest Road
Dallas, TX 75252
Contact: **Ms. Judi Glazer, Registrar**
(972) 248-3032
(972) 248-0695 FAX

Office Hours: 7:30 a.m. - 6:00 p.m.
E-MAIL: SSAJGlazer@aol.com
Web Site: N/A
MAPSCO: 5H

PHILOSOPHY OF SCHOOL

Solomon Schechter Academy is a Conservative Jewish Day School founded in 1979. The practices and beliefs of Conservative Judaism are presented positively and lived openly as an integral part of school life. Solomon Schechter Academy draws on the great diversity of Jewish life and welcomes Jewish students of varying religious backgrounds. From this diversity, we create awareness of the unity of *Klal Yisrael* (the Jewish people) in a community of Jewish learning where all of us are partners in building Jewish life of the future. We are committed to complete equality of opportunity for girls and boys in religious and secular life.

The school provides a warm nuturing environment for its children, together with an uncompromising emphasis on academic excellence in General Studies and Jewish Studies. Motivated from within, our children acquire a sense of self and accomplishment that allows for experiences of creativity, independent study, choice and responsibility. Through our emphasis of critical and intuitive thinking, as well as analysis and creative problem-solving, our children acquire the intellectual independence essential to succeed in a world of accelerating change.

CREDENTIALS

Accreditations: (see glossary) SACS
Awards and special recognition: (see glossary) N/A
Qualification of administrator: Minimum - master's degree
Qualification of faculty: Teacher academic degrees; people educated in Jewish and general studies and committed to helping children realize their potential; (many have master's degrees)

GENERAL

Alternative: No
College preparatory: No
Montessori: No
Nondenominational: No

155

Church affiliated: No
Denomination: Jewish Day School
Jewish: Yes
Other denominations: N/A
Student type: Co-ed
Grade category (for details see specific grades offered below): 1st - 8th
Infants: N/A
Preschool: Yes, 18 months to age 5
Kindergarten: Yes
Primary / Transition: N/A
Elementary: Yes
Secondary or Middle School: Yes
Specific grades offered: Preschool - 8th
Student teacher ratio average: 14:1
Classes offered per grade: N/A
Average class size: 14
Total enrollment: 535
Recommended grades to apply: N/A
School hours: 8:00 a.m. - 4:00 p.m. Grades 1st - 8th;
9:00 a.m. - 12:00 p.m. Preschool
Calendar school year: August - May
Uniforms required: N/A
Parental involvement opportunities and requirements: Active Parents'
Association; we encourage participation on all school committees.
Average SAT scores: N/A
Visitation procedures: See application materials
Personal appointments for touring the facility: Yes
Group tour dates: No
Open house dates: Yes
Classroom visits: N/A
Profit or non-profit: Non-profit

ADMISSIONS

Application form required: Yes
Forms required: Previous school records, report cards and medical records
Application deadline: Rolling admissions - classes are closed when registration is
reached
Application fee: $200 - Preschool; $300 - Elementary/Middle School
Contact: Ms. Judi Glazer, Registrar
Phone: (972) 248-3032
Student interview required: Yes
Parent interview required: Yes

Entrance test required: Some placement tests for Middle School
Specific tests administered: Applicants spend full day at school K - 7th
Accept test scores from other schools: N/A
Testing fee: N/A
Time of year testing is administered: N/A
Test dates offered: N/A
Out of state applicants: N/A
Notification by phone: N/A
Notification by mail: Yes

FINANCIAL

Preschool tuition: $2000 - $5000
Elementary tuition: $6200 - $7500
Secondary tuition: $8500 - $9700
Other tuition: N/A
Cash discounts: N/A
Personal check: Yes
Automatic bank draw: N/A
Credit cards: Visa, MasterCard
Monthly: Yes
Per semester: Yes
Annually: Yes
Financial assistance offered: Financial aid available for grades K - 8th.
Cancellation insurance: Yes
Sibling discount: None
Application acceptance deposit required: Yes

SERVICES

Before school care offered: Yes, 8:00 a.m. - 9:00 a.m. for preschool children
After school care offered: After care until 6:00 p.m.
Transportation provided: No bus transportation; car pools only
Lunch/snack program: Children provide their own snack.
Other: The computer lab consists of a classroom of multimedia computers and related instructional and demonstration hardware plus a modem for on-line services. Students attend at least weekly for direct instruction and for special projects. Computers are used to assist with the regular classroom curriculum, and special projects. All instructional activities relate to what students learn in general and Jewish studies. The instructors are certified teachers in the computer field. Students in grades K - 8th use the library as needed; library classes are part of the curriculum. The school has a full range of co-curricular and extra-curricular activities including interscholastic sports teams in the Middle School.

TRINITY CHRISTIAN ACADEMY

17001 Addison Rd.
Addison, TX   75001
Contact: Mary Helen Noland
(972) 931-8325
(972) 931-8923 FAX

Office Hours: 8:00 a.m. - 3:30 p.m.
E-MAIL: N/A

Web Site: www.trinitychristian.com
MAPSCO: 4U

PHILOSOPHY OF SCHOOL

Educating and developing the whole person for the glory of God.

CREDENTIALS

Accreditations: (see glossary) ACSI, SACS, TANS

Awards and special recognition: (see glossary) N/A

Qualification of administrator: College degree, Advanced degree, independent school background

Qualification of faculty: College degree, preferably advanced degrees, conservative, evangelical

GENERAL

Alternative: No
College preparatory: Yes
Montessori: No
Nondenominational: Yes
Church affiliated: No
Denomination: N/A
Jewish: N/A
Other denominations: N/A
Student type: Coed
Grade category (for details see specific grades offered below): 1st - 12th
Infants: N/A
Preschool: N/A
Kindergarten: Full Day
Primary / Transition: Yes
Elementary: Yes
Secondary or Middle School: Yes
Specific grades offered: Kindergarten - 12th

Other: Also have a half day Kindergarten

Student teacher ratio average: Upper school 11:1

Classes offered per grade: Lower School (1st -6th) 5 of each grade

Average class size: 18 - 20

Total enrollment: 1440

Recommended grades to apply: 1 year prior to enrollment

School hours: 8:00 a.m. - 3:30 p.m.

Calendar school year: August 15 - May 31

Uniforms required: Yes

Parental involvement opportunities and requirements: Parent-Teacher Fellowship, Booster Club, Academic Council, Fine Arts Council

Average SAT scores: 1140; ACT: 24

Visitation procedures: Request tour of campus - scheduled through Admissions Office

Personal appointments for touring the facility: Call the Admissions Office to arrange a tour. Tuesday Tours at Ten - tours given each Tuesday beginning September 7 - December 7 at 10:00 a.m.

Group tour dates: Tuesday Tours at Ten

Open house dates: Sunday, November 14, 2:00 p.m. - 4:00 p.m.

Classroom visits: Call for appointment

Profit or nonprofit: Non-profit

ADMISSIONS

Application form required: Yes

Forms required: Application for admission, recommendation forms, transcripts

Application deadline: January 28

Application fee: $100 - K, PFK; $75 - 1st - 12th

Contact: Mary Helen Noland

Phone: (972) 931 - 8325

Student interview required: Yes

Parent interview required: Yes

Entrance test required: Yes

Specific tests administered: Kindergarten: Missouri KIDS, 1st - 4th Grade: Stanford, Independent School Entrance Exam , Fifth and above: ISEE

Accept test scores from other schools: Yes

Testing fee: $75.00 ($100 for K)

Time of year testing is administered: January

Test dates offered: January 15 and January 29 (make up-emergency only)

Out of state applicants: N/A

Notification by phone: Yes; Wait pool - notified if accepted

Notification by mail: Yes, letter

Other: Interview required for students grades 9-12.

FINANCIAL

Preschool tuition: N/A
Elementary tuition: $3,700 - $7,400 (Grades K-8)
Secondary tuition: $8,150 - $8,600 (Grades 9-12)
Other tuition: N/A
Cash discounts: Yes, 25% ministerial discount
Personal check: Yes
Automatic bank draw: N/A
Credit cards: N/A
Monthly: Yes
Per semester: N/A
Annually: N/A
Financial assistance offered: Yes
Cancellation insurance: N/A
Sibling discount: N/A
Application acceptance deposit required: N/A

SERVICES

Before school care offered: N/A
After school care offered: N/A
Transportation provided: N/A
Lunch/snack program: Cafeteria available

WHITE ROCK NORTH SCHOOL

9727 White Rock Trail
Dallas, TX   75238
Contact: Amy Adams, Head of School
(214) 348-7410
(214) 348-3109 FAX

Office Hours:
9:00 a.m. - 6:00 p.m. Mon-Fri
E-MAIL: wrnsaaa@aol.com
Web Site: N/A
MAPSCO: 27K

PHILOSOPHY OF SCHOOL

To promote academic excellence, develop personal integrity, nurture individual artistic and imaginative expression coupled with an opportunity for intellectual development, physical development, character building and civic responsibility.

CREDENTIALS

Accreditations: (see glossary) SACS
Awards and special recognition: (see glossary) N/A
Qualification of administrator: Masters - Educational Administration
Qualification of faculty: Bachelor degree at minimum. Several teachers hold
    Master degrees and Doctorates.

GENERAL

Alternative: No
College preparatory: No
Montessori: No
Nondenominational: Yes
Church affiliated: No
Denomination: N/A
Jewish: N/A
Other denominations: N/A
Student type: Co-ed
Grade category (for details see specific grades offered below): Elementary
Infants: N/A
Preschool: Full Day
Kindergarten: Full Day
Primary / Transition: Yes
Elementary: Yes

Secondary or Middle School: N/A

Specific grades offered: Preschool - 8th grade

Other: Preschool - half days 8:30 a.m. - 12:30 p.m. also offered, reading taught in kindergarten.

Student teacher ratio average: 20:1

Classes offered per grade: N/A

Average class size: 15 students

Total enrollment: 350 students

Recommended grades to apply: K - 6th

School hours: 7:00 a.m. - 6:00 p.m.

Calendar school year: August 1999 - May 2000; Summer camp June - August

Uniforms required: Yes

Parental involvement opportunities and requirements: Mustang Club - parent organization. Participation at each grade level, school wide events.

Average SAT scores: N/A

Visitation procedures: Classrooms may be visited with approval of the Head of School.

Personal appointments for touring the facility: School tours may be scheduled by contacting Patti Griffith, (214) 348-7410. White Rock North School is shown on Wednesday at 9:00 a.m. and 10:00 a.m. All others by special appointment w/Head of School

Group tour dates: See above.

Open house dates: Saturday, August 15, 1999 and Saturday, February 19, 1999

Classroom visits: Classrooms may be visited with approval of the Head of School.

Profit or non-profit: Profit

ADMISSIONS

Application form required: Yes

Forms required: Application booklet, immunization form, emergency medical form.

Application deadline: Now enrolling for Fall 1999

Application fee: $50 per student, non-refundable

Contact: Patti Griffith

Phone: (214) 348-7410

Student interview required: Yes

Parent interview required: Yes

Entrance test required: Yes

Specific tests administered: Preschool: , Kindergarten: , 1st - 4th Grade: , Fifth and above: Stanford, ERB's, and CTP III

Accept test scores from other schools: Yes, depending on the date and type of the test. Approval is needed from the Head of School.

Testing fee: Grades $100 Kindergarten $75

Time of year testing is administered: January, February and summer months

Test dates offered: Tuesdays by appointment

Out of state applicants: May call for information or schedule a weekend tour.

Notification by phone: Yes

Notification by mail: Yes

FINANCIAL

Preschool tuition: $464-$453 per month

Elementary tuition: $410 per month

Secondary tuition: N/A

Other tuition: Kindergarten: $387 per month

Cash discounts: Yes **Description:** Annual & Bi-Annual discounts

Personal check: Yes

Automatic bank draw: Yes

Credit cards: Mastercard, Visa

Monthly: Yes

Per semester: Yes

Annually: Yes

Financial assistance offered: None

Cancellation insurance: N/A

Sibling discount: Yes, 5% of lesser tuition

Application acceptance deposit required: Yes

SERVICES

Before school care offered: Yes, beginning at 7:00 a.m.

After school care offered: Yes, extended care to 6 p.m.

Transportation provided: N/A

Lunch/snack program: Pre-school, pre-kindergarten and kindergarten students who participate in our Extended Care Program may enjoy a hot school lunch and AM and PM snack provided by the school.

Other: Kindergarten students not enrolled in Extended Care program and Grade school students must bring their own lunch, or they may purchase a school hot lunch ticket for $25.00 (11 meals).

163

THE WISE ACADEMY

6930 Alpha Road
Dallas, TX 75240
Contact: **Susan Horowitz, Head of School**
(972) 789-1800
(972) 789-1801 FAX

Office Hours: 8:00 a.m. - 4:00 p.m.
E-MAIL: headwise@msn.com
Web Site: N/A
MAPSCO: 15Q

PHILOSOPHY OF SCHOOL

The Isaac Mayer Wise Academy has been established to provide children with all of the intellectual tools needed to become independent thinkers and thoughtful, socially responsible members of both the general and Reform Jewish community. Wise Academy graduates will be prepared to excel in the most demanding academic environments, and to become creators, innovators and leaders in their futures.

CREDENTIALS

Accreditations: (see glossary) SACS candidate
Awards and special recognition: (see glossary) N/A
Qualification of administrator: M. Ed from University of North Texas, BA from the University of North Carolina, Texas Administrator certificate, Texas prek-6 Teacher Certificate
Qualification of faculty: Teaching certificates
Other: New School

GENERAL

Alternative: No
College preparatory: Yes
Montessori: No
Nondenominational: No
Church affiliated: No
Denomination: N/A
Jewish: Reform
Other denominations: N/A
Student type: Co-ed
Grade category (for details see specific grades offered below): Elementary
Infants: N/A
Preschool: N/A
Kindergarten: N/A

Primary / Transition: No

Elementary: Yes

Secondary or Middle School: N/A

Specific grades offered: First through fifth, adding one grade per year up to 8th.

Student teacher ratio average: 12:2

Classes offered per grade: 1

Average class size: 12

Total enrollment: 23

Recommended grades to apply: 1st - 5th

School hours: 8:30 a.m. - 3:30 p.m.

Calendar school year: August to the end of May

Uniforms required: Yes

Parental involvement opportunites and requirements: Parents will meet with teachers during scheduled conferences. Many volunteer opportunities for parent involvement are available. Parent organization

Average SAT scores: N/A

Visitation procedures: Please call the office, 972-789-1800, to schedule an appointment with the Head of the School.

Personal appointments for touring the facility: Upon request

Group tour dates: N/A

Open house dates: N/A

Classroom visits: We welcome classroom visits by parents by appointment only as scheduled by the admissions office.

Profit or non-profit: Non-profit

ADMISSIONS

Application form required: Yes

Forms required: The application form, school transcripts and teacher recommendations are required.

Application deadline: February 1, 2000

Application fee: $125.00

Contact: Susan Horowitz

Phone: (972) 789-1800

Student interview required: Yes

Parent interview required: Yes

Entrance test required: Yes

Specific tests administered: 1st - 5th Grade: ERB's for 2nd and up

Accept test scores from other schools: Yes. We participate in the Dallas Area Independent School testing program. Candidates may request that their test results be released to any other school to which they may be applying.

Testing fee: N/A

Time of year testing is administered: December, January

Test dates offered: TBA

Out of state applicants: Students who cannot test in Dallas must contact Wise Academy.

Notification by phone: N/A

Notification by mail: Yes, a notification letter will be mailed to all applicants who have met the above deadlines.

FINANCIAL

Preschool tuition: N/A

Elementary tuition: $7500

Secondary tuition: N/A

Other tuition: N/A

Cash discounts: N/A

Personal check: Yes

Automatic bank draw: N/A

Credit cards: N/A

Monthly: N/A

Per semester: Yes, billed the begining of each semester.

Annually: Yes

Financial assistance offered: Limited assisstance is available. An appointment with the Financial Director must be scheduled. Personal financial statement and SSS forms.

Cancellation insurance: N/A

Sibling discount: N/A

Application acceptance deposit required: $1000.00 upon receipt of contract.

SERVICES

Before school care offered: N/A

After school care offered: Yes, until 6:00 p.m.

Transportation provided: N/A

Lunch/snack program: N/A

SAES
Southwestern Association of Episcopal Schools

5952 Royal Lane, Suite 204
Dallas, Texas 75230
(214) 692-9872
(214) 692-9874 FAX
E-MAIL: saes@flash.net
Web Site: www.swaes.org

William P. Scheel, Ed.D.
Executive Director

The Southwestern Association of Episcopal Schools is a recognized member of TEPSAC (Texas Private Schools Accreditation Commission and is approved by the Commissioner of eduction. It is also recognized by NAIS (National Association of Independent Schools). SAES accredits Episcopal school in six states. Member schools of the association seeking accreditation must first make application for admission into the process, and then demonstrate that they meet the quality standards of the association though providing written documentation. Following approval of the documentation, the school conducts a thorough self-study which takes the better part of a year to complete. An on-site visit of three days' duration is made by a peer review team of no fewer than three qualified and trained educators. At the conclusion of the visit, the team chair makes a substantive report the school and to the Standards Committee of SAES. The Standards Committee makes a recommendation to the Executive Board of the Association, which makes the final decision to accredit or not the accredit the school. The on-site visit report becomes the school's guide for improvement in the ensuing years. To maintain accreditation, accredited schools make regular reports of progress.

All Saints Episcopal School (see Ch. 4)
Canterbury Episcopal School, The
Epiphany Day School
Episcopal School of Dallas, The (see Ch. 4)
Good Shepherd Episcopal School (see ISAS)
Holy Trinity Episcopal School

Parish Day School, The (see ISAS)
St. Alban's Episcopal School (see Ch. 4)
St. Andrew's Episcopal School
St. James Episcopal Montessori (see Montessori)
St. John's Episcopal School (see Ch. 4)
St. Vincent's Episcopal School

THE CANTERBURY EPISCOPAL SCHOOL

1708 North Westmoreland
DeSoto, TX 75115
Contact: Ron Ferguson, Headmaster
(972) 572-7200
(972) 572-7400 FAX

Office Hours: 7:45 a.m. - 4:30 p.m.
E-MAIL: N/A
Web Site: N/A
MAPSCO: 82H

PHILOSOPHY OF SCHOOL

The Canterbury Episcopal School inspires in each student a love of learning in preparation for college with an emphasis on academic excellence, spiritual development, appreciation of diversity and social responsibility.

CREDENTIALS

Accreditations: (see glossary) SAES (Southwestern Association of Episcopal Schools)
Awards and special recognition: (see glossary) N/A
Qualification of administrator: Master's degree (minimum)
Qualification of faculty: Bachelor's degree (minimum)
Other: Member of National Association of Episcopal Schools, National Association of Independent Schools

GENERAL

Alternative: No
College preparatory: Yes
Montessori: No
Nondenominational: No
Church affiliated: Yes
Denomination: Episcopal
Jewish: N/A
Other denominations: N/A
Student type: Co-ed
Grade category (for details see specific grades offered below): 1st - 12th
Infants: N/A
Preschool: N/A
Kindergarten: Full Day
Primary / Transition: No

Elementary: Yes

Secondary or Middle School: Yes

Specific grades offered: Kindergarten - grade 8 (high school scheduled to open fall 2000)

Student teacher ratio average: 12:1

Classes offered per grade: 2

Average class size: 16

Total enrollment: 240

Recommended grades to apply: N/A

School hours: 8:00 a.m. - 3:30 p.m.

Calendar school year: August - May

Uniforms required: Yes

Parental involvement opportunities and requirements: High involvement

Average SAT scores: N/A

Visitation procedures: N/A

Personal appointments for touring the facility: Available

Group tour dates: Available

Open house dates: November (or scheduled)

Classroom visits: Appointments

Profit or non-profit: Non-profit

ADMISSIONS

Application form required: Yes

Forms required: Application, health

Application deadline: Apply December - February

Application fee: No application fee

Contact: Ron Ferguson, Headmaster

Phone: (972) 572-7200

Student interview required: Yes

Parent interview required: Yes

Entrance test required: Yes

Specific tests administered: Kindergarten: , 1st - 4th Grade: , Fifth and above: Stanford Achievement, Otis-Lennon Ability

Accept test scores from other schools: No

Testing fee: $75

Time of year testing is administered: Winter/early spring testing schedule

Test dates offered: Yes, winter months

Out of state applicants: Yes

Notification by phone: N/A

Notification by mail: Parent conference scheduled immediately following testing & personal appointment when all documents are filed and contact/

acceptance is offered (if appropriate)

FINANCIAL

Preschool tuition: N/A
Elementary tuition: $5000 Kindergarten; $5450 grades 1-5
Secondary tuition: $5800 (Middle School)
Other tuition: N/A
Cash discounts: Yes
Personal check: Yes
Automatic bank draw: Yes
Credit cards: Yes
Monthly: Yes
Per semester: Yes
Annually: Yes
Financial assistance offered: Yes
Cancellation insurance: N/A
Sibling discount: N/A
Application acceptance deposit required: Enrollment fee of $ 400

SERVICES

Before school care offered: Yes, 7:30 a.m. - 7:45 a.m.
After school care offered: Yes, 3:00 p.m. - 6:00 p.m.
Transportation provided: N/A
Lunch/snack program: Snacks provided for primary grades; lunch program uses catering services.
Other: Library in school design; Enrichment curriculum and Extracurricular activities offered.

EPIPHANY DAY SCHOOL

421 Custer Road
Richardson, TX 75080
Contact: Alexis Clayton, Ed.D
(972) 690-0275
(972) 644-8116 FAX

Office Hours: 9:00 a.m. - 2:00 p.m.
E-MAIL: N/A
Web Site: N/A
MAPSCO: 17A

PHILOSOPHY OF SCHOOL

We believe that a child learns best when he or she is actively engaged with materials and experiences that are developmentally appropriate for that child. The goal of Epiphany Day School is to challenge students to construct meaning. To that end, we provide a rich environment of materials for children to explore and abundant opportunities for learning through discovery. Children are encouraged to learn how to learn and to think for themselves. Our small student/staff ratios facilitate a very individualized and child specific learning experience. We believe that the child's parents and teachers work in partnership with God, in this learning endeavor.

CREDENTIALS

Accreditations: (see glossary) NAEYC
Awards and special recognition: (see glossary) N/A
Qualification of administrator: Doctorate; certification
Qualification of faculty: College degree; certification; early childhood

GENERAL

Alternative: No
College preparatory: No
Montessori: No
Nondenominational: No
Church affiliated: Yes
Denomination: Episcopal
Jewish: N/A
Other denominations: Episcopal Church of the Epiphany
Student type: Co-ed
Grade category (for details see specific grades offered below): Preschool
Infants: N/A
Preschool: Half Day
Kindergarten: Extended Half Day

Primary / Transition: No
Elementary: N/A
Secondary or Middle School: N/A
Specific grades offered: 16 months - Kindergarten
Other: Kindergarten: Extended Half Day
Student teacher ratio average: 5:1 MDO; 10:1-12 Preschool; 12:1 K
Classes offered per grade: N/A
Average class size: 12
Total enrollment: 80
Recommended grades to apply: N/A
School hours: 9:00 a.m. - 1:00 p.m. MDO & PK; 9:00 a.m. - 2:00 p.m. K
Calendar school year: August - May
Uniforms required: No
Parental involvement opportunities and requirements: Parents' Club
Average SAT scores: N/A
Visitation procedures: N/A
Personal appointments for touring the facility: Offered
Group tour dates: Offered
Open house dates: N/A
Classroom visits: Offered
Profit or non-profit: Non-profit

ADMISSIONS

Application form required: Yes
Forms required: Ask director
Application deadline: Apply February-May
Application fee: $150 Preschool ; $100 MDO; $200 Kindergarten
Contact: Dr. Alexis Clayton, Director
Phone: (214) 690-0275
Student interview required: No
Parent interview required: No
Entrance test required: No
Specific tests administered: N/A
Accept test scores from other schools: No
Testing fee: N/A
Time of year testing is administered: N/A
Test dates offered: N/A
Out of state applicants: N/A
Notification by phone: Yes
Notification by mail: N/A

FINANCIAL

Preschool tuition: $1500 Preschool; $2300 1/2 day Kindergarten;
$2600 Kindergarten extended 1/2 day
Elementary tuition: $3000 Grade 1
Secondary tuition:
Other tuition: N/A
Cash discounts: N/A
Personal check: N/A
Automatic bank draw: N/A
Credit cards: N/A
Monthly: Yes
Per semester: N/A
Annually: N/A
Financial assistance offered: Limited
Cancellation insurance: N/A
Sibling discount: Yes, 5% for 2nd child; 7% for 3rd child
Application acceptance deposit required: N/A

SERVICES

Before school care offered: N/A
After school care offered: Yes, extended day program from 1:00 p.m. - 2:00 p.m.
Transportation provided: N/A
Lunch/snack program: Snacks provided
Other: Developmentally Appropriate Program with academic challenge, fieldtrips, chapel, creative dramatics, music

HOLY TRINITY EPISCOPAL SCHOOL

1524 Smirl Drive
Heath, TX   75032
Contact: **Dianna Fullerton, Interim Headmistress**
(972) 772-6919
Fax Number Not Available

Office Hours: 8:30 a.m. - 4:30 p.m.
E-MAIL: N/A
Web Site: holytrinityepiscopal.org
MAPSCO: N/A

PHILOSOPHY OF SCHOOL

Holy Trinity Episcopal School is a specialized ministry of the church in the field of education. It is the mission of the school to promote excellence in education guided by Christian principles; provide a moral and nurturing environment; foster self-esteem and self-discipline; further spiritual and personal growth; and offer unlimited academic opportunities. The program is designed to train the mind, strengthen the character, and enrich the spirit of each student in a Christian environment.

CREDENTIALS

Accreditations: (see glossary) Non-Public Private Schools, SAES
Awards and special recognition: (see glossary) Recognized as one of the outstanding new Episcopal schools in the U.S.A. by the National Association of Episcopal Schools
Qualification of administrator: N/A
Qualification of faculty: Bachelor's and Master's degree; certification in their assigned teaching field.
Other: Organization affiliations: National Association of Episcopal Schools; Southwestern Association of Episcopal Schools; National Association & Education of Young Children

GENERAL

Alternative: No
College preparatory: No
Montessori: No
Nondenominational: No
Church affiliated: No
Denomination: N/A
Jewish: N/A

Other denominations: N/A

Student type: Co-ed

Grade category (for details see specific grades offered below): N/A

Infants: N/A

Preschool: Half Day

Kindergarten: Full Day

Primary / Transition: Yes

Elementary: Yes

Secondary or Middle School: N/A

Specific grades offered: Pre-school (3 yr. olds) to 3rd grade

Student teacher ratio average: 8:1

Classes offered per grade: 1

Average class size: Pre-K:12; K:15; Grades 1-3:17

Total enrollment: 65

Recommended grades to apply: N/A

School hours: 8:30 a.m. - 3:30 p.m.

Calendar school year: September 1st to June 1st

Uniforms required: Yes

Parental involvement opportunities and requirements: The Parents' Association supports and assists the school through special projects and events during the school year. Parents are encouraged to share their special talents.

Average SAT scores: N/A

Visitation procedures: Arrangements to visit the school can be made through the office by calling (972) 772-6919.

Personal appointments for touring the facility: An appointment should be scheduled with Dianna Fullerton, Interim Headmistress.

Group tour dates: Call office (972) 772-6919 for appointment.

Open house dates: Open House's occur in the fall and the spring. Call the office for dates.

Classroom visits: To be arranged by the teacher or by the Headmistress.

Profit or non-profit: N/A

ADMISSIONS

Application form required: Yes

Forms required: HTES Application form

Application deadline: April 1st

Application fee: $200

Contact: Dianna Fullerton, Interim Headmistress

Phone: (972) 772-6919

Student interview required: Yes

Parent interview required: Yes

Entrance test required: Yes

Specific tests administered: Preschool: Gesell Developmental Evaluation, Kindergarten: Gesell Developmental Evaluation; Primer: Gesell Developmental Evaluation; 1st - 3rd Grade: Standardized achievement tests

Accept test scores from other schools: Yes, previous standardized achievement test from other schools accepted.

Testing fee: $75

Time of year testing is administered: Spring and Early Summer

Test dates offered: N/A

Out of state applicants: Test date will be made by appointment.

Notification by phone: Yes, some results will be given over the phone.

Notification by mail: Yes, test results will be sent with the acceptance letter.

FINANCIAL

Preschool tuition: Pre-School - $1650, Pre-K - $2600, Kindergarten - $3500

Elementary tuition: $3700

Secondary tuition: N/A

Other tuition: N/A

Cash discounts: Yes

Personal check: Yes

Automatic bank draw: N/A

Credit cards: MasterCard, Visa

Monthly: Yes

Per semester: Yes

Annually: Yes

Financial assistance offered: Scholarships are available. Interested parties must fill out paperwork by March of the proceeding school year.

Cancellation insurance: N/A

Sibling discount: Yes, 5% off of sibling tuitions.

Application acceptance deposit required: Yes

SERVICES

Before school care offered: No

After school care offered: No

Transportation provided: N/A

Lunch/snack program: Children bring their lunches.

ST. ANDREW'S EPISCOPAL SCHOOL

727 Hill Street
Grand Prairie, TX 75050
Contact: Betty Meek, Head of School
(972) 262-3817
(972) 264-3730 FAX

Office Hours: 9:00 a.m. - 4:00 p.m.
E-MAIL: N/A
Web Site: N/A
MAPSCO: 51D

PHILOSOPHY OF SCHOOL

To instill in the student a respect for God's word and His people and promote an atmosphere of caring and love for fellow beings; to provide an environment that recognizes the uniqueness and self-worth of each child; to provide an environment that prepares each student as an individual to live a creative, humane, and compassionate life, and to become a contributing member of society.

CREDENTIALS

Accreditations: (see glossary) SAES pending
Awards and special recognition: (see glossary) N/A
Qualification of administrator: Education background, master's degree in Education Administration
Qualification of faculty: College degree and certification (K-5)
Other: Accredited by Texas Dept. of Human Resources; in process of SAES accreditation.

GENERAL

Alternative: No
College preparatory: No
Montessori: No
Nondenominational: No
Church affiliated: Yes
Denomination: Episcopal
Jewish: N/A
Other denominations: N/A
Student type: Co-ed
Grade category (for details see specific grades offered below): Elementary
Infants: N/A
Preschool: Half Day

Kindergarten: Full Day
Primary / Transition: No
Elementary: Yes
Secondary or Middle School: N/A
Specific grades offered: 3 years - grade 5
Student teacher ratio average: 12:1
Classes offered per grade: N/A
Average class size: 10-14
Total enrollment: 90
Recommended grades to apply: N/A
School hours: 8:30 a.m. - 3:30 p.m.
Calendar school year: August - May
Uniforms required: Yes
Parental involvement opportunities and requirements: P.T.O program, spirit hours worked by parents
Average SAT scores: N/A
Visitation procedures: N/A
Personal appointments for touring the facility: Made by appointment.
Group tour dates: N/A
Open house dates: March
Classroom visits: By Appointment
Profit or non-profit: Non-profit

ADMISSIONS

Application form required: Yes
Forms required: Packet of admissions forms, health forms, etc.
Application deadline: Registration begins in Feb.
Application fee: $25.00
Contact: School office
Phone: (972) 262-3817
Student interview required: Yes
Parent interview required: Yes
Entrance test required: No
Specific tests administered: N/A
Accept test scores from other schools: Yes
Testing fee: N/A
Time of year testing is administered: N/A
Test dates offered: N/A
Out of state applicants: N/A
Notification by phone: N/A
Notification by mail: N/A

FINANCIAL

Preschool tuition: $2480.00
Elementary tuition: $3440.00
Secondary tuition: N/A
Other tuition: N/A
Cash discounts: N/A
Personal check: Yes
Automatic bank draw: N/A
Credit cards: Yes
Monthly: Yes
Per semester: Yes, quarterly
Annually: Yes
Financial assistance offered: Scholarship
Cancellation insurance: N/A
Sibling discount: Yes, 10%
Application acceptance deposit required: N/A

SERVICES

Before school care offered: Yes, begins at 7:00 a.m.
After school care offered: Yes, until 6:00 p.m.
Transportation provided: N/A
Lunch/snack program: Morning snacks & afternoon snacks for after-school care offered; students can bring their own lunches.
Other: Computers in classrooms, library, extracurricular and enrichment activities offered, Spanish, music, P.E.

ST.VINCENT'S EPISCOPAL SCHOOL

1300 Forest Ridge Drive
Bedford, TX 76022
Contact: **Janet Blakeman, Headmaster**
(817) 354-7979
(817) 354-5073 FAX

Office Hours: 8:00 a.m. - 4:00 p.m.
E-MAIL: sves@sves.org

Web Site: www.sves.org
MAPSCO: 54N

PHILOSOPHY OF SCHOOL

At St.Vincent's, we believe in balancing the developmental needs of children with strong academic requirements. Attention is given to building study habits and skills for success as will as providing spiritual direction. We believe that schools and parents must work together in positive and productive ways to maximize a child's potential. We believe there is something very special about our school. We are helping to mold the leaders of tomorrow.

CREDENTIALS

Accreditations: (see glossary) SAES, TANS
Awards and special recognition: (see glossary) N/A
Qualification of administrator: N/A
Qualification of faculty: N/A

GENERAL

Alternative: No
College preparatory: Yes
Montessori: No
Nondenominational: No
Church affiliated: Yes
Denomination: Episcopal
Jewish: N/A
Other denominations: N/A
Student type: Co-ed
Grade category (for details see specific grades offered below): Elementary
Infants: N/A
Preschool: Half Day
Kindergarten: Full Day
Primary / Transition: No

Elementary: Yes
Secondary or Middle School: N/A
Specific grades offered: 3 years - 6th grade
Student teacher ratio average: 13:1
Classes offered per grade: 2 in Elementary Grades
Average class size: 16
Total enrollment: 337
Recommended grades to apply: All Grades
School hours: 8:00 a.m. - 3:15 p.m.
Calendar school year: August 16, 1999 to May 26, 2000
Uniforms required: Yes
Parental involvement opportunities and requirements: Parent-Teacher Club
Library Volunteers Classroom Support
Average SAT scores: N/A
Visitation procedures: All visitors are required to check in at the office.
Personal appointments for touring the facility: Please call the school office to
arrange for a tour of the school. (817) 354-7979.
Group tour dates: N/A
Open house dates: Tentatively set for February 3, 2000 at 7:30 p.m.
Classroom visits: Visits need to be scheduled through the school office.
Profit or non-profit: No

ADMISSIONS

Application form required: Yes
Forms required: Completed Application Form Birth Certificate Shot Records
Previous School Records Previous Teacher Recommendation
Application deadline: N/A
Application fee: $50.00 for new students
Contact: Mrs. Lynn Buffington
Phone: (817) 354-7979
Student interview required: Yes
Parent interview required: Yes
Entrance test required: Yes
Specific tests administered: N/A
Accept test scores from other schools: Yes
Testing fee: $75.00
Time of year testing is administered: Spring/Summer/As Needed
Test dates offered: N/A
Out of state applicants: N/A
Notification by phone: N/A
Notification by mail: Yes

FINANCIAL

Preschool tuition: $1,615 - $2,735 Mornings Only

Elementary tuition: $4,400

Secondary tuition: N/A

Other tuition: N/A

Cash discounts: Yes

Personal check: Yes

Automatic bank draw: N/A

Credit cards: N/A

Monthly: N/A

Per semester: N/A

Annually: Yes, due June 1

Financial assistance offered: Scholarships are available to returning students

Cancellation insurance: Yes, Tuition Refund Plan - Dewar, Inc.

Sibling discount: N/A

Application acceptance deposit required: $50.00 New Students Only

Other: $75 Testing Fee K-6th for new students. $200 Deposit due upon signing contract. Applicable towards tuition.

SERVICES

Before school care offered: Yes, 7:30 a.m. - 8:00 a.m. - No Charge

After school care offered: Yes, 3:15 p.m. - 6:00 p.m.

Transportation provided: N/A

Lunch/snack program: Students may purchase a hot lunch or bring their own lunches.

Other: Camp Vincent - Summer Day Camp July 19 - 30. Call (817) 354-7979 for details.

TAAPS
Texas Alliance of Accredited Private Schools

137 Calhoun Plaza
Port Lavaca, Texas 77979
(361) 552-5757
(361) 552-1900 FAX

The Texas Alliance of Accredited Private Schools, a non-profit accreditation association, was organized in 1985. This organization serves both traditional and nontraditional elementary and secondary schools in the state of Texas. TAAPS is a member of the Texas Private School Accreditation Commission.

Schools seeking accreditation through TAAPS must have been in operation for three years before seeking an applicant visit. With a favorable applicant report, the school is encouraged to apply for the final accreditation visit. An annual report is the association's method of monitoring the school's continuing self-evaluation.

The Texas Alliance of Accredited Private Schools conducts an annual conference the last weekend of February. All member schools as well as guest schools are invited to attend.

Accredited members schools in the Dallas/Fort Worth area are:

Cambridge Square Private School of DeSoto (pending, see TDPRS)
Clariden School, The (pending)
Highland Park Presbyterian Day School
Hillier School of Highland Park Presbyterian Church (see Alternative)
J. Erik Jonsson Community School
Southwest Academy (see Alternative)
Yavneh Academy of Dallas (see Ch. 4)

THE CLARIDEN SCHOOL

1325 North White Chapel Blvd
Southlake, TX 76092
Contact: **Charlane Baccus**
(817) 481-7597
(817) 424-5561 FAX

Office Hours:
8:00 a.m. - 6:00 p.m.
E-MAIL: cbaccus@claridenschool.org
Web Site: www.claridenschool.org
MAPSCO: 11Z

PHILOSOPHY OF SCHOOL

Help children to become respectful, compassionate and contributing members of society by providing a strong academic, personal and social learning environment.

CREDENTIALS

Accreditations: (see glossary) AMI, TAAPS, TANS
Awards and special recognition: (see glossary) Grant for art program from Arts Council Northeast Tarrant County
Qualification of administrator: 30 plus years as owner/director of private school. AMI certification
Qualification of faculty: Classroom teachers-undergraduate degree, AMI cerification, many have their Masters.

GENERAL

Alternative: No
College preparatory: Yes
Montessori: Yes
Nondenominational: No
Church affiliated: No
Denomination: N/A
Jewish: N/A
Other denominations: N/A
Student type: Coed
Grade category (for details see specific grades offered below): Preschool - 12th
Infants: N/A
Preschool: Half Day
Kindergarten: Full Day
Primary / Transition: Yes
Elementary: Yes
Secondary or Middle School: Yes
Specific grades offered: Preschool age 3 - 12th grade

Student teacher ratio average: 16:1
Classes offered per grade: 1
Average class size: 16
Total enrollment: 85
Recommended grades to apply: All grades
School hours: 8:15 a.m. - 3:15 p.m.
Calendar school year: September.-May
Uniforms required: No
Parental involvement opportunites and requirements: Clariden Parent
  Organization Dad's Club
Average SAT scores: N/A
Visitation procedures: Must be made by appointment.
Personal appointments for touring the facility: Yes
Group tour dates: Periodically throughout the year
Open house dates: Periodically
Classroom visits: Must be made by appointment.
Profit or nonprofit: Non-profit

ADMISSIONS

Application form required: Yes
Forms required: School form Teacher recomendations 1st grade and above.
Application deadline: Ongoing
Application fee: $50.00
Contact: Charlane Baccus
Phone: (817) 481-7597
Student interview required: Yes
Parent interview required: Yes
Entrance test required: No
Specific tests administered: N/A
Accept test scores from other schools: Yes
Testing fee: N/A
Time of year testing is administered: N/A
Test dates offered: N/A
Out of state applicants: N/A
Notification by phone: N/A
Notification by mail: Yes, acceptance or nonacceptance is done through formal
  letter

FINANCIAL

Preschool tuition: $4,300.00
Elementary tuition: $5,400.00

Secondary tuition: $5,700.00
Other tuition: Middle/High $5,900.00, plus textbooks
Cash discounts: N/A
Personal check: Yes
Automatic bank draw: N/A
Credit cards: N/A
Monthly: Yes, through bank.
Per semester: N/A
Annually: Yes
Financial assistance offered: N/A
Cancellation insurance: N/A
Sibling discount: N/A
Application acceptance deposit required: $750.00

SERVICES

Before school care offered: N/A
After school care offered: Yes, 3:00 p.m. - 6:00 p.m.
Transportation provided: N/A
Lunch/snack program: Lunch Break 2 times per week. Pizza/Chicken

HIGHLAND PARK PRESBYTERIAN DAY SCHOOL

3821 University Blvd.
Dallas, TX 75205
Contact: **Carrie H. Parsons, Director**
(214) 559-5353
(214) 559-5357 FAX

Office Hours: 8:00 a.m. - 4:00 p.m.
E-MAIL: N/A
Web Site: N/A
MAPSCO: 35E

PHILOSOPHY OF SCHOOL

Highland Park Presbyterian Day School believes each child is God's creation and must be nurtured in biblically-based Christian love, acceptance, and reinforcement. We provide an enriching, productive school experience within this Christian environment.

CREDENTIALS

Accreditations: (see glossary) TAAPS
Awards and special recognition: (see glossary) N/A
Qualification of administrator: B.S. in Elementary Education; 27 years in the field of Education and educational consulting.
Qualification of faculty: All have degrees in early childhood education or elementary education
Other: Affiliated with TAEYC, DAEYC, & SECA

GENERAL

Alternative: No
College preparatory: No
Montessori: No
Nondenominational: Yes
Church affiliated: Yes
Denomination: Presbyterian
Jewish: N/A
Other denominations: N/A
Student type: Co-ed
Grade category (for details see specific grades offered below): Preschool - 4th Grade

Infants: N/A
Preschool: Yes
Kindergarten: Yes
Primary / Transition: Yes
Elementary: Yes
Secondary or Middle School: N/A
Specific grades offered: Pre-K (age 3)- 4th grade
Student teacher ratio average: 8:1
Classes offered per grade: N/A
Average class size: 12-14
Total enrollment: 325
Recommended grades to apply: 3 Years old (Beginner level)
School hours: 8:45 a.m. - 3:30 p.m.
Calendar school year: August - May
Uniforms required: Yes
Parental involvement opportunities and requirements: Parents' Council
Average SAT scores: N/A
Visitation procedures: N/A
Personal appointments for touring the facility: Call school office
Group tour dates: N/A
Open house dates: N/A
Classroom visits: By appointment
Profit or non-profit: Non-profit

ADMISSIONS

Application form required: Yes
Forms required: Immunization form and medical- consent form
Application deadline: Applications taken year round for wait list.
Application fee: Nonrefundable registration fee due @ enrollment
Contact: Day School Office
Phone: (214) 559-5353
Student interview required: Yes
Parent interview required: Yes
Entrance test required: Yes
Specific tests administered: Grade level assessment tests
Accept test scores from other schools: No
Testing fee: N/A
Time of year testing is administered: January for specific opening's
Test dates offered: N/A
Out of state applicants: N/A
Notification by phone: N/A

Notification by mail: Yes, letter to parents

FINANCIAL

Preschool tuition: $1820 - $5500
Elementary tuition: $1820 - $5500
Secondary tuition: N/A
Other tuition: Uniform, book bag costs, supply fee
Cash discounts: N/A
Personal check: N/A
Automatic bank draw: N/A
Credit cards: N/A
Monthly: N/A
Per semester: Yes, April 30 and July 15
Annually: N/A
Financial assistance offered: No
Cancellation insurance: Yes
Sibling discount: N/A
Application acceptance deposit required: N/A

SERVICES

Before school care offered: N/A
After school care offered: Yes, church's recreation department has a program
Transportation provided: N/A
Lunch/snack program: Lunch fee is optional; snacks provided by parents
Other: Technology lab, library

J. ERIK JONSSON COMMUNITY SCHOOL

106 E. 10th Street
Dallas, TX 75203
Contact: **Paige Conley**
(214) 915-1890
(214) 915-1863 FAX

Office Hours: 8:00 a.m. - 4:30 p.m.
E-MAIL: ralaniz@jonssonschool.org
Web Site: www.jonssonschool.org
MAPSCO: 54H

PHILOSOPHY OF SCHOOL

The J. Erik Jonsson Community School exists to develop and operate a transforming learning community for urban children and their families that values education and promotes academic excellence and social competence. JEJCS is a co-educational, multicultural, year-round, non-profit school. Students and staff strive for excellence through an active, engaged, rich learning environment using an across-subject-area integrated curriculum. Instructional teams and collaborative student groups are a hallmark of the program. JEJCS provides an emotionally supportive and safe environment for students. A full-time, on-site research department enables staff and students to refine and improve this innovative model for urban education.

CREDENTIALS

Accreditations: (see glossary) SACS, TAAPS
Awards and special recognition: (see glossary) N/A
Qualification of administrator: Graduate degree in education and/or school administration
Qualification of faculty: Degree from accredited college; Texas teacher certification; 41% of the staff have advanced degrees

GENERAL

Alternative: No
College preparatory: Accredited by SACS
Montessori: No, but principals used
Nondenominational: N/A
Church affiliated: N/A
Denomination: N/A
Jewish: N/A
Other denominations: N/A
Student type: Co-ed

Grade category (for details see specific grades offered below): Elementary

Infants: No

Preschool: Yes

Kindergarten: Yes

Primary / Transition: No

Elementary: Yes

Secondary or Middle School: No

Specific grades offered: Pre-Kindergarten - 6th

Student teacher ratio average: 10:1

Other: Within-grade-level and intra-grade-level teaching; two teachers in every classroom

Classes offered per grade: One per grade

Average class size: 25, with 2 teachers per class

Total enrollment: 200

Recommended grades to apply: All grades

School hours: 8:00 a.m. - 3:00 p.m.

Calendar school year: Year-round (August - June)

Uniforms required: Yes

Parental involvement opportunities and requirements: Parent Advisory Council; parental involvement is essential for student success; opportunities include parenting seminars, weekly discussion groups conducted in Spanish and English, and numerous volunteer activities

Average SAT scores: N/A

Visitation procedures: Call for appointment

Personal appointments for touring the facility: Yes

Group tour dates: N/A

Open house dates: Call for schedule

Classroom visits: Check in at office

Profit or non-profit: Non-profit

ADMISSIONS

Application form required: Yes

Forms required: Previous cumulative and assessment records

Application deadline: Open admissions; February preferred for following fall

Application fee: No admittance fee

Contact: Admissions Coordinator

Phone: (214) 915-1890

Student interview required: Yes

Parent interview required: Yes

Entrance test required: Reading assessment provided on campus, others as indicated

Specific tests administered: N/A
Accept test scores from other schools: Yes
Testing fee: No
Time of year testing is administered: Upon application
Test dates offered: Year round
Out of state applicants: N/A
Notification by phone: Yes
Notification by mail: Yes

FINANCIAL

Preschool tuition: Sliding scale based on family income
Elementary tuition: Sliding scale based on family income
Secondary tuition: N/A
Other tuition: Basic supplies including uniform provided by family; books and other expensive items provided by school
Cash discounts: No
Personal check: Yes
Automatic bank draw: No
Credit cards: N/A
Monthly: Yes
Per semester: No
Annually: No
Financial assistance offered: Flexible arrangements in financial crisis
Cancellation insurance: N/A
Sibling discount: Multiple siblings can attend for one sliding-scale fee
Application acceptance deposit required: No

SERVICES

Before school care offered: No; students can enter supervised building for breakfast at 7:30 a.m.
After school care offered: No
Transportation provided: Parents, DART, car pools
Lunch/snack program: No fee; breakfast and lunch served daily. Snacks provided for pre-kindergarten.
Other: Computer lab with internet access available with one computer per child. Computers available in each classroom. Outpatient family therapy available through Salesmanship Club Youth and Family Centers, Inc. Complete library/media center.

TCCED
Texas Catholic Conference Education Department

3725 Blackburn Street
P.O. Box 190507
Dallas, TX 75219
(214) 528-2360
(214) 522-1753 FAX
E-MAIL: dvasquez@cathdal.org
Web Site: www. cathdal.org

Mission Statement

The schools of the Roman Catholic Diocese of Dallas exist as the Church's response to the Gospel message "to teach as Jesus did." Each school espouses Catholic doctrine and the spirit of Vatican II in worship, community, justice, and social concerns. For a school to be Catholic, it must be seen and it must see itself as integral part of the Church's mission to spread God's word and bring all peoples to Christ, helping them to grow in faith and love. A school is designated "Catholic" only if it is canonically so stated by the Bishop of the Dioceses. The primary reason for Catholic schools to exist is to serve Catholic families in the Diocese of Dallas. All schools are to provide standards of religious and academic quality maintaining accreditation by the Texas Catholic Conference Education Department.

All Saints Catholic School (see Ch. 4)
Bishop Dunne Catholic High School
Bishop Lynch High School, Inc.
Christ the King School
Cistercian Preparatory School (see Ch. 4)
Good Shepherd Catholic School
Highlands School, The
Holy Family of Nazareth School (see Ch. 4)
Holy Trinity Catholic School
Immaculate Conception School (see Ch. 4)
Jesuit College Preparatory School (see Ch. 4)
Notre Dame of Dallas Schools, The (see Curriculum Alternative)

Prince of Peace Catholic School (see Ch. 4)
St. Bernard of Clairvaux School
St. Elizabeth of Hungary Catholic School (see Ch. 4)
St. John the Apostle Catholic School (see Ch. 4)
St. Mark's The Evangelist Catholic School (see Ch. 4)
St. Mary of Carmel (see Ch. 4)
St. Mary's Catholic School
St. Monica Catholic School
St. Patrick School (see Ch. 4)
St. Paul the Apostle
St. Phillip the Apostle Catholic School (see Ch. 4)
St. Pius Catholic School (see Ch. 4)
St. Rita School (see Ch. 4)
St. Thomas Aquinas School (see Ch. 4)
Ursuline Academy of Dallas, The (see ISAS)

BISHOP DUNNE CATHOLIC HIGH SCHOOL

3900 Rugged Drive *Office Hours:* 8:00 a.m. - 5:00 p.m. Mon. - Fri.
Dallas, TX 75224   *E-MAIL:* mroot@bdhs.org
Contact: Mario Root   *Web Site:* www.bdhs.org
(214) 339-6561 ext 292   *MAPSCO:* 36C
(214) 339-1438 FAX

PHILOSOPHY OF SCHOOL

The Bishop Dunne Catholic School community offers a comprehensive college preparatory curriculum for students of varied academic abilities. The Bishop Dunne community recognizes that a student's formation involves more than academic preparation. Students are nurtured to develop spiritually, physically, intellectually, and emotionally.

CREDENTIALS

Accreditations: (see glossary) Non Public Private Schools, TCCED

Awards and special recognition: (see glossary) Host site for National GEO-Tech Conference each Spring.

Qualification of administrator: Kate Dailey holds a Bachelor of Arts degree and a Masters of Education degree from the University of Queensland, Australia.

Qualification of faculty: 31 full-time faculty members on staff. All 31 faculty have bachelor's degrees. 14 hold master's degrees. 3 hold doctorate degrees.

Other: Technology rich instructional environment with 3 computer labs, networked computers in every classroom and technology skills integrated throughout the curriculum.

GENERAL

Alternative: No
College preparatory: Yes
Montessori: No
Nondenominational: No
Church affiliated: Yes
Denomination: Catholic
Jewish: N/A
Other denominations: N/A
Student type: Co-ed

Grade category (for details see specific grades offered below): Secondary

Infants: N/A

Preschool: N/A

Kindergarten: N/A

Primary / Transition: No

Elementary: N/A

Secondary or Middle School: Yes

Specific grades offered: Grades 7 - 12

Other: Bishop Dunne offers curriculum for college bound students.

Student Teacher ratio average: 11:1

Classes offered per grade: N/A

Average class size: Average size 18; no classes exceed 24 students.

Total enrollment: 560 for 1999-2000 school year.

Recommended grades to apply: 7-12

School hours: 8:00 a.m. - 3:20 p.m.

Calendar school year: August 9, 1999 - May 26, 2000

Uniforms required: Yes

Parental involvement opportunities and requirements: Parental involvement is
encouraged but not required. Parents work within the school community on
many boards and committees to further the development of our students. The
Home and School Association meets monthly and is responsible for the one
major fund raiser we have each year. The School Board meets monthly and
helps develop policy for the community. There are many opportunities for
parents and students to work on School Board committees throughout the
year.

Average SAT scores: Top quartile = 1149, 2nd quartile = 1053

Visitation procedures: N/A

Personal appointments for touring the facility: Contact Mario Root for an
opportunity to tour the facility.

Group tour dates: N/A

Open house dates: Open House will be Sunday November 7
from 2:00 p.m. to 4:00 p.m.

Classroom visits: Contact Mario Root for an opportunity to have your student
visit our campus for a day.

Profit or non-profit: Non-profit

Other: Ethnic diversity of Bishop Dunne Catholic High School: Hispanic - 44%
Anglo - 28% Black - 24% Asian - 4%

ADMISSIONS

Application form required: Yes

Forms required: 1. Application 2. Teacher recommendation from current math and English teacher 3. Copy of most recent report card 4. Copy of achievement test results that are less than one year old

Application deadline: February 25, 2000

Application fee: $35.00

Contact: Mario Root

Phone: (214) 339-6561 ext. 292

Student interview required: Yes

Parent interview required: Yes

Entrance test required: Yes

Specific tests administered: Secondary: STS High School Placement Test for incoming 8th and 9th grade students.

Accept test scores from other schools: Yes, if tested within the past 12 months.

Testing fee: (It is included with admissions fee.)

Time of year testing is administered: January and February

Test dates offered: Saturday, January 22, 2000 and Saturday, January 29, 2000

Out of state applicants: Complete admissions form and schedule an interview with Mario Root at any time.

Notification by phone: N/A

Notification by mail: Yes

FINANCIAL

Preschool tuition: N/A

Elementary tuition: N/A

Secondary tuition: Grades 9-12 tuition = $4800

Other tuition: 7th and 8th grade tuition = $3600.00

Cash discounts: N/A

Personal check: Yes

Automatic bank draw: N/A

Credit cards: N/A

Monthly: Yes, through Texas Catholic Credit Union

Per semester: N/A

Annually: Yes, July 1, 1999

Financial assistance offered: Financial aid application must be postmarked by April 15 each year to be considered for financial aid. If eligible, aid ranges from $600 to $2400 per year.

Cancellation insurance: N/A

Sibling discount: Yes, 5% for second child and 10% for third child

Application acceptance deposit required: $300 registration fee

SERVICES

Before school care offered: N/A

After school care offered: N/A

Transportation provided: Yes

Lunch/snack program: Full cafeteria offering plate lunches as well as a salad bar and a la carte selections

Other: 1. All students are issued e-mail accounts. 2. Yearbook, parking fees, Home and School membership, student admission to all sporting events, technology fees, etc. are included in an annual Activity fee of $225. 3. Progress reports are mailed home to families every two weeks. 4. All faculty are available for tutoring. Additionally, a part-time math tutor is available 4 times a week. 4. A full-time counselor is dedicated to working with students with learning differences. 5. All juniors will be enrolled in an SAT prep course in the spring of the year.

BISHOP LYNCH HIGH SCHOOL, INC.

9750 Ferguson Road
Dallas, TX 75228
Contact: Terry May
(214) 324-3607 ext 127
(214) 324-3600 FAX

Office Hours: 7:30 a.m. - 3:30 p.m.
E-MAIL: willt@mail.bishoplynch.org
Web Site: www.bishoplynch.org
MAPSCO: 38U

PHILOSOPHY OF SCHOOL

Faithful to Catholic truths and the Dominican heritage of scholarship and service, Bishop Lynch High School fosters the well-being of the total person by bringing together a diverse educational community that teaches students to seek truths and work for justice in the world.

CREDENTIALS

Accreditations: (see glossary) SACS, TCCAC - recognized by TEA

Awards and special recognition: (see glossary) National Merit 1980-1999: 25 National Merit Scholars, 35 National Merit Semi-Finalists, 71 National Commended Scholars. Regional School of Excellence U.S. Department of Education 1998, 1991. Meadows Foundation Community Service Awards 1998, 1996, 1991, 1985. TAPPS Sports Championships: 1998, 1997. 1996, 1995, 1994, 1993, 1992; 1998 Football state championship; 1998 Boys' basketball state finalist; 1999 Girls' track state championship; 1998 Boys' soccer district champions; 1998 wrestling state champions; 1998 golf state champions; 1999, 1998 swimming state championship; 1994 Softball regional championship; 1994, 1993 Girls' soccer regional championship;1994, 1993, 1992 Boys' and girls' cross country district championships; 1998 Boys' basketball state finalist; 1989-1999 Girls' basketball state championship

Qualification of administrator: M.A. with 18 years of service at Bishop Lynch

Qualification of faculty: B.A. degrees (35); M.A. degrees (33); Ph.D. degrees (4)

GENERAL

Alternative: No
College preparatory: Yes
Montessori: No
Nondenominational: No
Church affiliated: Yes

Denomination: Catholic
Jewish: Welcomed
Other denominations: Welcomed
Student type: Co-ed
Grade category (for details see specific grades offered below): Secondary
Infants: No
Preschool: No
Kindergarten: No
Primary / Transition: No
Elementary: No
Secondary or Middle School: Yes
Specific grades offered: 9th - 12th
Student teacher ratio average: 14:1
Classes offered per grade: N/A
Average class size: N/A
Total enrollment: 1038
Recommended grades to apply: Contact admissions office
School hours: 8:00 a.m. - 3:20 p.m.
Calendar school year: August - May
Uniforms required: Girls - white oxford shirt, plaid skirt; boys - white oxford shirt, gray slacks, tie
Parental involvement opportunities and requirements: School Board, Parents' Association, Band Boosters, Athletic Boosters. Choir Boosters
Average SAT scores: Consistently above state and national norms.
Visitation procedures: Contact admissions office (214) 324-3607 ext 127
Personal appointments for touring the facility: Contact admissions office
Group tour dates: December and January or contact admissions office
Open house dates: Sunday, November 21, 1999
Classroom visits: Contact admissions office
Profit or non-profit: Non-profit

ADMISSIONS

Application form required: Yes
Forms required: Application, standardized test scores, transcript, recommendation forms from teachers.
Application deadline: January for freshmen
Application fee: Yes
Contact: Admissions Office
Phone: (214) 324-3607 ext 127
Student interview required: Yes
Parent interview required: Yes

Entrance test required: Yes

Specific tests administered: ACT Explore

Accept test scores from other schools: For transfer students only.

Testing fee: Yes

Time of year testing is administered: January

Test dates offered: January 15, 2000 and January 22, 2000 for freshmen.

Out of state applicants: Yes

Notification by phone: No

Notification by mail: Freshmen - March 31st by letter

Other: Transfer - upon acceptance.

FINANCIAL

Preschool tuition: N/A

Elementary tuition: N/A

Secondary tuition: 1999 - 2000 $5450 (Catholic) $6485 (Non-Catholic)

Other tuition: Books ($500) per year; uniform $100

Cash discounts: No

Personal check: Yes

Automatic bank draw: No

Credit cards: Yes

Monthly: Through loan program, 11 monthly payments.

Per semester: N/A

Annually: Yes

Financial assistance offered: Catholic Diocese of Dallas Tuition Aid Program, Merit Scholars' Program, Opportunity and Achievement Scholarship Program

Cancellation insurance: No

Sibling discount: Yes

Application acceptance deposit required: Yes

Other: Payment in full by May 31st or guaranteed loan with local credit union.

SERVICES

Before school care offered: No

After school care offered: No

Transportation provided: Bus transportation available for Richardson, North Dallas, Collin County, N.W. Dallas, Rockwall, and Rowlett (fee involved)

Lunch/snack program: Plate lunch $2.25; also fresh sandwiches, hamburgers, french fries, salads, fruits, and drinks

Other: Two labs - networked with Novell; multiple computers networked in each classroom. Computers are IBM Pentium clones; upgraded each year.

CHRIST THE KING SCHOOL

4100 Colgate
Dallas, TX 75225
Contact: **Gwyne Bohren, Registrar**
(214) 365-1234
(214) 365-1236 FAX

Office Hours: 7:30 a.m. - 4:00 p.m.
E-MAIL: gbohren@cks.org
Web Site: www.cks.org
MAPSCO: 25Y

PHILOSOPHY OF SCHOOL

Conscious of the dignity of each student created in God's image, the primary concern of Christ the King School (CKS) is the development of the whole child. In "To Teach as Jesus Did", the United States bishops state: "...Educational programs for the young must strive to teach doctrine, to do so within the experience of Christian community, and to prepare individuals for Christian witness and service to others." With this in mind, CKS endeavors to provide every opportunity for children to grow spiritually, intellectually, physically, and emotionally, so they can take their places as responsible members of the church, the family, and society.

CREDENTIALS

Accreditations: (see glossary) TCCED
Awards and special recognition: (see glossary) Blue Ribbon
Qualification of administrator: M.A in education; United States Department of Education National Distinguished Principal Award
Qualification of faculty: Degrees and certification
Other: Affiliated with the Diocese of Dallas, NCEA, TCCED

GENERAL

Alternative: No
College preparatory: No
Montessori: No
Nondenominational: No
Church affiliated: Yes
Denomination: Catholic
Jewish: N/A
Other denominations: N/A
Student type: Coed
Grade category (for details see specific grades offered below): Elementary

Infants: N/A
Preschool: N/A
Kindergarten: Full Day
Primary / Transition: No
Elementary: Yes
Secondary or Middle School: Yes
Specific grades offered: K-through grade 8
Student teacher ratio average: 22:1 K; 22:1 grade 1; 25:1 grades 2 - 8
Classes offered per grade: 2 of each grade
Average class size: 25
Total enrollment: 425
Recommended grades to apply: N/A
School hours: 7:50 a.m. - 3:30 p.m.
Calendar school year: August - May
Uniforms required: Yes
Parental involvement opportunities and requirements: Many volunteer opportunities; boards
Average SAT scores: N/A
Visitation procedures: N/A
Personal appointments for touring the facility: Offered
Group tour dates: Offered
Open house dates: Offered
Classroom visits: Offered
Profit or nonprofit: Non-profit

ADMISSIONS

Application form required: Yes
Forms required: Admission form, teacher recommendation
Application deadline: Rolling admissions
Application fee: N/A
Contact: Ms. Gwyne Bohren, Director of Admissions
Phone: (214) 365-1234
Student interview required: Yes
Parent interview required: Yes
Entrance test required: Yes
Specific tests administered: N/A
Accept test scores from other schools: No
Testing fee: $ 50
Time of year testing is administered: February
Test dates offered: N/A
Out of state applicants: By appointment

Notification by phone: N/A
Notification by mail: Yes
Other: Parent and student interviews required for students in the 5th - 8th grade

FINANCIAL

Preschool tuition: N/A
Elementary tuition: $2600 per year for parishioners
Secondary tuition: N/A
Other tuition: More for non-parishioners
Cash discounts: N/A
Personal check: Yes
Automatic bank draw: Yes
Credit cards: N/A
Monthly: Yes
Per semester: Yes
Annually: Yes
Financial assistance offered: Yes
Cancellation insurance: N/A
Sibling discount: N/A
Application acceptance deposit required: Yes

SERVICES

Before school care offered: Yes, building opens at 7:30 a.m. with supervision.
After school care offered: Yes, from 3:30 p.m. - 6:00 p.m.
Transportation provided: N/A
Lunch/snack program: Snack for K-3; K-8 lunch fees vary by child.
Other: Computer lab, library, writing research lab, science lab, art and music in labs, enrichment curriculum and extracurricular activities offered.

GOOD SHEPHERD CATHOLIC SCHOOL

214 S. Garland Ave
Garland, TX   75040
Contact: David Ross, Principal
(972) 272-6533
(972) 272-0512 FAX

Office Hours: 7:30 a.m. - 4:00 p.m.
E-MAIL: goodsh@airmail.net
Web Site: N/A
MAPSCO: N/A

PHILOSOPHY OF SCHOOL

To offer a rigorous academic program in a catholic environment. Our three-fold purpose is faith, knowledge, and service.

CREDENTIALS

Accreditations: (see glossary) Texas Catholic Conference
Awards and special recognition: (see glossary) N/A
Qualification of administrator: Administrator's certificate; graduate degree
Qualification of faculty: Bachelor's degree and certification required; many have master's degrees

GENERAL

Alternative: No
College preparatory: No
Montessori: No
Nondenominational: No
Church affiliated: Yes
Denomination: Catholic Diocese of Dallas
Jewish: N/A
Other denominations: N/A
Student type: Co-ed
Grade category (for details see specific grades offered below): Elementary - Middle School
Infants: N/A
Preschool: N/A
Kindergarten: N/A
Primary / Transition: N/A
Elementary: Yes

Secondary or Middle School: Yes
Student teacher ratio average: 20:1
Classes offered per grade: N/A
Average class size: 20
Total enrollment: 365
Recommended grades to apply: N/A
School hours: 7:55 a.m. - 3:15 p.m. Pre-K - 4th; 7:55 a.m. - 3:25 p.m. 5th - 8th
Calendar school year: August - May
Uniforms required: Yes
Parental involvement opportunities and requirements: Parent-Teacher-Organization activities provide extensive involvement.
Average SAT scores: N/A
Visitation procedures: N/A
Personal appointments for touring the facility: N/A
Group tour dates: N/A
Open house dates: N/A
Classroom visits: N/A
Profit or non-profit: Non-profit

ADMISSIONS

Application form required: Yes
Forms required: Registration, test scores, report cards, birth certificate, baptismal record (if catholic)
Application deadline: February
Application fee: N/A
Contact: School office
Phone: (214) 272-6533
Student interview required: N/A
Parent interview required: N/A
Entrance test required: Yes
Specific tests administered: N/A
Accept test scores from other schools: N/A
Testing fee: $20
Time of year testing is administered: N/A
Test dates offered: N/A
Out of state applicants: N/A
Notification by phone: N/A
Notification by mail: Yes, within 2 weeks

FINANCIAL

Preschool tuition: N/A
Elementary tuition: $2100 Parishioner; $2950 Out-of-Parish; $3400 Non-catholic
Secondary tuition: N/A
Other tuition: Books: $100 per child; Uniform: according to Parker Uniform
   price list
Cash discounts: N/A
Personal check: N/A
Automatic bank draw: N/A
Credit cards: N/A
Monthly: Yes, 10 or 11 payments
Per semester: N/A
Annually: Yes, 5% discount if paid in full be specified date in June
Financial assistance offered: No
Cancellation insurance: No
Sibling discount: Yes
Application acceptance deposit required: N/A
Other: Parents Club Dues $5

SERVICES

Before school care offered: Yes
After school care offered: Yes
Transportation provided: Parents or car pools
Lunch/snack program: Lunch fee is $2.50.
Other: Macintosh computer lab available.

THE HIGHLANDS SCHOOL

1451 East Northgate Drive
Irving, TX 75062
Contact: **Susan Norton**
(972) 554-1980
(972) 721-1691 FAX

Office Hours: 8:00 a.m. - 4:30 p.m.
E-MAIL: n/a
Web Site:
www.thehighlandsschool.org
MAPSCO: 31B-H

PHILOSOPHY OF SCHOOL

The Highlands School is a private Catholic school directed by the Legionaries of Christ for boys and girls Pre-Kindergarten through Grade 12. An informed intellect, a moral character, and a vibrant spiritual life grow together for the integral formation of every student. A Highlands education prepares each individual to answer Christ's call to be true leaven in today's world.

The Highlands School has three essential and related missions: to teach the intellect, to educate the heart, to form the character. Semper Altius, the school's motto, sums up its spirit: Climb "Always Higher."

Teachers impart truth; students study, assimilate, and build upon it. Whether teaching facts and figures, religion, history or literature, The Highlands School proclaims that truth is the foundation of knowledge from which all other learning flows.

The child is not only mind, but heart and imagination, too. The Highlands School educates toward a view of the world, of nature, and of man in harmony with human and spiritual values. In creating lovely objects, through appreciation of music, and by reading fine books, young hearts are opened to the beautiful, the noble, and the just.

Character and virtue are formed by daily practice of responsibilities. Constant concern for justice, will-power to undertake what is difficult, fidelity to one's word, good manners, and personal responsibility for one's actions are the goals of The Highlands School.

The Highlands education is truly realized when it is the student who strives to reach his own potential under the direction of the teachers' examples and demands. The religious nature of the school emphasizes the individual's responsibility for his or her personal formation and development of natural talent.

CREDENTIALS

Accreditations: (see glossary) TCCED

Awards and special recognition: (see glossary) First PK-12 school run by Legionaries of Christ in the USA. Affiliated with inter- national network of Legionary Schools.

Qualification of administrator: Advanced degrees in administration.

Qualification of faculty: BA or BS minimum requirement.

Other: Teachers and Administrators also take a week long intensive course in Legionary pedagogy.

GENERAL

Alternative: No

College preparatory: Yes

Montessori: No

Nondenominational: No

Church affiliated: Yes

Denomination: Catholic

Jewish: N/A

Other denominations: N/A

Student type: Co-institutional

Grade category (for details see specific grades offered below): Preschool - 12th

Infants: N/A

Preschool: Full Day

Kindergarten: Full Day

Primary / Transition: No

Elementary: Yes

Secondary or Middle School: Yes

Specific grades offered: Preschool - 12th

Student teacher ratio average: 13:1

Classes offered per grade: 2 to 3

Average class size: 15

Total enrollment: 455

Recommended grades to apply: PK4, K, 1, 7, 9

School hours: 8:15 a.m. - 3:30 p.m.

Calendar school year: Mid-August through end of May

Uniforms required: Yes

Parental involvement opportunities and requirements: Very active Parents Club with various committees. All done on a volunteer basis.

Average SAT scores: 1200s

Visitation procedures: Arranged through Admissions Office. Student can spend a half-day with current grade, or in grade for following year.

Personal appointments for touring the facility: Call Admissions Office for a mutually convenient time.

Group tour dates: See below

Open house dates: November 7, 1999, January 23, 2000, February 27, 2000

Classroom visits: PK3&4 - Schedule through Admissions Office

Profit or non-profit: Non-profit

ADMISSIONS

Application form required: Yes

Forms required: Provided by school

Application deadline: March 1, 1999

Application fee: $50

Contact: Susan P. Norton

Phone: (972) 554-1980 x235

Student interview required: Yes

Parent interview required: Yes

Entrance test required: Yes

Specific tests administered: ISEE

Accept test scores from other schools: Yes When they are equivalent to ISEE

Testing fee: $79

Time of year testing is administered: December through April

Test dates offered: December 11, 1999, January 15, 2000, February 12, 2000, April 15, 2000

Out of state applicants: Can be done by mail

Notification by phone: Yes

Notification by mail: Yes, formal acceptance

FINANCIAL

Preschool tuition: $4900

Elementary tuition: $5200

Secondary tuition: $6100

Other tuition: $500 discount for Catholic families

Cash discounts: Yes **Description:** See below

Personal check: N/A

Automatic bank draw: Yes

Credit cards: N/A

Monthly: Yes, 10 months

Per semester: Yes, 2% discount

Annually: Yes, 5% discount

Financial assistance offered: Yes, SSS forms provided through Admissions Office. 4/14/00 deadline

Cancellation insurance: N/A
Sibling discount: Yes, 15% for 3rd, 4th; others free tuition
Application acceptance deposit required: N/A

SERVICES

Before school care offered: Yes, 7:30 a.m. - 8:15 a.m.
After school care offered: Yes, 3:30 p.m. - 5:00 p.m., 3:30 p.m. - 6:30 p.m.
Transportation provided: Limited; check with Admissions
Lunch/snack program: Full cafeteria. Parents provide snacks

HOLY TRINITY CATHOLIC SCHOOL

3815 Oak Lawn
Dallas, TX 75219
Contact: Ned Vanders, Principal
(214) 526-5113
(214) 526-4524 FAX

Office Hours: 8:00 a.m. - 4:30 p.m.
E-MAIL: N/A
Web Site: N/A
MAPSCO: 35X

PHILOSOPHY OF SCHOOL

The mission at Holy Trinity Catholic School is to provide each student the highest quality foundation of Catholic education. The school enriches the minds, bodies, and spirits of the children. The school produces students who are competitve in Catholic secondary schools, and who ultimately become productive citizens and wise leaders in society. In our rapidly changing urban community, the school reaches out to include and welcome those from the emerging cultural and ethnic diversity around us. The school's uniquely personal educational process encourages and motivates each student to strive for excellence.

CREDENTIALS

Accreditations: (see glossary) TCCED
Awards and special recognition: (see glossary) N/A
Qualification of administrator: Master's degree in educational administration
Qualification of faculty: College degree and teacher certification
Other: Affiliated with the National Catholic Education Association
and Texas Catholic Conference Education Department
(TCCED)

GENERAL

Alternative: No
College preparatory: No
Montessori: No
Nondenominational: No
Church affiliated: Yes
Denomination: Catholic
Jewish: N/A
Other denominations: N/A
Student type: Co-ed

Grade category (for details see specific grades offered below): Elementary

Infants: N/A

Preschool: Full Day

Kindergarten: Full Day

Primary / Transition: No

Elementary: Yes

Secondary or Middle School: N/A

Specific grades offered: Preschool (age 3) - grade 8

Student teacher ratio average: 18:1

Classes offered per grade: N/A

Average class size: 20

Total enrollment: 230

Recommended grades to apply: N/A

School hours: 7:45 a.m. - 3:30 p.m.

Calendar school year: Mid-August - end of May

Uniforms required: Yes

Parental involvement opportunites and requirements: PTO, volunteerism, and fundraising

Average SAT scores: N/A

Visitation procedures: N/A

Personal appointments for touring the facility: Offered

Group tour dates: N/A

Open house dates: N/A

Classroom visits: N/A

Profit or non-profit: Non-profit

ADMISSIONS

Application form required: Yes

Forms required: Birth certificate, baptismal certificate for Catholics, recent report card, recent achievement test scores

Application deadline: Apply mid-February - May of each year

Application fee: $185

Contact: School principal or school secretary

Phone: (214) 526-5113

Student interview required: No

Parent interview required: No

Entrance test required: Yes

Specific tests administered: 1st - 4th Grade: Placement test , Fifth and above: Placement test

Accept test scores from other schools: No

Testing fee: N/A

Time of year testing is administered: N/A
Test dates offered: N/A
Out of state applicants: N/A
Notification by phone: Yes
Notification by mail: Yes
Other: In person

FINANCIAL

Preschool tuition: N/A
Elementary tuition: Parishioner $2270; Non-Parishioner $2940
Secondary tuition: N/A
Other tuition: Non-Catholic $3400
Cash discounts: N/A
Personal check: N/A
Automatic bank draw: N/A
Credit cards: N/A
Monthly: Yes
Per semester: Yes
Annually: Yes
Financial assistance offered: Yes, but very limited
Cancellation insurance: N/A
Sibling discount: Yes
Application acceptance deposit required: N/A

SERVICES

Before school care offered: N/A
After school care offered: Yes, until 6:00 p.m.
Transportation provided: N/A
Lunch/snack program: Lunch fee $2.65; preschool through kindergarten bring morning snacks
Other: Computer lab, library, enrichment curriculum and extracurricular activities offered

ST. BERNARD OF CLAIRVAUX

1420 Old Gate Lane   *Office Hours:* 7:30 a.m. - 3:30 p.m.
Dallas, TX 75218   *E-MAIL:* www.non-profits.org/stbernard
Contact: **Margaret Schmoeckel**   *Web Site:* N/A
(214) 321-2897   *MAPSCO:* 37R
(214) 321-4060 FAX

PHILOSOPHY OF SCHOOL

We believe each child is a unique, loving, and spiritual individual. Each possesses the potential for learning and the ability to share these innate gifts.

At St. Bernard of Clairvaux School, we strive to create an open, loving atmosphere that will promote the growth of the whole child — spiritual, emotional, intellectual, physical and social.

To achieve these philosophical goals, St. Bernard of Clairvaux School sets forth the following objectives:
1. To teach religion as a way of life and provide Christian role models.
2. To provide opportunity to develop spiritually through worship, prayer, and service.
3. To promote a healthy self-image by giving positive reinforcement and consistency.
4. To meet individual academic and personal needs with warmth and love.
5. To promote appreciation of others by sharing cultural and traditional enrichment.

Once a student is registered and accepted into St. Bernard of Clairvaux School, it is understood that the student and parent agree to cooperate with the school's regulations and policies.

CREDENTIALS

Accreditations: (see glossary) TCCED
Awards and special recognition: (see glossary) N/A
Qualification of administrator: Must have at least a master's degree with three years teaching experience and an emphasis in administration
Qualification of faculty: College degree; 27% have master's degree or higher

GENERAL

Alternative: No
College preparatory: No
Montessori: No
Nondenominational: No
Church affiliated: Yes
Denomination: Catholic
Jewish: N/A
Other denominations: N/A
Student type: Co-ed
Grade category (for details see specific grades offered below): 1st - 12th
Infants: N/A
Preschool: N/A
Kindergarten: N/A
Primary / Transition: N/A
Elementary: Yes
Secondary or Middle School: Yes
Specific grades offered: Kindergarten - 8th
Student teacher ratio average: 20:1
Classes offered per grade: N/A
Average class size: N/A
Total enrollment: 360
Recommended grades to apply: N/A
School hours: 7:50 a.m. - 3:15 p.m.
Calendar school year: August - May
Uniforms required: Yes
Parental involvement opportunities and requirements: Home and School
    Association
Average SAT scores: N/A
Visitation procedures: N/A
Personal appointments for touring the facility: N/A
Group tour dates: N/A
Open house dates: N/A
Classroom visits: N/A
Profit or non-profit: Non-profit

ADMISSIONS

Application form required: Yes
Forms required: Registration packet
Application deadline: February
Application fee: $125-200 (Registration fee $125; books, activity fee $30)

Contact: Mr. Jack R. LaMar
Phone: (214) 321-2897
Student interview required: N/A
Parent interview required: N/A
Entrance test required: N/A
Specific tests administered: N/A
Accept test scores from other schools: N/A
Testing fee: N/A
Time of year testing is administered: N/A
Test dates offered: N/A
Out of state applicants: N/A
Notification by phone: N/A
Notification by mail: N/A
Other: Notification is usually done in person or by phone. If someone is not accepted, the principal works with parents for placement.

FINANCIAL

Preschool tuition: N/A
Elementary tuition: Parishioners $2090 with a reduction for more than one child; non-parishioners $2825; non-Catholic $3100
Secondary tuition: Parishioners $2090 with a reduction for more than one child; non-parishioners $2825; non-Catholic $3100
Other tuition: N/A
Cash discounts: N/A
Personal check: N/A
Automatic bank draw: N/A
Credit cards: N/A
Monthly: N/A
Per semester: N/A
Annually: Yes
Financial assistance offered: Limited
Cancellation insurance: Inquire at school office.
Sibling discount: Yes
Application acceptance deposit required: N/A
Other: Prepaid tuition; may pay the school directly or take a signature loan through the approved bank.

SERVICES

Before school care offered: No

After school care offered: Yes, 3:00 p.m. - 6:00 p.m.

Transportation provided: No

Lunch/snack program: Snacks for kindergarten classes only. $1.50 per day hot lunch.

Other: Computer lab available.

ST. MARY'S CATHOLIC SCHOOL

713 S. Travis
Sherman, TX 75090
Contact: **Francis Baird, Principal**
(903) 893-2127
(903) 813 - 5489 FAX

Office Hours: 7:30 a.m. - 4:00 p.m.
E-MAIL: stmarysch@texoma.net
Web Site: N/A
MAPSCO: N/A

PHILOSOPHY OF SCHOOL

Catholic education has its essential elements: message, community, and service. St. Mary's seeks the integration of this threefold dimension with the total educational process so the child may grow in the knowledge and love of God and in awareness of and commitment to the basic Christian values of love and service to neighbor.

CREDENTIALS

Accreditations: (see glossary) TCCED
Awards and special recognition: (see glossary) N/A
Qualification of administrator: B.S. in Elementary Education, M.Ed.
Qualification of faculty: Bachelor's degree in elementary education
Other: Accredited by the Texas Catholic Conference; Affiliated with TANS, NCEA

GENERAL

Alternative: No
College preparatory: No
Montessori: No
Nondenominational: No
Church affiliated: Yes
Denomination: Catholic
Jewish: N/A
Other denominations: N/A
Student type: Co-ed
Grade category (for details see specific grades offered below): Elementary
Infants: N/A
Preschool: Full Day
Kindergarten: Full Day

220

Primary / Transition: No
Elementary: Yes
Secondary or Middle School: N/A
Specific grades offered: Pre-K (age 3) - grade 6
Student teacher ratio average: 22:1
Classes offered per grade: N/A
Average class size: 22
Total enrollment: 150
Recommended grades to apply: N/A
School hours: 8:30 a.m. - 3:30 p.m.
Calendar school year: August - June
Uniforms required: Yes
Parental involvement opportunities and requirements: Home and school
association
Average SAT scores: N/A
Visitation procedures: N/A
Personal appointments for touring the facility: Offered
Group tour dates: N/A
Open house dates: N/A
Classroom visits: N/A
Profit or non-profit: Non-profit
Other: Uniforms: see handbook, page 12

ADMISSIONS

Application form required: Yes
Forms required: Birth certificate, shot record, baptismal certificate
Application deadline: Apply in spring.
Application fee: $200-registration-book fee
Contact: Frances Baird
Phone: (903) 893-2127
Student interview required: Yes
Parent interview required: Yes
Entrance test required: Yes
Specific tests administered: N/A
Accept test scores from other schools: No
Testing fee: N/A
Time of year testing is administered: Spring
Test dates offered: N/A
Out of state applicants: N/A
Notification by phone: N/A
Notification by mail: Yes

FINANCIAL

Preschool tuition: N/A

Elementary tuition: Catholic contributing $2100; Catholic non-contributing $2550; non-Catholic $2600

Secondary tuition: N/A

Other tuition: Uniform fee

Cash discounts: N/A

Personal check: N/A

Automatic bank draw: N/A

Credit cards: N/A

Monthly: Yes

Per semester: N/A

Annually: N/A

Financial assistance offered: Yes

Cancellation insurance: N/A

Sibling discount: Yes

Application acceptance deposit required: N/A

SERVICES

Before school care offered: Yes, 6:45 a.m. - 8:00 a.m.

After school care offered: Yes, 3:30 p.m. - 6:00 p.m.

Transportation provided: N/A

Lunch/snack program: Lunch fee: Preschool-grade 1 $1.35; grades 2-6 $1.85; snacks given at morning break

Other: Computer lab, library, enrichment curriculum and extracurricular activities offered

ST. MONICA
CATHOLIC SCHOOL

4140 Walnut Hill Lane
Dallas, TX 75229
Contact: **Roberta Allen, Secretary**
(214) 351-5688
(214) 352-2608 FAX

Office Hours: 8:00 a.m. - 4:00 p.m.
E-MAIL: offsms@cathedral.org
Web Site: www.stmonicaschool.org
MAPSCO: 24P

PHILOSOPHY OF SCHOOL

St. Monica Catholic School offers a challenging academic program that seeks to develop the whole child in a nurturing Catholic environment. The curriculum is enriched by an extensive technology and multimedia program, and an emphasis on the fine arts and languages.

CREDENTIALS

Accreditations: (see glossary) TCCED
Awards and special recognition: (see glossary)
Qualification of administrator: Doctor of Philosophy in Education
Qualification of faculty: All faculty are degreed and certified in area of assignment; nine hold advanced degrees.

GENERAL

Alternative: No
College preparatory: No
Montessori: No
Nondenominational: No
Church affiliated: Yes
Denomination: Catholic
Jewish: N/A
Other denominations: N/A
Student type: Co-ed
Grade category (for details see specific grades offered below): Elementary
Infants: N/A
Preschool: N/A
Kindergarten: Full Day
Primary / Transition: No

Elementary: Yes

Secondary or Middle School: Yes

Specific grades offered: Grades K-8

Student teacher ratio average: 25:1

Classes offered per grade: 4

Average class size: 25

Total enrollment: 850

Recommended grades to apply: Any

School hours: 8:00 a.m. to 4:00 p.m.

Calendar school year: August to May

Uniforms required: Yes

Parental involvement opportunities and requirements: PTO and Dad's Club

Average SAT scores: N/A

Visitation procedures: Call school office for an appointment; November and January Visitor's Days

Personal appointments for touring the facility: Call school office

Group tour dates: November and January of each year

Open house dates: November 12, 1999 and January 28, 2000

Classroom visits: Only during group tour days

Profit or non-profit: Non-profit

ADMISSIONS

Application form required: Yes

Forms required: N/A

Application deadline: Begins the end of January through spring

Application fee: $150.00 per student

Contact: Roberta Allen

Phone: (214) 351-5688

Student interview required: No

Parent interview required: No

Entrance test required: Yes

Specific tests administered: Kindergarten: Gesell School Readiness

Accept test scores from other schools: No

Testing fee: $25.00 per student

Time of year testing is administered: February

Test dates offered: February 7-12, 2000 or by appt.

Out of state applicants: N/A

Notification by phone: N/A

Notification by mail: Yes

FINANCIAL

Preschool tuition: N/A

Elementary tuition: $2,825 One child Parishioner for 1999-2000

Secondary tuition: N/A

Other tuition: N/A

Cash discounts: N/A

Personal check: N/A

Automatic bank draw: N/A

Credit cards: N/A

Monthly: Yes

Per semester: N/A

Annually: Yes

Financial assistance offered: Some available

Cancellation insurance: N/A

Sibling discount: Yes

Application acceptance deposit required: N/A

Other: N/A

SERVICES

Before school care offered: N/A

After school care offered: Yes, 3:30 p.m. - 6:00 p.m.

Transportation provided: N/A

Lunch/snack program: Hot lunches provided in cafeteria.

ST. PAUL THE APOSTLE

720 S. Floyd Road
Richardson, TX 75080
Contact: **Mary C. Williams, Principal**
(972) 235-3263
(972) 690-1542 FAX

Office Hours: 7:30 a.m. - 4:00 p.m.
E-MAIL: stpaul@airmail.net
Web Site: N/A
MAPSCO: 16H

PHILOSOPHY OF SCHOOL

St. Paul the Apostle School is committed to the development of the whole child and shares with parents the responsibility for the religious, intellectual, moral, physical, aesthetic, and social formation of the children.

CREDENTIALS

Accreditations: (see glossary) TCCED

Awards and special recognition: (see glossary) Blue Ribbon School of Excellence

Qualification of administrator: Master's degree in administration; certification in administration

Qualification of faculty: Degrees and certification

Other: Affiliated with the National Catholic Education Association, Texas Catholic Conference Education Department (TCCED), Middle School Teachers, Council for Exceptional Children

GENERAL

Alternative: No
College preparatory: No
Montessori: No
Nondenominational: No
Church affiliated: Yes
Denomination: Catholic
Jewish: N/A
Other denominations: N/A
Student type: Co-ed
Grade category (for details see specific grades offered below): Elementary
Infants: N/A
Preschool: N/A
Kindergarten: Full Day
Primary / Transition: No

Elementary: Yes
Secondary or Middle School: Yes
Specific grades offered: Kindergarten - grade 8
Student teacher ratio average: 22:1 approximately
Classes offered per grade: N/A
Average class size: 22
Total enrollment: 470
Recommended grades to apply: N/A
School hours: 7:45 a.m. - 3:20 p.m.
Calendar school year: August - May
Uniforms required: Yes
Parental involvement opportunities and requirements: Yes
Average SAT scores: N/A
Visitation procedures: N/A
Personal appointments for touring the facility: Offered
Group tour dates: N/A
Open house dates: N/A
Classroom visits: N/A
Profit or non-profit: Non-profit

ADMISSIONS

Application form required: Yes
Forms required: Registration and application
Application deadline: Applications taken year-round
Application fee: $135
Contact: Mary C. Williams, Principal
Phone: (214) 235-3263
Student interview required: Yes
Parent interview required: Yes
Entrance test required: No
Specific tests administered: N/A
Accept test scores from other schools: Yes, National Achievement Tests
Testing fee: N/A
Time of year testing is administered: Spring
Test dates offered: N/A
Out of state applicants: N/A
Notification by phone: N/A
Notification by mail: Yes
Other: Immediately upon registration; Student interviews required for
grades 5-8 only.

FINANCIAL

Preschool tuition: N/A

Elementary tuition: Parishioner (1) child $3036; non-parishioner (1) $3504; non-Catholic (1) $3960

Secondary tuition: N/A

Other tuition: Uniform fee; books included in registration fee.

Cash discounts: N/A

Personal check: Yes

Automatic bank draw: N/A

Credit cards: VISA, MasterCard, American Express

Monthly: Yes

Per semester: Yes

Annually: Yes

Financial assistance offered: Limited through Parish

Cancellation insurance: N/A

Sibling discount: Yes

Application acceptance deposit required: N/A

SERVICES

Before school care offered: Yes, 7:00 a.m. - 7:50 a.m.

After school care offered: Yes, 3:20 p.m. - 6:00 p.m.

Transportation provided: N/A

Lunch/snack program: Lunch fee $2.50 per day if child elects to purchase lunch at school.

Other: Computer lab, library, enrichment curriculum and extracurricular activities offered.

TSDA
Texas Conference of Seventh-Day Adventists

P.O. Box 800
Alvarado, TX 76009-0800
(817) 783-2223

The Seventh-Day Adventist School System began in the late 1800s and has developed into a world-wide system of education.

There are three schools located in the Dallas area: Dallas Adventist Junior Academy (4025 North Central Expressway, Dallas, Texas 75204) and Richardson Adventist School (1201 West Beltline Road, Richardson, Texas 75080). There is one school in Arlington: Burton Adventist Academy, 4611 Kelly-Elliot Road, Arlington, Texas 76017.

Each school is accredited through the Adventist Accrediting Association-the accrediting organization of Seventh-Day Adventist schools. New schools are evaluated during the second year of operation, and if they meet the requirements, they receive accreditation.

Each school is presented as an accredited school through the Texas SDA School System to the Texas Private School Accreditation Commission (TEPSAC). Each of these schools is then recognized by Texas Education Agency (TEA) in Austin as an accredited school.

The teachers of Seventh-Day Adventist schools are certified by the Seventh-Day Adventist Office of Education. Requirements must be met in order to receive this certification.

Therefore, each of the above-mentioned schools is accredited and has certified teachers. Students receive an education comparable to that required by TEA and religious instruction.

Richardson Adventist School

RICHARDSON ADVENTIST SCHOOL

1201 W. Beltline Road
Richardson, TX 75080
Contact: **Stephan Gray**
(972) 238-1183
(972) 644-3488 FAX

Office Hours: 7:30 a.m. - 5:00 p.m.
E-MAIL: ras120@airmail.net
Web Site: N/A
MAPSCO: 16B

PHILOSOPHY OF SCHOOL

The Richardson Adventist School is dedicated to providing all students with a Christ-centered educational experience designed to help them reach their fullest potential spiritually, mentally, physically, socially, and morally. We value the infinite worth of every individual and seek to provide a climate in which the development of personal excellence is practiced. Our mission is to prepare each student to be a lifelong seeker of knowledge and to live purposefully in service of God and man.

CREDENTIALS

Accreditations: (see glossary) TEA
Awards and special recognition: (see glossary) N/A
Qualification of administrator: College degrees, denominational certifications
Qualification of faculty: College degree; state and denominational certifications
Other: Also accredited by the Board of Regents of General Conference of Seventh-Day Adventist; Affiliated with the Texas Conference of Seventh-Day Adventist Schools

GENERAL

Alternative: No
College preparatory: No
Montessori: No
Nondenominational: No
Church affiliated: Yes
Denomination: Seventh-Day Adventists
Jewish: N/A
Other denominations: N/A
Student type: Co-ed

Grade category (for details see specific grades offered below): 1st - 12th

Infants: N/A

Preschool: N/A

Kindergarten: Yes

Primary / Transition: No

Elementary: Yes

Secondary or Middle School: Yes

Specific grades offered: Grades K - 10th

Student teacher ratio average: 15:1

Classes offered per grade: N/A

Average class size: 15

Total enrollment: 120

Recommended grades to apply: N/A

School hours: 8:30 a.m. - 3:30 p.m.

Calendar school year: July - May

Uniforms required: Yes

Parental involvement opportunities and requirements: Home and School (PTA) very active; volunteer program

Average SAT scores: N/A

Visitation procedures: Set appointment with principal.

Personal appointments for touring the facility: with principal

Group tour dates: with principal

Open house dates: N/A

Classroom visits: N/A

Profit or non-profit: Non-profit

ADMISSIONS

Application form required: Yes

Forms required: Application form, immunization

Application deadline: Apply any time (early registration January - April)

Application fee: $300 annual registration fee

Contact: Stephan Gray, Principal

Phone: (214) 238-1183

Student interview required: Yes

Parent interview required: Yes

Entrance test required: Yes

Specific tests administered: 1st - 10th grade: Individual testing

Accept test scores from other schools: Yes

Testing fee: N/A

Time of year testing is administered: N/A

Test dates offered: N/A

Out of state applicants: N/A
Notification by phone: Yes
Notification by mail: Yes

FINANCIAL

Preschool tuition: N/A
Elementary tuition: $2500/$250 per month/10 months
Secondary tuition: $3500/$350 per month/10 months
Other tuition: $50 technology fee
Cash discounts: N/A
Personal check: Yes
Automatic bank draw: N/A
Credit cards: N/A
Monthly: Yes
Per semester: N/A
Annually: N/A
Financial assistance offered: For worthy student
Cancellation insurance: N/A
Sibling discount: Yes
Application acceptance deposit required: Yes

SERVICES

Before school care offered: Yes, 7:00 a.m. - 8:15 a.m.; no charge
After school care offered: Yes, 3:45 p.m. - 6:00 p.m.; $25/week or $5/day
Transportation provided: N/A
Lunch/snack program: Lunch fee is $2.50 per lunch per day.
Other: Payments for after-school program due each Monday; computers in classroom, library for grades K - 10, enrichment curriculum and extracurricular activities available.

Additional Schools

These schools are not currently licensed or accredited. It is important to remember that accreditation is NOT MANDATORY in Texas. It is a voluntary process for the schools to select accreditation from an organization that meets their needs.

Academic Achievement Associates
Carlisle School, The
Coughs & Cuddles for Mildly Ill Children
Logos Academy
SMU Study Skills Classes (see Ch. 4)
St. Therese Academy

ACADEMIC ACHIEVEMENT ASSOCIATES

12820 Hillcrest Road, Suite 124 C
Dallas, TX 75230
Contact: **Dorothy Baxter**
(972) 490-6399
(972) 490-6416 FAX

Office Hours: 8:00 a.m. - 6:00 p.m. and evening tutoring/counseling
E-MAIL: aaadot@yahoo.com
Web Site: www.academicachievement.net
MAPSCO: 15R

PHILOSOPHY OF SCHOOL

Academic Achievement Associates is a group of teachers and counselors who work with individuals of all ages to overcome obstacles blocking them from achievement. We take students who need time out from a traditional educational setting and work with them to return to such a setting.

CREDENTIALS

Accreditations: (see glossary)
Awards and special recognition: (see glossary) N/A
Qualification of administrator: Teacher certification, Licensed Professional Counselor, Licensed Marriage & Family Therapist
Qualification of faculty: College degree, teacher certification
Other: Association of Educational Therapists, Orton Dyslexia Society. Our facility combines the hand-in-hand disciplines of education & counseling. High school students are able to receive a high school diploma through the Texas Tech guided education program.

GENERAL

Alternative: Yes
College preparatory: Yes
Montessori: No
Nondenominational: No
Church affiliated: No
Denomination: N/A
Jewish: N/A
Other denominations: N/A
Student type: Co-ed
Grade category (for details see specific grades offered below): 1st - 12th
Infants: N/A

Preschool: N/A
Kindergarten: N/A
Primary / Transition: No
Elementary: Yes
Secondary or Middle School: Yes
Specific grades offered: Kindergarten to adult
Student teacher ratio average: 1:1 or small groups
Classes offered per grade: Yes
Average class size: One-on-one
Total enrollment: Varies
Recommended grades to apply: N/A
School hours: 9:00 a.m. - 4:00 p.m.
Calendar school year: Year-round
Uniforms required: No
Parental involvement opportunities and requirements: Yes
Average SAT scores: N/A
Visitation procedures: N/A
Personal appointments for touring the facility: Yes
Group tour dates: N/A
Open house dates: N/A
Classroom visits: N/A
Profit or non-profit: Profit

ADMISSIONS

Application form required: Yes
Forms required: Varies with situation
Application deadline: none
Application fee: N/A
Contact: Dorothy Baxter, M.Ed., LPC, LMFT
Phone: (972) 490-6399
Student interview required: No
Parent interview required: No
Entrance test required: No
Specific tests administered: Kindergarten: For all students: complete psycho-
    educational available. Other tests: WRAT, Gilmore & Woodcock-Johnson
Accept test scores from other schools: No
Testing fee: Varies
Time of year testing is administered: N/A
Test dates offered: N/A
Out of state applicants: N/A
Notification by phone: N/A

Notification by mail: N/A

FINANCIAL

Preschool tuition: N/A
Elementary tuition: N/A
Secondary tuition: N/A
Other tuition: Varies with service
Cash discounts: N/A
Personal check: N/A
Automatic bank draw: N/A
Credit cards: No
Monthly: Yes
Per semester: Approximately $2500
Annually: N/A
Financial assistance offered: No
Cancellation insurance: N/A
Sibling discount: N/A
Application acceptance deposit required: N/A

SERVICES

Before school care offered: N/A
After school care offered: N/A
Transportation provided: N/A
Lunch/snack program: Vending machines, snack bar
Other: Computer Lab: Josten Educational CD-ROM software. After school tutoring offered.

THE CARLISLE SCHOOL

4705 West Lovers Lane
Dallas, TX 75209
Contact: **Dr. Richard Carlisle, Director**
(214) 351-1833
Fax Number Not Available

Office Hours: 7:30 a.m. - 6:00 p.m.
E-MAIL: N/A
Web Site: N/A
MAPSCO: 34B

PHILOSOPHY OF SCHOOL

The Carlisle School provides a caring environment for the learning process which serves each child individually as a bride between home and the more institutional structures of both private and public elementary schools. We use our combined 50 years of teaching to rise above the current stagnation in American education. In short, we are grounded in the traditional values of education.

CREDENTIALS

Accreditations: (see glossary) TDPRS, Curriculum Alternative
Awards and special recognition: (see glossary) N/A
Qualification of administrator: B.A., M.A., Ph.D. degrees, 30+ years of experience
Qualification of faculty: College degree, Montessori training

GENERAL

Alternative: No
College preparatory: No
Montessori: No
Nondenominational: No
Church affiliated: No
Denomination: N/A
Jewish: N/A
Other denominations: N/A
Student type: Co-ed
Grade category (for details see specific grades offered below): Pre-kindergarten - kindergarten
Infants: N/A
Preschool: Yes
Kindergarten: Yes
Primary / Transition: N/A
Elementary: N/A

Secondary or Middle School: N/A
Student teacher ratio average: Age 2, 4:1; age 3, 6:1; others, 10:1
Classes offered per grade: N/A
Average class size: Ratio determined
Total enrollment: 34
Recommended grades to apply: N/A
School hours: Before-school care: 7:30 a.m. - 9:00 a.m.; class: 9:00 a.m. - 3:00 p.m.; after-school care: 3:00 p.m. - 6:00 p.m.
Calendar school year: Year round program; September - May; June - August
Uniforms required: Yes
Parental involvement opportunities and requirements: N/A
Average SAT scores: N/A
Visitation procedures: N/A
Personal appointments for touring the facility: Call for appointment
Group tour dates: N/A
Open house dates: N/A
Classroom visits: N/A
Profit or non-profit: Non-profit

ADMISSIONS

Application form required: Yes
Forms required: Health certificate, application form, enrollment agreement
Application deadline: Open applications, year round
Application fee: Admission: $250; paper fee: $75
Contact: Dr. Richard Carlisle
Phone: (214) 351-1833
Student interview required: N/A
Parent interview required: N/A
Entrance test required: N/A
Specific tests administered: N/A
Accept test scores from other schools: N/A
Testing fee: N/A
Time of year testing is administered: N/A
Test dates offered: N/A
Out of state applicants: N/A
Notification by phone: N/A
Notification by mail: N/A
Other: Personal notification

FINANCIAL

Preschool tuition: Partial, $500/month; academic only, $550/month; full, $600/month. Tuitions include before/after school care.

Elementary tuition: N/A

Secondary tuition: N/A

Other tuition: Uniforms - girls: $30; boys; $20 (approximate costs); diapering fee: $50/month

Cash discounts: N/A

Personal check: N/A

Automatic bank draw: N/A

Credit cards: N/A

Monthly: N/A

Per semester: Yes, discount available

Annually: Yes, discount available

Financial assistance offered: Occasional scholarships available

Cancellation insurance: N/A

Sibling discount: Yes

Application acceptance deposit required: N/A

Other: N/A

SERVICES

Before school care offered: Yes, 7:30 a.m. - 9:00 a.m.

After school care offered: Yes, 3:00 p.m. - 6:00 p.m.

Transportation provided: Available within immediate area

Lunch/snack program: Before school, at 3:00 p.m., and at 5:00 p.m.

Other: Challenging programs in reading, social studies, humanities, and math for grades K through 6, June-August each summer; Spanish throughout curriculum.

COUGHS AND CUDDLES FOR MILDLY ILL CHILDREN

6100 W. Parker Rd.
Plano, TX 75093
Contact: Rose Marie Oliphant
(972) 608-8585
(972) 608-8587 FAX

Office Hours: 6:30 a.m. - 6:30 p.m.
E-MAIL: N/A
Web Site: N/A
MAPSCO: 656F

PHILOSOPHY OF SCHOOL

If your child isn't feeling well or has an injury that prevents attendance at a regular childcare facility, call Coughs & Cuddles at Presbyterian Hospital of Plano. We provide a warm, comfortable atmosphere where your child can receive attention from nurses and other trained childcare providers.

CREDENTIALS

Accreditations: (see glossary)
Awards and special recognition: (see glossary) N/A
Qualification of administrator: College degree
Qualification of faculty: Teacher & nurse-college degrees

GENERAL

Alternative: Yes
College preparatory: No
Montessori: No
Nondenominational: No
Church affiliated: Yes
Denomination: N/A
Jewish: N/A
Other denominations: Church affiliated: Faith-based
Student type: Coed
Grade category (for details see specific grades offered below): Preschool - 12th
Infants: Yes
Preschool: Yes
Kindergarten: Yes

Primary / Transition: No
Elementary: Yes
Secondary or Middle School: Yes
Specific grades offered: Preschool - 10th
Student teacher ratio average: N/A
Classes offered per grade: N/A
Average class size: N/A
Total enrollment: N/A
Recommended grades to apply: N/A
School hours: 6:30 a.m. - 6:30 p.m.
Calendar school year: Year-round
Uniforms required: No
Parental involvement opportunities and requirements: N/A
Average SAT scores: N/A
Visitation procedures: N/A
Personal appointments for touring the facility: N/A
Group tour dates: N/A
Open house dates: N/A
Classroom visits: N/A
Profit or nonprofit: Non-profit

ADMISSIONS

Application form required: Yes
Forms required: N/A
Application deadline: None
Application fee: N/A
Contact: Rose Marie Oliphant
Phone: (972) 608-8585
Student interview required: No
Parent interview required: No
Entrance test required: No
Specific tests administered: N/A
Accept test scores from other schools: No
Testing fee: N/A
Time of year testing is administered: N/A
Test dates offered: N/A
Out of state applicants: N/A
Notification by phone: N/A
Notification by mail: N/A

FINANCIAL

Preschool tuition: $6 per hour, 4 hour minimum
Elementary tuition: $6 per hour, 4 hour minimum
Secondary tuition: N/A
Other tuition: N/A
Cash discounts: N/A
Personal check: Yes
Automatic bank draw: N/A
Credit cards: Visa, MasterCard, American Express, Discover
Monthly: N/A
Per semester: N/A
Annually: N/A
Financial assistance offered: N/A
Cancellation insurance: N/A
Sibling discount: N/A
Application acceptance deposit required: N/A

SERVICES

Before school care offered: Yes, from 6:30 a.m.
After school care offered: Yes, until 6:30 p.m.
Transportation provided: N/A
Lunch/snack program: Yes
Other: Emergency/back-up child care

LOGOS ACADEMY

10919 Royal Haven
Dallas, TX 75229
Contact: **Director of Admission**
(214) 357-2995
(214) 357-0880 FAX

Office Hours: 8:00 a.m. - 3:30 p.m. M-F
E-MAIL: N/A
Web Site: N/A
MAPSCO: 23G

PHILOSOPHY OF SCHOOL

Offers an integrated classical and Christ-centered college preparatory curriculum with the goal of preparing graduating students to be effective leaders and ambassadors for Jesus Christ.

CREDENTIALS

Accreditations: (see glossary) ACCS in progress
Awards and special recognition: (see glossary) N/A
Qualification of administrator: N/A
Qualification of faculty: Degreed in field.
Other: Member ACSI, ACCS, ERB

GENERAL

Alternative: No
College preparatory: Yes
Montessori: No
Nondenominational: Yes
Church affiliated: No
Denomination: N/A
Jewish: N/A
Other denominations: N/A
Student type: Co-ed
Grade category (for details see specific grades offered below): N/A
Infants: N/A
Preschool: N/A
Kindergarten: N/A
Primary / Transition: No
Elementary: N/A
Secondary or Middle School: Yes
Specific grades offered: 7th - 12th
Other: Classical, Christian

Student teacher ratio average: 15:1

Classes offered: Integrated humanities, literature, history, philosophy, art and music along with Latin, French, math, science, logic, rhetoric, bible, drama and P.E.,

Average class size: 13

Total enrollment: 70

Recommended grades to apply: Applications are accepted for any grade.

School hours: 8:00 a.m. - 3:30 p.m. Monday - Friday

Calendar school year: August 16 - May 19

Uniforms required: Yes

Parental involvement opportunities and requirements: Parent Teacher Fellowship

Average SAT scores: N/A

Visitation procedures: Please call office to schedule appointment.

Personal appointments for touring the facility: Please call office to schedule appointment.

Group tour dates: Call the office to make an appointment.

Open house dates: November 11, 1999, January 31, 2000 - 7:30 p.m.

Classroom visits: Please call office to schedule appointment.

Profit or non-profit: Non-profit

ADMISSIONS

Application form required: Yes

Forms required: Admissions packet

Application deadline: Applications accepted year round.

Application fee: $75

Contact: Lori Prior

Phone: (214) 357-2995

Student interview required: Yes

Parent interview required: Yes

Entrance test required: Yes, standardized test scores

Specific tests administered: No

Accept test scores from other schools: Yes, standardized test

Testing fee: No

Time of year testing is administered: N/A

Test dates offered: N/A

Out of state applicants: Follow same procedure.

Notification by phone: N/A

Notification by mail: Yes, letter of acceptance sent.

FINANCIAL

Preschool tuition: N/A
Elementary tuition: N/A
Secondary tuition: $6100 (99-2000 year)
Other tuition: Book and supply fees
Cash discounts: N/A
Personal check: Yes
Automatic bank draw: N/A
Credit cards: N/A
Monthly: N/A
Per semester: N/A
Annually: Yes, in two installments.
Financial assistance offered: Scholarships available.
Cancellation insurance: No
Sibling discount: No
Application acceptance deposit required: N/A

SERVICES

Before school care offered: No
After school care offered: No
Transportation provided: No
Lunch/snack program: Hot lunch available three times per week.

ST. THERESE ACADEMY

2700 Finley Road
Irving, TX 75062
Contact: Mrs. Ellen Thomas, Headmaster
(972) 252-3000
(972) 570 - 1986 FAX

Office Hours: 8:00 a.m. - 4:00 p.m.
E-MAIL: N/A
Web Site: N/A
MAPSCO: 31A-C

PHILOSOPHY OF SCHOOL

The emphasis of St. Therese Academy is on the unfolding of 2000 years of Western Christian civilization rooted in the Catholic tradition.

CREDENTIALS

Accreditations: (see glossary) NAPCIS pending

Awards and special recognition: (see glossary) First Graduating Class (1999) awarded $100,000* in merit based college scholarships; (*approximation)

Qualification of administrator: Degree in education with Texas State Certification, extensive teaching and school management experience

Qualification of faculty: Dedicated Christians who have college degrees

Other: Member TAPPS (Texas Association of Private and Parochial Schools); approved candidate for accreditation through NAPCIS (National Association of Private Catholic Independent Schools), 2640 Third Ave., Sacramento, CA 95818.

GENERAL

Alternative: No
College preparatory: Yes
Montessori: No
Nondenominational: No
Church affiliated: No
Denomination: Christian
Jewish: N/A
Other denominations: We teach in the Catholic tradition; however, other denominations are accepted.
Student type: Co-ed
Grade category (for details see specific grades offered below): Preschool - 12th
Infants: N/A
Preschool: Half and Full Day
Kindergarten: Half and Full Day

Primary / Transition: No
Elementary: Yes
Secondary or Middle School: Yes
Specific grades offered: Pre-primary - 12th grade
Student teacher ratio average: 15:1
Classes offered per grade: Generally one, sometimes two
Average class size: 15
Total enrollment: 160
Recommended grades to apply: K, 1st, 3rd, 6th, 7th, 9th
School hours: 8:00 a.m. - 3:30 p.m.
Calendar school year: Labor Day - Memorial Day
Uniforms required: Yes
Parental involvement opportunities and requirements: Yes
Average SAT scores: 1275
Visitation procedures: Call for appointment for tour/interview.
Personal appointments for touring the facility: Yes
Group tour dates: N/A
Open house dates: Every February; call for details.
Classroom visits: Yes, by appointment
Profit or non-profit: Non-profit 501 (c) 3 corp

ADMISSIONS

Application form required: Yes
Forms required: Application, Prospective Parent Questionnaire, immunization, emergency release, transcript
Application deadline: August 15
Application fee: $200
Contact: Mrs. Ellen Thomas or Mrs. Erika Choffel
Phone: (214) 252-3000
Student interview required: Yes
Parent interview required: Yes
Entrance test required: Yes
Specific tests administered: N/A
Accept test scores from other schools: Yes, standardized tests
Testing fee: $50
Time of year testing is administered: Call for appointment.
Test dates offered: By appointment
Out of state applicants: Yes
Notification by phone: N/A
Notification by mail: Yes
Other: Interviews required for students in grades 5-12.

FINANCIAL

Preschool tuition: 1/2 day $2750/year; additional 1/2 day $1000/year

Elementary tuition: 1st & 2nd child PP-8 $2750; 3rd $1700; 4th $1500; 5th+ free

Secondary tuition: Grades 9-12, $3200, $75 science lab fee, no multiple child discounts in high school

Other tuition: N/A

Cash discounts: N/A

Personal check: Yes

Automatic bank draw: N/A

Credit cards: Visa, MasterCard

Monthly: Yes, 10 payments

Per semester: N/A

Annually: Yes, 5% discount for tuition paid in full by July 1st.

Financial assistance offered: Yes (not available for first year families)

Cancellation insurance: N/A

Sibling discount: Yes, **see above

Application acceptance deposit required: $200 registration fee to confirm spot

SERVICES

Before school care offered: N/A

After school care offered: Yes, Extended Day Program 3:45 p.m. - 6 p.m. (see below)

Transportation provided: N/A

Lunch/snack program: Hot lunch M - F for extra fee. Students can bring own lunches each day.

Other: Art, Music, P.E., Spanish, library, computers, clubs grades 7-12. High school sports offered in TAPPS. Extended Day Program: Registration $20/ child, $35/week for 3+ days/week/child.

Alternative Schools

An alternative school is an educational facility that implements an individualized or alternative curriculum to meet the specific needs of its students. ASESA and SAILS are recognized accrediting organizations for these schools.

Arbor Acre Preparatory School
Autistic Treatment Center (see Ch. 4)
Bending Oaks High School
Bridgeway School
Buckingham North Christian School
Dallas Academy
Dallas Learning Center
Fairhill School and Diagnostic Assessment Center
Glen Lakes Academy
Happy Hill Farm Academy/Home
Highland Academy
Hillier School of Highland Park Presbyterian Church
Keystone Academy
Meadowview School
Notre Dame of Dallas School, The (see Curriculum Alternative)
Oak Hill Academy
Preston Hollow Presbyterian School
Rise School of Dallas, The (see Curriculum Alternative)
Shelton School and Evaluation Center
Southwest Academy
Vanguard Preparatory School
Walden Preparatory School
Winston School, The

ARBOR ACRE
PREPARATORY SCHOOL

8000 South Hampton Road   *Office Hours:* 8:00 a.m. - 4:30 p.m.
Dallas, TX 75232   *E-MAIL:* N/A
Contact: Mary Beth Cunningham   *Web Site:* N/A
(972) 224-0511   *MAPSCO:* 73D
(972) 224-0511; CALL FIRST FAX

PHILOSOPHY OF SCHOOL

To provide educational services to children with average or above-average I.Q's.
To provide a successful learning situation for language-learning-different children.

CREDENTIALS

Accreditations: (see glossary) Non Public Private Schools, SACS, TACLD, TEA
Awards and special recognition: (see glossary) N/A
Qualification of administrator: Master's degree, LLD certification, language therapist
Qualification of faculty: Teachers with college degrees and experience
Other: Curriculum is individualized using state-approved textbooks & the Scottish Rite Dyslexia Training Program's intensive phonics program and effective remedial methods & concepts.

GENERAL

Alternative: Yes
College preparatory: Yes
Montessori: No
Nondenominational: No
Church affiliated: No
Denomination: N/A
Jewish: N/A
Other denominations: N/A
Student type: Coed
Grade category (for details see specific grades offered below): Elementary
Infants: N/A
Preschool: Full Day
Kindergarten: Full Day

Primary / Transition: Yes
Elementary: Yes
Secondary or Middle School: Yes
Specific grades offered: Pre-K (4 year old) - 8th
Other: Private language therapy for dyslexic students.
Student teacher ratio average: 12:1
Classes offered per grade: 1
Average class size: 12
Total enrollment: 100
Recommended grades to apply: N/A
School hours: 8:00 a.m. - 3:10 p.m.
Calendar school year: Third week in August - May.
Uniforms required: Yes
Parental involvement opportunities and requirements: Yes
Average SAT scores: N/A
Visitation procedures: Call for appointment.
Personal appointments for touring the facility: Yes
Group tour dates: N/A
Open house dates: N/A
Classroom visits: Yes
Profit or nonprofit: Non-profit
Other: Students with average or above-average ability having dyslexia or ADD
are accepted. The structure of small classrooms/Alphabetic- Phonics method
of teaching reading & language skills have proven successful for these
children. Our students are readily accepted into both private and public high
schools.

ADMISSIONS

Application form required: Yes
Forms required: Application, health records, report card, test scores.
Application deadline: March - July
Application fee: $400
Contact: Mary B. Cunningham
Phone: (972) 224-0511
Student interview required: Yes
Parent interview required: Yes
Entrance test required: Yes
Specific tests administered: Fifth and above: Reading Comprehension, Math,
Language, Spelling to determine grade placement.
Accept test scores from other schools: Yes
Testing fee: $25.00

Time of year testing is administered: March - July, by appointment.
Test dates offered: N/A
Out of state applicants: N/A
Notification by phone: Yes, phone call approximately one week after testing.
Notification by mail: N/A

FINANCIAL

Preschool tuition: $2700
Elementary tuition: K: $2700, 1 - 8: $3500
Secondary tuition: N/A
Other tuition: Art fee, computer fee, cost of field trips.
Cash discounts: N/A
Personal check: Yes
Automatic bank draw: N/A
Credit cards: N/A
Monthly: Yes
Per semester: Yes
Annually: Yes
Financial assistance offered: Sliding scale scholarships available.
Cancellation insurance: N/A
Sibling discount: Yes
Application acceptance deposit required: Yes
Other: Previous school records and test scores.

SERVICES

Before school care offered: Yes, from 7:00 a.m.
After school care offered: Yes, 3:00 p.m. - 6:00 p.m.
Transportation provided: N/A
Lunch/snack program: Snacks given mid-morning & late afternoon. $2.50 - $3.00 per day for lunch or can bring lunch.
Other: Computer Lab: computers & printers, keyboarding taught in 4th grade, word processing taught, lab open before & after school. Library open for reference books & general reading (5800 books).

BENDING OAKS HIGH SCHOOL

11884 Greenville Avenue, Suite 120
Dallas, TX 75243
Contact: **Brandy McNamara**
(972) 669-0000
(972) 669-8149 FAX

Office Hours:
9:00 a.m. - 4:00 p.m.
E-MAIL: info@bohs.com
Web Site: www.bohs.com
MAPSCO: 16Z

PHILOSOPHY OF SCHOOL

Bending Oaks High School was founded by a group of teachers who believe many students cannot reach their potential in a large classroom setting. They designed the school for limited enrollment to ensure the availability of the teacher's assistance without sacrificing the sharing of ideas in the classroom.

CREDENTIALS

Accreditations: (see glossary) SACS
Awards and special recognition: (see glossary) N/A
Qualification of administrator: Principal - Ph.D. and extensive teaching experience in private and public schools
Qualification of faculty: Texas certification or advanced degree
Other: Recognized by Texas Education Agency, National Association of Secondary School Principals, College Board, & Texas Association of College Admissions Counselors

GENERAL

Alternative: Yes
College preparatory: Yes
Montessori: No
Nondenominational: Yes
Church affiliated: No
Denomination: N/A
Jewish: N/A
Other denominations: N/A
Student type: Co-ed
Grade category (for details see specific grades offered below): Secondary
Infants: N/A
Preschool: N/A

Kindergarten: N/A
Primary / Transition: No
Elementary: N/A
Secondary or Middle School: Yes
Specific grades offered: Grades 9 - 12
Student teacher ratio average: Approximately 6:1
Classes offered per grade: N/A
Average class size: 6
Total enrollment: 75
Recommended grades to apply: N/A
School hours: 9:00 a.m. - 3:30 p.m.
Calendar school year: August - June
Uniforms required: No
Parental involvement opportunities and requirements: Welcomed and
    encouraged
Average SAT scores: 1050
Visitation procedures: Prospective students are encouraged to visit classes
Personal appointments for touring the facility: Individual appointments offered
Group tour dates: N/A
Open house dates: N/A
Classroom visits: N/A
Profit or non-profit: Profit

ADMISSIONS

Application form required: Yes
Forms required: School records, transcripts, and health records
Application deadline: Year-round enrollment
Application fee: $75.00
Contact: Admissions office
Phone: (972) 669-0000
Student interview required: Yes
Parent interview required: Yes
Entrance test required: No
Specific tests administered: Secondary: Educational Diagnostic Testing,
    if necessary.
Accept test scores from other schools: Yes
Testing fee: N/A
Time of year testing is administered: N/A
Test dates offered: N/A
Out of state applicants: N/A
Notification by phone: N/A

Notification by mail: N/A

FINANCIAL

Preschool tuition: N/A
Elementary tuition: N/A
Secondary tuition: $ 10,000
Other tuition: N/A
Cash discounts: N/A
Personal check: Yes
Automatic bank draw: N/A
Credit cards: Yes
Monthly: Yes, budgeting program available.
Per semester: Yes
Annually: Yes
Financial assistance offered: No
Cancellation insurance: N/A
Sibling discount: N/A
Application acceptance deposit required: See Application Fee

SERVICES

Before school care offered: N/A
After school care offered: N/A
Transportation provided: N/A
Lunch/snack program: N/A
Other: Enrichment Curriculum and Enrichment Activities offered;
    computer lab and library.

BRIDGEWAY SCHOOL

7808 Clodus Fields Drive　　*Office Hours:* 8:00 a.m. - 5:00 p.m.
Dallas, TX 75251　　*E-MAIL:* info@bridgewayschool.com
Contact: **Tami Whitington or Margie English**　　*Web Site:*
(214) 991-9504 or (972) 770-0845　　www.bridgewayschool.com
(214) 991-2417 FAX　　*MAPSCO:* 16W

PHILOSOPHY OF SCHOOL

The Bridgeway School provides a therapeutic academic program for students who may be experiencing emotional/behavioral problems or learning difficulties who need a structured environment.

CREDENTIALS

Accreditations: (see glossary) Southern Association of Colleges and Schools
Awards and special recognition: (see glossary) N/A
Qualification of administrator: Principal-M.Ed. in educational administration; state-certified; alternative-education experience
Qualification of faculty: College degree (master's degree preferred; most have master's degrees); teacher certification and/or work-related experience

GENERAL

Alternative: Yes
College preparatory: No
Montessori: No
Nondenominational: N/A
Church affiliated: No
Denomination: N/A
Jewish: N/A
Other denominations: N/A
Student type: Co-ed
Grade category (for details see specific grades offered below): Secondary
Infants: N/A
Preschool: N/A
Kindergarten: N/A
Primary / Transition: N/A
Elementary: N/A
Secondary or Middle School: Yes
Specific grades offered: 7th - 12th

Student teacher ratio average: 8:1

Classes offered per grade: N/A

Average class size: 8

Total enrollment: 50

Recommended grades to apply: All

School hours: 8:30 a.m. - 2:15 p.m.

Calendar school year: Year-round

Uniforms required: No

Parental involvement opportunities and requirements: Parent-teacher reporting conferences

Average SAT scores: N/A

Visitation procedures: N/A

Personal appointments for touring the facility: Yes

Group tour dates: By appointment

Open house dates: N/A

Classroom visits: By appointment

Profit or non-profit: Profit

ADMISSIONS

Application form required: Yes

Forms required: Previous school records; immunization records; previous academic and/or psychological testing results; drug testing results

Application deadline: Year-round enrollment

Application fee: $250

Contact: Tami Whitington, Principal or Margie English, School Liaison

Phone: (972) 331-9504 or (972) 770-0845

Student interview required: Yes

Parent interview required: Yes

Entrance test required: No

Specific tests administered: Individualized and as needed; all students must have a drug test before enrolling at Bridgeway School.

Accept test scores from other schools: N/A

Testing fee: N/A

Time of year testing is administered: N/A

Test dates offered: N/A

Out of state applicants: N/A

Notification by phone: N/A

Notification by mail: N/A

Other: Students must be in a therapeutic treatment program or in counseling while attending Bridgeway School.

FINANCIAL

Preschool tuition: N/A
Elementary tuition: N/A
Secondary tuition: $6000 - $8000 per year
Other tuition: $125 book & activity fee, $35 drug test, $25 notebook/backpack fee
Cash discounts: No
Personal check: Yes
Automatic bank draw: No
Credit cards: Visa, MasterCard, Discover, American Express
Monthly: $600 - $800 per month
Per semester: $3000 - $4000 per semester
Annually: N/A
Financial assistance offered: No
Cancellation insurance: No
Sibling discount: No
Application acceptance deposit required: N/A

SERVICES

Before school care offered: No
After school care offered: No
Transportation provided: No
Lunch/snack program: Students may bring lunch or eat in cafeteria.
Other: Computers are utilized in the classrooms for instructional reinforcement of core subjects, keyboarding, word processing, and graphic arts. Research/ resources available through modem access to outside electronic sources and use of community libraries.

To enable its students to succeed, Bridgeway School seeks to:
- improve attention skills
- enhance learning skills
- modify behavior
- improve self-esteem
- increase school attendance
- control impulsive behavior
- develop interpersonal communication skills

Bridgeway School provides an alternative educational program for students with emotional problems or learning difficulties that prevent them from functioning well as a traditional academic setting.

Bridgeway School provides a transition for secondary-school students who are in out-patient therapy (individual and/or family counseling) and need a school program that emphasizes close interaction with teachers in small, structured classes with individualized instruction. When students are ready to return to their home schools, Bridgeway School's liaison assists the students and parents in contacting the home school to make the transition as comfortable and successful as possible.

Bridgeway provides an Academic Intervention School for students whom:
- have been professionally advised to seek intervention away from their current school in order to become emotionally stabilized
- have been suspended for a period of time from their school; this may be a self-referral or made by a school

Students in the Intervention Program:
- must adhere to weekly or random drug test if substance abuse is an issue
- agree to see a professional counselor or be enrolled in an out patient program

Extracurricular Activities & Enrichment Curriculum
- Theater arts program
- Cultural outgoings
- Community service projects

Bridgeway uses a therapeutic approach to help students develop coping and academic skills through structured classes, individualized behavior modification and individualized curriculum.

BUCKINGHAM NORTH CHRISTIAN SCHOOL

801 W. Buckingham
Garland, TX 75040
Contact: Veronica Marshall
(972) 495-0851
(972) 530-1315 FAX

Office Hours: 8:30 a.m. - 3:30 p.m.
E-MAIL: N/A
Web Site: N/A
MAPSCO: N/A

PHILOSOPHY OF SCHOOL

Our mission is to work with the home in providing a quality academic education based on Godly principles and integrated with a Christian view of God.

CREDENTIALS

Accreditations: (see glossary) TACLD
Awards and special recognition: (see glossary) N/A
Qualification of administrator: M.Ed., Texas Teaching Certificate
Qualification of faculty: Teaching Certificate, Minimum bachelor's degree
Other: We are a member of ACSI

GENERAL

Alternative: No
College preparatory: Yes
Montessori: No
Nondenominational: No
Church affiliated: Yes
Denomination: Assembly of God
Jewish: N/A
Other denominations: N/A
Student type: Co-ed
Grade category (for details see specific grades offered below): N/A
Infants: N/A
Preschool: N/A
Kindergarten: Half Day
Primary / Transition: Yes
Elementary: Yes
Secondary or Middle School: N/A

Specific grades offered: N/A

Student teacher ratio average: 16:1

Classes offered per grade: Regular academics (language arts, math, science, social studies, spelling, literature, Bible) plus computers, library, art, drama, Spanish, P.E.

Average class size: 15 in Kindergarten; 26 in 1st - 6th

Total enrollment: 182

Recommended grades to apply: Kindergarten

School hours: 8:20 a.m. - 3:15 p.m.

Calendar school year: August 19 - May 20

Uniforms required: No

Parental involvement opportunities and requirements: Many volunteer opportunities, Parent/Teacher Fellowship

Average SAT scores: 2.5 years above grade level

Visitation procedures: Call for appointment

Personal appointments for touring the facility: Call for appointment

Group tour dates: N/A

Open house dates: March 9, 2000

Classroom visits: By appointment

Profit or non-profit: Non-profit

ADMISSIONS

Application form required: Yes

Forms required: School form

Application deadline: N/A

Application fee: $165, Kindergarten; $215, 1st - 6th

Contact: Sherry Bacher

Phone: (972) 495-0851

Student interview required: Yes

Parent interview required: Yes

Entrance test required: Yes

Specific tests administered: Kindergarten: school-designed, 1st - 6th: school-designed

Accept test scores from other schools: No

Testing fee: None

Time of year testing is administered: By appointment

Test dates offered: N/A

Out of state applicants: Accepted

Notification by phone: Yes

Notification by mail: N/A

FINANCIAL

Preschool tuition: N/A

Elementary tuition: Kindergarten $1280, 1st - 6th $2380

Secondary tuition: N/A

Other tuition: N/A

Cash discounts: Yes, $50 if paid in full before September 1.

Personal check: Yes

Automatic bank draw: N/A

Credit cards: N/A

Monthly: Yes

Per semester: Yes

Annually: Yes

Financial assistance offered: None

Cancellation insurance: No

Sibling discount: Yes, 10% - 2nd child; 20% - 3rd child; 50% - 4th child.

Application acceptance deposit required: N/A

SERVICES

Before school care offered: N/A

After school care offered: N/A

Transportation provided: N/A

Lunch/snack program: Sack lunches. Pizza, etc. provided by volunteers.

DALLAS ACADEMY

950 Tiffany Way
Dallas, TX   75218
Contact: **Jim Richardson, Director**
(214) 324 - 1481
(214) 327 - 8537 FAX

Office Hours: 8:00 a.m. - 3:30 p.m.
E-MAIL: mail@dallas-academy.com

Web Site: www.dallas-academy.com
MAPSCO: 37H

PHILOSOPHY OF SCHOOL

Dallas Academy offers a structured multisensory program for students with diagnosed learning differences. We believe that structure is the main factor for success at the Academy. The classes provide a quiet, nurturing environment to students who in the past have had trouble with concentration and short attention spans. By incorporating a strong curriculum and a wide variety of extra-curricular activities, Dallas Academy strives to graduate students with good self-esteem and a positive direction in their lives.

CREDENTIALS

Accreditations: (see glossary) COPSES, SACS, TAAPS, TACLD
Awards and special recognition: (see glossary) N/A
Qualification of administrator: B.S. M.S. 24 hrs. Post Masters Supervisors and Administrators Certification
Qualification of faculty: 2/3 masters degrees, all special education qualified

GENERAL

Alternative: No
College preparatory: Yes
Montessori: No
Nondenominational: No
Church affiliated: No
Denomination: N/A
Jewish: N/A
Other denominations: N/A
Student type: Co-ed
Grade category (for details see specific grades offered below): Secondary
Infants: N/A
Preschool: N/A
Kindergarten: N/A
Primary / Transition: No

Elementary: N/A
Secondary or Middle School: Yes
Specific grades offered: 7th - 12th grade
Student teacher ratio average: 7:1
Classes offered per grade: N/A
Average class size: 9-12 students per class
Total enrollment: 140
Recommended grades to apply: 7th - 12th
School hours: 8:30 a.m. - 3:00 p.m.
Calendar school year: August - May
Uniforms required: Yes
Parental involvement opportunities and requirements: Organized Parent Group with many fun, volunteer opportunities; Booster Club for athletics
Average SAT scores: 900
Visitation procedures: Please call the office to set up an appointment and bring updated testing when you visit.
Personal appointments for touring the facility: We would love for you and your child to visit our campus. Please contact Mr. Jim Richardson for an appointment.
Group tour dates: N/A
Open house dates: N/A
Classroom visits: Yes
Profit or non-profit: Non-profit

ADMISSIONS

Application form required: Yes
Forms required: Please contact school.
Application deadline: Rolling Admissions
Application fee: Registration Fee $500.00 (non refundable)
Contact: Jim Richardson
Phone: (214) 324-1481
Student interview required: Yes
Parent interview required: Yes
Entrance test required: Yes
Specific tests administered: Secondary: Diagnostic Testing by a professional within the last three years
Accept test scores from other schools: Yes, if school is accredited
Testing fee: N/A
Time of year testing is administered: N/A
Test dates offered: N/A
Out of state applicants: Yes

Notification by phone: N/A
Notification by mail: N/A

FINANCIAL

Preschool tuition: N/A
Elementary tuition: N/A
Secondary tuition: $8200.00
Other tuition: N/A
Cash discounts: Yes
Personal check: Yes
Automatic bank draw: Yes
Credit cards: Mastercard, Visa
Monthly: Yes
Per semester: Yes
Annually: Yes
Financial assistance offered: Yes, through the admissions process
Cancellation insurance: N/A
Sibling discount: Yes, $500.00.
Application acceptance deposit required: Yes

SERVICES

Before school care offered: N/A
After school care offered: N/A
Transportation provided: N/A
Lunch/snack program: Yes, school lunch is available by catering service. Order monthly.
Other: Van transportation to North Dallas, Plano, and Richardson

DALLAS LEARNING CENTER

1021 Newberry Drive, Suite 1   *Office Hours:* 9:00 a.m. - 3:00 p.m.
Richardson, TX 75080   *E-MAIL:* N/A
Contact: **Kathleen Herrin-Kinard, Director**   *Web Site:* N/A
(972) 231-3723   *MAPSCO:* 6Z
(972) 231-8810 FAX (Call before faxing)

PHILOSOPHY OF SCHOOL

The Dallas Learning Center is dedicated to providing students with positive learning experiences that emphasize the needs of the individual. The Dallas Learning Center achieves this by offering a structured, yet comfortable, environment that promotes academic and personal growth.

CREDENTIALS

Accreditations: (see glossary) NCACS, Alternative
Awards and special recognition: (see glossary) N/A
Qualification of administrator: Master's degree and 15 years of teaching experience
Qualification of faculty: College degrees, certification, and experience in working with learning-differenced students and accelerated students.

GENERAL

Alternative: Yes
College preparatory: Yes
Montessori: No
Nondenominational: Yes
Church affiliated: No
Denomination: N/A
Jewish: N/A
Other denominations: N/A
Student type: Co-ed
Grade category (for details see specific grades offered below): Middle School and Secondary
Infants: N/A
Preschool: N/A
Kindergarten: N/A

266

Primary / Transition: No
Elementary: N/A
Secondary or Middle School: Yes
Specific grades offered: 6th - 12th
Student teacher ratio average: 6:1
Classes offered per grade: Unlimited, based on students progress.
Average class size: 1:1 and 6:1
Total enrollment: 40
Recommended grades to apply: 6th - 12th grade
School hours: 9:00 a.m. - 3:00 p.m.
Calendar school year: August - May (Summer School - June and July)
Uniforms required: No
Parental involvement opportunities and requirements: Phone contact once per week.
Average SAT scores: Available upon request.
Visitation procedures: Interview followed by one or two visit days.
Personal appointments for touring the facility: Call for appointment.
Group tour dates: N/A
Open house dates: September and February
Classroom visits: Call for appointment
Profit or non-profit: Profit

ADMISSIONS

Application form required: Application form required at interview.
Forms required: Transcript from previous school.
Application deadline: Open enrollment
Application fee: None
Contact: Kathleen Herrin-Kinard
Phone: (214) 231-3723
Student interview required: Yes
Parent interview required: Yes
Entrance test required: No
Specific tests administered: N/A
Accept test scores from other schools: N/A
Testing fee: N/A
Time of year testing is administered: N/A
Test dates offered: N/A
Out of state applicants: Open enrollment
Notification by phone: Yes, within one day of visit
Notification by mail: No

FINANCIAL

Preschool tuition: N/A
Elementary tuition: N/A
Secondary tuition: $5000 per semester
Other tuition: Middle school tuition: $4500 per semester
Cash discounts: No
Personal check: Yes
Automatic bank draw: No
Credit cards: No
Monthly: Yes, interest-free financing
Per semester: Yes
Annually: No
Financial assistance offered: One scholarship per year
Cancellation insurance: No
Sibling discount: No
Application acceptance deposit required: Deposit required to secure placement.

SERVICES

Before school care offered: N/A
After school care offered: N/A
Transportation provided: N/A
Lunch/snack program: Students bring a sack lunch. Vending machines available.
Other: Individualized, accelerated programs to allow students to graduate from high school early and to make up credit deficiencies. Tutorials and home school programs also available.

FAIRHILL SCHOOL AND DIAGNOSTIC ASSESSMENT CENTER

16150 Preston Road
Dallas, TX 75248
Contact: **Jane Sego, Executive Director**
(972) 233-1026
(972) 233-8205 FAX

Office Hours: 8:00 a.m. - 4:30 p.m.
E-MAIL: fairhill@airmail.net
Web Site:
http://web2.airmail.net/fairhill
MAPSCO: 5T

PHILOSOPHY OF SCHOOL

Fairhill is a private, nonprofit college preparatory school serving students in grades one through twelve. Fairhill's primary purpose is to provide a superior education for students of average and above intelligence who have been diagnosed with a learning difference such as Dyslexia, Dysgraphia, Dyscalculia, or Attention Deficit Disorder. While they possess the intellectual potential to succeed academically, often at superior levels, because of a learning difference, these students have experienced great frustration in traditional school environments. The result is that their academic performance does not reflect their potential. Fairhill's staff works to develop strategies to help individual students "learn to learn" through a multi-sensory approach to teaching, a small student/teacher ratio, and a warm, supportive atmosphere. At Fairhill, each student is recognized as an individual with distinct strengths and weaknesses. Students are taught to maximize their strengths and to employ tools and processes that minimize their weaknesses. A Fairhill education is designed for the whole child, to develop a firm foundation in problem-solving and critical thinking skills that will enhance emotional, social, and academic development.

CREDENTIALS

Accreditations: (see glossary) SACS
Awards and special recognition: (see glossary) N/A
Qualification of administrator: M.Ed.
Qualification of faculty: Degreed and certified

GENERAL

Alternative: Yes
College preparatory: Yes

Montessori: No
Nondenominational: Yes
Church affiliated: No
Denomination: N/A
Jewish: N/A
Other denominations: N/A
Student type: Co-ed
Grade category (for details see specific grades offered below): 1st - 12th
Infants: N/A
Preschool: N/A
Kindergarten: N/A
Primary / Transition: No
Elementary: Yes
Secondary or Middle School: Yes
Specific grades offered: 1st - 12th
Student teacher ratio average: 7:1
Classes offered per grade: 1, grades 1-3; 2, grades 4-12
Average class size: 10
Total enrollment: 225
Recommended grades to apply: N/A
School hours: 8:15 a.m. - 3:15 p.m. MTTF, 8:15 a.m. - 2:15 p.m. W
Calendar school year: Traditional school calendar
Uniforms required: Yes
Parental involvement opportunities and requirements: Yes; Parent Council, Annual Fund, Spring Gala
Average SAT scores: N/A
Visitation procedures: 1 day student visit
Personal appointments for touring the facility: Yes
Group tour dates: N/A
Open house dates: N/A
Classroom visits: N/A
Profit or non-profit: Non-profit

ADMISSIONS

Application form required: Yes
Forms required: N/A
Application deadline: N/A
Application fee: $50.00
Contact: Carla Stanford, Gr. 1-7; Kay Wendell, Gr. 8-12
Phone: (972) 233-1026
Student interview required: Yes

Parent interview required: Yes
Entrance test required: No
Specific tests administered: N/A
Accept test scores from other schools: Yes
Testing fee: N/A
Time of year testing is administered: N/A
Test dates offered: N/A
Out of state applicants: Yes
Notification by phone: Yes
Notification by mail: Yes
Other: Diagnostic test required for admission.

FINANCIAL

Preschool tuition: N/A
Elementary tuition: $9200 - $9300
Secondary tuition: $9500
Other tuition: N/A
Cash discounts: N/A
Personal check: Yes
Automatic bank draw: N/A
Credit cards: N/A
Monthly: N/A
Per semester: N/A
Annually: Yes
Financial assistance offered: Yes
Cancellation insurance: N/A
Sibling discount: N/A
Application acceptance deposit required: Yes, $500

SERVICES

Before school care offered: N/A
After school care offered: N/A
Transportation provided: N/A
Lunch/snack program: Yes
Other: Diagnostic assessment available to applicant and the general public.

GLEN LAKES ACADEMY

6000 Custer Road, Building 7
Plano, TX   75023
Contact: **Cara Hill**
(972) 517-7498
(972) 517-0133 FAX

Office Hours:
8:00 a.m. - 3:45 p.m.
E-MAIL: N/A
Web Site: www.glenlakesacademy.com
MAPSCO: 658E

PHILOSOPHY OF SCHOOL

Glen Lakes Academy seeks to combine therapeutic practice with education to create a new model of training for children and youth. The school is committed to helping individuals who exhibit symptoms of ADD/ADHD. In addition to a challenging curriculum, Glen Lakes Academy offers a low student-teacher ratio, multisensory learning, parent support groups, outside ADD/ADHD speakers, and continuous monitoring of progress. We also offer a fine arts program (art/drama), computer classes, study skills and weekly sessions addressing concerns, such as anger management, impulse control, listening skills, social behavior, following directions, making and keeping friends, and coping with frustration.

CREDENTIALS

Accreditations: (see glossary) SACS pending
Awards and special recognition: (see glossary) N/A
Qualification of administrator: N/A
Qualification of faculty: College degree; suitable experience

GENERAL

Alternative: Yes
College preparatory: No
Montessori: No
Nondenominational: Yes
Church affiliated: No
Denomination: N/A
Jewish: N/A
Other denominations: N/A
Student type: Co-ed
Grade category (for details see specific grades offered below): Elementary
Infants: N/A
Preschool: N/A
Kindergarten: N/A

Primary / Transition: No
Elementary: Yes
Secondary or Middle School: N/A
Specific grades offered: 2nd - 9th for '99-'00 school year
Student teacher ratio average: 10:1
Classes offered per grade: 1 section per grade, except 6th grade which has two
Average class size: 13 maximum. However, most classes significantly below.
Total enrollment: 85
Recommended grades to apply: N/A
School hours: 8:30 a.m. - 3:30 p.m.
Calendar school year: Late August - Early June
Uniforms required: Yes
Parental involvement opportunities and requirements: Yes
Average SAT scores: N/A
Visitation procedures: Children to visit classroom for 3-5 days as an active participant prior to application being accepted for school term.
Personal appointments for touring the facility: Offered
Group tour dates: Offered
Open house dates: N/A
Classroom visits: N/A
Profit or non-profit: Profit

ADMISSIONS

Application form required: Yes
Forms required: Previous transcripts, copies of testing for student file.
Application deadline: Enrollment process begins February 1st
Application fee: $50
Contact: Cara R. Hill
Phone: (972) 517-7498 ext 111
Student interview required: Yes
Parent interview required: Yes
Entrance test required: Yes
Specific tests administered: 1st - 4th Grade: ADD/ADHD, psychological evaluation, Fifth and above: ADD/ADHD, psychological evaluation.
Accept test scores from other schools: Yes
Testing fee: N/A
Time of year testing is administered: N/A
Test dates offered: N/A
Out of state applicants: N/A
Notification by phone: Yes
Notification by mail: Yes, after interview.

FINANCIAL

Preschool tuition: N/A
Elementary tuition: $9,400 plus $600 supply fee
Secondary tuition: $9,400 plus $2,000 supply fee
Other tuition: N/A
Cash discounts: N/A
Personal check: Yes
Automatic bank draw: N/A
Credit cards: MasterCard, Visa
Monthly: Yes, $725/month, August - May.
Per semester: Yes
Annually: Yes
Financial assistance offered: Yes, limited.
Cancellation insurance: N/A
Sibling discount: Yes, 10% off tuition.
Application acceptance deposit required: $3,000

SERVICES

Before school care offered: N/A
After school care offered: N/A
Transportation provided: N/A
Lunch/snack program: Hot lunch program available for additional fee.
Other: Computer, enrichment curriculum and extracurricular activities offered.

HAPPY HILL FARM ACADEMY/HOME

HC51 - Box 56
Granbury, TX 76048
Contact: **Todd L. Shipman, President/Chief Financial Officer**
(254) 897-4822
(254) 897-7650 FAX

Office Hours: 8:30 a.m. - 5:00 p.m.
E-MAIL: N/A
Web Site: www.weblifepro.com/happyhill
MAPSCO: N/A

PHILOSOPHY OF SCHOOL

Happy Hill Farm Academy/Home is a year-round, residential treatment center, childcare facility, offering a unique boarding school environment for children & adolescents. Though interdenominational in approach, there are strong moral, ethical and spiritual underpinnings to the entire academic & vocational programs.

CREDENTIALS

Accreditations: (see glossary) SACS, TAAPS
Awards and special recognition: (see glossary) N/A
Qualification of administrator: Bachelor's degree, master's degree, & administrative certification
Qualification of faculty: Teaching degree, Texas certification
Other: Located 40 miles south of Ft. Worth on State Highway 144

GENERAL

Alternative: Yes
College preparatory: Yes
Montessori: No
Nondenominational: No
Church affiliated: No
Denomination: N/A
Jewish: N/A
Other denominations: N/A
Student type: Co-ed
Grade category (for details see specific grades offered below): 1st - 12th
Infants: N/A
Preschool: N/A
Kindergarten: Full Day
Primary / Transition: No

Elementary: N/A
Secondary or Middle School: Yes
Specific grades offered: K - grade 12
Student teacher ratio average: 6:1
Classes offered per grade: N/A
Average class size: 6 - 8
Total enrollment: 110
Recommended grades to apply: N/A
School hours: 8:30 a.m. - 3:05 p.m.
Calendar school year: Year-round, residential facility
Uniforms required: Yes
Parental involvement opportunities and requirements: Yes
Average SAT scores: 1000
Visitation procedures: N/A
Personal appointments for touring the facility: Yes
Group tour dates: N/A
Open house dates: N/A
Classroom visits: N/A
Profit or non-profit: Non-profit
Other: N/A

ADMISSIONS

Application form required: Yes
Forms required: Family history, admissions application
Application deadline: Continual admissions
Application fee: N/A
Contact: Office, social worker
Phone: Metro (817) 572-9736
Student interview required: Yes
Parent interview required: Yes
Entrance test required: No
Specific tests administered: N/A
Accept test scores from other schools: No
Testing fee: N/A
Time of year testing is administered: N/A
Test dates offered: N/A
Out of state applicants: N/A
Notification by phone: Yes
Notification by mail: Yes

FINANCIAL

Preschool tuition: N/A
Elementary tuition: Verify with school office
Secondary tuition: Verify with school office
Other tuition: All fees included
Cash discounts: N/A
Personal check: N/A
Automatic bank draw: N/A
Credit cards: N/A
Monthly: N/A
Per semester: N/A
Annually: N/A
Financial assistance offered: Scholarships available
Cancellation insurance: N/A
Sibling discount: N/A
Application acceptance deposit required: N/A
Other: N/A

SERVICES

Before school care offered: Yes, 24-hour, year-round boarding school program.
After school care offered: Yes, 24-hour residential facility.
Transportation provided: Yes
Lunch/snack program: Lunch and snacks

HIGHLAND ACADEMY

1231 W. Beltline Road
Richardson, TX 75080
Contact: **Lynda Handlogten**
(972) 238-7567
(972) 238-7647 FAX

Office Hours: 8:00 a.m. - 3:00 p.m.
E-MAIL: highland@cyberramp.net
Web Site: N/A
MAPSCO: 12D

PHILOSOPHY OF SCHOOL

To provide a complete, customized, elementary education for intelligent children with language-learning difficulties, A.D.D., and giftedness.

CREDENTIALS

Accreditations: (see glossary) ASESA

Awards and special recognition: (see glossary) N/A

Qualification of administrator: Ph.D. in special education, certified educational diagnostician, America's Phonics certification, academic language-therapy certification

Qualification of faculty: Teacher certifications in elementary and special education, undergraduate and graduate degrees in education

GENERAL

Alternative: Yes
College preparatory: No
Montessori: No
Nondenominational: No
Church affiliated: No
Denomination: N/A
Jewish: N/A
Other denominations: N/A
Student type: Co-ed
Grade category (for details see specific grades offered below) : Elementary
Infants: N/A
Preschool: N/A
Kindergarten: Full Day
Primary / Transition: No
Elementary: Yes
Secondary or Middle School: N/A
Specific grades offered: K - Grade 8

Student teacher ratio average: 8:1
Classes offered per grade: N/A
Average class size: 8
Total enrollment: 60
Recommended grades to apply: N/A
School hours: 8:30 a.m. - 2:30 p.m.
Calendar school year: Late August - May 31
Uniforms required: Yes
Parental involvement opportunities and requirements: Hot lunch, field trips, class parties, reading to students, specialized presentations and workshops
Average SAT scores: N/A
Visitation procedures: N/A
Personal appointments for touring the facility: Offered
Group tour dates: Group appointments offered
Open house dates: N/A
Classroom visits: N/A
Profit or non-profit: Inquire with school

ADMISSIONS

Application form required: Yes
Forms required:
Application deadline: N/A
Application fee: Included in tuition
Contact: Dr. Lynda K. Handlogten, Director
Phone: (214) 238-7567
Student interview required: No
Parent interview required: Yes
Entrance test required: No
Specific tests administered: N/A
Accept test scores from other schools: Yes
Testing fee: N/A
Time of year testing is administered: N/A
Test dates offered: N/A
Out of state applicants: N/A
Notification by phone: Yes
Notification by mail: N/A

FINANCIAL

Preschool tuition: N/A
Elementary tuition: $8500 - $9100
Secondary tuition: N/A

Other tuition: N/A
Cash discounts: Yes
Personal check: Yes
Automatic bank draw: N/A
Credit cards: N/A
Monthly: Yes
Per semester: Yes
Annually: Yes
Financial assistance offered: Limited
Cancellation insurance: N/A
Sibling discount: N/A
Application acceptance deposit required: N/A

SERVICES

Before school care offered: N/A

After school care offered: Yes, after school tutorials as needed

Transportation provided: N/A

Lunch/snack program: Snack for kindergarten & first grade, hot lunch 2-3 times per month

Other: Computers: Windows 98, all networked, Internet in all classrooms, annual technology update; Library: more then 1,000 literature/reference volumes.

HILLIER SCHOOL OF HIGHLAND PARK PRESBYTERIAN CHURCH

3821 University Blvd.
Dallas, TX 75205
Contact: Larry Evans, Principal
(214) 559-5363
(214) 559-5377 FAX

Office Hours: 8:00 a.m. - 4:00 p.m.
E-MAIL: Evans@hppc.org
Web Site: N/A
MAPSCO: P35-F

PHILOSOPHY OF SCHOOL

Hillier School seeks to serve children in grades one through eighth with learning disabilities in a loving, Christian school environment. We have been faithfully fulfilling this mission for the last 30 years.

CREDENTIALS

Accreditations: (see glossary) TAAPS, TANS
Awards and special recognition: (see glossary) N/A
Qualification of administrator: B.S. - Certified Academic Language Therapist
Qualification of faculty: Degreed teachers

GENERAL

Alternative: Yes
College preparatory: No
Montessori: No
Nondenominational: No
Church affiliated: Yes
Denomination: Presbyterian
Jewish: N/A
Other denominations: We accept students of all faiths on an equal basis.
Student type: Co-ed
Grade category (for details see specific grades offered below): Elementary
Infants: N/A
Preschool: N/A
Kindergarten: N/A
Primary / Transition: No

Elementary: Yes

Secondary or Middle School: Yes

Specific grades offered: 1st - 8th

Other: Hillier offers children with learning disabilities a positive, nurturing, environment, an appropriate, accredited academic curriculum and the school-wide structure necessary to ensure a successful scholastic experience. Scottish Rite Hospital's highly acclaimed Language Therapy Program is included in our basic tuition for children with dyslexia and/or related disorders.

Student teacher ratio average: 8:1

Classes offered per grade: N/A

Average class size: 8

Total enrollment: 60 - 65

Recommended grades to apply: All grades accepted

School hours: 8:30 a.m. - 3:00 p.m.

Calendar school year: August 16, 1999 - May 25, 2000

Uniforms required: Yes

Parental involvement opportunities and requirements: Parents' Club offers many opportunities for families to become involved with the school. Individual volunteers help in other ways, too.

Average SAT scores: N/A

Visitation procedures: Arrange visitation through Larry Evans, principal.

Personal appointments for touring the facility: Please call for individual appointment with Larry Evans, principal.

Group tour dates: N/A

Open house dates: September 16, 1999, 7:00 p.m. - 8:30 p.m. March 2, 2000, 7:00 p.m. - 8:30 p.m.

Classroom visits: Classroom visits can be arranged at anytime through Larry Evans, principal.

Profit or non-profit: Non-profit

ADMISSIONS

Application form required: Yes

Forms required: Hillier School will provide application form upon request.

Application deadline: Rolling admissions - accept at any time

Application fee: $300

Contact: Cindy Clower, Secretary

Phone: (214) 559-5363

Student interview required: Yes

Parent interview required: Yes

Entrance test required: No

Specific tests administered: N/A

Accept test scores from other schools: Yes, we require an outside professional diagnosis of learning disability based on an appropriate psycho-educational battery of tests to begin the enrollment procedure.

Testing fee: N/A

Time of year testing is administered: N/A

Test dates offered: N/A

Out of state applicants: Yes

Notification by phone: Yes

Notification by mail: N/A

FINANCIAL

Preschool tuition: N/A

Elementary tuition: $7005 a year

Secondary tuition: $7005 a year

Other tuition: N/A

Cash discounts: N/A

Personal check: Yes

Automatic bank draw: Yes

Credit cards: N/A

Monthly: Yes

Per semester: Yes

Annually: Yes

Financial assistance offered: Scholarships available on a "need basis" for students diagnosed with dyslexia who need the Language Therapy Program.

Cancellation insurance: N/A

Sibling discount: Yes, only one registration fee charged per family.

Application acceptance deposit required: N/A

SERVICES

Before school care offered: Yes, on individual basis through principal

After school care offered: Yes, 3:00 p.m. - 5:45 p.m. through church program

Transportation provided: N/A

Lunch/snack program: Children bring their own lunches daily. Milk is provided. Every other Friday the Parents' Club serves a hot lunch.

KEYSTONE ACADEMY

6506 Frankford Rd.
Dallas, TX 75252
Contact: **Helen Werner, Director and Founder**
(972) 250-4455
(972) 250-4960 FAX

Office Hours: 8:00 a.m. - 4:30 p.m.
E-MAIL: kacademy@juno.com
Web Site: http://gtesupersite.com/keystone
MAPSCO: 659W

PHILOSOPHY OF SCHOOL

Keystone Academy, a private school, is a high quality unique educator with a fresh approach, unparalleled in the public, private, secular or Christian sectors. Its uniqueness lies in cultivating the "whole" learning challenged child cognitively, physically, emotionally, socially, and spiritually. Keystone's goal for each child, as he is created in the image of God, is to be transformed by God's grace for His glory. Parents, students and teachers work as a cooperative team to tailor an individualized program so each person progresses at their own rate and develops a sense of self worth that is securely based on biblical principles. The child grows into the person God has designed for His purposes in a caring and firm environment that provides multisensory, integrated experiences. Keystone's distinctive learning approach that accepts and teaches to children's differences and equips them individually in all spheres of development is a most unique opportunity in education today.

CREDENTIALS

Accreditations: (see glossary) ACSI, ACST, ASESA, SACS, TANS
Awards and special recognition: (see glossary) N/A
Qualification of administrator: 18 years administration, certified with MA equivalent.
Qualification of faculty: All degreed teachers

GENERAL

Alternative: Yes
College preparatory: No
Montessori: No
Nondenominational: Yes
Church affiliated: No
Denomination: N/A
Jewish: N/A
Other denominations: N/A
Student type: Co-ed

Grade category (for details see specific grades offered below): Elementary

Infants: N/A

Preschool: N/A

Kindergarten: Full Day

Primary / Transition: No

Elementary: Yes

Secondary or Middle School: Yes

Specific grades offered: Kindergarten - 8th

Student teacher ratio average: 7:1

Classes offered per grade: N/A

Average class size: 6

Total enrollment: 45

Recommended grades to apply: K - 8

School hours: 8:30 a.m. - 3:00 p.m.

Calendar school year: August 23, 1999 - May 25, 2000

Uniforms required: Yes

Parental involvement opportunities and requirements: Help with class needs, help in lunch program, assistance with field trips and assist in library.

Average SAT scores: N/A

Visitation procedures: Call office for appointment to visit class.

Personal appointments for touring the facility: Call anytime to tour building.

Group tour dates: Open

Open house dates: September - 2nd week

Classroom visits: Appointments can be made with the office.

Profit or non-profit: Non-profit

ADMISSIONS

Application form required: Yes

Forms required: Call the office for the information packet to be mailed.

Application deadline: Open

Application fee: $500.00 admission fee

Contact: Helen Werner

Phone: (972) 250-4455

Student interview required: Yes

Parent interview required: Yes

Entrance test required: Yes

Specific tests administered: Kindergarten: Brigance Comprehensive Test for all levels, Psychological Test WISC; 1st - 4th Grade: Brigance Test for all levels, Psychological Test WISC; Fifth and above: Brigance Test for all levels, Psychological Test WISC

Accept test scores from other schools: Yes

Testing fee: None

Time of year testing is administered: August and upon entrance through the year

Test dates offered: Dates open as needed 1st week of August

Out of state applicants: N/A

Notification by phone: Yes, contact parent for an interview

Notification by mail: Yes

FINANCIAL

Preschool tuition: N/A

Elementary tuition: K- $7,500 for 10 months, 1 - 6 $8900 for 10 months; 7-8 $9,100 for 10 months; or a 12 month option is available

Secondary tuition: N/A

Other tuition: After school care is $45 a week.

Cash discounts: N/A

Personal check: Yes

Automatic bank draw: N/A

Credit cards: N/A

Monthly: Yes

Per semester: N/A

Annually: Yes, as some desire

Financial assistance offered: Yes, to needy families

Cancellation insurance: N/A

Sibling discount: Yes, depends on needs

Application acceptance deposit required: $500

SERVICES

Before school care offered: Yes, 8:00 a.m. - 8:30 a.m.

After school care offered: Yes, 3:00 p.m. - 6:00 p.m.

Transportation provided: N/A

Lunch/snack program: Only on Friday a hot meal is served.

Other: Tutoring, Monthly Parent Seminars

MEADOWVIEW SCHOOL

2419 Franklin
Mesquite, TX 75150
Contact: **Beverly Presley, Director**
(972) 289-1831
(972) 289-8730 FAX

Office Hours: 8:00 a.m. - 4:00 p.m.
E-MAIL: mvschool@flash.net

Web Site: www.flash.net/~mvschool
MAPSCO: 49A-B

PHILOSOPHY OF SCHOOL

Meadowview School provides a quality educational foundation for intelligent children who learn differently through specialized instruction, programs, and services in a nurturing and positive learning environment. Meadowview School strives to build a better future for children with learning differences by breaking the cycle of frustration and failure.

CREDENTIALS

Accreditations: (see glossary) ASESA, COPSES

Awards and special recognition: (see glossary) N/A

Qualification of administrator: Master's degree in education with certifications in learning and language disabilities

Qualification of faculty: Some are certified in learning disabilities with many years of teaching experience. Others are certified teachers with special training.

GENERAL

Alternative: Yes
College preparatory: No
Montessori: No
Nondenominational: Yes
Church affiliated: No
Denomination: N/A
Jewish: N/A
Other denominations: N/A
Student type: Co-ed
Grade category (for details see specific grades offered below): Elementary
Infants: N/A
Preschool: N/A
Kindergarten: N/A
Primary / Transition: No

Elementary: Yes

Secondary or Middle School: Yes

Specific grades offered: Grades 1 - 8

Student teacher ratio average: 10:1

Classes offered per grade: Full range of academic subjects are taught in each.

Average class size: 10

Total enrollment: 75+

Recommended grades to apply: N/A

School hours: 8:00 a.m. - 3:00 p.m.

Calendar school year: August - May

Uniforms required: Yes

Parental involvement opportunities and requirements: Meadowview School has a very strong and active parent/teacher organization. Parents are encouraged to participate in school events and fund raising projects.

Average SAT scores: N/A

Visitation procedures: A prospective parent will be given a personal tour of the school by the director of the school. Tours are scheduled by appointment.

Personal appointments for touring the facility: Tours are available by appointment with the school director.

Group tour dates: N/A

Open house dates: N/A

Classroom visits: Special arrangements are to be made with the school director.

Profit or non-profit: Non-profit

ADMISSIONS

Application form required: Yes

Forms required: N/A

Application deadline: Apply March 1 for the next year.

Application fee: A non-refundable $50 application fee is required.

Contact: Beverly Presley, Director of Meadowview School

Phone: (972) 289-1831

Student interview required: No

Parent interview required: Yes

Entrance test required: Yes

Specific tests administered: 1st - 4th Grade: Diagnostic evaluations , Fifth and above: Diagnostic evaluations.

Accept test scores from other schools: Yes, current diagnostic evaluations which include intelligence and academic assessments are required for all applicants. Testing will be accepted from public schools or private agencies if testing is complete.

Testing fee: $450 for complete evaluation

Time of year testing is administered: Anytime
Test dates offered: N/A
Out of state applicants: N/A
Notification by phone: Yes
Notification by mail: N/A
Other: Varies

FINANCIAL

Preschool tuition: N/A
Elementary tuition: $7300
Secondary tuition: N/A
Other tuition: N/A
Cash discounts: Yes, discount only for early payment.
Personal check: Yes
Automatic bank draw: Yes
Credit cards: Mastercard or Visa
Monthly: Yes, 10 payments of $730
Per semester: N/A
Annually: Yes, $400 discount if paid in full by July 1, 1999.
Financial assistance offered: Partial scholarships available on a limited basis. Scholarships are based on financial need.
Cancellation insurance: N/A
Sibling discount: N/A
Application acceptance deposit required: A non-refundable $150 enrollment fee is required

SERVICES

Before school care offered: N/A
After school care offered: N/A
Transportation provided: N/A
Lunch/snack program: A hot lunch program is provided by Food for Thought. Parents order for the month in advance.
Other: Computer lab, library, enrichment classes, and extracurricular activities offered

OAK HILL ACADEMY

6464 E. Lovers Lane
Dallas, TX 75214
Contact: **Pam Quarterman, Director**
(214) 368-0664
(214) 346-9866 FAX

Office Hours: 8:00 a.m. - 4:00 p.m.
E-MAIL: oakhillphq@aol.com
Web Site: N/A
MAPSCO: 36D

PHILOSOPHY OF SCHOOL

Oak Hill Academy is dedicated to providing success-oriented, individualized programming with focus on the development of the WHOLE child. Multisensory/ interactive strategies are implemented in a structured environment. Each child is actively involved in the learning process and competition is de-emphasized.

CREDENTIALS

Accreditations: (see glossary) ASESA, COPSES

Awards and special recognition: (see glossary) Carole Hill, Director Emeritus, winner of the Scott Murray Excellence in Education Award

Qualification of administrator: 20 years experience, Master's of Medical Science degree, Emory University; certified and licensed speech and language pathologist; Executive Board Member of the Dallas Branch of the International Dyslexia Assoc.

Qualification of faculty: Degreed/advanced degreed, creative, experienced, and dedicated faculty; many hold certification in academic language therapy, speech/language pathology, Montessori training, and various specific pedagogical methodologies.

GENERAL

Alternative: Yes
College preparatory: No
Montessori: No
Nondenominational: Yes
Church affiliated: No
Denomination: N/A
Jewish: N/A
Other denominations: N/A
Student type: Co-ed
Grade category (for details see specific grades offered below): Preschool - 12th
Infants: N/A

Preschool: Half Day
Kindergarten: Full Day
Primary / Transition: Yes
Elementary: Yes
Secondary or Middle School: N/A
Specific grades offered: Preschool - 8th
Other: Full Day Preschool also available
Student teacher ratio average: 8:1
Classes offered per grade: N/A
Average class size: Maximum of 12
Total enrollment: 115
Recommended grades to apply: N/A
School hours: 8:30 a.m. - 3:15 p.m. (1:45 Fridays)
Calendar school year: Mid-August through May/Summer program available
Uniforms required: Yes
Parental involvement opportunities and requirements: No requirements - parents are encouraged to volunteer by reading in the library, serving lunch, chaperoning field trips, etc. Parent education sessions are scheduled through out the year.
Average SAT scores: N/A
Visitation procedures: Please call the school office to arrange a personal tour and visit with the administrator.
Personal appointments for touring the facility: Appointments of approximately an hour in length are a welcome part of our admissions process. This is an opportunity for parents to share insights regarding their child and ask questions about Oak Hill.
Group tour dates: All tours are individually scheduled.
Open house dates: N/A
Classroom visits: N/A
Profit or non-profit: Profit

ADMISSIONS

Application form required: No
Forms required: N/A
Application deadline: N/A
Application fee: N/A
Contact: Pam Quarterman or Suzanne Eades
Phone: (214) 368-0664
Student interview required: Yes
Parent interview required: Yes
Entrance test required: No

Specific tests administered: N/A
Accept test scores from other schools: No
Testing fee: N/A
Time of year testing is administered: N/A
Test dates offered: N/A
Out of state applicants: N/A
Notification by phone: N/A
Notification by mail: N/A

FINANCIAL

Preschool tuition: $5,100 part-day/ $6,100 full-day
Elementary tuition: $7,900
Secondary tuition: N/A
Other tuition: N/A
Cash discounts: Yes
Personal check: Yes
Automatic bank draw: N/A
Credit cards: N/A
Monthly: Yes
Per semester: Yes
Annually: Yes
Financial assistance offered: The Director of Oak Hill works with many families to make their tuition payments affordable. Financial aid is offered in varying amounts, depending on the need of the family and the limitations of the school budget.
Cancellation insurance: N/A
Sibling discount: N/A
Application acceptance deposit required: There is a non-refundable registration fee of $600.

SERVICES

Before school care offered: N/A
After school care offered: N/A
Transportation provided: N/A
Lunch/snack program: A hot lunch program is offered on Tuesdays & Thursdays through Whole Foods Market and on Fridays through Fuddruckers Restaurant.
Other: An after-school band program is available for the Middle School students on Mondays and Fridays. After school sports teams are organized in soccer, basketball, softball, track for 4th - 8th grades.

PRESTON HOLLOW PRESBYTERIAN SCHOOL

9800 Preston Road
Dallas, TX 75230
Contact: **Sheila Phaneuf, Director**
(214) 368-3886
(214) 368-2255 FAX

Office Hours: 8:00 a.m. - 4:00 p.m.
E-MAIL: s.phaneuf@phps.org
Web Site: www.phps.org
MAPSCO: 25P

PHILOSOPHY OF SCHOOL

To provide a positive, nurturing, individualized teaching approach to remediate children's learning weaknesses, build on their strengths, and teach them compensating skills. Ours is a structured, multisensory program geared to maximize the learning potential of bright children diagnosed with learning differences. Ours is a full academic program which addresses all aspects of curriculum. Our goal is to return our students to the mainstream of education.

CREDENTIALS

Accreditations: (see glossary) ASESA

Awards and special recognition: (see glossary) N/A

Qualification of administrator: M.Ed. in L.D. and E.D. and 32 years' experience in the L.D. field (25 years at Preston Hollow)

Qualification of faculty: Degree and certification in special education with a concentration in learning disabilities

Other: Affiliated with the Learning Disabilities Association, Attention-Deficit Disorder Association, Texas Computer Education Association, Council for Exceptional Children (division for learning disabilities), International Reading Association

GENERAL

Alternative: Yes
College preparatory: Yes
Montessori: No
Nondenominational: We accept children of all faiths.
Church affiliated: Yes
Denomination: Presbyterian
Jewish: N/A
Other denominations: N/A

Student type: Co-ed
Grade category (for details see specific grades offered below): Elementary
Infants: N/A
Preschool: N/A
Kindergarten: N/A
Primary / Transition: No
Elementary: Yes
Secondary or Middle School: N/A
Specific grades offered: Grades 1 - 6
Student teacher ratio average: 5:1
Classes offered per grade: 2
Average class size: 8-9
Total enrollment: 106
Recommended grades to apply: N/A
School hours: 8:15 a.m. - 2:45 p.m. (grades 1 - 3); 8:15 a.m. - 3:15 p.m.
    (grades 4 - 6)
Calendar school year: Late August - late May
Uniforms required: Yes
Parental involvement opportunities and requirements: Very active parents' club
    which sponsors three parent meetings with speakers, an annual family sock
    hop, an annual fundraiser, a school directory publication, a school yearbook
    publication, a library organization, daily cafeteria servers, etc.
Average SAT scores: N/A
Visitation procedures: Arranged on individual basis
Personal appointments for touring the facility: Yes
Group tour dates: N/A
Open house dates: N/A
Classroom visits: Arranged on individual basis
Profit or non-profit: Non-profit

ADMISSIONS

Application form required: Yes
Forms required: Copy of diagnostic testing, school records, and
    teacher-recommendation form
Application deadline: Begin applications in November prior to fall semester
Application fee: N/A
Contact: Sheila Phaneuf or Kay Burns
Phone: (214) 368-3886
Student interview required: Yes
Parent interview required: Yes
Entrance test required: Must have had previous diagnostic testing

Specific tests administered: N/A
Accept test scores from other schools: N/A
Testing fee: N/A
Time of year testing is administered: N/A
Test dates offered: N/A
Out of state applicants: N/A
Notification by phone: Yes
Notification by mail: Yes
Other: In person

FINANCIAL

Preschool tuition: N/A
Elementary tuition: Annual or semi-annual $8500; monthly $8925
Secondary tuition: N/A
Other tuition: N/A
Cash discounts: N/A
Personal check: N/A
Automatic bank draw: Yes
Credit cards: N/A
Monthly: Yes, 10 payments
Per semester: Yes
Annually: Yes
Financial assistance offered: No
Cancellation insurance: N/A
Sibling discount: N/A
Application acceptance deposit required: N/A

SERVICES

Before school care offered: N/A
After school care offered: N/A
Transportation provided: N/A
Lunch/snack program: Lunch fee is $3.25 per day (optional); students may bring their own lunches.
Other: Computer lab, library, art, music, P.E. and drama and afterschool art and sports programs offered.

SHELTON SCHOOL AND EVALUATION CENTER

15720 Hillcrest
Dallas, TX 75248
Contact: **Diann Slaton, Admission Director**
(972) 774 - 1772
(972)991-3977 FAX

Office Hours: 8:00 a.m. - 4:00 p.m.
E-MAIL: webmaster@shelton.org
Web Site: www.shelton.org
MAPSCO: 34B

PHILOSOPHY OF SCHOOL

The June Shelton School is an independent, nonsectarian, coeducational, nonprofit school that seeks to provide excellence in education to learning-different children (preschool-grade12). The School offers this population a full, broad-based curriculum with a strong academic orientation and a nurturing family atmosphere which considers the physical, social, emotional, and social growth of each student.

CREDENTIALS

Accreditations: (see glossary) SACS
Awards and special recognition: (see glossary) N/A
Qualification of administrator: Master's degree and over 26 years' experience in teaching, therapy, testing and administrative work
Qualification of faculty: Bachelor's degree (or above) plus specialized multisensory training
Other: Also accredited by SAIS; Affiliated with TANS, COPSES, TACLD, International Dyslexia Association, ALTA

GENERAL

Alternative: Yes
College preparatory: No
Montessori: No
Nondenominational: Yes
Church affiliated: No
Denomination: N/A
Jewish: N/A
Other denominations: N/A
Student type: Co-ed
Grade category (for details see specific grades offered below): Preschool - 12th
Infants: N/A

Preschool: Full Day
Kindergarten: N/A
Primary / Transition: Yes
Elementary: Yes
Secondary or Middle School: Yes
Specific grades offered: Preschool - grade 12
Student teacher ratio average: 6:1
Classes offered per grade: N/A
Average class size: 10
Total enrollment: 640
Recommended grades to apply: N/A
School hours: 8:10 a.m. - 3:20 p.m. (Mon-Thurs); 8:10 a.m. - 2:20 p.m. (Fri)
Calendar school year: Mid-August - May
Uniforms required: Yes
Parental involvement opportunities and requirements: The Parent Council, Dads' Club, parent-education courses
Average SAT scores: N/A
Visitation procedures: Call admission office for information.
Personal appointments for touring the facility: Call admission office for information.
Group tour dates: Call admission office for information.
Open house dates: N/A
Classroom visits: Call admission office for information.
Profit or non-profit: Non-profit

ADMISSIONS

Application form required: Yes
Forms required: Verify with school
Application deadline: Apply year round if openings; most apply Nov-March
Application fee: $50
Contact: Diann Slaton, Director of Admission
Phone: (972) 774-1772
Student interview required: No
Parent interview required: No
Entrance test required: Yes
Specific tests administered: 1st - 4th Grade: Psycho-educational diagnostic testing required, Fifth and above: Psycho-educational diagnostic testing required, Secondary: Psycho-educational diagnostic testing required
Accept test scores from other schools: No
Testing fee: N/A
Time of year testing is administered: N/A

Test dates offered: N/A
Out of state applicants: N/A
Notification by phone: Yes
Notification by mail: N/A
Other: Within one week after a 3-day student visit; by phone call or conference

FINANCIAL

Preschool tuition: $5700
Elementary tuition: T/1-12 $9670
Secondary tuition: N/A
Other tuition: Fees $500-$950; Matriculate $575; uniform $75
Cash discounts: N/A
Personal check: N/A
Automatic bank draw: N/A
Credit cards: N/A
Monthly: N/A
Per semester: Yes
Annually: N/A
Financial assistance offered: Yes, limited
Cancellation insurance: Yes
Sibling discount: No
Application acceptance deposit required: $950 deposit due Feb.,
    balance due July

SERVICES

Before school care offered: N/A
After school care offered: Yes, until 6:00 p.m.
Transportation provided: N/A
Lunch/snack program: Lunch Program; Children bring mid-morning snacks
Other: 6 computer labs, 2 libraries, Enrichment Curriculum and Extracurricular
    Activities offered; Summer School; Speech/Language/Hearing Clinic;
    Evaluation Center; Scholars Tutoring Program

SOUTHWEST ACADEMY

600 S. Jupiter
Allen, TX 75002-4065
Contact: **Beverly Dooley, Ph.D, Executive Director, Principal**
    Peggy Signall, M.Ed., Vice Principal
(972) 359-6646
(972) 359-8291 FAX

Office Hours: 8:00 a.m. - 4:00 p.m.
E-MAIL: swacad@buz.net
Web Site: N/A
MAPSCO: Allen

PHILOSOPHY OF SCHOOL

To help children feel lovable and capable and to love learning.

CREDENTIALS

Accreditations: (see glossary) ASESA, SACS candidate, TANS
Awards and special recognition: (see glossary) Teacher Training Center,
    Evaluation Center
Qualification of administrator: Ph.D
Qualification of faculty: Bachelors or Masters degree
Other: Certified Academic Language Therapists; Montessori-certified teacher;
    Certified Educational Diagnostician

GENERAL

Alternative: Private
College preparatory: Yes
Montessori: Yes
Nondenominational: Yes
Church affiliated: Bible courses offered
Denomination: N/A
Jewish: N/A
Other denominations: N/A
Student type: Co-ed
Grade category (for details see specific grades offered below): Elementary,
    Middle School
Infants: N/A
Preschool: Full Day
Kindergarten: Half Day and Full Day
Primary / Transition: Yes
Elementary: Yes
Secondary or Middle School: Yes

Specific grades offered: Preschool - 8th
Other: Preschool
Student teacher ratio average: 12:1
Classes offered per grade: 2
Average class size: 9
Total enrollment: 70
Recommended grades to apply: Preschool - 8th
School hours: 8:45 a.m. - 3:30 p.m.
Calendar school year: August - May
Uniforms required: Yes
Parental involvement opportunities and requirements: PTO, University Days, 4 fund raisers
Average SAT scores: N/A
Visitation procedures: Call for appointment
Personal appointments for touring the facility: Yes
Group tour dates: Fall and Spring
Open house dates: Fall and Spring
Classroom visits: Fall and Spring
Profit or non-profit: Non-profit

ADMISSIONS

Application form required: Yes
Forms required: Application and registration
Application deadline: N/A
Application fee: $100
Contact: Beverly Dooley, Ph.D. or Peggy Signall, M.Ed.
Phone: (972) 359-6646
Student interview required: Yes
Parent interview required: Yes
Entrance test required: Yes
Specific tests administered: Preschool: Montessori Readiness Interview; Kindergarten: WISC-III, Woodcock-Johnson-R, Revised ITPA, Beary: VMI; Primer: WISC-III, Woodcock-Johnson-R, Revised ITPA, Beary: VMI; 1st - 4th Grade: VISC-III, Woodcock-Johnson-R, Revised ITPA, Beary: VMI; 5th and above: WISC-III, Woodcock-Johnson-R
Accept test scores from other schools: Yes, if current
Testing fee: $150
Time of year testing is administered: All year
Test dates offered: By appointment - all year
Out of state applicants: Yes
Notification by phone: Yes, personal feedback session

Notification by mail: Yes

FINANCIAL

Preschool tuition:	Tuition 10/mo	Registration Fee	Supply Fee	TOTAL
3 year olds, 2 day	$250/mo	$125	$150	**$2775**
3 year olds, 3 day	$300/mo	$125	$150	**$3275**
3 year olds, 5 day	$350/mo	$125	$150	**$3775**
4 year olds, 3 day	$450/mo	$125	$200	**$4825**
4 year olds, 5 day	$550/mo	$125	$250	**$5875**
Elementary tuition:	**Tuition**	**Registration Fee**	**Supply Fee**	
Kindergarten, 5 day	$6000	$125	$250	
First Grade	$6250	$125	$350	
Second Grade	$6250	$125	$350	
Third Grade	$6250	$125	$350	
Fourth Grade	$6500	$125	$400	
Fifth Grade	$6500	$125	$400	
Sixth Grade	$7250	$125	$500	
Secondary tuition:	**Tuition**	**Registration Fee**	**Supply Fee**	
Seventh Grade	$7250	$125	$500	
Eighth Grade	$7250	$125	$500	

Other tuition: After school lab $35 per hour

Cash discounts: Yes

Personal check: Yes

Automatic bank draw: Yes

Credit cards: Visa, MasterCard

Monthly: Yes, bank draft

Per semester: Yes

Annually: Yes

Financial assistance offered: Scholarships - limited

Cancellation insurance: No

Sibling discount: Yes

Application acceptance deposit required: Yes, $100 due at the time the student's application is submitted to the school.

Other: For Kindergarten - 8th grade there is a $150 Admissions, Orientation & Testing Fee and a $200 Enrollment Fee (one time fee) The registration fee is due at the time the student is accepted.

SERVICES

Before school care offered: Yes, 8:00 a.m. - 9:00 a.m.
After school care offered: No
Transportation provided: Yes, from Central and Forest
Lunch/snack program: Yes

VANGUARD PREPARATORY SCHOOL

4240 Omega
Dallas, TX   75244
Contact: **Rosalind Funderburgh**
(972) 404-1616
(972) 404-1641 FAX

Office Hours: 8:05 a.m. - 4:00 p.m.
E-MAIL: N/A
Web Site: N/A
MAPSCO: 14L

PHILOSOPHY OF SCHOOL

Vanguard Preparatory School serves children of normal intelligence who are experiencing social, emotional, behavioral, or academic delays. We offer a highly individualized program in a therapeutic milieu that emphasizes development of academic skills, and behavioral and social abilities to build successful relationships and foster scholastic achievement.

CREDENTIALS

Accreditations: (see glossary) Alternative Schools, ASESA, SACS
Awards and special recognition: (see glossary) N/A
Qualification of administrator: Master's degree in special-education administration; minimum of 5 years' experience with special population
Qualification of faculty: College degree; certification; minimum of 3 years' experience

GENERAL

Alternative: Yes
College preparatory: Yes
Montessori: No
Nondenominational: Yes
Church affiliated: No
Denomination: N/A
Jewish: N/A
Other denominations: N/A
Student type: Co-ed
Grade category (for details see specific grades offered below): Preschool - 12th
Infants: N/A
Preschool: Full Day
Kindergarten: Full Day

Primary / Transition: No
Elementary: Yes
Secondary: Yes
Specific grades offered: PreK - grade 12
Student teacher ratio average: 4:1
Classes offered per grade: N/A
Average class size: 8
Total enrollment: 105
Recommended grades to apply: N/A
School hours: 8:30 a.m. - 3:00 p.m.
Calendar school year: August 1 (year round school)
Uniforms required: No
Parental involvement opportunities and requirements: Active parent-support
    group
Average SAT scores: N/A
Visitation procedures: Call for appointment
Personal appointments for touring the facility: Offered
Group tour dates: N/A
Open house dates: N/A
Classroom visits: Mandatory for admission
Profit or non-profit: Profit
Other: Uniforms required for Upper School only.

ADMISSIONS

Application form required: Yes
Forms required: N/A
Application deadline: Apply April 1
Application fee: $450/ admission & testing
Contact: Rosalind Funderburgh
Phone: (214) 404-1616
Student interview required: Yes
Parent interview required: Yes
Entrance test required: Yes
Specific tests administered: Preschool, Kindergarten, 1st - 4th, 5th and above,
    Secondary: Individual psycho-educational battery required
Accept test scores from other schools: Yes
Testing fee: N/A
Time of year testing is administered: N/A
Test dates offered: N/A
Out of state applicants: N/A
Notification by phone: Yes

Notification by mail: N/A

Other: Individual conference with parents

FINANCIAL

Preschool tuition: $845/month

Elementary tuition: $875/month

Secondary tuition: $1150/month

Other tuition: N/A

Cash discounts: Yes **Description:** For semester or discount for annual payment.

Personal check: Yes

Automatic bank draw: N/A

Credit cards: Yes

Monthly: Yes

Per semester: Yes

Annually: Yes

Financial assistance offered: Limited scholarships

Cancellation insurance: N/A

Sibling discount: Yes

Application acceptance deposit required: Yes

SERVICES

Before school care offered: Yes

After school care offered: Yes

Transportation provided: N/A

Lunch/snack program: Snacks Pre K and Elementary

Other: One computer per 5 children, library offered.

WALDEN PREPARATORY SCHOOL

14552 Montfort Drive
Dallas, TX   75240
Contact: Pamala Stone
(972) 233-6883
(972) 458-4553 FAX

Office Hours: 8:00 a.m. - 4:00 p.m.
E-MAIL: waldenprep@aol.com
Web Site: N/A
MAPSCO: 15

PHILOSOPHY OF SCHOOL
Small classes or individualized instruction with special accelerated program.

CREDENTIALS
Accreditations: (see glossary) SACS
Awards and special recognition: (see glossary) N/A
Qualification of administrator: College degrees
Qualification of faculty: College degrees

GENERAL
Alternative: Yes
College preparatory: Yes
Montessori: No
Nondenominational: N/A
Church affiliated: No
Denomination: N/A
Jewish: N/A
Other denominations: N/A
Student type: Co-ed
Grade category (for details see specific grades offered below): N/A
Infants: N/A
Preschool: N/A
Kindergarten: N/A
Primary / Transition: No
Elementary: N/A
Secondary or Middle School: Yes
Specific grades offered: 9th - 12th
Student teacher ratio average: 8:1

Classes offered per grade: N/A
Average class size: 6 - 8
Total enrollment: 55 - 65
Recommended grades to apply: N/A
School hours: 9:00 a.m. - 4:00 p.m.
Calendar school year: Traditional school calendar
Uniforms required: No
Parental involvement opportunities and requirements: Parents' organization
Average SAT scores: N/A
Visitation procedures: Appointment with Director
Personal appointments for touring the facility: Offered
Group tour dates: N/A
Open house dates: N/A
Classroom visits: Offered
Profit or non-profit: Non-profit

ADMISSIONS

Application form required: Yes
Forms required: Application; high school transcripts
Application deadline: Ongoing enrollment
Application fee: No
Contact: Pamala Stone
Phone: (972) 233-6883
Student interview required: Yes
Parent interview required: Yes
Entrance test required: No
Specific tests administered: N/A
Accept test scores from other schools: Yes
Testing fee: N/A
Time of year testing is administered: N/A
Test dates offered: N/A
Out of state applicants: N/A
Notification by phone: N/A
Notification by mail: N/A
Other: Done during initial interview

FINANCIAL

Preschool tuition: N/A
Elementary tuition: N/A
Secondary tuition: $7000 + $500 enrollment fee
Other tuition: N/A

Cash discounts: N/A
Personal check: Yes
Automatic bank draw: N/A
Credit cards: N/A
Monthly: N/A
Per semester: N/A
Annually: Yes
Financial assistance offered: No
Cancellation insurance: N/A
Sibling discount: N/A
Application acceptance deposit required: N/A

SERVICES

Before school care offered: N/A
After school care offered: N/A
Transportation provided: N/A
Lunch/snack program: N/A
Other: Computers in classrooms

THE WINSTON SCHOOL

bright students who learn differently®

5707 Royal Lane
Dallas, TX   75229
Contact: Amy C. Smith
(214) 691-6950
(214) 691-1509 FAX

Office Hours: 8:00 a.m. - 4:00 p.m.
E-MAIL: admissions@winston-school.org
Web Site: www.winston-school.org
MAPSCO: 25E

PHILOSOPHY OF SCHOOL

The environment and curriculum of The Winston School is designed for *bright students who learn differently.*® Since learning differences are unique to the individual and may be manifested in various academic areas, each person deserves the opportunity to learn in the manner appropriate for his or her own distinctive style. As cornerstones of our philosophy, the Winston community believes: Learning requires self-discipline. Learning requires active, mental participation of the student. Learning focuses on long term goals. Learning is enhanced by understanding one's particular strengths and weaknesses in the learning process. Learning is the process of continual elaboration on the student's knowledge base. Learning requires courage and tenacity. Learning strengthens self-esteem. The Winston community, which includes the Board of Trustees, faculty, and staff, is dedicated to developing a student's strengths, to conquering weaknesses, to instilling confidence, and to helping each student reach his or her full potential. A variety of assessment processes and teaching methods are utilized to assist students in satisfying their unique cognitive needs. Concept development, specific skills, learning strategies, study skills, and problem solving are taught in a balanced curriculum across academic subject areas.

CREDENTIALS

Accreditations: (see glossary) Alternative Schools, ISAS, NAIS
Awards and special recognition: (see glossary) N/A
Qualification of administrator: Pamela K. Murfin, Ph.D., Head of School.
   Rebbie Evans, B.S.W., M.Ed., Certified Educational Diagnostician, Head of Lower School and Middle School.
   Richard Hayse, MA, Head of Upper School
Qualification of faculty: All faculty members are degreed with Bachelor's degrees. 33% of faculty have Master's degrees. Head of School and School Psychologist each hold a Ph.D.

GENERAL

Alternative: Yes

College preparatory: Yes

Montessori: No

Nondenominational: Yes

Church affiliated: No

Denomination: N/A

Jewish: N/A

Other denominations: The Winston School is Interdenominational.

Student type: Co-ed

Grade category (for details see specific grades offered below): 1st - 12th

Infants: N/A

Preschool: N/A

Kindergarten: N/A

Primary / Transition: No

Elementary: Yes

Secondary or Middle School: Yes

Specific grades offered: LS: grades 1 to 6; MS: grades 7 and 8; US: grades 9 - 12

Other: We are a school for students of average to superior intelligence with a diagnosed learning difference.

Student teacher ratio average: 8:1

Classes offered per grade: N/A

Average class size: 10

Total enrollment: 230

Recommended grades to apply: 1-12

School hours: 8:10 a.m. - 3:30 p.m.

Calendar school year: August to May

Uniforms required: No

Parental involvement opportunities and requirements: PTO and Development volunteer opportunities

Average SAT scores: 1040

Visitation procedures: 3-day visit required

Personal appointments for touring the facility: Call Amy C. Smith (214) 691-6950

Group tour dates: Individual tours only

Open house dates: March 14, 2000 from 7:00 p.m. to 8:30 p.m.

Classroom visits: By appointment.

Profit or non-profit: Non-profit

ADMISSIONS

Application form required: Yes

Forms required: Full battery of Psychoeducational testing including I.Q., diagnostic achievement testing and language testing.

Application deadline: Year round

Application fee: $150.00

Contact: Amy C. Smith

Phone: (214) 691-6950

Student interview required: Yes

Parent interview required: Yes

Entrance test required: No

Specific tests administered: N/A

Accept test scores from other schools: Yes

Testing fee: $750.00

Time of year testing is administered: Year round

Test dates offered: By appointment

Out of state applicants: Yes

Notification by phone: Yes

Notification by mail: Yes

FINANCIAL

Preschool tuition: N/A

Elementary tuition: $9,350 to 11,500

Secondary tuition: $11,850

Other tuition: Book Fees-LS/$375; MS/ $525; US/$650

Cash discounts: N/A

Personal check: Yes

Automatic bank draw: N/A

Credit cards: Mastercard, Visa, & American Express

Monthly: Yes, 7 payments

Per semester: Yes, 2 payments

Annually: Yes

Financial assistance offered: Financial assistance available. Application can be made by calling at the beginning of January.

Cancellation insurance: Yes

Sibling discount: N/A

Application acceptance deposit required: $750

SERVICES

Before school care offered: N/A

After school care offered: Yes, 3:45 p.m. to 6:00 p.m.

Transportation provided: N/A

Lunch/snack program: Hot meals prepared at school daily. Sandwiches and chips available. Salad bar, baked potatoes, soup, fresh fruit, and yogurt served daily. Aftercare program provides snacks each day.

Curriculum Alternative

A curriculum alternative is an educational facility that implements a specialized curriculum which is unique to that school.

Covenant Classical School
Dallas International School (see Ch. 4)
Highlander-Carden School, The
Notre Dame of Dallas School, The
Rise School, The
Star Bright Academy

COVENANT CLASSICAL SCHOOL

6401 Garland Ave.
Fort Worth, TX 76116
Contact: **Linda Shook**
(817) 731-6447
(817) 731-6447 FAX

Office Hours: 8:00 a.m. - 2:00 p.m.
E-MAIL: ccsfw@flash.net
Web Site: N/A
MAPSCO: 89R

PHILOSOPHY OF SCHOOL

Covenant Classical School bases its educational philosophy on the Christian worldview that uses the Bible as the foundation and guide to evaluate knowledge, the world, and the whole of life. The classical system begins with the Trivium, which emphasizes the basic classical scholastic categories of grammar, logic, and rhetoric. Classical teaching techniques develop the whole child, academically, artistically, culturally, socially, and spiritually. Our school is an institution of learning established to provide quality academic training in an atmosphere wherein Christ is acknowledged and honored.

CREDENTIALS

Accreditations: (see glossary) ACCS in progress
Awards and special recognition: (see glossary) N/A
Qualification of administrator: N/A
Qualification of faculty: Minimum B.A./B.S., master's degree preferred in appropriate field
Other: Pending membership in Association of Christian and Classical Schools

GENERAL

Alternative: No
College preparatory: No
Montessori: No
Nondenominational: No
Church affiliated: No
Denomination: N/A
Jewish: N/A
Other denominations: N/A
Student type: Co-ed
Grade category (for details see specific grades offered below): Elementary

Infants: N/A

Preschool: N/A

Kindergarten: Half Day

Primary / Transition: N/A

Elementary: Yes

Secondary or Middle School: N/A

Specific grades offered: Kindergarten - 5th

Other: Classical and Christian school

Student teacher ratio average: 7:1

Classes offered per grade: 1

Average class size: Varies

Total enrollment: Not available at this time

Recommended grades to apply: Kindergarten - 5th

School hours: Kindergarten: Mon., Tues., and Thurs. 8:00 a.m. - Noon,
1st - 5th: Mon. - Thurs. 8:00 a.m. - 2:00 p.m.,
4th and 5th: Fri. 8:00 a.m. - Noon

Calendar school year: September 1, 1999 - May 26, 2000

Uniforms required: Yes

Parental involvement opportunities and requirements: Required to donate one
to two hours each week

Average SAT scores: N/A

Visitation procedures: By appointment

Personal appointments for touring the facility: By appointment

Group tour dates: By appointment

Open house dates: November 9, 1999 and January 25, 2000

Classroom visits: By appointment; also November 11, 1999 and January 27, 2000

Profit or non-profit: Non-profit

ADMISSIONS

Application form required: Yes

Forms required: Contact CCS to obtain application packet

Application deadline: N/A

Application fee: $50

Contact: Linda Shook

Phone: (817) 731-6447

Student interview required: Yes

Parent interview required: Yes

Entrance test required: Yes

Specific tests administered: Kindergarten - 5th: CCS admissions test

Accept test scores from other schools: Submit test scores with CCS application
packet

Testing fee: $50 (included in admissions fee)
Time of year testing is administered: Year round
Test dates offered: By appointment
Out of state applicants: As needed
Notification by phone: N/A
Notification by mail: Yes
Other: Personal interview

Non-Discriminatory Policy

CCS admits students of any race, color, national, and ethnic origin to all rights, privileges, programs and activities made available to students at the school. It does not discriminate on the basis of race, color, national or ethnic origin in administration of its educational policies, admissions policies, scholarship programs, and athletic and other school-administered programs.

FINANCIAL

Preschool tuition: N/A
Elementary tuition: Kindergarten: $1800; 1st - 3rd: $3300; 4th - 5th: $3800
Secondary tuition: N/A
Other tuition: N/A
Cash discounts: N/A
Personal check: Yes
Automatic bank draw: N/A
Credit cards: N/A
Monthly: Yes
Per semester: Yes
Annually: Yes
Financial assistance offered: N/A
Cancellation insurance: No
Sibling discount: No
Application acceptance deposit required: N/A

SERVICES

Before school care offered: No
After school care offered: No
Transportation provided: No
Lunch/snack program: N/A

THE HIGHLANDER-CARDEN SCHOOL

9120 Plano Road
Dallas, TX 75238
Contact: **Dr. Betty Woodring, Director**
(214) 348-3220
N/A FAX

Office Hours: 8:00 a.m. - 4:00 p.m.
E-MAIL: N/A
Web Site: N/A
MAPSCO: 28J

PHILOSOPHY OF SCHOOL

It is a wise teacher who makes learning a joy, but an even wiser one who makes each of God's children feel special.

CREDENTIALS

Accreditations: (see glossary) Curriculum Alternative
Awards and special recognition: (see glossary) Accredited by Carden
Qualification of administrator: Ph.D. in Elementary Education and Computer Science
Qualification of faculty: Minimum of bachelor's degree with additional Carden Curriculum training
Other: Affiliated with ACSD, ATE, TATE, and Phi Delta Kappa

GENERAL

Alternative: Yes
College preparatory: No
Montessori: No
Nondenominational: Yes
Church affiliated: No
Denomination: N/A
Jewish: N/A
Other denominations: N/A
Student type: Co-ed
Grade category (for details see specific grades offered below): Elementary
Infants: N/A
Preschool: Half Day; Pre-K I: 3 half days, Pre-K II: 2 half days
Kindergarten: Half Day, 5 half days
Primary / Transition: No

Comments: Pre-K - grade 6
Elementary: Yes
Secondary or Middle School: N/A
Specific grades offered: 1st - 6th
Student teacher ratio average: 8:1 - 20:1
Classes offered per grade: N/A
Average class size: 17
Total enrollment: 300+
Recommended grades to apply: N/A
School hours: 8:15 a.m. - 3:15 p.m.
Calendar school year: August - May
Uniforms required: Yes
Parental involvement opportunities and requirements: Parents' Club
Average SAT scores: N/A
Visitation procedures: N/A
Personal appointments for touring the facility: Offered
Group tour dates: Offered
Open house dates: N/A
Classroom visits: N/A
Profit or non-profit: Profit

ADMISSIONS

Application form required: Yes
Forms required: Health, enrollment, directory, emergency form, field trip form
Application deadline: Apply after January 1
Application fee: $35-$50
Contact: Betty G. Woodring, Ph.D.
Phone: (214) 348-3220
Student interview required: No
Parent interview required: No
Entrance test required: Yes
Specific tests administered: Kindergarten: Learning styles, 1st - 4th Grade: ITBS, Fifth and above: ITBS
Accept test scores from other schools: No
Testing fee: N/A
Time of year testing is administered: N/A
Test dates offered: N/A
Out of state applicants: N/A
Notification by phone: Yes
Notification by mail: N/A

FINANCIAL

Preschool tuition: N/A
Elementary tuition: Grades 1-3 $4500, grades 4-6 $4700
Secondary tuition: N/A
Other tuition: N/A
Cash discounts: N/A
Personal check: Yes
Automatic bank draw: N/A
Credit cards: N/A
Monthly: Yes
Per semester: Yes
Annually: Yes
Financial assistance offered: No
Cancellation insurance: N/A
Sibling discount: Yes
Application acceptance deposit required: N/A

SERVICES

Before school care offered: N/A
After school care offered: N/A
Transportation provided: N/A
Lunch/snack program: Lunch fee; school provides snacks for pre-kindergarten and kindergarten, not for elementary students
Other: Computer lab, library, enrichment curriculum and extracurricular activities offered

THE NOTRE DAME OF DALLAS SCHOOLS

2018 Allen Street
Dallas, TX 75204
Contact: **Theresa Francis, Principal**
(214) 720-3911
(214) 720-3913 FAX

Office Hours: 8:00 a.m. - 4:00 p.m.
E-MAIL: notredame.dallas@worldnet.att.net
Web Site: home.att.net/~notredame.dallas
MAPSCO: 45B

PHILOSOPHY OF SCHOOL

The mission of Notre Dame is twofold: to provide quality, individualized education to students with mental disabilities and to maximize their integration into society.

CREDENTIALS

Accreditations: (see glossary) TCCED, TEA
Awards and special recognition: (see glossary) N/A
Qualification of administrator: Master's degree in special education and 20 years' experience with special-needs population
Qualification of faculty: Certified in special education
Other: CEC, ASCD

GENERAL

Alternative: Yes
College preparatory: No
Montessori: No
Nondenominational: Yes
Church affiliated: No
Denomination: Catholic
Jewish: N/A
Other denominations: All accepted
Student type: Co-ed
Grade category (for details see specific grades offered below): Ungraded 3 - 21
Infants: N/A
Preschool: Full Day
Kindergarten: Full Day
Primary / Transition: No
Elementary: Yes

Secondary or Middle School: Yes, vocational training 18 and over.
Specific grades offered: Ungraded; ages 3-21
Student teacher ratio average: 5:1
Classes offered per grade: N/A
Average class size: 10
Total enrollment: 125
Recommended grades to apply: N/A
School hours: 8:30 a.m. - 3:00 p.m.
Calendar school year: August - May
Uniforms required: Yes, for elementary students
Parental involvement opportunities and requirements: Yes, volunteer work at
 school and for fundraisers
Average SAT scores: N/A
Visitation procedures: N/A
Personal appointments for touring the facility: Offered
Group tour dates: N/A
Open house dates: N/A
Classroom visits: N/A
Profit or non-profit: Non-profit

ADMISSIONS

Application form required: Yes
Forms required: Placement application, medical, psychological and educational
 records
Application deadline: Apply throughout the year
Application fee: $100
Contact: Theresa Francis, Principal
Phone: (214) 720-3911
Student interview required: Yes
Parent interview required: Yes
Entrance test required: No
Specific tests administered: N/A
Accept test scores from other schools: No
Testing fee: N/A
Time of year testing is administered: N/A
Test dates offered: N/A
Out of state applicants: N/A
Notification by phone: N/A
Notification by mail: Yes

FINANCIAL

Preschool tuition: $3800
Elementary tuition: $3800
Secondary tuition: $3800
Other tuition: N/A
Cash discounts: N/A
Personal check: Yes
Automatic bank draw: N/A
Credit cards: Yes
Monthly: Yes, 10 month schedule
Per semester: N/A
Annually: N/A
Financial assistance offered: Tuition assistance available
Cancellation insurance: N/A
Sibling discount: N/A
Application acceptance deposit required: N/A

SERVICES

Before school care offered: Yes, 7:30 a.m. - 8:15 a.m.
After school care offered: Yes, until 6:00 p.m. for students ages 6 to 16
Transportation provided: Yes
Lunch/snack program: Hot lunch fee: $2.00; milk: $.50
Other: Parent support groups, computers in each classroom; library, and
    extracurricular activities offered, Special Olympics; parent support groups.

THE RISE SCHOOL
OF DALLAS

5923 Royal Lane
Dallas, TX 75230
Contact: **Carol Kratville**
(214) 373-4666
(214) 373-6545 FAX

Office Hours: 8:00 a.m. - 4:00 p.m.
E-MAIL: risedal@swbell.net
Web Site: www.riseschool.com
MAPSCO: 36C

PHILOSOPHY OF SCHOOL

All children can learn together and achieve their highest functioning potential within a nurturing, stimulating, and developmentally appropriate environment.

CREDENTIALS

Accreditations: (see glossary)

Awards and special recognition: (see glossary) Modeled after the RISE Program of the Stallings Center at the University of Alabama.

Qualification of administrator: Masters degreed, licensed, and certified speech-language pathologist with 24 years experience.

Qualification of faculty: Teachers are master's degreed early childhood special educators, or bachelor degree with extensive experience.

Other: Licensed speech, occupational and music therapists, with physical therapy consultants

GENERAL

Alternative: No
College preparatory: No
Montessori: No
Nondenominational: Yes
Church affiliated: No
Denomination: N/A
Jewish: N/A
Other denominations: N/A
Student type: Co-ed
Grade category (for details see specific grades offered below): Preschool
Infants: N/A
Preschool: Full Day

Kindergarten: N/A
Primary / Transition: No
Elementary: N/A
Secondary or Middle School: N/A
Specific grades offered: N/A
Other: Preschool for children with Down Syndrome or other disabilities and for those without disabilities.
Teacher student ratio average: 3:1
Classes offered per grade: N/A
Average class size: Up to 10 children
Total enrollment: Current capacity 50
Recommended grades to apply: N/A
School hours: 8:30 a.m. - 12:30 p.m. and 8:30 a.m. - 2:30 p.m.
Calendar school year: 12 months
Uniforms required: No
Parental involvement opportunities and requirements: Volunteer opportunities; frequent and on-going parent communication
Average SAT scores: N/A
Visitation procedures: Call Rise to set up an appointment with the Director, Carol Kratville.
Personal appointments for touring the facility: Call Rise to set up an appointment with the Director, Carol Kratville.
Group tour dates: Special arrangements would need to be made.
Open house dates: N/A
Classroom visits: 9:00 a.m. - 11:30 a.m., preferred
Profit or non-profit: Non-profit

ADMISSIONS

Application form required: Yes
Forms required: Pre-enrollment packet will need to be submitted with application, child release, emergency authorization, medical exam and tuition agreement.
Application deadline: N/A
Application fee: N/A
Contact: Carol Kratville, Director
Phone: (214) 373-4666
Student interview required: No
Parent interview required: Yes
Entrance test required: Yes
Specific tests administered: Includes, but not limited to: AEPS, HELP, Rise Checklist

Accept test scores from other schools: Yes

Testing fee: N/A

Time of year testing is administered: At time of enrollment with parents involved

Test dates offered: N/A

Out of state applicants: N/A

Notification by phone: Yes, appointment following evaluation to develop Individual Program Plan.

Notification by mail: N/A

FINANCIAL

Preschool tuition: $455 - $720 Monthly

Elementary tuition: N/A

Secondary tuition: N/A

Other tuition: N/A

Cash discounts: N/A

Personal check: Yes

Automatic bank draw: N/A

Credit cards: N/A

Monthly: Yes

Per semester: N/A

Annually: N/A

Financial assistance offered: Available for those who qualify based on a family's net household income and the number of persons in household.

Cancellation insurance: N/A

Sibling discount: N/A

Application acceptance deposit required: No

SERVICES

Before school care offered: N/A

After school care offered: N/A

Transportation provided: N/A

Lunch/snack program: Morning and afternoon snacks are provided for all students. Parents send a lunch daily.

STAR BRIGHT ACADEMY

6000 Custer Road, Bldg. 5
Plano, TX 75023
Contact: **Karen Morrell**
(972) 517-6730
(972) 379-7056 FAX

Office Hours: 10:00 am - 9:00 p.m.
(Mon. - Thurs.)
E-MAIL: star97bp.abigplanet.com
Web Site: N/A
MAPSCO: 36C

PHILOSOPHY OF SCHOOL

We provide individualized instruction to maximize success.

CREDENTIALS

Accreditations: (see glossary) Curriculum Alternative

Awards and special recognition: (see glossary) N/A

Qualification of administrator: Certified teacher; 26 years experience

Qualification of faculty: All college-degree educators, many with masters or Ph.D.s

GENERAL

Alternative: Yes
College preparatory: No
Montessori: No
Nondenominational: Yes
Church affiliated: No
Denomination: N/A
Jewish: N/A
Other denominations: N/A
Student type: Co-ed
Grade category (for details see specific grades offered below): 1st - 12th
Infants: N/A
Preschool: N/A
Kindergarten: N/A
Primary / Transition: No
Elementary: Yes
Secondary or Middle School: Yes
Specific grades offered: N/A
Student teacher ratio average: 30:7
Classes offered per grade: 1 (4th), 2 (5th), 1 each (6th-9th)
Average class size: 5

Total enrollment: 30

Recommended grades to apply: 4 - 10

School hours: 8:30 a.m. - evening

Calendar school year: August 18 - May 21

Uniforms required: No

Parental involvement opportunities and requirements: Parents usually provide transportation and may drive on field trips.

Average SAT scores: We give the IOWA.

Visitation procedures: Visitors are welcome at all times.

Personal appointments for touring the facility: Daily Monday - Friday 9:00 a.m. - 9:00 p.m.

Group tour dates: Daily Monday - Friday 9:00 a.m. - 9:00 p.m.

Open house dates: N/A

Classroom visits: N/A

Profit or non-profit: N/A

ADMISSIONS

Application form required: Yes

Forms required: Entrance-registration form, former school transcripts

Application deadline: July 1st and December 1st

Application fee: $25

Contact: Karen Morrell

Phone: (972) 517-6730

Student interview required: Yes

Parent interview required: Yes

Entrance test required: Yes

Specific tests administered: 1st - 4th Grade: IOWA Test of Basic Skills, 5th and above: IOWA Test of Basic Skills

Accept test scores from other schools: Yes

Testing fee: $100.00

Time of year testing is administered: Ongoing

Test dates offered: Scheduled monthly

Out of state applicants: N/A

Notification by phone: N/A

Notification by mail: N/A

FINANCIAL

Preschool tuition: N/A

Elementary tuition: N/A

Secondary tuition: N/A

Other tuition: Varies with # of students - currently $475/month

Cash discounts: N/A
Personal check: Yes
Automatic bank draw: N/A
Credit cards: MasterCard, Visa
Monthly: Yes
Per semester: N/A
Annually: N/A
Financial assistance offered: N/A
Cancellation insurance: N/A
Sibling discount: N/A
Application acceptance deposit required: N/A

SERVICES

Before school care offered: N/A
After school care offered: N/A
Transportation provided: Yes
Lunch/snack program: Students may bring lunch and/or snacks; Drinks $.50
Other: Transportation provided to & from WOGA and Infinite Bounds gyms

Montessori Schools

What is the Montessori method?

1. The method is a means of scientific assistance to the total development of the child: social, intellectual, psychic, physical. Academic development is not a concern of the method, for it follows naturally in the child who has the experiences essential to the fulfillment of the aforementioned aspects of development.

2. The environment is carefully prepared so that the child's sense of order is fulfilled by having a special place for each item, with apparatus arranged in categories. There are not distracting decorations or excess materials to clutter the room.

3. Activities with scientifically designed learning apparatus take place in the "prepared environment." Use of these didactic materials is demonstrated by the teacher to each child individually. Once a demonstration has been given, self-teaching is possible as the child uses the apparatus which has built-in control of error, allowing self-correction. There are special materials for care of the environment (practical life), education of the senses, language (reading, grammar, vocabulary), mathematics, geography, history, handwork, natural and experimental science.

4. Concentration develops through work with the hands, leading to self-discipline and independence through self-direction. "Normalization" is the term used by Montessori.

5. There is freedom of choice within well-defined limits. The child may choose to:
  • work alone or with others
  • select any activity after a lesson has been given
  • continue an activity as long as desired with any material
  • pursue a wide range of activities according to individual interests and needs
  • socialize with children of several ages
  • exercise self-discipline in an atmosphere of trust and faith in the child
  • solve his/her own problems
  • meet challenges through the exercise of independence and self-reliance which enhances the development of exercise self-esteem.

What are the goals of Montessori education?

The proper application of Montessori's method permits the child to develop a positive self-concept, self-discipline, respect for others, respect for the environment, and to maintain the innate natural love of learning.

What are the qualities of the Ideal Montessori teacher?

The teacher knows Montessori's principles of child development as well as those of other major theorists; understands the uses, purposes and sequences of materials in all areas of learning; observes objectively to be able to give the appropriate lesson at the proper time; presents short, interesting lessons and demonstrations; sets appropriate limits and always enforces them equally; provides beautiful learning materials and maintains the simple, orderly environment; respects the personal dignity of each child; and displays a sense of humility, keeping one's own personality in abeyance.

What are the characteristics of Montessori education?

1. Learning is active, not passive.

2. Teacher control is replaced by the child's self-control.

3. The natural interests of each child are followed rather than subjecting an entire class to a pre-determined syllabus or daily lesson plan.

4. Acquisition of teacher-determined facts by rote memory is replaced by understanding of concepts through work with the Montessori learning materials.

5. Montessori education is concerned with the total development of each individual child rather than accenting academic achievement.

Jane Dutcher
President
Montessori Educators International, Inc.
P.O. Box 143
Cordova, TN 38018

Montessori schools included in this text are listed below:

A Child's Garden Montessori (see Ch. 4)
Amberwood Montessori Academy (see Ch. 4)
Andrew Austin School
Ashbury Academy - Montessori AMI
Clariden School, The (see TAAPS)
Country Day Montessori School
Dallas Montessori Academy
Dallas North Montessori School, The (see Ch. 4)
East Dallas Community School (see Ch. 4)
Good Shepherd Montessori (see Ch. 4)

Highland Meadow Montessori Academy
Lakemont Academy (see SACS)
Meadowbrook School
Montessori Children's House and School
Montessori Episcopal School (see Ch. 4)
Montessori of Las Colinas
Montessori School of North Dallas
Montessori School of Park Cities (see Ch. 4)
Montessori School - Pleasant Grove (see Ch. 4)
Montessori School of Westchester
North Garland Montessori School (see Ch. 4)
Preston Meadows Montessori
Redeemer Montessori School
St. Alcuin Montessori
St. Christopher Montessori
St. James Episcopal Montessori
Trinity Episcopal Preschool (see Ch. 4)
West Plano Montessori School
Westwood Montessori School
White Rock Montessori School
White Rock North School (see SACS)
Windsong Montessori School

ANDREW AUSTIN MONTESSORI SCHOOL

10206 Webb Chapel Road
Dallas, TX 75229
Contact: **Fran Bradshaw**
(214) 350-3371

Office Hours: 8:30 a.m. - 4:30 p.m.
E-MAIL: Fbradshaw@andrewaustinschool.com
Web Site: www.andrewaustinschool.com
MAPSCO: N/A

PHILOSOPHY OF SCHOOL

We look at the guidance of the whole child through development of his/her self. The focus is on the environment and atmosphere of the classroom as one of quiet nurturing, respect for the child's natural desire to learn, and appreciation of individual strengths and differences. This foundation, begun in preschool, assists the child to develop as inquisitive and independent learners that have an excitement and joy for learning, and to develop a sense of community responsibility.

CREDENTIALS

Accreditations: (see glossary) AMITOT pending, Montessori
Awards and special recognition: (see glossary) N/A
Qualification of administrator: Masters level - Education, AMS certified
Qualification of faculty: Montessori Certification

GENERAL

Alternative: No
College preparatory: No
Montessori: Yes
Nondenominational: No
Church affiliated: No
Denomination: N/A
Jewish: N/A
Other denominations: N/A
Student type: Co-ed
Grade category (for details see specific grades offered below): Preschool - 9th
Infants: No
Preschool: Half Day and Full Day
Kindergarten: Half Day and Full Day
Primary / Transition: N/A

Elementary: N/A

Secondary or Middle School: Yes

Specific grades offered: Kindergarten - 9th grade

Student teacher ratio average: 10:1

Classes offered per grade: Age grouping

Average class size: Sizes vary

Total enrollment: Varies

Recommended grades to apply: All open

School hours: 8:30 a.m. - 3:15 p.m.

Calendar school year: September - May

Uniforms required: No

Parental involvement opportunities and requirements: Regularly scheduled parent information meetings and participation in school activities and clubs. We offer a variety of extra-curricular activities as well as before and after school care.

Average SAT scores: N/A

Visitation procedures: Call to set up an appointment. Parents only on initial visit. There is a one- to three- day visit that will allow your child to meet the teacher and other students in the class.

Personal appointments for touring the facility: Please call for an appointment.

Group tour dates: Individual only.

Open house dates: None scheduled

Classroom visits: By appointment

Profit or non-profit: Profit

ADMISSIONS

Application form required: Yes

Forms required: Yes

Application deadline: Year round

Application fee: A $200 testing and application fee for the visit and assessment.

Contact: Fran Bradshaw

Phone: (214) 350-3371

Student interview required: Yes

Parent interview required: Yes

Entrance test required: No

Specific tests administered: N/A

Accept test scores from other schools: N/A

Testing fee: A $200 testing and application fee for the visit and assessment.

Time of year testing is administered: N/A

Test dates offered: N/A

Out of state applicants: N/A

Notification by phone: N/A
Notification by mail: Yes

FINANCIAL

Preschool tuition: $480
Elementary tuition: $500 - $550
Secondary tuition: $750
Other tuition: Extended care, $100
Cash discounts: N/A
Personal check: Yes
Automatic bank draw: N/A
Credit cards: N/A
Monthly: N/A
Per semester: Yes
Annually: Yes, 100% upon notification of acceptance
Financial assistance offered: Infrequently
Cancellation insurance: No
Sibling discount: No
Application acceptance deposit required:

SERVICES

Before school care offered: Yes
After school care offered: Yes
Transportation provided: No
Lunch/snack program: Sack lunch program. Natural snacks provided.
Other: Extracurricular activities offered.

ASHBURY ACADEMY - MONTESSORI AMI

219 Executive Way
DeSoto, TX 75115
Contact: **Lakshmi Witharane**
(972) 780-4700
(972) 780-4700 FAX

Office Hours: 8:30 a.m. - 4:00 p.m.
E-MAIL: sajiniw@aol.com
Web Site: N/A
MAPSCO: N/A

PHILOSOPHY OF SCHOOL

Individualized, self-paced learning environment which allows each child to follow his own curiosity and natural desire and joy of learning.

CREDENTIALS

Accreditations: (see glossary) AMI, Montessori
Awards and special recognition: (see glossary) Music, Art & Craft
Qualification of administrator: Bachelors degree, law degree, Montessori training - primary and elementary
Qualification of faculty: Bachelor's degree and Montessori training
Other: Licensed by AMITOT

GENERAL

Alternative: No
College preparatory: No
Montessori: Yes
Nondenominational: Yes
Church affiliated: No
Denomination: N/A
Jewish: N/A
Other denominations: N/A
Student type: Co-ed
Grade category (for details see specific grades offered below): N/A
Infants: N/A
Preschool: Half Day & Full Day
Kindergarten: Full Day
Primary / Transition: Yes
Elementary: Yes

Secondary or Middle School: N/A
Specific grades offered: 18 months - 12 years (6th grade)
Other: Planning to offer school up to age 15 in the year 2000.
Student teacher ratio average: Toddler 6:1; primary and elementary 10:1
Classes offered per grade: 2 Toddler, 1 Primary, 1 Elementary
Average class size: Toddlers 6/teacher; Primary 20/ 2 teachers;
    Elementary 12-15/ 2 teachers
Total enrollment: 60
Recommended grades to apply: Toddler and Primary Elementary,
    18 months - 12 years
School hours: 8:30 a.m. - 3:00 p.m./ Before and after school available
Calendar school year: Academic Year: August - May (following the DeSoto ISD
    schedule); Summer Enrichment: June and July
Uniforms required: Yes
Parental involvement opportunities and requirements: Encourage parent
    support in social and academic development.
Average SAT scores: N/A
Visitation procedures: Observation by appointment any day.
Personal appointments for touring the facility: Yes, any day
Group tour dates: N/A
Open house dates: N/A
Classroom visits: By appointment
Profit or non-profit: Profit

ADMISSIONS

Application form required: Yes
Forms required: School forms
Application deadline: All year
Application fee: $50
Contact: Lakshmi Witharane
Phone: (972) 780-4700
Student interview required: Yes
Parent interview required: Yes
Entrance test required: Yes, if coming from another Montessori school
Specific tests administered: Preschool: Screening, Kindergarten: Screening,
    Primary and Elementary: Screening and Testing
Accept test scores from other schools: N/A
Testing fee: N/A
Time of year testing is administered: All year
Test dates offered: N/A
Out of state applicants: N/A

Notification by phone: Yes
Notification by mail: Yes

FINANCIAL

Preschool tuition: Toddler (18 months - 3 years) $3950 - $5100:
   Primary (3 years - 6 years) $3850 - $5000
Elementary tuition: Transition/Elementary (6 - 12 years) $4200 - $5300
Secondary tuition: N/A
Other tuition: Summer Program same price as school year tuition. Use of after/
   before or day care with notice will be $5.00/hour or $20/day. Payment will be
   due before or on day of use.
Cash discounts: Yes
Personal check: Yes
Automatic bank draw: N/A
Credit cards: N/A
Monthly: Yes, ten monthly installments. The first payment is due with the contract
   on May 1, 1999.
Per semester: N/A
Annually: Yes, 10% discount
Financial assistance offered: N/A
Cancellation insurance: No
Sibling discount: Yes, 10% for second child
Application acceptance deposit required: Enrollment Fee (non-refundable/non-
   deductible from tuition) $100
Other: Late fee - payments received after the 5th of each month is $15. Return
   check fee is $20. Re-enrollment Fee (reserve placement subsequent years)
   $50. For late pick-up - $1 per minute after 5:30 p.m. (with or without notice)

SERVICES

Before school care offered: Yes, 7:30 a.m. - 8:30 a.m.
After school care offered: Yes, 3:00 p.m. - 5:30 p.m.
Transportation provided: No
Lunch/snack program: Parents provide lunch.

COUNTRY DAY MONTESSORI SCHOOL

2305 Plaza Dr.
Rockwall, TX 75032
Contact: **Margaret Lyman**
(972) 771-6680
(972) 722-6680 FAX

Office Hours: 8:00 a.m. - 5:00 p.m. M-F
E-MAIL: CDMSchool@aol.com
Web Site: cdmontessori.qpg.com
MAPSCO: 30C-D

PHILOSOPHY OF SCHOOL

Our primary goal is to "empower" children: to nurture in them the feeling that school is a responsive environment and that they are vital forces in it. We specialize in fostering independent, happy, and capable children who are comfortably challenged.

CREDENTIALS

Accreditations: (see glossary) NPSA, TDPRS

Awards and special recognition: (see glossary) Wal-Mart: Teacher of the Year Award - 1996; Who's Who - 1995-1999

Qualification of administrator: Masters level - Education, AMS certified, 10 year teacher

Qualification of faculty: Montessori Certification

Other: Masters level Reading Specialist, certified Musikgarten instructor, bachelors level art instructor.

GENERAL

Alternative: No
College preparatory: No
Montessori: Yes
Nondenominational: No
Church affiliated: No
Denomination: N/A
Jewish: N/A
Other denominations: N/A
Student type: Co-ed
Grade category (for details see specific grades offered below): N/A
Infants: No
Preschool: Half Day and Full Day

Kindergarten: Half Day and Full Day
Primary / Transition: Yes
Elementary: No
Secondary or Middle School: No
Specific grades offered: Preschool (3 years) - Kindergarten
Student teacher ratio average: 10:1
Classes offered per grade: 2 Preschool, 3 Kindergarten
Average class size: 30 Preschool, 20 Kindergarten
Total enrollment: 120
Recommended grades to apply: N/A
School hours: 8:30 a.m. - 3:30 p.m., Extended day 6:30 a.m. - 6:30 p.m.
Calendar school year: Kindergarten: September - May, Preschool: Year round
Uniforms required: Yes, Kindergarten only.
Parental involvement opportunities and requirements: October Fall Carnival, reader, listener, Room Mother/Dad parties.
Average SAT scores: N/A
Visitation procedures: Appointment preferred 9:00 a.m. Monday - Friday. Parent only on initial visit.
Personal appointments for touring the facility: Preferred, but not required.
Group tour dates: Individual only.
Open house dates: Ist week in December (annually). By appointment.
Classroom visits: By appointment.
Profit or non-profit: Profit

ADMISSIONS

Application form required: Yes
Forms required: School Forms: 1. Prospective student information form (Preschool) 2. Kindergarten application form (Kindergarten)
Application deadline: Year round
Application fee: $50: 1st child, $30: 2nd child, $20: 3rd child
Contact: Margaret Lyman
Phone: (972) 771-6680
Student interview required: Yes
Parent interview required: Yes
Entrance test required: No
Specific tests administered: Kindergarten: Placement only (Reading)
Accept test scores from other schools: N/A
Testing fee: N/A
Time of year testing is administered: N/A
Test dates offered: N/A
Out of state applicants: N/A

Notification by phone: Yes, in person on date of visit if space is available.

Notification by mail: Confirmation only.

FINANCIAL

Preschool tuition: $2040 - $4335 annual (12 months)

Elementary tuition: Kindergarten - $4000 - $4160 (9 months), includes reading lab fees

Secondary tuition: N/A

Other tuition: Activity Fee: Preschool $25/semester, $35/summer; ages 6-10 $25/semester, $85/summer; Year Round Extended Day $15/week

Cash discounts: N/A

Personal check: Yes

Automatic bank draw: N/A

Credit cards: Mastercard + 4% handling, Visa + 4% handling

Monthly: Yes, Kindergarten: $352 - $436, reading lab fees not included.

Per semester: Yes, Kindergarten $1552 - $1940, reading lab fees not included.

Annually: Yes, Kindergarten: $3041 - $3802, reading lab fees not included.

Financial assistance offered: Infrequently

Cancellation insurance: No

Sibling discount: Yes, 5%

Application acceptance deposit required: Yes, $50

Other: Short visit required.

SERVICES

Before school care offered: Yes, 6:30 a.m. - 8:30 a.m.

After school care offered: Yes, 3:30 p.m. - 6:30 p.m.

Transportation provided: Yes, to RISD schools.

Lunch/snack program: Sack lunch program. Natural snacks provided.

Other: Extracurricular classes: dance, gymnastics, Musikgarten, Spanish, art.

DALLAS MONTESSORI ACADEMY

5757 Samuell Blvd.
Dallas, TX 75228
Contact: James & Dina Paulik, President and Director
(214) 388-0091
(214) 388-3415 FAX

Office Hours: 8:00 a.m. - 5:00 p.m.
E-MAIL: N/A
Web Site: N/A
MAPSCO: 48F

PHILOSOPHY OF SCHOOL

The Dallas Montessori Academy educates children from preschool through eighth grade. We adhere to the psychology, philosophy, and pedagogy of Dr. Maria Montessori. The goal of Montessori education is to assist the child in the positive development of a flexible personality. We prepare children to meet tomorrow's challenges in a culturally diverse global society.

CREDENTIALS

Accreditations: (see glossary) AMS
Awards and special recognition: (see glossary) N/A
Qualification of administrator: AMS Certification; M.Ed.
Qualification of faculty: College degree; AMS certification

GENERAL

Alternative: No
College preparatory: No
Montessori: Yes
Nondenominational: No
Church affiliated: No
Denomination: N/A
Jewish: N/A
Other denominations: N/A
Student type: Co-ed
Grade category (for details see specific grades offered below): N/A
Infants: N/A
Preschool: Half Day
Kindergarten: Full Day
Primary / Transition: No
Elementary: Yes

Secondary or Middle School: N/A
Specific grades offered: Pre-primary (ages 3-6) - Grade 8
Student teacher ratio average: Pre-primary 12:1, elementary 15:1
Classes offered per grade: N/A
Average class size: Pre-primary = 24, elementary = 21
Total enrollment: 150
Recommended grades to apply: N/A
School hours: 8:30 a.m. - 3:00 p.m.
Calendar school year: August-May and summer school
Uniforms required: Yes
Parental involvement opportunities and requirements: Parents' Support Group, room parents and scouts
Average SAT scores: N/A
Visitation procedures: N/A
Personal appointments for touring the facility: Individual interview
Group tour dates: N/A
Open house dates: N/A
Classroom visits: N/A
Profit or non-profit: Profit

ADMISSIONS

Application form required: Yes
Forms required: Previous school reports
Application deadline: N/A
Application fee: $75 application fee
Contact: James or Dina Paulik
Phone: (214) 388-0091
Student interview required: No
Parent interview required: No
Entrance test required: No
Specific tests administered: N/A
Accept test scores from other schools: No
Testing fee: N/A
Time of year testing is administered: N/A
Test dates offered: N/A
Out of state applicants: N/A
Notification by phone: N/A
Notification by mail: N/A
Other: Conference with parent and child.

FINANCIAL

Preschool tuition: N/A
Elementary tuition: $3755 - $5100
Secondary tuition: N/A
Other tuition: Book/supply fee $200 per semester, uniforms
Cash discounts: N/A
Personal check: N/A
Automatic bank draw: N/A
Credit cards: N/A
Monthly: Yes, 10 monthly payments.
Per semester: N/A
Annually: Yes
Financial assistance offered: N/A
Cancellation insurance: N/A
Sibling discount: Yes
Application acceptance deposit required: N/A

SERVICES

Before school care offered: Yes, 7:00 a.m. - 8:30 a.m.
After school care offered: Yes, 3:00 p.m. - 6:00 p.m.
Transportation provided: N/A
Lunch/snack program: School provides snack, Signature-Services lunches at $40/month
Other: Private lessons in piano and violin; private art lessons, fieldtrips

HIGHLAND MEADOW MONTESSORI ACADEMY

1060 Highland Street
Southlake, TX 76092
Contact: Pat McCormick
(817) 488-2138

Office Hours: 8:30 a.m. - 3:00 p.m.
Mon. - Fri.
E-MAIL: N/A
Web Site: N/A
MAPSCO: N/A

PHILOSOPHY OF SCHOOL

Montessori

CREDENTIALS

Accreditations: (see glossary) AMS
Awards and special recognition: (see glossary) N/A
Qualification of administrator: Business degree, Montessori certification
Qualification of faculty: College degree, Montessori certification

GENERAL

Alternative: No
College preparatory: No
Montessori: Yes
Nondenominational: No
Church affiliated: No
Denomination: N/A
Jewish: N/A
Other denominations: N/A
Student type: Co-ed
Grade category (for details see specific grades offered below): Elementary
Infants: N/A
Preschool: Yes
Kindergarten: Yes
Primary / Transition: N/A
Elementary: Yes
Secondary or Middle School: N/A
Specific grades offered: 2 years - 6th grade
Student teacher ratio average: 10 or 11:1

Classes offered per grade: N/A
Average class size: 18
Total enrollment: 110
Recommended grades to apply: N/A
School hours: 8:30 a.m. - 3:00 p.m. (class); extended care (7:30 a.m. - 6:30 p.m.)
Calendar school year: August - May
Uniforms required: Yes
Parental involvement opportunities and requirements: N/A
Average SAT scores: N/A
Visitation procedures: N/A
Personal appointments for touring the facility: Yes, many volunteer programs.
Group tour dates: N/A
Open house dates: N/A
Classroom visits: N/A
Profit or non-profit: Non-profit

ADMISSIONS

Application form required: Yes
Forms required: Immunization
Application deadline: Year round
Application fee: New student registration fee $150.
Contact: Pat McCormick
Phone: (817) 488-2138
Student interview required: N/A
Parent interview required: N/A
Entrance test required: N/A
Specific tests administered: N/A
Accept test scores from other schools: N/A
Testing fee: N/A
Time of year testing is administered: N/A
Test dates offered: N/A
Out of state applicants: N/A
Notification by phone: N/A
Notification by mail: Yes

FINANCIAL

Preschool tuition: Range $3600 - $4800
Elementary tuition: Range $2300 - $5000
Secondary tuition: N/A
Other tuition: N/A
Cash discounts: N/A

Personal check: N/A
Automatic bank draw: N/A
Credit cards: N/A
Monthly: Yes, 12 month plan.
Per semester: N/A
Annually: Yes
Financial assistance offered: No
Cancellation insurance: No
Sibling discount: No
Application acceptance deposit required: $25

SERVICES

Before school care offered: Yes, 7:30 a.m. - 8:30 a.m.
After school care offered: Yes, 3:15 p.m. - 6:30 p.m.
Transportation provided: No
Lunch/snack program: Snacks provided

MEADOWBROOK SCHOOL

5414 Northwest Highway
Dallas, TX 75220
Contact: **Sharon L. Goldberg**
(214) 369-4981
(214) 363-4981 FAX

Office Hours: 9:00 a.m. - 3:00 p.m.
E-MAIL: N/A
Web Site: N/A
MAPSCO: 24Y

PHILOSOPHY OF SCHOOL

Meadowbrook is an academic facility modeled after the English traditional school using Montessori materials. It is dedicated to giving children a firm academic foundation with a special focus on the three R's. It is an individualized program that works on self-esteem and a meaningful relationship among child, teacher, and parent. It offers children a choice within a controlled environment.

CREDENTIALS

Accreditations: (see glossary) Academic
Awards and special recognition: (see glossary) N/A
Qualification of administrator: B.S and master's degrees
Qualification of faculty: College degree, certification, trained by Meadowbrook, Montessori
Other: Texas Department of Human Services

GENERAL

Alternative: No
College preparatory: No
Montessori: No
Nondenominational: No
Church affiliated: No
Denomination: N/A
Jewish: N/A
Other denominations: N/A
Student type: Co-ed
Grade category (for details see specific grades offered below): N/A
Infants: N/A
Preschool: Half Day
Kindergarten: Half Day
Primary / Transition: No
Elementary: N/A

Secondary or Middle School: N/A

Specific grades offered: 3 years - Kindergarten

Student teacher ratio average: 9:1

Classes offered per grade: 2 classes per grade

Average class size: Maximum 19 students per class

Total enrollment: 110

Recommended grades to apply: N/A

School hours: 9:00 a.m. - 11:45 a.m.; 12:15 p.m. - 3:00 p.m.

Calendar school year: Day after Labor Day - end of May

Uniforms required: No

Parental involvement opportunities and requirements: Parent's Club, encouraged to participate

Average SAT scores: N/A

Visitation procedures: N/A

Personal appointments for touring the facility: N/A

Group tour dates: Small group orientation for prospective Meadowbrook parents twice a month

Open house dates: N/A

Classroom visits: Within group orientaion

Profit or non-profit: Profit

Other: Privately owned by Trish M. Fusch.

ADMISSIONS

Application form required: Yes

Forms required: Registration form, medical emergency form, health

Application deadline: Any time during school year

Application fee: $500 due 2/1 to reserve class space

Contact: Sharon Goldberg, Diane Eyles

Phone: (214) 369-4981

Student interview required: No

Parent interview required: No

Entrance test required: No

Specific tests administered: Admission tests for 2nd and 3rd year program

Accept test scores from other schools: No

Testing fee: N/A

Time of year testing is administered: N/A

Test dates offered: N/A

Out of state applicants: N/A

Notification by phone: Yes

Notification by mail: Yes, registration form mailed

FINANCIAL

Preschool tuition: $3850

Elementary tuition: $4050 - half day Kindergarten

Secondary tuition: N/A

Other tuition: Tuition due April 1

Cash discounts: N/A

Personal check: Yes

Automatic bank draw: N/A

Credit cards: N/A

Monthly: N/A

Per semester: N/A

Annually: Yes

Financial assistance offered: N/A

Cancellation insurance: N/A

Sibling discount: N/A

Application acceptance deposit required: YES, $500

SERVICES

Before school care offered: N/A

After school care offered: N/A

Transportation provided: N/A

Lunch/snack program: Room mothers provide snack lists.

Other: Simply Science after-school science program offered every 8 weeks from 3:00 p.m. - 4:30 p.m. Instructors are Diane Eyles and Lesley Armstrong.

MONTESSORI CHILDREN'S HOUSE AND SCHOOL

7335 Abrams Road
Dallas, TX   75231
Contact: Kristina Geiser Wood
(214) 348-6276
(214) 348-6628 FAX

Office Hours: 8:00 a.m. - 3:00 p.m.
E-MAIL: N/A
Web Site: N/A
MAPSCO: 27N

PHILOSOPHY OF SCHOOL

Montessori Children's House and School's enrollment is limited to 3-6 year old children because this 3 year period represents such a crucial stage in a child's social, academic and emotional development. Combining children of this age span in one classroom with the same peers and teacher during the three year program creates a stable educational community, allows younger children to be motivated by observing older children at work on progressively more complex and abstract lessons, and fosters older children's confidence and self-esteem through their role in the classroom as models. The Montessori classroom environment incorporates a wide array of academic concrete manipulatives with a multi-sensory approach to learning. The foundation of the Montessori learning philosophy is the recognition of and respect for children's individuality, which dictates that each child is encouraged to pursue active, self-motivated exploration of the materials, making their own choices, following their innate interests, and proceeding at their own pace. The Montessori classroom imbues each child with self-dependence and confidence and creates an enthusiastic lifelong learner, all characteristics which help the child excel in any environment they encounter throughout life, whether social, academic or professional.

CREDENTIALS

Accreditations: (see glossary) AMI, Montessori
Awards and special recognition: (see glossary) N/A
Qualification of administrator: B.A. 1976; J.D. 1980
Qualification of faculty: AMI certified teaching staff

GENERAL

Alternative: No
College preparatory: No
Montessori: Yes

Nondenominational: Yes
Church affiliated: No
Denomination: N/A
Jewish: N/A
Other denominations: N/A
Student type: Co-ed
Grade category (for details see specific grades offered below): Preschool/ Kindergarten
Infants: N/A
Preschool: Half Day
Kindergarten: Full Day
Primary / Transition: No
Elementary: N/A
Secondary: N/A
Specific grades offered: Preschool & Kindergarten
Other: 3-4 1/2 year old children are in the Montessori classroom from 8:15 a.m. - 11:20 a.m. 4 1/2 - 6 year old children are in the Montessori classroom from 8:15 a.m. - 2:20 p.m. The school also offers before & after class care from 7:30 a.m. - 8:15 a.m. & from 11:30 a.m. - 6:00 p.m.
Teacher student ratio average: 12.5:1 or 25:2
Classes offered per grade: After school classes in Spanish and gymnastics
Average class size: 25
Total enrollment: 75
Recommended grades to apply: At age 2-2 1/2
School hours: 7:30 a.m. - 6:00 p.m.
Calendar school year: August - May, a summer program is also available
Uniforms required: No
Parental involvement opportunities and requirements: Parent's Club is a social and fund-raising group. Classroom parents meet with teacher to address particular teacher/classroom needs.
Average SAT scores: N/A
Visitation procedures: Available daily, please call in advance.
Personal appointments for touring the facility: Daily, with administrator. Please call to schedule an appointment.
Group tour dates: N/A
Open house dates: N/A
Classroom visits: 9:00 a.m. - 9:30 a.m daily after November 1 Appointments are necessary.
Profit or non-profit: Non-profit

ADMISSIONS

Application form required: Yes

Forms required: One application form with general information and child's information

Application deadline: January, for following school year

Application fee: None

Contact: Kristina Geiser Wood

Phone: (214) 348-6276

Student interview required: No

Parent interview required: Yes

Entrance test required: No

Specific tests administered: N/A

Accept test scores from other schools: No

Testing fee: N/A

Time of year testing is administered: N/A

Test dates offered: N/A

Out of state applicants: N/A

Notification by phone: N/A

Notification by mail: Yes

FINANCIAL

Preschool tuition: $365 per month or $1,550 per semester for morning students (8:15 a.m. - 11:30 a.m. for 3-4 1/2 years old, approximately)

Elementary tuition: $542 per month or $2,300 per semester for extended day students (8:15 a.m. - 2:30 p.m. for 4 1/2-6 years old, approximately)

Secondary tuition: N/A

Other tuition: Yes, amount depends on extent of before or after school care elected.

Cash discounts: N/A

Personal check: Yes

Automatic bank draw: No

Credit cards: No

Monthly: Yes

Per semester: Yes

Annually: Yes

Financial assistance offered: Up to one-half of Montessori tuition is available. Apply in December for following year.

Cancellation insurance: No

Sibling discount: No

Application acceptance deposit required: Yes, $250

SERVICES

Before school care offered: 7:30 a.m. - 8:15 a.m.

After school care offered: 11:30 a.m. - 2:30 p.m. or 11:30 a.m. - 6:00 p.m.
for morning students; 2:30 p.m. - 6:00 p.m. for extended day students. Cost
ranges from $65 - $305 per month and depends on the amount of time needed.

Transportation provided: No

Lunch/snack program: Children bring their own lunches. The school does
provide a snack in the morning for all students, and in the afternoon for after-
school care children.

MONTESSORI SCHOOL OF LAS COLINAS

4961 N. O'Connor Road
Irving, TX 75062
Contact: Jo Harris, Director
(972) 717-0417
(972) 717-6737 FAX

Office Hours: 8:00 a.m. - 6:00 p.m.
E-MAIL: N/A
Web Site: www.montessori.com
MAPSCO: N/A

PHILOSOPHY OF SCHOOL

To see the child as a "total being" with equal importance to the physical, mental and spriritual nature of the child. We follow the philosophy of Maria Montessori and remain guides to the child who "light the pathway as the child determines the direction."

CREDENTIALS

Accreditations: (see glossary) MACTE
Awards and special recognition: (see glossary) N/A
Qualification of administrator: 20 years experience in directing and teaching
Qualification of faculty: Certified Montessorians, interns

GENERAL

Alternative: No
College preparatory: No
Montessori: Yes
Nondenominational: No
Church affiliated: No
Denomination: N/A
Jewish: N/A
Other denominations: N/A
Student type: Co-ed
Grade category (for details see specific grades offered below): Preschool
Infants: Yes
Preschool: Yes
Kindergarten: Yes
Primary / Transition: N/A
Elementary: N/A
Secondary or Middle School: N/A

Specific grades offered: 6 weeks - 6 years old

Student teacher ratio average: Depends on age level

Classes offered per grade: N/A

Average class size: 1 - 12 months: 1-4; 12 - 18 months: 1-5; 18 months - 2 years old: 1-7; 2 - 3 years old: 1-8; 3 - 6 years old: 1-13

Total enrollment: 140 when full

Recommended grades to apply: N/A

School hours: 6:30 a.m. - 6:30 p.m.

Calendar school year: All year school

Uniforms required: No

Parental involvement opportunities and requirements: Parent education nights, luncheons and festivals

Average SAT scores: N/A

Visitation procedures: N/A

Personal appointments for touring the facility: Please call

Group tour dates: N/A

Open house dates: Please call

Classroom visits: N/A

Profit or non-profit: Profit

ADMISSIONS

Application form required: Yes

Forms required: Yes

Application deadline: Open enrollment, as space available

Application fee: $100 registration fee first year/ $50 registration fee subsequent years

Contact: Jo Harris

Phone: (214) 717-0417

Student interview required: N/A

Parent interview required: Yes

Entrance test required: N/A

Specific tests administered: N/A

Accept test scores from other schools: N/A

Testing fee: N/A

Time of year testing is administered: N/A

Test dates offered: N/A

Out of state applicants: N/A

Notification by phone: Yes

Notification by mail: Yes

FINANCIAL

Preschool tuition: Determined by programs enrolled in
Elementary tuition: N/A
Secondary tuition: N/A
Other tuition: N/A
Cash discounts: N/A
Personal check: Yes
Automatic bank draw: N/A
Credit cards: N/A
Monthly: Yes
Per semester: N/A
Annually: N/A
Financial assistance offered: No
Cancellation insurance: No
Sibling discount: N/A
Application acceptance deposit required: N/A

SERVICES

Before school care offered: Yes
After school care offered: Yes
Transportation provided: No
Lunch/snack program: Snacks and lunch provided by school.

MONTESSORI SCHOOL OF NORTH DALLAS

18303 Davenport
Dallas, TX 75252
Contact: **Reena Khandpur, Director**
(972) 985-8844
(972) 673-0118 FAX

Office Hours: 7:00 a.m. - 6:00 p.m.
E-MAIL: info@montessorischool.com
Web Site: www.montessorischool.com
MAPSCO: 5G

PHILOSOPHY OF SCHOOL

The main purpose in establishing the Montessori School of North Dallas is to provide a carefully planned, stimulating environment which will help our children develop within themselves an excellent foundation for creative learning. Each child is guided individually in each subject according to his/her own individual requirements.

CREDENTIALS

Accreditations: (see glossary) Montessori
Awards and special recognition: (see glossary) N/A
Qualification of administrator: Master's degree and Montessori certification
Qualification of faculty: Montessori certification
Other: AMS Affiliated

GENERAL

Alternative: No
College preparatory: No
Montessori: Yes
Nondenominational: Yes
Church affiliated: No
Denomination: N/A
Jewish: N/A
Other denominations: N/A
Student type: Co-ed
Grade category (for details see specific grades offered below): Preschool - 1st
Infants: N/A
Preschool: Full Day
Kindergarten: Full Day
Primary / Transition: Yes

Elementary: Yes
Secondary or Middle School: N/A
Specific grades offered: Preschool - Grade 1
Student teacher ratio average: Toddlers 14-16:2, primary & elementary 24-26:2
Classes offered per grade: N/A
Average class size: Toddlers 14-16, primary & elementary 24-26
Total enrollment: 210
Recommended grades to apply: N/A
School hours: 7:00 a.m. - 6:00 p.m.
Calendar school year: August - May
Uniforms required: No
Parental involvement opportunities and requirements: Yes
Average SAT scores: N/A
Visitation procedures: By appointment
Personal appointments for touring the facility: Individual appointments offered
Group tour dates: N/A
Open house dates: N/A
Classroom visits: N/A
Profit or non-profit: Profit

ADMISSIONS

Application form required: Yes
Forms required: Registration, medical, emergency
Application deadline: Open application
Application fee: Registration & supply fee
Contact: Reena Khandpur
Phone: (972) 985-8844
Student interview required: No
Parent interview required: No
Entrance test required: Yes
Specific tests administered: N/A
Accept test scores from other schools: No
Testing fee: N/A
Time of year testing is administered: Anytime prior to enrollment
Test dates offered: N/A
Out of state applicants: N/A
Notification by phone: N/A
Notification by mail: N/A
Other: Personal contact

FINANCIAL

Preschool tuition: Depends on program selected
Elementary tuition: Depends on program selected
Secondary tuition: N/A
Other tuition: N/A
Cash discounts: N/A
Personal check: Yes
Automatic bank draw: N/A
Credit cards: N/A
Monthly: Yes
Per semester: Yes
Annually: Yes
Financial assistance offered: No
Cancellation insurance: N/A
Sibling discount: N/A
Application acceptance deposit required: N/A

SERVICES

Before school care offered: Yes, 7:00 a.m. - 8:30 a.m.
After school care offered: Yes, 3:00 p.m. - 6:00 p.m.
Transportation provided: N/A
Lunch/snack program: Morning and afternoon snacks provided
Other: Computer classes offered to all students ages 4 and above. Excellent selection of books, cassettes and computer software available at on-site computer room and library. Spanish classes offered to all student ages 3 and above.

MONTESSORI SCHOOL OF WESTCHESTER

290 E. Westchester Parkway
Grand Prairie, TX 75052
Contact: Amy Rose
(972) 262-1053
(972) 262-4123 FAX

Office Hours: Mon. - Fri.
9:00 a.m. - 5:00 p.m.
E-MAIL: N/A
Web Site: www.montessoriunlimited.com
MAPSCO: 61Q

PHILOSOPHY OF SCHOOL

A Montessori environment dedicated to parent child relationship and growth of total child.

CREDENTIALS

Accreditations: (see glossary) Texas Department of Human Services, MEPI Internship School
Awards and special recognition: (see glossary) N/A
Qualification of administrator: Montessori certified, early childhood
Qualification of faculty: College degree and Montessori certification

GENERAL

Alternative: No
College preparatory: No
Montessori: Yes
Nondenominational: No
Church affiliated: No
Denomination: N/A
Jewish: N/A
Other denominations: N/A
Student type: Co-ed
Grade category (for details see specific grades offered below): Preschool
Infants: N/A
Preschool: Yes
Kindergarten: Yes
Primary / Transition: N/A
Elementary: N/A
Secondary or Middle School: N/A

Specific grades offered: Preschool and Kindergarten
Student teacher ratio average: N/A
Classes offered per grade: N/A
Average class size: N/A
Total enrollment: N/A
Recommended grades to apply: N/A
School hours: 6:30 a.m. - 6:30 p.m.
Calendar school year: N/A
Uniforms required: N/A
Parental involvement opportunities and requirements: Yes
Average SAT scores: N/A
Visitation procedures: N/A
Personal appointments for touring the facility: N/A
Group tour dates: N/A
Open house dates: Offered annually
Classroom visits: N/A
Profit or non-profit: Profit
Other: Parent education seminars offered annually.

ADMISSIONS

Application form required: Yes
Forms required: City, state and school forms
Application deadline: Open enrollment based upon availability
Application fee: Registration fee $100
Contact: Amy Rose
Phone: (972) 262-1053
Student interview required: N/A
Parent interview required: N/A
Entrance test required: N/A
Specific tests administered: N/A
Accept test scores from other schools: N/A
Testing fee: N/A
Time of year testing is administered: N/A
Test dates offered: N/A
Out of state applicants: N/A
Notification by phone: Yes, or in person
Notification by mail: N/A

FINANCIAL

Preschool tuition: $6900 Toddlers (18 months - 3 years); $4860 Morning class;
 $5220 Extended day class; $6360 Full day program
Elementary tuition: N/A
Secondary tuition: N/A
Other tuition: N/A
Cash discounts: N/A
Personal check: Yes
Automatic bank draw: N/A
Credit cards: N/A
Monthly: N/A
Per semester: N/A
Annually: N/A
Financial assistance offered: None
Cancellation insurance: N/A
Sibling discount: N/A
Application acceptance deposit required: N/A

SERVICES

Before school care offered: Yes
After school care offered: Yes
Transportation provided: No
Lunch/snack program: Lunch fee included in tuition. Lunch and snack served
 family style.
Other: Extracurricular activity optional. Fully equipped classrooms; all
 Montessori materials are available.

PRESTON MEADOWS MONTESSORI SCHOOL

6912 Ohio Drive
Plano, TX   75024
Contact: Sheila Sherwood
(972) 596-7094
(972) 596-8665 FAX

Office Hours: 8:00 a.m. - 5:00 p.m.
E-MAIL: N/A
Web Site: N/A
MAPSCO: N/A

PHILOSOPHY OF SCHOOL

We believe that every child is an individual learner, who should be encouraged to work at their own pace on projects they initiate. Children learn better when they are given the opportunity to choose and discover in their own way.

CREDENTIALS

Accreditations: (see glossary) MEPI
Awards and special recognition: (see glossary) N/A
Qualification of administrator: Certified Montessori degreed professional
Qualification of faculty: Certified Montessori teachers

GENERAL

Alternative: No
College preparatory: No
Montessori: Yes
Nondenominational: No
Church affiliated: No
Denomination: N/A
Jewish: N/A
Other denominations: N/A
Student type: Co-ed
Grade category (for details see specific grades offered below): Preschool
Infants: N/A
Preschool: Yes
Kindergarten: Yes
Primary / Transition: N/A
Elementary: N/A
Secondary or Middle School: N/A
Specific grades offered: Preschool - Kindergarten

Student teacher ratio average: 13:1
Classes offered per grade: N/A
Average class size: 25
Total enrollment: N/A
Recommended grades to apply: One year before child is 3 years.
School hours: 6:30 a.m. - 6:30 p.m.
Calendar school year: August - May
Uniforms required: No
Parental involvement opportunities and requirements: Volunteering
Average SAT scores: N/A
Visitation procedures: N/A
Personal appointments for touring the facility: N/A
Group tour dates: N/A
Open house dates: N/A
Classroom visits: N/A
Profit or non-profit: Profit

ADMISSIONS

Application form required: Yes
Forms required: Enrollment application
Application deadline: N/A
Application fee: Yes
Contact: Sheila Sherwood
Phone: (972) 569-7094
Student interview required: N/A
Parent interview required: N/A
Entrance test required: N/A
Specific tests administered: N/A
Accept test scores from other schools: N/A
Testing fee: N/A
Time of year testing is administered: N/A
Test dates offered: N/A
Out of state applicants: N/A
Notification by phone: N/A
Notification by mail: N/A

FINANCIAL

Preschool tuition: Full $585; 3/4 $460; 1/2 $410
Elementary tuition: N/A
Secondary tuition: N/A
Other tuition: N/A

Cash discounts: N/A
Personal check: Yes
Automatic bank draw: N/A
Credit cards: N/A
Monthly: N/A
Per semester: N/A
Annually: N/A
Financial assistance offered: N/A
Cancellation insurance: N/A
Sibling discount: N/A
Application acceptance deposit required: N/A
Other: N/A

SERVICES

Before school care offered: N/A
After school care offered: N/A
Transportation provided: No
Lunch/snack program: Morning and afternoon snack offered.
Other: Counseling and evaluation available annually.

REDEEMER MONTESSORI SCHOOL

120 E. Rochelle
Irving, TX 75062
Contact: Susan Story, Director
(972) 257-3517
(972) 255-4173 FAX

Office Hours: 8:00 a.m. - 4:00 p.m.
E-MAIL: N/A
Web Site: N/A
MAPSCO: 31B-G

PHILOSOPHY OF SCHOOL

Redeemer Montessori School is dedicated to giving children the opportunity to develop to the fullest of their potential so that they experience the joy and success of learning, enabling them to create a framework for a lifetime of cognitive and effective development.

CREDENTIALS

Accreditations: (see glossary) AMS
Awards and special recognition: (see glossary) N/A
Qualification of administrator: Degreed
Qualification of faculty: Lead teachers; Montessori certification

GENERAL

Alternative: No
College preparatory: No
Montessori: Yes
Nondenominational: Yes
Church affiliated: No
Denomination: N/A
Jewish: N/A
Other denominations: N/A
Student type: Co-ed
Grade category (for details see specific grades offered below): Elementary
Infants: N/A
Preschool: Half Day and Full Day
Kindergarten: Full Day
Primary / Transition: Yes
Elementary: Yes
Secondary or Middle School: N/A

Specific grades offered: 2 1/2 years - grade 5
Student teacher ratio average: 3-6 years 22:2; elementary 24:2
Classes offered per grade: N/A
Average class size: 3-6 years 22; elementary 20-24
Total enrollment: 120
Recommended grades to apply: N/A
School hours: 7:30 a.m. - 6:00 p.m.
Calendar school year: August - May
Uniforms required: No
Parental involvement opportunities and requirements: Volunteer Parents
Average SAT scores: N/A
Visitation procedures: Contact office
Personal appointments for touring the facility: Call school for appointment
Group tour dates: Call school for appointment
Open house dates: N/A
Classroom visits: Contact office
Profit or non-profit: Non-profit

ADMISSIONS

Application form required: Yes
Forms required: Application, health forms, emergency forms
Application deadline: Re-enrollment in March for fall
Application fee: $175; ($100 continuing student)
Contact: Susan Story
Phone: (972) 257-3517
Student interview required: No
Parent interview required: No
Entrance test required: No
Specific tests administered: N/A
Accept test scores from other schools: N/A
Testing fee: N/A
Time of year testing is administered: N/A
Test dates offered: N/A
Out of state applicants: N/A
Notification by phone: N/A
Notification by mail: N/A

FINANCIAL

Preschool tuition: $3450 (half day); $4400 (full day)
Elementary tuition: $4600
Secondary tuition: N/A

Other tuition: N/A
Cash discounts: N/A
Personal check: N/A
Automatic bank draw: N/A
Credit cards: N/A
Monthly: Yes
Per semester: Yes
Annually: Yes
Financial assistance offered: Limited
Cancellation insurance: N/A
Sibling discount: Yes, 10%
Application acceptance deposit required: N/A

SERVICES

Before school care offered: Yes, 7:30 a.m. - 8:30 a.m.
After school care offered: Yes, 3:00 p.m. - 6:00 p.m.
Transportation provided: N/A
Lunch/snack program: Snacks given in mid-morning for pre-primary, after-school care.
Other: Spanish, physical education, music, art offered.

ST. ALCUIN MONTESSORI

6144 Churchill Way
Dallas, TX 75230
Office Hours: 7:30 a.m. - 5:00 p.m.
E-MAIL: peg@saintalcuin.org
Contact: **Peggy Larson, Director of Admission**
(972) 239-1745
(972) 934-8727 FAX
Web Site: www.saintalcuin.org
MAPSCO: 15U

PHILOSOPHY OF SCHOOL

A Montessori education allows each child to follow his or her own curiosity and supports a natural desire for and enjoyment of learning. Children within a three-year age span are purposefully grouped to foster a sense of community and to serve as models for one another. Each child is allowed to develop to the fullest of his or her own potential, often exceeding the bounds associated with traditional methods of education. The St. Alcuin student has the opportunity to achieve a deep understanding of all academic basics and other subjects in an interrelated manner. He or she develops a love for learning, a self-assurance, and self-motivation which serve as a preparation not only for secondary and higher education, but also for all of life.

CREDENTIALS

Accreditations: (see glossary) AMI, ISAS
Awards and special recognition: (see glossary) N/A
Qualification of administrator: M.Ed., Association Montessori Internationale certification
Qualification of faculty: College, Association Montessori Internationale certification

GENERAL

Alternative: No
College preparatory: No
Montessori: Yes
Nondenominational: Yes
Church affiliated: No
Denomination: N/A
Jewish: N/A
Other denominations: N/A
Student type: Co-ed
Grade category (for details see specific grades offered below): Preschool - 8th

Infants: Yes
Preschool: Full Day
Kindergarten: Full Day
Primary / Transition: No
Elementary: Yes
Secondary or Middle School: Yes
Specific grades offered: 18 months - 14 years (grade 8)
Student Teacher ratio average: 13:1
Classes offered per grade: N/A
Average class size: 26
Total enrollment: 515
Recommended grades to apply: N/A
School hours: 8:15 a.m. - 3:15 p.m.
Calendar school year: End of August - end of May
Uniforms required: No
Parental involvement opportunities and requirements: Active parents' club
Average SAT scores: N/A
Visitation procedures: N/A
Personal appointments for touring the facility: Individual interview
Group tour dates: Group orientation on Wednesday mornings.
Open house dates: N/A
Classroom visits: N/A
Profit or non-profit: Non-profit

ADMISSIONS

Application form required: Yes
Forms required: Previous school reports
Application deadline: Ongoing enrollment; decisions made early spring
Application fee: $50
Contact: Admission Office, Peggy Larson
Phone: (972) 239-1745
Student interview required: Yes
Parent interview required: Yes
Entrance test required: No
Specific tests administered: N/A
Accept test scores from other schools: No
Testing fee: N/A
Time of year testing is administered: N/A
Test dates offered: N/A
Out of state applicants: N/A
Notification by phone: N/A

Notification by mail: Yes; majority of acceptance letters in March and April; others as space becomes available

FINANCIAL

Preschool tuition: $4500 (toddlers) - $6900 (primary)
Elementary tuition: $7625 - $7839
Secondary tuition: $9930 (middle school)
Other tuition: N/A
Cash discounts: N/A
Personal check: N/A
Automatic bank draw: N/A
Credit cards: N/A
Monthly: Yes, 9 payments with 10% interest
Per semester: N/A
Annually: N/A
Financial assistance offered: Yes
Cancellation insurance: Yes
Sibling discount: N/A
Application acceptance deposit required: N/A

SERVICES

Before school care offered: Yes, begins at 7:00 a.m.
After school care offered: Yes, until 6:00 p.m.
Transportation provided: N/A
Lunch/snack program: Snacks: Parents provide one week per year for preschool.
Other: Computer lab, library, enrichment curriculum and extracurricular activities offered.

ST. CHRISTOPHER MONTESSORI

7900 Lovers Lane
Dallas, TX 75225
Contact: **Bettye or Becky Meyerson**
(214) 363-9391
(214) 363-2795 FAX

Office Hours: 7:30 a.m. - 6:00 p.m. M-F
E-MAIL: N/A
Web Site: N/A
MAPSCO: N/A

PHILOSOPHY OF SCHOOL

St. Christopher Montessori School is in harmony with the philosophy and teachings of Dr. Montessori. Our goal is to provide an environment that is rich with materials and the opportunity to explore learning as a journey. The child explores their environment through lessons designed to guide the child into the learning process. This fosters positive self-esteem, self-discipline, creativity, and independence. These attributes all combine to build a life long love of learning.

CREDENTIALS

Accreditations: (see glossary) AMS
Awards and special recognition: (see glossary) N/A
Qualification of administrator: Degreed. AMS, MACTE
Qualification of faculty: Degreed, AMS, MACTE

GENERAL

Alternative: No
College preparatory: No
Montessori: Yes
Nondenominational: Yes
Church affiliated: No
Denomination: N/A
Jewish: N/A
Other denominations: N/A
Student type: Co-ed
Grade category (for details see specific grades offered below): Elementary
Infants: No
Preschool: Half Day & Full Day
Kindergarten: Half Day & Full Day
Primary / Transition: Yes

Elementary: Yes
Secondary or Middle School: No
Specific grades offered: Preschool - 3rd Grade
Student teacher ratio average: 2 yr. class 5:1, 3-5 yr. class 10:1
Classes offered per grade: N/A
Average class size: N/A
Total enrollment: N/A
Recommended grades to apply: N/A
School hours: 7:30 a.m. - 6:00 p.m.
Calendar school year: September - May + Summer Program
Uniforms required: Yes, elementary level only.
Parental involvement opportunities and requirements: Parents are encouraged to participate in their child's school experience. Call the office to inquire about opportunities to lend your special talents.
Average SAT scores: N/A
Visitation procedures: Call office to reserve time for observations.
Personal appointments for touring the facility: Call office to set-up an appointment to tour the facility.
Group tour dates: As requested.
Open house dates: N/A
Classroom visits: As requested
Profit or non-profit: Non-profit

ADMISSIONS

Application form required: Yes
Forms required: Parents will receive information packet upon request.
Application deadline: N/A
Application fee: N/A
Contact: Bettye or Becky Meyerson
Phone: (214) 363-9391
Student interview required: Yes
Parent interview required: Yes
Entrance test required: Yes, Elementary level only.
Specific tests administered: N/A
Accept test scores from other schools: Yes
Testing fee: N/A
Time of year testing is administered: N/A
Test dates offered: N/A
Out of state applicants: N/A
Notification by phone: Yes
Notification by mail: Yes

FINANCIAL

Preschool tuition: Upon request

Elementary tuition: Upon request

Secondary tuition: N/A

Other tuition: Depending on class requested $ 250.00 - $ 375.00 per month. Additional charge for before/after school care.

Cash discounts: No

Personal check: Yes

Automatic bank draw: No

Credit cards: No

Monthly: Yes

Per semester: Yes

Annually: Yes

Financial assistance offered: N/A

Cancellation insurance: No

Sibling discount: Yes, 10% off sibling's monthly tuition.

Application acceptance deposit required: Yes

SERVICES

Before school care offered: Yes, 7:30 a.m. - 9:00 a.m.

After school care offered: Yes, 12:00 p.m./3:30 p.m. - 6:00 p.m.

Transportation provided: No

Lunch/snack program: Snacks will be provided by the school. Children bring their own lunches.

ST. JAMES EPISCOPAL MONTESSORI

9845 McCree
Dallas, TX 75238
Contact: **Lisa Wilson, Adm. Assistant**
(214) 348-1349
(214) 348-1368 FAX

Office Hours: 7:30 a.m. - 3:30 p.m.
E-MAIL: N/A
Web Site: N/A
MAPSCO: 27U

PHILOSOPHY OF SCHOOL

To offer a high quality Montessori education from an Episcopal perspective. The goal of the school is to develop the mind, body, and spirit of each individual to the fullest capacity. To achieve this goal, a well qualified faculty is dedicated to using the Montessori method to nurture children and their academic and spiritual abilities.

CREDENTIALS

Accreditations: (see glossary) Montessori, NAIS, SAES, TEPSAC
Awards and special recognition: (see glossary) N/A
Qualification of administrator: B.S. Ed UNT, Certified Teacher
Qualification of faculty: Primary-Association Montessori International (AMI) certification; elementary - AMS certification and college degree
Other: Affiliated with Association Montessori International, National Association of Episcopal Schools (NAES), Southwest Association of Episcopal Schools (SAES), Licensed by Texas Dept. of Protective and Regulatory Services

GENERAL

Alternative: No
College preparatory: No
Montessori: Yes
Nondenominational: No
Church affiliated: Yes
Denomination: Episcopal
Jewish: N/A
Other denominations: N/A
Student type: Co-ed
Grade category (for details see specific grades offered below): Elementary
Infants: N/A

Preschool: Full Day
Kindergarten: Full Day
Primary / Transition: No
Elementary: Yes
Secondary or Middle School: N/A
Specific grades offered: Preschool (age 2 - kindergarten); elementary (1st - 6th)
Student teacher ratio average: 5:1, 8:1; 13:1, 15:1
Classes offered per grade: N/A
Average class size: Toddler: 10, PS-K: 21; grades 1-6:15
Total enrollment: 80
Recommended grades to apply: N/A
School hours: 8:15 a.m. - 3:15 p.m.
Calendar school year: R.I.S.D. school calendar
Uniforms required: Yes
Parental involvement opportunities and requirements: Yes
Average SAT scores: N/A
Visitation procedures: N/A
Personal appointments for touring the facility: N/A
Group tour dates: Tours accompanied by principal
Open house dates: N/A
Classroom visits: N/A
Profit or non-profit: Non-profit
Other: Uniforms required for age 3 - elementary students

ADMISSIONS

Application form required: Yes
Forms required: Registration, health forms, previous school records, medical permission forms
Application deadline: March 1
Application fee: $200
Contact: Barbara Moore, Principal
Phone: (214) 348-1349
Student interview required: Yes
Parent interview required: Yes
Entrance test required: Yes
Specific tests administered: Kindergarten: IOWA Test of Basic Skills, 1st - 6th Grade: IOWA Test of Basic Skills
Accept test scores from other schools: No
Testing fee: N/A
Time of year testing is administered: Spring
Test dates offered: N/A

Out of state applicants: N/A
Notification by phone: N/A
Notification by mail: Yes
Other: Entrance test required for Elementary grade.

FINANCIAL

Preschool tuition: $2730 - $4610 annually
Elementary tuition: $4860 annually
Secondary tuition: N/A
Other tuition: N/A
Cash discounts: N/A
Personal check: Yes
Automatic bank draw: Yes
Credit cards: N/A
Monthly: Yes
Per semester: Yes
Annually: Yes
Financial assistance offered: Some scholarships are available.
Cancellation insurance: N/A
Sibling discount: Yes
Application acceptance deposit required: Yes

SERVICES

Before school care offered: Yes, 7:30 a.m. - 8:15 a.m.
After school care offered: Yes, 3:30 p.m. - 6:00 p.m.; 11:30 a.m. - 3:30 p.m. for morning students
Transportation provided: N/A
Lunch/snack program: Students bring lunches; snacks sent from home on a rotating scheduled basis.
Other: Computers, library, P.E., music, Spanish

WEST PLANO MONTESSORI SCHOOL

3425 Ashington Lane
Plano, TX 75023
Contact: **J. P. Khandpur, Director**
(972) 618-8844
(972) 398-1798 FAX

Office Hours: 7:00 a.m. - 6:00 p.m.
E-MAIL: info@montessorischool.com
Web Site: www.montessorischool.com
MAPSCO: 657C

PHILOSOPHY OF SCHOOL

The main purpose in establishing West Plano Montessori School is to provide a carefully planned, stimulating environment which will help our children develop within themselves an excellent foundation for creative learning. Each child is guided individually in each subject according to his/her own individual requirements.

CREDENTIALS

Accreditations: (see glossary) Montessori
Awards and special recognition: (see glossary) N/A
Qualification of administrator: Bachelor's or master's degree & Montessori certification
Qualification of faculty: Montessori certification
Other: AMS Affiliated

GENERAL

Alternative: No
College preparatory: No
Montessori: Yes
Nondenominational: Yes
Church affiliated: No
Denomination: N/A
Jewish: N/A
Other denominations: N/A
Student type: Co-ed
Grade category (for details see specific grades offered below): Pre-school - 1st
Infants: N/A
Preschool: Full Day
Kindergarten: Full Day

Primary / Transition: Yes
Elementary: Yes
Secondary or Middle School: N/A
Specific grades offered: Preschool - Grade 1
Student teacher ratio average: Toddler 14-16:2; Primary/Elementary 24-26:2
Classes offered per grade: N/A
Average class size: Toddlers:14-16; Primary/Elementary: 24-26
Total enrollment: 135
Recommended grades to apply: N/A
School hours: 7:00 a.m. - 6:00 p.m.
Calendar school year: August - May
Uniforms required: No
Parental involvement opportunities and requirements: Yes
Average SAT scores: N/A
Visitation procedures: By appointment
Personal appointments for touring the facility: Individual appointments offered
Group tour dates: N/A
Open house dates: N/A
Classroom visits: N/A
Profit or non-profit: Profit

ADMISSIONS

Application form required: Yes
Forms required: Registration, medical, emergency
Application deadline: Open Application
Application fee: Registration & supply fee
Contact: J.P Khandpur
Phone: (972) 618-8844
Student interview required: No
Parent interview required: No
Entrance test required: Yes
Specific tests administered: N/A
Accept test scores from other schools: No
Testing fee: N/A
Time of year testing is administered: Any time prior to enrollment
Test dates offered: N/A
Out of state applicants: N/A
Notification by phone: N/A
Notification by mail: N/A
Other: Personal contact

FINANCIAL

Preschool tuition: Depends on program selected
Elementary tuition: Depends on program selected
Secondary tuition: N/A
Other tuition: N/A
Cash discounts: N/A
Personal check: Yes
Automatic bank draw: N/A
Credit cards: N/A
Monthly: Yes
Per semester: Yes
Annually: Yes
Financial assistance offered: No
Cancellation insurance: N/A
Sibling discount: N/A
Application acceptance deposit required: N/A

SERVICES

Before school care offered: Yes, 7:00 a.m. - 8:30 a.m.
After school care offered: Yes, 3:00 p.m. - 6:00 p.m.
Transportation provided: N/A
Lunch/snack program: Morning/afternoon snacks provided
Other: Computer classes offered to all students ages 4 and above. Excellent selection of books, cassettes and computer software available at on-site computer room and library. Spanish classes offered to all students ages 3 and above.

WESTWOOD MONTESSORI SCHOOL

13618 Gamma Road
Dallas, TX 75244
Contact: **Heather Lourcey**
(972) 239-8598
(972) 239-1028 FAX

Office Hours: 8:30 a.m. - 3:30 p.m.
E-MAIL: wms1a@airmail.net
Web Site: www.Westwoodschool.com
MAPSCO: 14K

PHILOSOPHY OF SCHOOL

Westwood is best known for our ability to provide an atmosphere where academics are stressed and each student's uniqueness is cherished. The Westwood environment promotes the development of social skills, emotional growth, physical fitness, and cognitive preparation. High academic standards are achieved in an atmosphere that fosters independent thinking, personal responsibility, freedom of choice, self-esteem, love, and respect.

CREDENTIALS

Accreditations: (see glossary) AMI
Awards and special recognition: (see glossary) N/A
Qualification of administrator: College degree plus Montessori certification for all grades, college instructor
Qualification of faculty: College degree plus Montessori certification
Other: Licensed by A.M.I. Teachers of Texas

GENERAL

Alternative: No
College preparatory: No
Montessori: Yes
Nondenominational: N/A
Church affiliated: No
Denomination: N/A
Jewish: N/A
Other denominations: N/A
Student type: Co-ed
Grade category (for details see specific grades offered below): 1st - 12th
Infants: N/A

Preschool: Half Day and Full Day
Kindergarten: Full Day
Primary / Transition: No
Elementary: Yes
Secondary or Middle School: Yes
Specific grades offered: Preschool to grade 8
Other: Part-time preschool also offered
Student teacher ratio average: 10:1
Classes offered per grade: N/A
Average class size: 20
Total enrollment: 160
Recommended grades to apply: N/A
School hours: 7:15 a.m. - 6:00 p.m.
Calendar school year: 9 months
Uniforms required: No
Parental involvement opportunities and requirements: Parents Booster Club
Average SAT scores: N/A
Visitation procedures: N/A
Personal appointments for touring the facility: Individual appointments with Assistant Administrator Individual tours are recommended.
Group tour dates: N/A
Open house dates: January of each year
Classroom visits: N/A
Profit or non-profit: Profit

ADMISSIONS

Application form required: Yes
Forms required: Application, parent essay, prior records
Application deadline: March 1
Application fee: $150
Contact: Heather Lourcey, Assistant Administrator
Phone: (972) 239-8598
Student interview required: Yes
Parent interview required: Yes
Entrance test required: Yes
Specific tests administered: 1st - 4th Grade: Applicants take a grade achievement test for elementary placement and have an on-campus interview. , Fifth and above: Applicants take a grade achievement test for elementary placement and have an on-campus interview.
Accept test scores from other schools: No
Testing fee: N/A

Time of year testing is administered: N/A
Test dates offered: N/A
Out of state applicants: N/A
Notification by phone: N/A
Notification by mail: Yes, in April
Other: April 1

FINANCIAL

Preschool tuition: $3,400 - $4,400
Elementary tuition: $5,400 - $6,200
Secondary tuition: $6,600
Other tuition: Books - supply list each semester
Cash discounts: N/A
Personal check: Yes
Automatic bank draw: N/A
Credit cards: N/A
Monthly: Yes
Per semester: Yes
Annually: Yes
Financial assistance offered: Advanced elementary level only
Cancellation insurance: N/A
Sibling discount: Yes
Application acceptance deposit required: Yes

SERVICES

Before school care offered: Yes, 7:15 a.m. - 8:45 a.m.
After school care offered: Yes, 3:15 p.m. - 6:00 p.m.
Transportation provided: Yes
Lunch/snack program: School provides snack refreshments for preschool and after-school care students.
Other: Transportation provided to after school activities. Summer camp and enrichment programs are available. Graduates attend both private and public high schools and experience a positive transition. Many are noted as strong leaders and graduate with honors.

WHITE ROCK MONTESSORI SCHOOL

1601 Oates Drive
Dallas, TX 75228
Contact: **Sue Henry, Director**
(214) 324-5580
(214) 324-5671 FAX

Office Hours: 8:30 a.m. - 5:00 p.m.
E-MAIL: wrmschool@aol.com
Web Site: N/A
MAPSCO: 38U

PHILOSOPHY OF SCHOOL

The only valid impulse to learning is the self-motivation of the child. The adult prepares the environment, directs the activity, functions as the authority, and offers the stimulation, but it is the child who must be motivated by the work itself to persist in his/her given task. Towards this end, the work is individualized and self-paced. Each child is encouraged to express himself/herself creatively and to develop to his/her own fullest potential.

CREDENTIALS

Accreditations: (see glossary) AMS

Awards and special recognition: (see glossary) N/A

Qualification of administrator: B.A., all levels of Texas State Teachers Certification, AMS certification, 24 years professional experience in teaching

Qualification of faculty: Must have degrees and AMS certification or the equivalent; 25% of the staff have master's degrees.

Other: Accreditation: North American Montessori Teacher Association, National Middle School Association

GENERAL

Alternative: No
College preparatory: Yes
Montessori: Yes
Nondenominational: Yes
Church affiliated: No
Denomination: N/A
Jewish: N/A
Other denominations: N/A
Student type: Co-ed
Grade category (for details see specific grades offered below): Preschool

Infants: N/A
Preschool: Half Day
Kindergarten: Full Day
Primary / Transition: No
Elementary: Yes
Secondary or Middle School: Yes
Specific grades offered: PK-Grade 8
Student teacher ratio average: Preschool, lower elementary and middle school, 12:1; upper elementary, 18:1
Classes offered per grade: N/A
Average class size: 23, Preschool and lower elementary; 18 upper elementary and middle school
Total enrollment: 150
Recommended grades to apply: N/A
School hours: Preschool, 8:30 a.m. - 11:30 a.m.; K-6th, 8:30 a.m. - 3:00 p.m.; middle school, 8:30 a.m. - 3:30 p.m. (before and after school care 7:00 a.m. - 8:30 a.m. and 3:00 p.m. - 6:00 p.m.)
Calendar school year: August-May
Uniforms required: No
Parental involvement opportunities and requirements: Parents' organization, parent volunteers
Average SAT scores: N/A
Visitation procedures: Call for appointment
Personal appointments for touring the facility: Yes
Group tour dates: N/A
Open house dates: N/A
Classroom visits: Classrooms are open.
Profit or non-profit: Non-profit

ADMISSIONS

Application form required: Yes
Forms required: Yes
Application deadline: Ongoing for waiting list
Application fee: N/A
Contact: Sue Henry
Phone: (214) 324-5580
Student interview required: Yes
Parent interview required: Yes
Entrance test required: No
Specific tests administered: N/A
Accept test scores from other schools: Yes

Testing fee: N/A
Time of year testing is administered: N/A
Test dates offered: N/A
Out of state applicants: N/A
Notification by phone: Yes, following interview with parents and child.
Notification by mail: N/A

FINANCIAL

Preschool tuition: 1/2 Day, $2896.00; Extended Day, $4632.00
Elementary tuition: Lower, $4944.00; Upper, $5114.00
Secondary tuition: Middle School, $5952
Other tuition: N/A
Cash discounts: N/A
Personal check: Yes
Automatic bank draw: N/A
Credit cards: N/A
Monthly: Yes
Per semester: Yes
Annually: Yes
Financial assistance offered: Limited
Cancellation insurance: No
Sibling discount: No
Application acceptance deposit required: $150 deposit when child enrolls ($100 of which is applied to the first tuition payment)

SERVICES

Before school care offered: Yes, 7:00 a.m. - 8:30 a.m.
After school care offered: Yes, 3:00 p.m. - 6:00 p.m.
Transportation provided: N/A
Lunch/snack program: Snack provided for preschool children and after-school children.
Other: White Rock Montessori believes in integrating computer use into the day-to-day environment; therefore, computers are located within the classrooms rather than in a lab setting. Each classroom has a computer center with computer, printer and color monitor. Children are moved towards computer literacy at their own pace and are encouraged to use the computer when appropriate as a tool as they go about their daily work. White Rock Montessori puts great emphasis on its ever-growing library. The school maintains a lending library for parents. After-school activities include piano, dance, Indian Guides, yoga, Boy and Girl Scouts; fifth and sixth grade students have a spring camp out; middle school students take an annual 3 day canoe trip.

386

WINDSONG MONTESSORI SCHOOL

2825 Valley View #100
Farmers Branch, TX 75234
Contact: **Julia "Jere" Albanesi**
(972) 620-2466
(972) 620-2466 FAX

Office Hours: 7:30 a.m. - 6:00 p.m.
E-MAIL: N/A
Web Site: N/A
MAPSCO: 14Y

PHILOSOPHY OF SCHOOL

The Windsong Montessori School offers a unique individualized program. At the Windsong Montessori School, there is an enduring commitment to Dr. Montessori's method education. The goal of the school is to give students the foundation for developing a strong reasoning ability, an exceptional method for studying effectively, and a deep-rooted love of learning. The depth to which any topic can be understood is limited only by a student's interest and ability. The core curriculum, which includes math, geometry, reading, writing, and spelling, is highly individualized and carefully monitored to ensure each student's maximum individual program.

CREDENTIALS

Accreditations: (see glossary) Licensed by (A.M.I.T.O.T.), AMI Teachers of
    Texas, Montessori
Awards and special recognition: (see glossary) N/A
Qualification of administrator: B.A. degree, Montessori certification
Qualification of faculty: Certified Montessori teachers, Montessori interns

GENERAL

Alternative: No
College preparatory: No
Montessori: Yes
Nondenominational: No
Church affiliated: No
Denomination: N/A
Jewish: N/A
Other denominations: N/A
Student type: Co-ed
Grade category (for details see specific grades offered below): Elementary

Infants: N/A
Preschool: Half Day and Full Day
Kindergarten: Half Day and Full Day
Primary / Transition: No
Elementary: Yes
Secondary or Middle School: N/A
Specific grades offered: Preschool (age 2 1/2) - grade 5
Student teacher ratio average: 11:1
Classes offered per grade: N/A
Average class size: 22
Total enrollment: 75
Recommended grades to apply: N/A
School hours: 8:30 a.m. - 3:30 p.m.
Calendar school year: Academic year August-May, Summer school June-Aug
Uniforms required: No
Parental involvement opportunities and requirements: Opportunities for field trip support, reader-listeners, but not required
Average SAT scores: N/A
Visitation procedures: Call for appointment requested, but usually not necessary
Personal appointments for touring the facility: Yes
Group tour dates: N/A
Open house dates: Fall & Spring
Classroom visits: Yes
Profit or non-profit: Profit

ADMISSIONS

Application form required: Yes
Forms required: Application forms and previous school records
Application deadline: Open year-round, Feb, March & April ideal
Application fee: $150 (covers testing also)
Contact: Julia ("Jere") Albanesi
Phone: (972) 620-2466
Student interview required: Yes
Parent interview required: Yes
Entrance test required: Yes
Specific tests administered: N/A
Accept test scores from other schools: No
Testing fee: Included in application fee
Time of year testing is administered: Year round
Test dates offered: Year round
Out of state applicants: Yes

Notification by phone: Yes
Notification by mail: Yes
Other: By conference, specific tests administered: Albanesi Educational Center Standardized Curriculum Tests

FINANCIAL

Preschool tuition: $4500/Academic year
Elementary tuition: $5220/Academic year
Secondary tuition: N/A
Cash discounts: Yes, 5% prepayment discount on academic year tuition
Personal check: Yes
Automatic bank draw: N/A
Credit cards: N/A
Monthly: Yes
Per semester: Yes
Annually: Yes, with 5% prepayment discount for academic year tuition & fees
Financial assistance offered: 10% discount on tuition for additional students of same family enrolled at the same time
Cancellation insurance: N/A
Sibling discount: Yes, 10% discount on tuition
Application acceptance deposit required: Yes

SERVICES

Before school care offered: Yes, 7:30 a.m. - 8:30 a.m.
After school care offered: Yes, 3:30 p.m. - 6:00 p.m.
Transportation provided: N/A
Lunch/snack program: Snack, (Pizza) Friday

TDPRS
Texas Department of Protective and Regulatory Services

Minimum standards for regulating child care facilities are developed and monitored by the Texas Department of Protective and Regulatory Services.

Anderson Private School for the Gifted and Talented, The
Ashleys Private School
Bent Tree Child Development Center (see NAEYC)
Bent Tree Episcopal School
Beth Torah Preschool and Kindergarten
Burton Adventist Academy (see Ch. 4)
Callier Child Development Center (see Ch. 4)
Cambridge Square Private School of DeSoto
Carlisle School, The (see Additional schools)
Children's World (see Ch. 4)
Children's Center of First Community Church (see Ch. 4)
Christ Our Savior Lutheran School (see Ch. 4)
Christian Childhood Development Center (see Ch. 4)
Country Day Montessori (see Montessori)
Dallas North Montessori School (see Ch. 4)
daVinci School, The
DeSoto Private School
Discovery School at Canyon Creek Presbyterian Church (see Ch. 4)
East Dallas Development Center (see Ch. 4)
Fair Oaks Day School (see Ch. 4)
Fellowship Christian Academy (see Ch. 4)
First Christian Elementary and Preschool
First United Methodit Church Day School (see NAEYC)
Fulton Academy of Rockwall, The
Glen Oaks School (see NAEYC)
Harrington School, The (see Ch. 4)
Hillcrest Academy (see SACS)
Lakewood Presbyterian School (see Ch. 4)
Lakewood United Methodist Learning Center (see Ch. 4)
Little Red Schoolhouse (see Ch. 4)
Maryview/Meritor Academy (see Ch. 4)

Meadowbrook School (see Montessori)

North Dallas Day School (see Ch. 4)

Northbrook School

NorthPark Presbyterian Day School

Palisades Day School (see Ch. 4)

Pathfinders College Preparatory (see Ch. 4)

The Peanut Gallery (see Ch. 4)
> Carrollton, Colony, Galleria, Greenville, Rosemeade Parkway, Walnut Hill

Prestonwood Christian Academy

Primrose School of Chase Oaks (see Ch. 4)

Prince of Peace Christian School (see Ch. 4)

Providence Christian School of Texas

Rowlett Christian Academy (see Ch. 4)

Rosemeade Baptist Christian School

Sloan School (see Ch. 4)

Smart Start Early Childhood Education Center (see Ch. 4)

Trinity Episcopal Preschool (see Ch. 4)

THE ANDERSON PRIVATE SCHOOL FOR THE GIFTED AND TALENTED

14900 White Settlement Road *Office Hours:* 8:30 a.m. - 4:30 p.m.
Fort Worth, TX 76108   *E-MAIL:* N/A
Contact: **LeVonna Anderson**   *Web Site:* N/A
(817) 448-8484   *MAPSCO:* West of 573 (not mapped)

PHILOSOPHY OF SCHOOL

To provide a unique haven for precocious children where the primary focus is not upon learning but upon motivation through immersion in a nurturing , sensitive and stimulating environment.

CREDENTIALS

Accreditations: (see glossary) TDPRS (Licensed by the Texas Department of Protective & Regulatory Services.)

Awards and special recognition: (see glossary) 1999 National Merit Scholarship Finalist

Qualification of administrator: Ed.D. Baylor University, M.Ed. Abilene Christian University, B.S. Hardin-Simmons University

Qualification of faculty: Gifted adults working in diverse academic disciplines and fields of enrichment for which they harbor a passion are recruited in lieu of certified educators.

GENERAL

Alternative: No
College preparatory: Yes
Montessori: No
Nondenominational: No
Church affiliated: No
Denomination: N/A
Jewish: N/A
Other denominations: N/A
Student type: Co-ed
Grade category (for details see specific grades offered below): K - 12th

Infants: N/A

Preschool: N/A

Kindergarten: Full Day

Primary / Transition: N/A

Elementary: Yes

Secondary or Middle School: Yes

Specific grades offered: N/A

Other: Special school for the Gifted, Talented and Creative. Core scholastic subjects are highly accelerated and compacted. Frequent pre and post testing qualifies children for rapid acceleration. Mastery is attained at 90% and recorded in continuous progress profiles. Traditional grades and report cards are not issued.

Student teacher ratio average: Highly variable

Classes offered per grade: Varied

Average class size: Varied

Total enrollment: 22

Recommended grades to apply: All open

School hours: 8:30 a.m. - 3:15 p.m.

Calendar school year: September 1 - May 25

Uniforms required: Yes

Parental involvement opportunities and requirements: Parents are required to read to their children or listen to their children read aloud one hour each evening in lieu of homework.

Average SAT scores: 1470

Visitation procedures: The Anderson School maintains an open door policy. You may visit at any time. Please call for an appointment.

Personal appointments for touring the facility: School tours are typically provided on Sunday afternoons. Please call for an appointment.

Group tour dates: Sunday afternoons

Open house dates: None scheduled

Classroom visits: Our open door policy permits classroom visitation at any time.

Profit or non-profit: Profit

ADMISSIONS

Application form required: Yes

Forms required: Enrollment information, emergency authorization, Transportation consent, immunization, physical exam, medication authorization, parent inventory of characteristics, parental permission, signed acknowledgment, portfolio, and interview with the school psychologist.

Application deadline: We accept applications throughout the year.

Application fee: The non-refundable application fee is $125.

Contact: Dr. William C. Anderson
Phone: (817) 448-8484
Student interview required: Yes, also an interview with the school psychologist.
Parent interview required: Yes, also an interview with the school psychologist.
Entrance test required: No
Specific tests administered: N/A
Accept test scores from other schools: Yes. In lieu of specific test scores, a portfolio of information about the applicant is required. This may include test data, historical records, samples of creative production, awards, recognitions, letters of recommendation, contact sheets, or other evidence of aptitude, achievement or potential.
Testing fee: N/A
Time of year testing is administered: N/A
Test dates offered: N/A
Out of state applicants: N/A
Notification by phone: N/A
Notification by mail: Yes

FINANCIAL

Preschool tuition: N/A
Elementary tuition: $6150
Secondary tuition: $6150
Other tuition: N/A
Cash discounts: N/A
Personal check: Yes
Automatic bank draw: N/A
Credit cards: N/A
Monthly: N/A
Per semester: Yes, 60% for the first semester, 40% for the second semester
Annually: Yes, 100% upon notification of acceptance
Financial assistance offered: The school accepts children participating in the Children's Scholarship Fund.
Cancellation insurance: No
Sibling discount: No
Application acceptance deposit required: Yes

SERVICES

Before school care offered: No

After school care offered: No

Transportation provided: No

Lunch/snack program: Students bring their lunch to school.

Other: A brochure is available. Participation in academic endeavor is limited to fifty percent of time in school. The remaining time is dedicated to enrichment activities including weekly study trips and adventure trips each semester.

ASHLEYS PRIVATE SCHOOL

310 W. Beltline Rd.
Cedar Hill, TX 75104
Contact: Sharon Ashley
(972) 291-1313
(972) 293-8056 FAX

Office Hours: 8:00 a.m. - 4:00 p.m.
E-MAIL: N/A
Web Site: N/A
MAPSCO: N/A

PHILOSOPHY OF SCHOOL

A place where minds develop anchored by truths and educational excellence surrounds the most precious of all investments - your child.

CREDENTIALS

Accreditations: (see glossary) TDPRS

Awards and special recognition: (see glossary) N/A

Qualification of administrator: Degreed and accredited college and continuing education hours required yearly.

Qualification of faculty: Teachers for K-4 same as administrator.

GENERAL

Alternative: No
College preparatory: No
Montessori: No
Nondenominational: No
Church affiliated: No
Denomination: N/A
Jewish: N/A
Other denominations: N/A
Student type: Co-ed
Grade category (for details see specific grades offered below): N/A
Infants: N/A
Preschool: Half day and Full day
Kindergarten: Half day and Full day
Primary / Transition: N/A
Elementary: Yes
Secondary or Middle School: N/A

Specific grades offered: Preschool - 4th

Other: Academic. Wanted: Academically centered students and parents.

Student teacher ratio average: 12:1

Classes offered per grade: Multiple sections Preschool - K/ Single sections
    1st - 4th

Average class size: 18

Total enrollment: 200

Recommended grades to apply: N/A

School hours: Class schedule 8:00 a.m. - 3:15 p.m.

Calendar school year: Late August - May

Uniforms required: Yes, Kindergarten - 4th only.

Parental involvement opportunities and requirements: Conferences,
    chaperones, open door policy.

Average SAT scores: Above national average.

Visitation procedures: Open door policy

Personal appointments for touring the facility: Arrange through office

Group tour dates: N/A

Open house dates: Fall (open door policy)

Classroom visits: Scheduled conferences and open door policy

Profit or non-profit: Profit

ADMISSIONS

Application form required: Yes

Forms required: Enrollment, medical, past scores or records (K-4)

Application deadline: N/A

Application fee: $40

Contact: Sharon Ashley

Phone: (972) 291-1313

Student interview required: Yes

Parent interview required: Yes

Entrance test required: Yes, very informal - no fee

Specific tests administered: Yes

Accept test scores from other schools: Yes

Testing fee: $30

Time of year testing is administered: Spring (for enrolled students)

Test dates offered: N/A

Out of state applicants: N/A

Notification by phone: Yes

Notification by mail: N/A

FINANCIAL

Preschool tuition: $3500/year
Elementary tuition: $3500-$4500/year
Secondary tuition: N/A
Other tuition: N/A
Cash discounts: Yes
Personal check: Yes
Automatic bank draw: N/A
Credit cards: N/A
Monthly: Yes
Per semester: Yes
Annually: Yes
Financial assistance offered: N/A
Cancellation insurance: No
Sibling discount: No
Application acceptance deposit required: N/A
Other: Also offer weekly tuition payments. Our families set up their own preferred payment plan.

SERVICES

Before school care offered: Yes, 6:00 a.m. - class time.
After school care offered: Yes, class dismissal - 6:00 p.m.
Transportation provided: No
Lunch/snack program: Hot lunches provided daily and two snacks, student may bring own lunch.

BENT TREE
EPISCOPAL SCHOOL

17405 Muirfield Dr.
Dallas, TX 75287
Contact: **Gayla Jones**
(972) 248-6505
(972) 248-6575

Office Hours: 8:30 a.m. - 2:30 p.m.
E-MAIL: N/A
Web Site: N/A
MAPSCO: 36C

PHILOSOPHY OF SCHOOL

Our philosophy and goals incorporate excellence in teaching and curriculum with emphasis upon character development and learning skills necessary to excel in life's endeavors. BTES focuses on the development of the child as a whole - programs are provided to enhance academic skill, socialization, emotional development and spiritual growth.

- BTES adopts a child centered, hands-on, learning-through-play concept of teaching.
- BTES staff has created a curriculum which has its basis in the theories of Piaget and Vigotsky. Scaffolding, constructivism and child-centered curriculum provide our foundation.
- All teaching is done through love - love for children, love of learning and love for the life God had given each of us.

CREDENTIALS

Accreditations: (see glossary) TDPRS
Awards and special recognition: (see glossary) N/A
Qualification of administrator: N/A
Qualification of faculty: N/A

GENERAL

Alternative: No
College preparatory: No
Montessori: No
Nondenominational: Yes
Church affiliated: Yes
Denomination: Episcopal
Jewish: N/A

Other denominations: Our student body is comprised of children from many different religious backgrounds. Children of all faiths are accepted and respected.

Student type: Co-ed

Grade category (for details see specific grades offered below): N/A

Infants: N/A

Preschool: Half Day

Kindergarten: Full Day

Primary / Transition: No

Elementary: No

Secondary or Middle School: No

Specific grades offered: 2 years - Kindergarten

Student teacher ratio average: 6:1=2's; 10:1=3's; 12:1=4's and up

Classes offered per grade: 2's and 3's = 2 classes; 4's and up = 1 class

Average class size: 2's = 6; 3's = 10; 4's and up = 12

Total enrollment: 66

Recommended grades to apply: 2 year - K

School hours: 9:00 a.m. - 12:15 p.m./ 9:00 a.m. - 2:00 p.m. K

Calendar school year: September - May

Uniforms required: Yes

Parental involvement opportunities and requirements: BTES Parent's Association

Average SAT scores: N/A

Visitation procedures: Open - check with office

Personal appointments for touring the facility: Flexible - call office to schedule

Group tour dates: N/A

Open house dates: N/A

Classroom visits: Flexible - call to schedule

Profit or non-profit: Non-profit

ADMISSIONS

Application form required: Yes

Forms required: BTES application form

Application deadline: Accepted throughout the year, recommended by February 1

Application fee: $50.00

Contact: Gayla Jones

Phone: (972) 248-6505

Student interview required: Yes

Parent interview required: Yes

Entrance test required: No

Specific tests administered: N/A

Accept test scores from other schools: Yes. Testing may be required in cases of special needs children. All previous testing must be submitted with application.

Testing fee: N/A

Time of year testing is administered: N/A

Test dates offered: N/A

Out of state applicants: N/A

Notification by phone: Yes

Notification by mail: Yes

Other: Waiting list kept and parents called as places become available.

FINANCIAL

Preschool tuition: $1600 - 4500 yearly

Elementary tuition: N/A

Secondary tuition: N/A

Other tuition: Enrollment Fees

Cash discounts: N/A

Personal check: Yes

Automatic bank draw: N/A

Credit cards: N/A

Monthly: Yes, 10 equal payments, June - March

Per semester: Yes, discount available

Annually: Yes, discount available

Financial assistance offered: Limited scholarships available

Cancellation insurance: No

Sibling discount: Yes, % offered for 3 or more siblings enrolled

Application acceptance deposit required: Recommend application submitted by February 1, acceptance by March 1.

SERVICES

Before school care offered: N/A

After school care offered: N/A

Transportation provided: N/A

Lunch/snack program: Parent provided

Other: Extended hours Tuesday and Wednesday until 2:00 p.m.

BETH TORAH PRESCHOOL & KINDERGARTEN

720 Lookout Drive
Richardson, TX 75080
Contact: **Ester Cohen**
(972) 234-1549
(972) 783-1463 FAX

Office Hours: 8:30 a.m. - 3:00 p.m.
E-MAIL: info@dfwprivateschools.com
Web Site: N/A
MAPSCO: 7K

PHILOSOPHY OF SCHOOL

To provide a conservative Jewish atmosphere where children can develop a positive self-image and love of learning.

CREDENTIALS

Accreditations: (see glossary) TDPRS
Awards and special recognition: (see glossary) N/A
Qualification of administrator: Degree - early childhood development
Qualification of faculty: College degrees
Other: United Synagogue Affiliation

GENERAL

Alternative: No
College preparatory: No
Montessori: No
Nondenominational: No
Church affiliated: No
Denomination: N/A
Jewish: Conservative
Other denominations: N/A
Student type: Co-ed
Grade category: (for details see specific grades offered below): Preschool
Infants: N/A
Preschool: Half Day
Kindergarten: Half Day
Primary / Transition: No
Elementary: N/A
Secondary or Middle School: N/A
Specific grades offered: Preschool

Student teacher ratio average: 6:1

Classes offered per grade: N/A

Average class size: 12

Total enrollment: 1

Recommended grades to apply: N/A

School hours: 9:00 a.m. - 1:00 p.m., K: 9:00 a.m. - 2:00 p.m.

Calendar school year: Late August through May

Uniforms required: No

Parental involvement opportunities and requirements: Many opportunities to volunteer.

Average SAT scores: N/A

Visitation procedures: N/A

Personal appointments for touring the facility: Individual appointments offered.

Group tour dates: N/A

Open house dates: N/A

Classroom visits: N/A

Profit or non-profit: Non-profit

ADMISSIONS

Application form required: Yes

Forms required:

Application deadline: Rolling admissions (if space permits)

Application fee: Yes

Contact: Esther Cohen

Phone: (214) 234-1549 ext. 222

Student interview required: No

Parent interview required: No

Entrance test required: No

Specific tests administered:

Accept test scores from other schools: No

Testing fee: N/A

Time of year testing is administered: N/A

Test dates offered: N/A

Out of state applicants: N/A

Notification by phone: N/A

Notification by mail: N/A

FINANCIAL

Preschool tuition: $4250 for 5-day program

Elementary tuition: N/A

Secondary tuition: N/A

Other tuition: Other options available
Cash discounts: N/A
Personal check: N/A
Automatic bank draw: N/A
Credit cards: N/A
Monthly: N/A
Per semester: N/A
Annually: N/A
Financial assistance offered: Limited basis.
Cancellation insurance: N/A
Sibling discount: N/A
Application acceptance deposit required: N/A

SERVICES

Before school care offered: Yes, arrangements made upon request.
After school care offered: Yes, 1:00 p.m. - 2:00 p.m.
Transportation provided: N/A
Lunch/snack program: School provides snacks; child provides lunch except for 4 times a year when school provides hot lunch.
Other: 3 year, 4 years & K have computer lab/weekly instruction; children check out books weekly, parents read aloud during library time, music specialist, Hebrew specialist.

CAMBRIDGE SQUARE PRIVATE SCHOOL OF DESOTO

1121 East Pleasant Run Road
DeSoto, TX 75115
Contact: Mary Lowrey
(972) 224-5596
(972) 617-3074 FAX

Office Hours: 6:30 a.m. - 6:00 p.m.
E-MAIL: N/A
Web Site: N/A
MAPSCO: 74W

PHILOSOPHY OF SCHOOL

To encourage and guide each child to develop his/her greatest potential in a secure, loving, and stimulating environment.

CREDENTIALS

Accreditations: (see glossary) TAAPS pending, TDPRS
Awards and special recognition: (see glossary) N/A
Qualification of administrator: Master's degree
Qualification of faculty: Bachelor's degree required in major teaching field

GENERAL

Alternative: No
College preparatory: No
Montessori: No
Nondenominational: No
Church affiliated: No
Denomination: N/A
Jewish: N/A
Other denominations: N/A
Student type: Co-ed
Grade category (for details see specific grades offered below): Preschool - Middle School
Infants: N/A
Preschool: Yes
Kindergarten: Yes
Primary / Transition: N/A

Elementary: Yes
Secondary or Middle School: Yes
Specific grades offered: 3-year-olds - 8th
Student teacher ratio average: 12:1
Classes offered per grade: N/A
Average class size: 12
Total enrollment: 250
Recommended grades to apply: N/A
School hours: 8:00 a.m. - 3:30 p.m.
Calendar school year: Mid-August - May
Uniforms required: No
Parental involvement opportunities and requirements: N/A
Average SAT scores: N/A
Visitation procedures: N/A
Personal appointments for touring the facility: N/A
Group tour dates: N/A
Open house dates: N/A
Classroom visits: N/A
Profit or non-profit: Profit

ADMISSIONS

Application form required: Yes
Forms required: N/A
Application deadline: March through July as space allows
Application fee: Yes
Contact: Mary Lowrey
Phone: (214) 224-5596
Student interview required: N/A
Parent interview required: N/A
Entrance test required: N/A
Specific tests administered: N/A
Accept test scores from other schools: N/A
Testing fee: N/A
Time of year testing is administered: N/A
Test dates offered: N/A
Out of state applicants: N/A
Notification by phone: N/A
Notification by mail: N/A
Other: Parents will be notified within two weeks of receiving application and
transcripts.

FINANCIAL

Preschool tuition: $3000

Elementary tuition: $3000

Secondary tuition: $3000

Other tuition: Books (approximately $125)

Cash discounts: N/A

Personal check: N/A

Automatic bank draw: N/A

Credit cards: N/A

Monthly: Yes

Per semester: Yes

Annually: Yes

Financial assistance offered: No

Cancellation insurance: No

Sibling discount: N/A

Application acceptance deposit required: N/A

SERVICES

Before school care offered: Yes, 6:30 a.m. - 8:00 a.m.

After school care offered: Yes, 3:30 p.m. - 6:00 p.m.

Transportation provided: No

Lunch/snack program: Provided by school.

Other: Networked IBM computer units with CD ROM and laser printer; Apple computers in classroom.

THE da Vinci SCHOOL

5442 La Sierra Drive
Dallas, TX 75231
Contact: **Mary Ann Greene - Director**
(214) 373-9504
(214) 691-4603 FAX

Office Hours: 8:00 a.m. - 5:30 p.m.
E-MAIL: N/A

Web Site: Davincischool.org
MAPSCO: 26K

PHILOSOPHY OF SCHOOL

"Where great minds start in little bodies." The da Vinci School recognizes that children begin learning the moment they are born. Professionals everywhere agree that the early years of life are an especially sensitive time for establishing basic skills and for fostering joy, ability, and interest in learning. The da Vinci School provides its students with a unique environment and experiences that advance equally intellectual, physical, emotional, psychological, social, artistic (creative), and practical life growth.

CREDENTIALS

Accreditations: (see glossary) TDPRS

Awards and special recognition: (see glossary) N/A

Qualification of administrator: Degree in psychology, 28 years experience in early childhood development and education, gifted education from birth to sixth grade, and parent/baby education

Qualification of faculty: K and above must have degrees and experience; pre school-degree is required, but experience and other qualifications are considered; a psychologist screens the staff for positive and supportive attitudes toward children and learning; staff must be versatile and creative in their teaching

Other: Have not sought accreditation, licensed by the Texas Department of Human Services.

GENERAL

Alternative: No
College preparatory: No
Montessori: No
Nondenominational: Yes
Church affiliated: No
Denomination: N/A
Jewish: N/A

Other denominations: N/A
Student type: Co-ed
Grade category (for details see specific grades offered below): Kindergarten
Infants: Yes
Preschool: Half Day
Kindergarten: Full Day
Primary / Transition: Yes
Elementary: N/A
Secondary or Middle School: N/A
Specific grades offered: 18 months - kindergarten and primer
Other: Kindergarten: 8:45 a.m. - 2:15 p.m.
Student teacher ratio average: Ranges from 5:1 to 14:1
Classes offered per grade: N/A
Average class size: Ranges from 5-14
Total enrollment: 90
Recommended grades to apply: N/A
School hours: 8:45 a.m. - 2:15 p.m.
Calendar school year: Sept. - May (Camp: June & July)
Uniforms required: No
Parental involvement opportunities and requirements: Active, involved parents
 with high priority on welfare of their child and his/her education; Parent's
 Association; parents and children benefit greatly from our parent education
 classes, which are available as soon as the child is born.
Average SAT scores: N/A
Visitation procedures: N/A
Personal appointments for touring the facility: Call to schedule observation of
 classes and discussion with director; appointments available days, evenings,
 or weekends if necessary to accommodate both parents.
Group tour dates: N/A
Open house dates: Early February
Classroom visits: N/A
Profit or non-profit: Non-profit

ADMISSIONS

Application form required: Yes
Forms required: Registration, immunization, enrollment application/information,
 tuition contract.
Application deadline: Apply March through school year
Application fee: $250
Contact: Mary Ann Engel-Greene
Phone: (214) 373-9504

Student interview required: Yes
Parent interview required: Yes
Entrance test required: No
Specific tests administered: N/A
Accept test scores from other schools: No
Testing fee: N/A
Time of year testing is administered: N/A
Test dates offered: N/A
Out of state applicants: N/A
Notification by phone: N/A
Notification by mail: N/A

FINANCIAL

Preschool tuition: $160-$380/month for nine months
Elementary tuition: $487/month K and primer for nine months
Secondary tuition: N/A
Other tuition: Consumables fee
Cash discounts: N/A
Personal check: N/A
Automatic bank draw: N/A
Credit cards: N/A
Monthly: Yes
Per semester: N/A
Annually: Yes
Financial assistance offered: N/A
Cancellation insurance: N/A
Sibling discount: Yes, inquire at school.
Application acceptance deposit required: N/A

SERVICES

Before school care offered: Yes, 8:00 a.m..
After school care offered: Yes, limited - until 3:00 p.m.
Transportation provided: N/A
Lunch/snack program: Daily morning snack provided-wholesome foods, no sugar, 100% fruit juice; snacks often complement unit or theme in curriculum.
Other: Computer class is regular part of kindergarten and primer; optional for 3 and 4 year olds.

DESOTO PRIVATE SCHOOL

301 E. Beltline Road
DeSoto, TX 75115
Contact: **Kenneth or Carolyn Larson, Owners**
(972) 223-6450
(972) 230-0629 FAX

Office Hours: 6:30 a.m. - 6:00 p.m.
E-MAIL: N/A
Web Site: N/A
MAPSCO: 84F

PHILOSOPHY OF SCHOOL

To meet the individual needs and differences of each student (DeSoto Private School is concerned with the development of the whole child.)

CREDENTIALS

Accreditations: (see glossary) TDPRS
Awards and special recognition: (see glossary) N/A
Qualification of administrator: College degree
Qualification of faculty: College degree required for teachers K5 - grade 6
Other: Affiliated with TACCA, NAEYC

GENERAL

Alternative: No
College preparatory: No
Montessori: No
Nondenominational: Yes
Church affiliated: No
Denomination: N/A
Jewish: N/A
Other denominations: N/A
Student type: Co-ed
Grade category (for details see specific grades offered below): Elementary
Infants: N/A
Preschool: Full Day
Kindergarten: Full Day
Primary / Transition: No
Elementary: Yes
Secondary or Middle School: N/A
Specific grades offered: Preschool (age 3) - grade 6
Student teacher ratio average: 12:1
Classes offered per grade: N/A

Average class size: 8 (3K) - 21 (primary)
Total enrollment: 600
Recommended grades to apply: N/A
School hours: 8:00 a.m. - 3:30 p.m.; extended day care until 6:00 p.m.
Calendar school year: August - May
Uniforms required: Yes
Parental involvement opportunities and requirements: Yes
Average SAT scores: N/A
Visitation procedures: N/A
Personal appointments for touring the facility: Individual appointments offered
Group tour dates: N/A
Open house dates: N/A
Classroom visits: N/A
Profit or non-profit: Profit

ADMISSIONS

Application form required: Yes
Forms required: Enrollment forms, medical report
Application deadline: Apply in March; school year begins in August
Application fee: Yes
Contact: Kenneth or Carolyn Larson
Phone: (972) 223-6450
Student interview required: No
Parent interview required: No
Entrance test required: Yes
Specific tests administered: N/A
Accept test scores from other schools: No
Testing fee: Yes
Time of year testing is administered: March
Test dates offered: N/A
Out of state applicants: N/A
Notification by phone: N/A
Notification by mail: Yes, by letter

FINANCIAL

Preschool tuition: N/A
Elementary tuition: $3100
Secondary tuition: N/A
Other tuition: N/A
Cash discounts: N/A
Personal check: N/A

Automatic bank draw: N/A
Credit cards: N/A
Monthly: Yes
Per semester: N/A
Annually: N/A
Financial assistance offered: No
Cancellation insurance: N/A
Sibling discount: Yes
Application acceptance deposit required: N/A

SERVICES

Before school care offered: Yes, 6:30 a.m. - 8:00 a.m.
After school care offered: Yes, 3:30 p.m. - 6:00 p.m.
Transportation provided: N/A
Lunch/snack program: There is a lunch fee.
Other: Computer lab and library; extracurricular activities and enrichment
curriculum.

FIRST CHRISTIAN ELEMENTARY AND PRESCHOOL

1109 Brown Street
Waxahachie, TX 75165
Contact: Joanne Bronson
(972) 937-1952
(972) 937-1997 FAX

Office Hours: 8:00 a.m. - 5:00 p.m.
E-MAIL: frstchrsch@aol.com
Web Site: N/A
MAPSCO: Ellis Co., pg. 1081, section X

PHILOSOPHY OF SCHOOL

To provide a superior academic program in a Christian atmosphere for all students.

CREDENTIALS

Accreditations: (see glossary) TDPRS

Awards and special recognition: (see glossary) Students consistently admitted to G/T programs and honors classes in middle school and high school. Also among top graduates of Waxahachie High School and area schools.

Qualification of administrator: Master's Degree in Education (Also Master's in Religion-Theory preferred)

Qualification of faculty: Grade School: B.A. Preschool: B.A. preferred. Will consider high school with some college.

Other: ACSI: Application for accreditation being prepared. NAEYC: Accreditation in progress. Preschool founded in 1982. Elementary founded in 1987.

GENERAL

Alternative: No
College preparatory: No
Montessori: No
Nondenominational: No
Church affiliated: Yes
Denomination: Christian church (Disciples of Christ)
Jewish: All faiths accepted.
Other denominations: N/A
Student type: Co-ed

Grade category (for details see specific grades offered below): N/A

Infants: Yes

Preschool: Full Day

Kindergarten: Full Day

Primary / Transition: No

Elementary: Yes

Secondary or Middle School: No

Specific grades offered: K-5 through 5th grade

Student teacher ratio average: 12:1

Classes offered per grade: 1 or 2

Average class size: 12

Total enrollment: 125

Recommended grades to apply: N/A

School hours: 8:00 a.m. to 3:00 p.m.

Calendar school year: August to June 1

Uniforms required: Yes

Parental involvement opportunities and requirements: Parent-Teacher Organization library volunteers room parent

Average SAT scores: N/A

Visitation procedures: Prior notification to the school office and approval by Headmaster/Mistress

Personal appointments for touring the facility: Yes, call school office for appointment.

Group tour dates: N/A

Open house dates: the Sunday before school opens in August, also in early December and early Spring (usually March)

Classroom visits: Yes, with permission and prior notification to the Headmistress.

Profit or non-profit: Non-profit Parochial School

ADMISSIONS

Application form required: Yes

Forms required: Medical records, previous school records if applicable, notarized field trip forms

Application deadline: July 15th or when classes are full

Application fee: Preschool: $100, Grades: $150

Contact: Rev. Joanne Bronson or Rev. Dr. Gary Bronson

Phone: (972) 937-1952 or (972) 937-1953

Student interview required: Yes

Parent interview required: Yes

Entrance test required: No

Specific tests administered: Preschool: Houghton-Mifflin, Kindergarten &

Primer: C.A.T.
Accept test scores from other schools: Yes
Comments: Provided that the scores are provided through a nationally recognized service, ie., C.A.T., I.T.B.S., TAAS
Testing fee: $50
Time of year testing is administered: April
Test dates offered: Varying
Out of state applicants: N/A
Notification by phone: Yes
Notification by mail: Yes, if unable to reach by phone

FINANCIAL

Preschool tuition: $2650/year
Elementary tuition: $2950/year
Secondary tuition: N/A
Other tuition: N/A
Cash discounts: Yes, 5%
Personal check: Yes
Automatic bank draw: Yes
Credit cards: MasterCard, Visa, American Express
Monthly: Yes
Per semester: N/A
Annually: Yes
Financial assistance offered: Yes, limited and by personal interview
Cancellation insurance: No
Sibling discount: Yes, 5%
Application acceptance deposit required: N/A

SERVICES

Before school care offered: Yes, 7:00 a.m. - 8:00 a.m.
After school care offered: Yes, 3:00 p.m. - 5:30 p.m.
Transportation provided: No
Lunch/snack program: Cafeteria - hot lunch programs, morning/afternoon snacks for Preschool
Other: Instrumental music, beginning band program, sports in season by request, nurse on staff, also professional counselor available.

THE FULTON ACADEMY OF ROCKWALL

1623 Laurence
Rockwall, TX 75032
Contact: **Norma Morris**
(972) 772-4445
(972) 772-9558 FAX

Office Hours: 8:00 a.m. - 5:00 p.m. M - F
E-MAIL: N/A
Web Site: N/A
MAPSCO: 30C - X

PHILOSOPHY OF SCHOOL

Mission: To foster community spirit and instill in every girl and boy a love of learning, a deep sense of self-worth and confidence, and a responsibility for themselves, their community and their country.

CREDENTIALS

Accreditations: (see glossary) Non Public Private Schools, TEA

Awards and special recognition: (see glossary) Who's Who (Educator) Mr. Underwood '98, National Geography Bee State Finalist '97, National Spelling Bee - County Winner '99 , Who's Who (Executives & Prof.) Norma Morris

Qualification of administrator: Kansas State Teachers College, Kansas St. Univ. Montessori Certification - San Francisco State University, 21 years Montessori school administration, 12 years Elementary Montessori school administration

Qualification of faculty: Degreed, Montessori certified

Other: Affiliation: International Montessori Society Accreditation: National Private School Assn.

GENERAL

Alternative: No
College preparatory: Yes
Montessori: Yes
Nondenominational: Yes
Church affiliated: No
Denomination: N/A
Jewish: N/A
Other denominations: N/A
Student type: Co-ed
Grade category (for details see specific grades offered below): Elementary

Infants: N/A
Preschool: N/A
Kindergarten: N/A
Primary / Transition: No
Elementary: Yes
Secondary or Middle School: Yes
Specific grades offered: 1st - 8th grades
Other: Grade Category: Middle School. Preschool and Kindergarten see Country Day Montessori School, Rockwall, TX.
Student teacher ratio average: 13 :1
Classes offered per grade: Grades 1-3: 2 multi-age classes, 4-8: 2 multi-age
Average class size: 20
Total enrollment: 85
Recommended grades to apply: All
School hours: 8:30 a.m. - 3:30 p.m. M - F; Extended day offered
Calendar school year: Aug - May , Summer Camp > 3 week sessions
Uniforms required: Yes
Parental involvement opportunities and requirements: Parent/Faculty Club, Room Parents (Parties) , Special projects - Christmas float, Orientation, fundraising, Parent Conferences (2 times annually)
Average SAT scores: N/A
Visitation procedures: 1. Parents meet with Executive Director. 2. Students visit full day for testing and interviews.
Personal appointments for touring the facility: Tours available 8:00 a.m. - 5:00 p.m., M - F. Weekend tours given upon request - by appointment.
Group tour dates: By appointment only
Open house dates: February each year
Classroom visits: Year round by appointment
Profit or non-profit: Non-profit
Other: New 14 acre campus.

ADMISSIONS

Application form required: Yes
Forms required: Application Form
Application deadline: Considered year-round
Application fee: N/A
Contact: Norma Morris
Phone: (972) 772-4445
Student interview required: Yes
Parent interview required: Yes
Entrance test required: Yes

Specific tests administered: Primer: Montessori-based achievement tests primarily for placement purposes. Admission based on desire to achieve academic potential more than test scores. , 1st - 4th Grade: Montessori-based achievement tests primarily for placement purposes. Admission based on desire to achieve academic potential more than test scores. , Fifth and above: Montessori-based achievement tests primarily for placement purposes. Admission based on desire to achieve academic potential more than test scores.

Accept test scores from other schools: Yes, prefer Stanford Achievement Test, 9th edition

Testing fee: $30

Time of year testing is administered: Year-round (on day of student visit)

Test dates offered: By appointment

Out of state applicants: Will test on weekend if needed (by appointment)

Notification by phone: Yes, if needed

Notification by mail: Yes, unless unusual circumstances

FINANCIAL

Preschool tuition: N/A

Elementary tuition: Grades 1 - 3 ($4550); 4 - 6 ($5,050); 7 - 8 ($6,150)

Secondary tuition: N/A

Other tuition: Bi-annual and monthly pay schedules available.

Cash discounts: N/A

Personal check: Yes

Automatic bank draw: N/A

Credit cards: N/A

Monthly: Yes

Per semester: Yes

Annually: Yes

Financial assistance offered: Yes, partial only

Cancellation insurance: N/A

Sibling discount: Yes, 10 % family discount

Application acceptance deposit required: Within 5 days of on-site visit and testing results

SERVICES

Before school care offered: Yes, at Country Day Montessori School, 6:30 a.m. - 8:00 a.m.

After school care offered: Yes, on site 3:30 p.m. - 6:30 p.m.

Transportation provided: Yes

Lunch/snack program: Sack lunch program at present

Other: Transportation Provided before school to Fulton from CDMS

NORTHPARK PRESBYTERIAN DAY SCHOOL

9555 N. Central Expressway
Dallas, TX 75231
Contact: Claire Wood
(214) 361-8024
(214) 361-5398 FAX

Office Hours: 9:00 a.m. - 3:00 p.m.
E-MAIL: N/A
Web Site: N/A
MAPSCO: 26F

PHILOSOPHY OF SCHOOL

NorthPark Presbyterian Day School strives to provide young children opportunities to grow and develop physically, mentally, socially, and spiritually and to develop their senses of self-worth and identity within the context of Christian faith. We do not discriminate on the basis of race or color for hiring or enrollment.

CREDENTIALS

Accreditations: (see glossary)

Awards and special recognition: (see glossary) N/A

Qualification of administrator: M.Ed. in Elementary and Early Childhood; 20 years teaching experience; Director since 1987

Qualification of faculty: Most have degrees; others have more than three years' experience, several master's degrees.

Other: Affiliated with NAEYC, DAEYC, MNKA

GENERAL

Alternative: No
College preparatory: No
Montessori: No
Nondenominational: No
Church affiliated: Yes
Denomination: Presbyterian
Jewish: N/A
Other denominations: N/A
Student type: Co-ed
Grade category (for details see specific grades offered below): Kindergarten

Infants: N/A
Preschool: Half Day
Kindergarten: Half Day
Primary / Transition: No
Elementary: N/A
Secondary or Middle School: N/A
Specific grades offered: One-year - kindergarten
Student teacher ratio average: 2's 6-8:1; 3's 8-10:1; 4's 12:1; K 16:1
Classes offered per grade: N/A
Average class size: 6-12 (varies according to age)
Total enrollment: 165
Recommended grades to apply: N/A
School hours: 9:00 a.m. -12:00 p.m. (M, T); 9:00 a.m. - 2:00 a.m. (W, Th ,F)
Calendar school year: September - May
Uniforms required: No
Parental involvement opportunities and requirements: Ongoing volunteer
    activities (optional participation)
Average SAT scores: N/A
Visitation procedures: N/A
Personal appointments for touring the facility: Individual appointments with
    Director or with teachers
Group tour dates: N/A
Open house dates: N/A
Classroom visits: N/A
Profit or non-profit: Non-profit

ADMISSIONS

Application form required: Yes
Forms required: Health, emergency
Application deadline: Apply January-February
Application fee: Yes
Contact: Claire Wood, Director
Phone: (214) 361-8024
Student interview required: No
Parent interview required: No
Entrance test required: No
Specific tests administered: N/A
Accept test scores from other schools: No
Testing fee: N/A
Time of year testing is administered: N/A
Test dates offered: N/A

Out of state applicants: N/A
Notification by phone: Yes
Notification by mail: Yes
Other: By mid-March, Student Application Required parents encouraged to visit school.

FINANCIAL

Preschool tuition: 1 day (9:00 a.m. - 2p.m.) $75; 2 days $100; 3 days $125; 5 days $200
Elementary tuition: Kindergarten $200
Secondary tuition: N/A
Other tuition: Optional school bag $5; optional school pictures $9
Cash discounts: N/A
Personal check: N/A
Automatic bank draw: N/A
Credit cards: Yes
Monthly: Yes
Per semester: Yes
Annually: Yes
Financial assistance offered: No
Cancellation insurance: N/A
Sibling discount: N/A
Application acceptance deposit required: N/A

SERVICES

Before school care offered: N/A
After school care offered: N/A
Transportation provided: N/A
Lunch/snack program: Lunch Bunch (12:00 pm-2:00 pm); Wednesday, Thursday, & Friday-students bring their lunches; $25 per month; Snacks: provided by parents and school
Other: Enrichment curriculum offered.

PRESTONWOOD CHRISTIAN ACADEMY

15720 Hillcrest
Dallas, TX 75248
Contact: **Donna Mowrey, Principal**
(972) 404-9796
(972) 661-9886 FAX

Office Hours: 8:00 a.m. - 4:30 p.m.
E-MAIL: N/A
Web Site: pwbc.org/pca.html
MAPSCO: 5Z

PHILOSOPHY OF SCHOOL

To provide an academically challenging environment with a college preparatory curriculum, centered on Biblical truths, for the purpose of developing students into leaders who recognize their God-given gifts and ultimately use their lives to serve Christ and their communities.

CREDENTIALS

Accreditations: (see glossary)
Awards and special recognition: (see glossary) N/A
Qualification of administrator: College degree, advanced degree, teaching background
Qualification of faculty: Certified, college degree, preferably advanced degree, Evangelical

GENERAL

Alternative: No
College preparatory: Yes
Montessori: No
Nondenominational: Yes
Church affiliated: Yes
Denomination: Baptist
Jewish: N/A
Other denominations: N/A
Student type: Co-ed
Grade category (for details see specific grades offered below): N/A
Infants: N/A
Preschool: Full Day, 2, 3, 5 days available
Kindergarten: Half Day and Full Day
Primary / Transition: Yes

Elementary: Yes
Secondary or Middle School: Yes
Specific grades offered: Preschool - 10th
Student teacher ratio average: 17:1
Classes offered per grade: N/A
Average class size: 15
Total enrollment: 510
Recommended grades to apply: 1 year prior to enrollment
School hours: 8:55 a.m. - 3:55 p.m.
Calendar school year: August - May
Uniforms required: Yes
Parental involvement opportunities and requirements: Parent-Teacher
    Fellowship, Council & Committees
Average SAT scores: N/A
Visitation procedures: Schedule through Admissions Office
Personal appointments for touring the facility: Call admissions office to
    arrange a tour
Group tour dates: November 2, 1999, January 25, 2000, February 15, 2000 at
    9:30 a.m. in the Prayer Chapel
Open house dates: November 2, 1999, January 25, 2000, February 15, 2000 at
    9:30 a.m. in the Prayer Chapel
Classroom visits: Call admissions office to arrange a visit
Profit or non-profit: Non-profit

ADMISSIONS

Application form required: Yes
Forms required: Recommendation from former teacher and principal.
Application deadline: N/A
Application fee: $100.00
Contact: Sharron Shaw
Phone: (972) 404-9796 ext 403
Student interview required: Yes
Parent interview required: Yes
Entrance test required: Yes
Specific tests administered: SAT for grades K-10th; Missouri Kids for
    Kindergarten
Accept test scores from other schools: No
Testing fee: Included in application fee
Time of year testing is administered: Year round
Test dates offered: Call for appointment
Out of state applicants: Can be done on-line at www.pwbc.org/pca

Notification by phone: N/A
Notification by mail: Yes

FINANCIAL

Preschool tuition: $1,770 (2 Day), 2,495(3 Day) & 3,950 (5 Day)
Elementary tuition: $5,015 - $5,615 (Grades 1 - 5)
Secondary tuition: $5,615 - $7,135 (Grades 6 - 10)
Other tuition: $300 one-time admission fee, $200 matriculation fee
Cash discounts: Yes, 2% paid annually in advance.
Personal check: Yes
Automatic bank draw: N/A
Credit cards: N/A
Monthly: Yes, 10 equal installments
Per semester: N/A
Annually: Yes
Financial assistance offered: N/A
Cancellation insurance: N/A
Sibling discount: Yes
Application acceptance deposit required: Yes

SERVICES

Before school care offered: Yes
After school care offered: Yes
Transportation provided: All car pool.
Lunch/snack program: Cafeteria meals - optional
Other: Extra curricular activities: football, volleyball, basketball, golf, tennis, drill
team, cheerleading, band. Facilities/services provided: two computer labs, one
for lower and one for upper; library; nurse on staff, school counselor.
Curriculum: content, college-preparatory.

PROVIDENCE CHRISTIAN SCHOOL OF TEXAS

5002 W. Lovers Lane
Dallas, TX 75209
Mailing address:
P.O. Box 25068, Dallas, TX 75225
Contact: **James R. O'Dea**
(214) 691-1030
(214) 691-9189 FAX

Office Hours: 7:30 a.m. - 4:00 p.m.
E-MAIL: jodea6654@aol.com
Web Site: N/A
MAPSCO: 26L

PHILOSOPHY OF SCHOOL

Providence Christian School of Texas offers its students an education that is both classical and Christian. The school offers a rich humanities/arts/social studies curriculum that integrates the study of literature and the arts with the study of history and geography. The mathematics-and-science program enables the student to master the content and skills necessary to participate knowledgeably in the scientific and technological discussions of the modern world. Students are encouraged to develop a world view that integrates Christian faith with all areas of learning.

CREDENTIALS

Accreditations: (see glossary)
Awards and special recognition: (see glossary) N/A
Qualification of administrator: Bachelor's degree (minimum)
Qualification of faculty: Bachelor's degree (minimum)
Other: Affiliated with TANS

GENERAL

Alternative: No
College preparatory: Yes
Montessori: No
Nondenominational: Yes
Church affiliated: Yes
Denomination: Christian
Jewish: N/A
Other denominations: N/A
Student type: Co-ed

Grade category (for details see specific grades offered below): Elementary
Infants: N/A
Preschool: Full Day
Kindergarten: N/A
Primary / Transition: No
Elementary: Yes
Secondary or Middle School: Yes
Specific grades offered: Grades 1 - 9 and Enrichment Preschool
Student teacher ratio average: 12:1
Classes offered per grade: N/A
Average class size: 16
Total enrollment: 450
Recommended grades to apply: N/A
School hours: 8:10 a.m. - 2:40 p.m.
Calendar school year: August (last week) - May
Uniforms required: Yes
Parental involvement opportunities and requirements: Parents' Council
  Organization
Average SAT scores: N/A
Visitation procedures: N/A
Personal appointments for touring the facility: N/A
Group tour dates: N/A
Open house dates: N/A
Classroom visits: N/A
Profit or non-profit: Non-profit

ADMISSIONS

Application form required: Yes
Forms required: Birth certificate, medical form, parental authorization.
Application deadline: Apply December to February
Application fee: $50
Contact: Kathy Stewart, Director of Admissions
Phone: (214) 691-1030
Student interview required: No
Parent interview required: Yes
Entrance test required: Yes
Specific tests administered: N/A
Accept test scores from other schools: No
Testing fee: N/A
Time of year testing is administered: January & February & as needed
Test dates offered: N/A

Out of state applicants: N/A
Notification by phone: N/A
Notification by mail: Yes, letter sent on March 1.

FINANCIAL

Preschool tuition: $600 - $1300
Elementary tuition: Grades 1-3 $4550; 4-6 $4950; 7-8 $5750
Secondary tuition: Grade 9 $5750
Other tuition: Uniform cost
Cash discounts: N/A
Personal check: N/A
Automatic bank draw: N/A
Credit cards: N/A
Monthly: N/A
Per semester: N/A
Annually: Yes, due in full by 1st class day.
Financial assistance offered: Yes
Cancellation insurance: N/A
Sibling discount: N/A
Application acceptance deposit required: N/A

SERVICES

Before school care offered: N/A
After school care offered: N/A
Transportation provided: N/A
Lunch/snack program: N/A
Other: Computer lab, library, enrichment curriculum and extracurricular activities offered.

ROSEMEADE BAPTIST CHRISTIAN SCHOOL

1225 E. Rosemeade Pkwy.
Carrollton, TX 75007
Contact: Sharon Potter, School Administrator
(972) 492-4253
(972) 394-7519 FAX

Office Hours: 7:45 a.m. - 4:00 p.m.
E-MAIL: dspotter@msn.com
Web Site: N/A
MAPSCO: 653Y

PHILOSOPHY OF SCHOOL
To provide a Christ-centered educational program to PreK 3, PreK 4, and K-5 students.

CREDENTIALS
Accreditations: (see glossary) TDPRS
Awards and special recognition: (see glossary) N/A
Qualification of administrator: Master's in Mid-Management
Qualification of faculty: Degreed and certified
Other: Elementary School member of Association of Christian School
    International

GENERAL
Alternative: No
College preparatory: No
Montessori: No
Nondenominational: No
Church affiliated: Yes
Denomination: Baptist
Jewish: N/A
Other denominations: Affiliated with Rosemeade Baptist Church
Student type: Co-ed
Grade category (for details see specific grades offered below): Elementary
Infants: N/A
Preschool: Yes
Kindergarten: Half Day
Primary / Transition: No
Elementary: Yes

Secondary or Middle School: N/A
Specific grades offered: K-5
Other: Preschool 12 months - 4 years
Student teacher ratio average: 18:1
Classes offered per grade: N/A
Average class size: 14-18
Total enrollment: N/A
Recommended grades to apply: N/A
School hours: 8:15 a.m. - 3:15 p.m.
Calendar school year: August - May
Uniforms required: Yes
Parental involvement opportunities and requirements: Active PTF
Average Stanford Achievement Test scores: 70-90 Percentiles
Visitation procedures: Call
Personal appointments for touring the facility: Call
Group tour dates: N/A
Open house dates: January
Classroom visits: Upon Request
Profit or non-profit: Non-profit

ADMISSIONS

Application form required: No
Forms required: Yes, after admission.
Application deadline: N/A
Application fee: N/A
Contact: Sharon Potter
Phone: (972) 492-4253
Student interview required: No
Parent interview required: No
Entrance test required: Yes
Specific tests administered: Kindergarten: MKIDS, 1st - 5th Grade: Stanford Achievement Test
Accept test scores from other schools: Yes
Testing fee: $30.00
Time of year testing is administered: Spring
Test dates offered: Individually administered
Out of state applicants: Call school for information packet or E-mail for pack
Notification by phone: Yes
Notification by mail: N/A
Other: Open Enrollment begins in February.

FINANCIAL

Preschool tuition: From $1330.00 to $2450.00 for 3's and 4's
Elementary tuition: K = $2350.00 1-5=$3470.00
Secondary tuition: N/A
Other tuition: Before and After Care varies
Cash discounts: N/A
Personal check: Yes
Automatic bank draw: Yes
Credit cards: No
Monthly: Yes, 10 or 12 month plan
Per semester: Yes
Annually: Yes, receives 5% discount.
Financial assistance offered: Yes
Cancellation insurance: N/A
Sibling discount: Yes, 10%
Application acceptance deposit required: Yes $250.00 for K, $300 for 1-5
Other: Book Fees: K, $150.00 1-5, $200.00

SERVICES

Before school care offered: Yes, beginning at 7:00 a.m.
After school care offered: Yes, until 6:00 p.m.
Transportation provided: N/A
Lunch/snack program: All snacks for Preschool provided. Elementary lunch program through Twelve Oaks Catering.
Other: Choir and String programs

Chapter 2
Categorized by School Grade

In this chapter, all the DFW schools are listed by school grade to facilitate your research.

We have provided you with a listing of all educational facilities that we could locate. Schools which provided detailed information have their contact information listed here and the page number to reference the additional information. Some of the schools listed did not furnish information for this publication. For information on those schools, you are referred to Chapter 4, "Alphabetical Listing of Schools", which provides their contact information.

CATEGORIZED BY SCHOOL GRADES

INFANT/TODDLER

MDO - Kindergarten

First United Methodist Church Day School   Page(s): 114-117
    801 W. Ave. B at Glenbrook
    Garland, TX 75040
    Phone: (972) 494-3096 or (972) 272-3471
    Grades: 3 years - Kindergarten, MDO

Schreiber Methodist Preschool   Ch.4

Westminister Presbyterian Preschool & Kindergarten   Page(s): 130-132
    8200 Devonshire Drive
    Dallas, Texas 75209
    Phone: (214) 350-6155
    Grades: 2 years - Kindergarten, MDO

MDO - 6th grade

Our Redemeer Lutheran School   Page(s): 94-96
    7611 Park Lane
    Dallas, TX 75225
    Phone: (214) 368-1465
    Grades: 3 years - 6th grade, MDO

6 weeks - 2 years

Peanut Gallery, The (Galleria)   Ch.4

6 weeks - 4 years

Primrose School at Chase Oaks   Ch.4

6 weeks - Kindergarten (5 years)

Highland Park United Methodist Child Development   Ch.4
East Dallas Developmental Center   Ch.4
Lakewood United Methodist Developmental Learning Center   Ch.4
Montessori School of Park Cities   Ch.4
Peanut Gallery, The (Richardson)   Ch.4
Peanut Gallery, The (Walnut Hill)   Ch.4

6 weeks - 1st grade

Montessori School of Las Colinas   Page(s): 354-356
4961 N. O'Connor Blvd.
Irving, TX 75062
Phone: (972) 717-0417
Grades: 6 weeks - 1st grade

6 weeks - 2nd grade

North Dallas Day School   Ch.4

6 weeks - 6th grade (12 years)

Peanut Gallery, The (Colony)   Ch.4
Peanut Gallery, The (Carrollton)   Ch.4
Peanut Gallery, The (Rosemeade Pkwy)   Ch.4

5 months - 4 years

Christian Childhood Development Center   Ch.4

6 months - Kindergarten

Buckingham North Christian School   Page(s): 260-262
801 W. Buckingham
Garland, Texas 75040
Phone: (972) 495-0851
Grades: 6 months—Kindergarten
Temple Emanu-El Preschool   Ch.4

6 months - 1st grade

Lovers Lane United Methodist Church   Page(s): 124-126
9200 Inwood Road
Dallas, TX 75220
Phone: (214) 691-4721
Grades: 6 months - 1st grade

1 year - Kindergarten

Fair Oaks Day School
NorthPark Presbyterian Day School
   9555 N. Central Expressway
   Dallas, Texas 75231
   Phone: (214) 361-8024
   Grades: 1 year - Kindergarten

14 months - 8th grade

Selwyn School
   3333 University Drive West
   Denton, TX 76207
   Phone: (940) 382-6771
   Grades: 13 months - 8th grade

15 months - Preschool

Early Learning Center of First Christian Church

16 months - Kindergarten

Epiphany Day School
   421 Custer Road
   Richardson, Texas 75080
   Phone: (972) 690-0275
   Grades: 16 months - Kindergarten

Jewish Community Center of Dallas

18 months - Kindergarten

daVinci School, The
   5442 La Sierra Drive
   Dallas, Texas 75231
   Phone: (214) 373-9504
   Grades: 18 months - K - primer
Glenwood Day School
   2446 Apollo
   Garland, TX 75044
   Phone: (972) 530-4460
   Grades: 18 months - Kindergarten

18 months - Kindergarten - continued
Northaven Co-operative Preschool and Kindergarten   Ch.4

18 months - 6th grade

Ashbury Academy - Montessori AMI   Page(s): 335-337
219 Executive Way
DeSoto, TX 75115
Phone: (972) 780-4700
Grades: 18 months - 6th grade
Children's World   Ch.4
Fellowship Christian Academy   Ch.4
Good Shepard Montessori School   Ch.4

18 months - 8th grade

Akiba Academy   Page(s): 139-141
6210 Churchill Drive
Dallas, Texas 75230
Phone: (972) 239-7248
Grades: 18 months - 8th grade
Lakemont Academy   Page(s): 152-154
3993 West Northwest Highway
Dallas, Texas 75220
Phone: (214) 351-6404
18 months - 8th grade
St. Alcuin Montessori   Page(s): 369-371
6144 Churchill Way
Dallas, TX 75230
Phone: (972) 239-1745
Grades:18 months - 8th grade
Solomon Schechter Academy of Dallas   Page(s): 155-157
18011 Hillcrest Road
Dallas, TX 75252
Phone: (972) 248-3032
Grades: 18 months - 8th grade

18 Months - 12th grade

Buckingham Private School   Page(s): 52-54
701 State Street
Garland, TX 75040
Phone: (972) 272-4638
Grades: 18 months - 12th grade

PRESCHOOL/KINDERGARTEN PROGRAMS

2 years - 4 years

Creative Preschool Co-Op   Page(s): 108-110
 1210 W. Beltline Road
 Richardson, TX 75080
 Phone: (972) 234-4791
 Grades : 2 years - 4 years
Preston-Royal Preschool   Ch.4
Smart Start Early Childhood Education Center   Ch.4

2 years - 5 years (Kindergarten)

Bent Tree Episcopal School   Page(s): 399-401
 17405 Muirfield Drive
 Dallas, TX 75287
 Phone: (972) 248-6505
 Grades: 2 years - Kindergarten
Callier Child Development Preschool   Ch.4
Trinity Episcopal Preschool   Ch.4

2 years - 1st grade (6 years)

Carlisle School, The   Page(s): 237-239
 4705 West Lovers Lane
 Dallas, TX 75209
 Phone: (214) 351-1833
 Grades: 2 years - 6 years
Montessori School of North Dallas   Page(s): 357-359
 18303 Davenport
 Dallas, Texas 75252
 Phone: (972) 985-8844
 Grades: 2 years - 1st grade
West Plano Montessori School   Page(s): 378-380
 3425 Ashington Lane
 Plano, TX 75023
 Phone: (972) 618-8844
 Grades: 2 years - 1st grade

2 years - 2nd grade

Montessori Episcopal School   Ch.4

2 years - 3rd grade

St. Christopher Montessori   Page(s): 372-374
    7900 Lovers Lane
    Dallas, Texas 75225
    Phone: (214) 363-9391
    Grades: 2 years - 3rd grade

2 years - 4th grade

Child's Garden Montessori School, A   Ch.4
Glen Oaks School   Page(s): 118-120
    12105 Plano Road
    Dallas, TX 75243
    Phone: (972) 231-3135
    Grades: 2 years - 4th grade
Northbrook School   Page(s): 127-129
    5608 Northaven Road
    Dallas, Texas 75230
    Phone: (214) 369-8330
    Grades: 2 years - 4th grade

2 years - 5th grade

Christ Our Savoir Lutheran School   Ch.4
Maryview/ Meritor Academy   Ch.4

2 years - 6th grade

Highland Meadow Montessori Academy   Page(s): 344-346
    1060 Highland Street
    Southlake, TX 76092
    Phone: (817) 488-2138
    Grades: 2 years - 6th grade
St. James Episcopal Montessori   Page(s): 375-377
    9845 McCree
    Dallas, TX 75238
    Phone: (214) 348-1349
    Grades: 2 years - 6th grade

2 years - 8th grade

Country Day School of Arlington   Ch.4

2 years - 12th grade

Alpha Academy   Page(s): 52-54
  701 State Street
  Garland, TX 75040
  Phone: (972) 272-2173
  Grades: 2 years - 12th grade
Evangel Temple Christian School   Ch.4

2 1/2 years - 5 years

Children's Center of First Community Church   Ch.4

2 1/2 years - 3rd grade

Sloan School   Ch.4

2 1/2 years - 5th grade

Redeemer Montessori School   Page(s): 366-368
  120 E. Rochelle
  Irving, TX 75062
  Phone: (972) 257-3517
  Grades: 2 1/2 years - 5th grade
White Rock North School   Page(s): 161-163
  9727 White Rock Trail
  Dallas, TX 75238
  Phone: (214) 348-7410
  Grades: 2 1/2 years - 5th grade
Windsong Montessori School   Page(s): 387-389
  2825 Valley View #100
  Farmers Branch, TX 75234
  Phone: (972) 620-2466
  Grades: 2 1/2 years - 5th grade

2 1/2 years - 6th grade

Amberwood Montessori Academy   Ch.4

Pre-school and Kindergarten

Bent Tree Child Development Center   Page(s): 102-104
  17275 Addison Road
  Addison, TX 75001
  Phone: (972) 931-0868
  Grades: Preschool - Kindergarten

439

PRESCHOOL AND GRADES

3 years - Kindergarten

First United Methodist Church Day School   Page(s): 114-117
    801 W. Ave. B at Glenbrook
    Garland, TX 75040
    Phone: (972) 494-3096 or (972) 272-3471
    Grades: 3 years - Kindergarten

3 years - 1st grade

Little Red Schoolhouse   Ch.4

3 years - 3rd grade

Dallas North Montessori School, The   Ch.4
East Dallas Community School   Ch.4
Holy Trinity Episcopal School   Page(s): 175-177
    1524 Smirl Drive
    Rockwall, Texas 75032
    Phone: (972) 772-6919
    Grades: 3 years - 3rd grade
North Garland Montessori School   Ch.4

3 years - 4th grade

Highland Park Presbyterian Day School   Page(s): 188-190
    3821University Blvd.
    Dallas, Texas 75205
    Phone: (214) 559-5353
    Grades: 3 years - 4th grade
Lamplighter School, The   Ch. 4

3 years - 5th grade

Children's Workshop, The   Page(s): 105-107
    1409 14th Street
    Plano, Texas 75074
    Phone: (972) 424-1932
    Grades: 3 years - 5th grade

441

3 years - 5th grade - continued
St. Andrew's Episcopal School   Page(s): 178-180
   727 Hill Street
   Grand Prairie, Texas 75050
   Phone: (972) 262-3817
   Grades: 3 years - 5th grade

3 years - 6th grade

Cross of Christ Lutheran School   Page(s): 85-87
   512 N. Cockrell Hill
   DeSoto, Texas 75115
   Phone: (972) 223-9586
   Grades: 3 years - 6th grade
DeSoto Private School   Page(s): 411-413
   301 E. Beltline Road
   DeSoto, Texas 75115
   Phone: (972) 223-6450
   Grades: 3 years - 6th grade
Discovery School at Canyon Creek Presbyterian Church   Ch.4
Grace Academy of Dallas   Page(s): 34-36
   11306 A Inwood Road
   Dallas, TX 75229
   Phone: (214) 696-5648
   Grades: 3 years - 6th grade
Highlander-Carden School   Page(s): 317-319
   9120 Plano Road
   Dallas, Texas 75238
   Phone: (214) 348-3220
   Grades: 3 years - 6th grade
Holy Cross Lutheran School   Page(s): 88-90
   11425 Marsh Lane
   Dallas, Texas 75229
   Phone: (214) 358-4396
   Grades: 3 years - 6th grade
Parish Day School, The   Page(s): 70-72
   14115 Hillcrest Road
   Dallas, Texas 75240
   Phone: (972) 239-8011; (800) 909-9081
   Grades: 3 years - 6th grade
St. Mary's Catholic School   Page(s): 220-222
   713 S. Travis
   Sherman, Texas 75090
   Phone: (903) 893-2127
   Grades: 3 years - 6th grade

3 years - 6th grade - continued
St. Philip's School   Ch.4
St. Vincent's Episcopal School   Page(s): 181-183
 1300 Forest Ridge Drive
 Bedford, Texas 76022
 Phone: (817) 354-7979
 Grades: 3 years - 6th grade
Scofield Christian School   Page(s): 40-42
 7730 Abrams Road
 Dallas, Texas 75231
 Phone: (214) 349-6843
 Grades: 3 years—6th grade

3 years - 8th grade

Cambridge Square Private School of DeSoto   Page(s): 405-407
 1121 East Pleasant Run Road
 DeSoto, TX 75115
 Phone: (214) 224-5596
 Grades: 3 years - 8th grade
Dallas Montessori Academy   Page(s): 341-343
 5757 Samuell Blvd.
 Dallas, Texas 75228
 Phone: (214) 388-0091
 Grades: 3 years - 8th grade
Faith Lutheran School   Ch.4
Good Shepherd Catholic School   Page(s): 206-208
 214 S. Garland Ave.
 Garland, TX 75040
 Phone: (972) 272-6533
 Grades: 3 years - 8th grade
Hillcrest Academy, The   Page(s): 148-151
 12302 Park Central Drive
 Dallas, Texas 75251
 Phone: (972) 788-0292
 Grades: 3 years - 8th grade
Holy Trinity Catholic School   Page(s): 213-215
 3815 Oak Lawn
 Dallas, Texas 75219
 Phone: (214) 526-5113
 Grades: 3 years - 8th grade
Immaculate Conception School   Ch.4
Prince of Peace Christian School   Ch.4

4 years - 6th grade

Eastlake Christian School   Page(s): 28-30
    721 Easton
    Dallas, Texas 75218
    Phone: (214) 349-4547
    Grades: 4 years - 6th grade
J. Erik Jonsson Community School   Page(s): 191-193
    110 E. Tenth Street
    Dallas, TX 75203
    Phone: (214) 915-1890
    Grades: 4 years - 6th grade
White Lake School, The   Ch.4

4 years - 7th grade

Glenview Christian School   Ch.4

4 years - 8th grade

Arbor Acre Preparatory School   Page(s): 250-252
    8000 South Hampton Road
    Dallas, Texas 75232
    Phone: (972) 224-0511
    Grades: 4 years - 8th grade
Good Shepherd Episcopal School   Page(s): 60-63
    11122 Midway
    Dallas, Texas 75229
    Phone: (214) 357-1610 ext. 215
    Grades: 4 years - 8th grade

4 years - 8th grade - continued

Holy Family of Nazareth School   Ch.4
Oak Hill Academy   Page(s): 290-292
    6464 E. Lovers Lane
    Dallas, TX 75214
    Phone: (214) 368-0664
    Grades: 4 years - 8th grade
St. John's Episcopal School   Ch.4
St. Mary of Carmel   Ch.4
St. Paul Lutheran   Ch.4

4 years - 9th grade

Providence Christian School of Texas   Page(s): 426-428
   5002 W. Lovers Lane
   Dallas, Texas 75209
   Phone: (214) 691-1030
   Grades: 4 years - 9th grade

4 years - 10th grade

Prestonwood Christian Academy   Page(s): 423-425
   15720 Hillcrest
   Dallas, Texas 75248
   Phone: (972) 404-9796
   Grades: 4 years - 10th grade

4 years - 12th grade

Bethany Christian School   Ch.4
Canyon Creek Academy   Ch.4
Covenant Christian Academy   Ch.4
Dallas Christian School   Page(s): 134-136
   1515 Republic Parkway
   Mesquite, TX 75150
   Phone: (972) 270-5495
   Grades: 4 years - 12th grade
Fort Worth Christian School   Ch.4
Gospel Lighthouse Christian Academy   Ch.4
Hockaday School, The   Ch.4
Metropolitan Christian School   Ch.4
St. Therese Academy   Page(s): 246-248
   2700 Finley Road
   Irving, Texas 75062
   Phone: (972) 252-3000
   Grades: 4 years - 12th
Texas Christian Academy   Page(s): 43-45
   915 WEB
   Arlington, TX 76011
   Phone: (817) 274-5201
   Grades: 4 years - 12th grade
Trinity Lyceum   Page(s): 46-48
   805 Secretary Drive
   Arlington, TX 76015
   Phone: (817) 469-6895
   Grades: 4 years - 12th

4 years - 12th grade - continued
Vanguard Preparatory School   Page(s): 303-305
    4240 Omega
    Dallas, TX 75244
    Phone: (972) 404-1616
    Grades: Preschool - 12th

Kindergarten Only

Montessori School of Pleasant Grove   Ch.4

KINDERGARTEN & GRADES

Kindergarten - 5th grade

Covenant Classical School   Page(s): 314-316
    6401 Garland Avenue
    Fort Worth, TX 76116
    Phone: (817) 731-6447
    Grades: K - 5th grade
First Christian Elementary & Preschool   Page(s): 414-416
    1109 Brown Street
    Waxahachie, Texas 75165
    Phone: (972) 937-1952
    Grades: Kindergarten - 5th
Rosemeade Baptist Christian School   Page(s): 429-431
    1225 E. Rosemeade Pkwy.
    Carrollton, Texas 75007
    Phone: (972) 492-4253
    Grades: Kindergarten - 5th

Kindergarten - 8th grade

All Saints Catholic School   Ch. 4
Canterbury Episcopal School, The   Page(s): 169-171
    1708 North Westmoreland
    DeSoto, TX 75115
    Phone: (972) 572-7200
    Grades: Kindergarten - 8th grade
Christ The King School   Page(s): 203-205
    4100 Colgate
    Dallas, Texas 75225
    Phone: (214) 365-1234
    Grades: Kindergarten - 8th

Kindergarten—10th grade

Richardson Adventist School   Page(s): 230-232
  1201 W. Beltline Road
  Richardson, Texas 75080
  Phone: (972) 238-1183
  Grades: Kindergarten—10th grade

Kindergarten—12th grade

All Saints Episcopal School   Ch.4
Anderson Private School for the Gifted and Talented, The   Page(s): 392-395
  14900 White Settlement Road
  Fort Worth, TX 76108
  Phone: (817) 448-8484
  Grades: Kindergarten - 12th grade
Burton Adventist Academy   Ch.4
First Baptist Academy   Page(s): 31-33
  Box 868
  Dallas, Texas 75221
  Phone: (214) 969-2488
  Grades: Kindergarten - 12th grade
Fort Worth Country Day School   Ch.4
Garland Christian Academy   Ch.4
Happy Hill Farm Academy/ Home   Page(s): 275-277
  HC51- Box 56
  Granbury, TX 76048
  Phone: (254) 897-4822
  Grades: Kindergarten - 12th
Lakehill Preparatory School   Page(s): 64-66
  2720 Hillside Drive
  Dallas, Texas 75214
  Phone: (214) 826-2931
  Grades: Kindergarten - 12th grade
Liberty Christian School   Ch.4
Shady Grove Christian Academy   Ch.4
Trinity Christian Academy   Page(s): 158-160
  17001 Addison Road
  Addison, TX 75001
  Phone: (972) 931-8325
  Grades: Kindergarten - 12th grade
Trinity Valley School   Page(s): 77-79
  7500 Dutch Branch Road
  Ft. Worth, TX 76132
  Phone: (817) 321-0100
  Grades: Kindergarten - 12th grade

PRIMER PROGRAMS— AFTER KINDERGARTEN BEFORE 1ST GRADE

ELEMENTARY PROGRAMS

1st - 4th grade

Wise Academy, The   Page(s): 164-166
6930 Alpha Road
Dallas, Texas 75240
Phone: (972) 789-1800
Grades: 1st - 4th

1st - 6th grade

Preston Hollow Presbyterian School   Page(s): 293-295
9800 Preston Road
Dallas, TX 75230
Phone: (214) 368-3886
Grades: 1st - 6th

1st - 8th grade

Fulton Academy of Rockwall, The   Page(s): 417-419
1623 Laurence
Rockwall, Texas 75032
Phone: (972) 772-4445
Grades: 1st - 8th

Hillier School of Highland Park Presbyterian Church   Page(s): 281-283
3821 University Blvd.
Dallas, TX 75205
Phone: (214) 559-5363
Grades: 1st - 8th

Meadowview School   Page(s): 287-289
2419 Franklin
Mesquite, Texas 75150
Phone: (972) 289-1831
Grades: 1st grade - 8th grade

1st - 12th grade programs

ChristWay Academy   Ch.4

1st - 12th grade programs - continued

Fairhill School & Diagnostic Assessment Center Page(s): 269-271
  16150 Preston Road
  Dallas, Texas 75248
  Phone: (972) 233-1026
  Grades: 1st - 12th
St. Mark's School Of Texas Page(s): 73
  10600 Preston Road
  Dallas, Texas 75230
  Phone: (214) 346-8700
  Grades: 1st grade - 12th grade
Star Bright Academy Page(s): 326-328
  6000 Custer Road, Bldg 5
  Dallas, Texas 75023
  Phone: (972) 517-6730
  Grades: 1st - 12th
Winston School, The Page(s): 309-312
  5707 Royal Lane
  Dallas, Texas 75229
  Phone: (214) 691-6950
  Grades: 1st - 12th

2nd - 9th grade

Glen Lakes Academy Page(s): 272-274
  6000 Custer Road, Building 7
  Plano, Texas 75023
  Phone: (972) 517-7498
  Grades: 2nd - 9th

MIDDLE SCHOOL PROGRAMS

5th - 12th Grades

Cistercian Preparatory School Ch.4

7th - 12th Grades

Bishop Dunne Catholic High School Page(s): 196-199
  3900 Rugged Drive
  Dallas, TX 75224
  Phone: (214) 339-6561
  Grades: 7th grade - 12th grade
Bridgeway School Page(s): 256-259
  7808 Clodus Fields Drive
  Dallas, TX 75251
  Phone: (214) 770-0845
  Grades: 7th grade - 12th grade

Dallas Academy   Page(s): 263-265
    950 Tiffany Way
    Dallas, TX 75218
    Phone: (214) 324-1481
    Grades: 7th grade - 12th grade
Lakewood Presbyterian School   Ch.4
Liberty Christian High School   Ch.4
Logos Academy   Page(s): 243-245
    10919 Royal Haven
    Dallas, Texas 75229
    Phone: (214) 357-2995
    Grades: 7th grade - 12th grade
Lutheran High School   Page(s): 91-93
    8494 Stults Road
    Dallas, TX 75243
    Phone: (214) 349-8912
    Grades: 7th - 12th
Southern Methodist University Study Skills Classes   Ch.4

JUNIOR HIGH PROGRAMS

8th - 12th Grades

Alexander School, The   Page(s): 142-144
    409 International Parkway
    Richardson, Texas 75081
    Phone: (972) 690-9210
    Grades: 8th - 12th

HIGH SCHOOL PROGRAMS

9th - 12th grade

Bending Oaks High School   Page(s): 253-255
    11884 Greenville Avenue, Suite 120
    Dallas, TX 75243
    Phone: (972) 669-0000
    Grades: 9th grade - 12th grade
Bishop Lynch High School, Inc.   Page(s): 200-202
    9750 Ferguson Road
    Dallas, TX 75228
    Phone: (214) 324-3607
    Grades: 9th grade - 12th grade

9th - 12th grade - continued

Dallas Learning Center   Page(s): 266-268
    1021 Newberry Drive, Suite 1
    Richardson, TX 75080
    Phone: (972) 231-3723
    Grades: 12th grade - 9th grade

Jesuit College Preparatory School   Ch.4

Ursuline Academy of Dallas   Page(s): 80-82
    4900 Walnut Hill Lane
    Dallas, TX 75229
    Phone: (214) 363-6551
    Grades: 9th - 12th

Walden Preparatory School   Page(s): 306-308
    14552 Monfort Drive
    Dallas, TX 75240
    Phone: (972) 233-6883
    Grades: 9th - 12th

Yavneh Academy of Dallas   Ch.4

SPECIAL NEEDS SCHOOLS

Academic Achievement Associates   Page(s): 234-236
    12820 Hillcrest Road, Suite 124 C
    Dallas, Texas 75230
    Phone: (972) 490-6399
    Grades: Kindergarten - Adult

Autistic Treatment Center   Ch.4

Coughs & Cuddles for Mildly Ill Children   Page(s): 240-242
    6100 W. Parker Road
    Plano, Texas 75093
    Phone: (972) 608-8585
    Ages: 6 weeks - 16 years

Notre Dame of Dallas Schools, The   Page(s): 320-322
    2018 Allen Street
    Dallas, TX 75204
    Phone: (214) 720-3911
    Grades: 3 years - 21 years

PATHfinders College Preparatory   Ch. 4

Rise School of Dallas, The   Page(s): 323-325
    Preschool for children with Down's Syndrome and other disabilities
    5923 Royal Lane
    Dallas, TX 75230
    Phone: (214) 373-4666
    Grades: Preschool

Chapter 3
School Locations and Maps

In this chapter, all the DFW schools are grouped geographically to help you find a school near your home. The listings are arranged alphabetically by town name or neighborhood. Within these categories, schools are listed by zip code for your convenience.

The maps have been provided by MAPSCO and MAPSCO reference numbers appear with the contact information of the schools.

CATEGORIZED BY ZIP CODE

ADDISON

75001

Bent Tree Child Development Center
75001, Addison
Page(s): 102-104

Greenhill School
75001, Addison
See Ch. 4

Trinity Christian Academy
75001, Addison
Page(s): 158-160

ALLEN

75002

Southwest Academy
75002, Allen
Page(s): 299-302

ARLINGTON

76011

Country Day School of Arlington
76011, Arlington
See Ch. 4

Texas Christian Academy
76011, Arlington
Page(s): 158-160

76013

Oakridge School, The
76013, Arlington
Page(s): 67-69

St. Alban's Episcopal School
76013, Arlington
See Ch. 4

76015

Trinity Lyceum
76015, Arlington
Page(s): 46-48

76017

Burton Adventist Academy
76017, Arlington
See Ch. 4

BEDFORD

76022

St. Vincent's Episcopal School
76022, Bedford
Page(s): 181-183

CARROLLTON

75006

Carrollton Christian Academy
75006, Carrollton
Page(s): 145-147

Child's Garden Montessori School, A
75006, Carrollton
See Ch. 4

75007

Peanut Gallery, The
75007, Carrollton
See Ch. 4

Peanut Gallery, The
75007, Carrollton
See Ch. 4

Prince of Peace Christian School
75007, Carrollton
See Ch. 4

Rosemeade Baptist Christian School
75007, Carrollton
Page(s): 429-431

CEDAR HILL

75104

Ashleys Private School
75104, Cedar Hill
Page(s): 396-398

Trinity Christian School
75104, Cedar Hill
Page(s): 55-57

COLLEYVILLE

76034

Covenant Christian Academy
76034, Colleyville
See Ch. 4

COLONY

75056

Peanut Gallery, The
75056, Colony
See Ch. 4

COPPELL

75019

Christ Our Savior Lutheran School
75019, Coppell
See Ch. 4

Smart Start Early Childhood Education Center
75019, Coppell
See Ch. 4

DALLAS

75203

J. Erik Jonsson Community School
75203, Dallas
Page(s): 191-193

75204

Notre Dame of Dallas Schools, The
75204, Dallas
Page(s): 320-322

St. Thomas Aquinas
75204, Dallas
See Ch. 4

75205

Highland Park Presbyterian Day School
75205, Dallas
Page(s): 188-190

Highland Park United Methodist Child Development
75205, Dallas
See Ch. 4

Hillier School of Highland Park Presbyterian Church
75205, Dallas
Page(s): 281-283

75206

East Dallas Developmental Center
75206, Dallas
See Ch. 4

75208

Tyler Street Christian Academy
75208, Dallas
See Ch. 4

75209

Carlisle School, The
75209, Dallas
Page(s): 237-239

Montessori School of Park Cities
75209, Dallas
See Ch. 4

Providence Christian School of Texas
75209, Dallas
Page(s): 426-428

Westminster Presbyterian Preschool and Kindergarten
75209, Dallas
Page(s): 130-132

75211

Gospel Lighthouse Christian Academy
75211, Dallas
See Ch. 4

75212

St. Mary of Carmel
75212, Dallas
See Ch. 4

75214

Children's Center of First Community Church, The
75214, Dallas
See Ch. 4

Lakehill Preparatory School
75214, Dallas
Page(s): 64-66

Lakewood Presbyterian School
75214, Dallas
See Ch. 4

Lakewood United Methodist Developmental Learning Center
75214, Dallas
See Ch. 4

Oak Hill Academy
75214, Dallas
Page(s): 290-292

Zion Lutheran School
75214, Dallas
Page(s): 97-99

75215

St. Phillip's School
75215, Dallas
See Ch. 4

75217

Metropolitan Christian School
75217, Dallas
See Ch. 4

Montessori School of Pleasant Grove
75217, Dallas
See Ch. 4

75218

Dallas Academy
75218, Dallas
Page(s): 263-265

Eastlake Christian School
75218, Dallas
Page(s): 28-30

St. Bernard of Clairvaux
75218, Dallas
Page(s): 216-219

St. John's Episcopal School
75218, Dallas
See Ch. 4

75219

Holy Trinity Catholic School
75219, Dallas
Page(s): 213-215

75220

Lakemont Academy
75220, Dallas
Page(s): 152-154

Lover's Lane United Methodist Church
75220, Dallas
Page(s): 124-126

75220 continued

Meadowbrook School
75220, Dallas
Page(s): 347-349

75221

First Baptist Academy
75221, Dallas
Page(s): 31-33

75223

East Dallas Community School
75223, Dallas
See Ch. 4

75224

Bishop Dunne Catholic High School
75224, Dallas
Page(s): 196-199

St. Elizabeth of Hungary Catholic School
75224, Dallas
See Ch. 4

75225

Christ the King School
75225, Dallas
Page(s): 203-205

Our Redeemer Lutheran School
75225, Dallas
Page(s): 94-96

St. Christopher Montessori
75225, Dallas
Page(s): 372-374

Temple Emanu-El Preschool
75225, Dallas
See Ch. 4

75225

Yavneh Academy of Dallas
75225, Dallas
See Ch. 4

75227

St. Phillip the Apostle Catholic School
75227, Dallas
See Ch. 4

75228

Bishop Lynch High School, Inc.
75228, Dallas
Page(s): 200-202

Dallas Montessori Academy
75228, Dallas
Page(s): 341-343

St. Pius X Catholic School
75228, Dallas
See Ch. 4

White Rock Montessori School
75228, Dallas
Page(s): 384-386

75229

Andrew Austin School
75229, Dallas
Page(s): 332-334

Creative School, The - Walnut Hill United Methodist Church
75229, Dallas
Page(s): 111-113

Episcopal School of Dallas
75229, Dallas
See Ch. 4

75229 continued

Good Shepherd Episcopal School
75229, Dallas
Page(s): 60-63

Grace Academy of Dallas
75229, Dallas
Page(s): 34-36

Hockaday School, The
75229, Dallas
See Ch. 4

Holy Cross Lutheran School
75229, Dallas
Page(s): 88-90

Lamplighter School, The
75229, Dallas
See Ch. 4

Logos Academy
75229, Dallas
Page(s): 243-245

Preston-Royal Preschool
75229, Dallas
See Ch. 4

St. Monica Catholic School
75229, Dallas
Page(s): 223-225

Ursuline Academy of Dallas
75229, Dallas
Page(s): 80-82

Winston School, The
75229, Dallas
Page(s): 309-312

75230

Academic Achievement Associates
75230, Dallas
Page(s): 234-236

Akiba Academy
75230, Dallas
Page(s): 139-141

Dallas International School
75230, Dallas
See Ch. 4

Jewish Community Center of Dallas
75230, Dallas
See Ch. 4

Northaven Co-operative Preschool & Kindergarten
75230, Dallas
See Ch. 4

Northbrook School
75230, Dallas
Page(s): 127-129

Preston Hollow Presbyterian School
75230, Dallas
Page(s): 293-295

Rise School of Dallas, The
75230, Dallas
Page(s): 323-325

St. Alcuin Montessori
75230, Dallas
Page(s): 369-371

St. Mark's School of Texas
75230, Dallas
Page(s): 73

75231

daVinci School, The
75231, Dallas
Page(s): 408-410

Fair Oaks Day School
75231, Dallas
See Ch. 4

Liberty Christian High School
75231, Dallas
See Ch. 4

Montessori Children's House and School
75231, Dallas
Page(s): 350-353

NorthPark Presbyterian Day School
75231, Dallas
Page(s): 420-422

Peanut Gallery, The
75231, Dallas
See Ch. 4

Scofield Christian School
75231, Dallas
Page(s): 40-42

75232

Arbor Acre Preparatory School
75232, Dallas
Page(s): 250-252

Fellowship Christian Academy
75232, Dallas
See Ch. 4

75235

Callier Child Development Preschool
75235, Dallas
See Ch. 4

75238

Christian Childhood Development Center
75238, Dallas
See Ch. 4

Highlander-Carden School, The
75238, Dallas
Page(s): 317-319

St. James Episcopal Montessori
75238, Dallas
Page(s): 375-377

St. Patrick School
75238, Dallas
See Ch. 4

White Rock North Montessori School
75238, Dallas
Page(s): 161-163

75240

Parish Day School, The
75240, Dallas
Page(s): 70-72

Peanut Gallery, The
75240, Dallas
See Ch. 4

Walden Preparatory School
75240, Dallas
Page(s): 306-308

Wise Academy, The
75240, Dallas
Page(s): 164-166

75243

Autistic Treatment Center
75243, Dallas
See Ch. 4

75243 continued

Bending Oaks High School
75243, Dallas
Page(s): 253-255

Glen Oaks School
75243, Dallas
Page(s): 118-120

Lutheran High School
75243, Dallas
Page(s): 91-93

North Dallas Day School
75243, Dallas
See Ch. 4

Phoenix Academy
75243, Dallas
See Ch. 4

75244

Jesuit College Preparatory School
75244, Dallas
See Ch. 4

St. Rita School
75244, Dallas
See Ch. 4

Schreiber Methodist Preschool
75244, Dallas
See Ch. 4

Vanguard Preparatory School
75244, Dallas
Page(s): 303-305

Westwood Montessori School
75244, Dallas
Page(s): 381-383

75248

All Saints Catholic School
75248, Dallas
See Ch. 4

Fairhill School and Diagnostic Assessment Center
75248, Dallas
Page(s): 269-271

Prestonwood Christian Academy
75248, Dallas
Page(s): 423-425

Shelton School and Evaluation Center
75248, Dallas
Page(s): 296-298

75251

Bridgeway School
75251, Dallas
Page(s): 256-259

Hillcrest Academy
75251, Dallas
Page(s): 148-151

75252

Keystone Academy
75252, Dallas
Page(s): 284-286

Montessori School of North Dallas
75252, Dallas
Page(s): 357-359

Solomon Schechter Academy of Dallas
75252, Dallas
Page(s): 155-157

<u>75275</u>

Southern Methodist University Study Skills Classes
75275, Dallas
See Ch. 4

<u>75287</u>

Bent Tree Episcopal School
75287, Dallas
Page(s): 399-401

DENTON

<u>76207</u>

Liberty Christian School
76207, Denton
See Ch. 4

Selwyn School
76207, Denton
Page(s): 74-76

DESOTO

<u>75115</u>

Ashbury Academy - Montessori AMI
75115, DeSoto
Page(s): 335-337

Cambridge Square Private School of DeSoto
75115, DeSoto
Page(s): 405-407

Canterbury Episcopal School
75115, DeSoto
Page(s): 169-171

Cross of Christ Lutheran School
75115, DeSoto
Page(s): 85-87

75115 continued

DeSoto Private School
75115, DeSoto
Page(s): 411-413

Maryview/ Meritor Academy
75115, DeSoto
See Ch. 4

DUNCANVILLE

75116

ChristWay Academy
75116, Duncanville
See Ch. 4

FARMERS BRANCH

75234

Harrington School, The
75234, Farmers Branch
See Ch. 4

Windsong Montessori School
75234, Farmers Branch
Page(s): 387-389

FORT WORTH

76102

St. Paul Lutheran
76102, Fort Worth
See Ch. 4

76103

White Lake School, The
76103, Fort Worth
See Ch. 4

76108

All Saints Episcopal School
76108, Fort Worth
See Ch. 4

Anderson Private School for the Gifted and Talented, The
76108, Fort Worth
Page(s): 392-395

76109

Fort Worth Country Day School
76109, Fort Worth
See Ch. 4

Trinity Episcopal Preschool
76109, Fort Worth
See Ch. 4

76116

Covenant Classical School
76116, Fort Worth
Page(s): 314-316

Redeemer Lutheran School
76116, Fort Worth
See Ch. 4

76132

Trinity Valley School
76132, Fort Worth
Page(s): 77-79

76137

Glenview Christian School
76137, Fort Worth
See Ch. 4

76180

Fort Worth Christian School
76180, Fort Worth
See Ch. 4

St. John the Apostle Catholic School
76180, Fort Worth
See Ch. 4

FRISCO

75034

Legacy Christian Academy
75034, Frisco
Page(s): 37-39

GARLAND

75040

Alpha Academy
75040, Garland
Page(s): 52-54

Buckingham North Christian School
75040, Garland
Page(s): 260-262

Buckingham Private School
75040, Garland
Page(s): 52-54

First United Methodist Church Day School
75040, Garland
Page(s): 114-117

Garland Christian Academy
75040, Garland
See Ch. 4

75040 continued

Good Shepherd Catholic School
75040, Garland
Page(s): 206-208

North Garland Montessori School
75040, Garland
See Ch. 4

75044

Glenwood Day School
75044, Garland
Page(s): 121-123

GRANBURY

76048

Happy Hill Farm Academy/Home
76048, Granbury
Page(s): 275-277

GRAND PRAIRIE

75050

St. Andrew's Episcopal School
75050, Grand Prairie
Page(s): 178-180

Immaculate Conception School
75050, Grand Prairie
See Ch. 4

Shady Grove Christian Academy
75050, Grand Prairie
See Ch. 4

<u>**75051**</u>

Evangel Temple Christian School
75051, Grand Prairie
See Ch. 4

Montessori School of Westchester
75052, Grand Prairie
Page(s): 360-362

IRVING

<u>**75014**</u>

Cistercian Preparatory School
75014, Irving
See Ch. 4

<u>**75061**</u>

Amberwood Montessori Academy
75061, Irving
See Ch. 4

<u>**75062**</u>

Children's World
75062, Irving
See Ch. 4

Highlands School, The
75062, Irving
Page(s): 209-212

Holy Family of Nazareth School
75062, Irving
See Ch. 4

Montessori School of Las Colinas
75062, Irving
Page(s): 354-356

Redeemer Montessori School
75062, Irving
Page(s): 366-368

75062 continued

St. Therese Academy
75062, Irving
Page(s): 246-248

Sloan School
75062, Irving
See Ch. 4

LEWISVILLE

75067

Montessori Episcopal School
75067, Lewisville
See Ch. 4

MCKINNEY

75070

Good Shepherd Montessori School
75070, McKinney
See Ch. 4

MESQUITE

75149

Little Red Schoolhouse
75149, Mesquite
See Ch. 4

75150

Dallas Christian School
75150, Mesquite
Page(s): 134-136

Meadowview School
75150, Mesquite
Page(s): 287-289

PLANO

75023

Glen Lakes Academy
75023, Plano
Page(s): 272-274

Primrose School at Chase Oaks
75023, Plano
See Ch. 4

Star Bright Academy
75023, Plano
Page(s): 326-328

West Plano Montessori School
75023, Plano
Page(s): 278-280

75024

Preston Meadows Montessori
75024, Plano
Page(s): 263-265

Children's Workshop, The
75074, Plano
Page(s): 105-107

Faith Lutheran School
75074, Plano
See Ch. 4

Bethany Christian School
75075, Plano
See Ch. 4

Palisades Day School
75075, Plano
See Ch. 4

75093

Coughs and Cuddles for Mildly Ill Children
75093, Plano
Page(s): 240-242

Prince of Peace Catholic School
75093, Plano
See Ch. 4

RICHARDSON

75080

Beth Torah Preschool & Kindergarten
75080, Richardson
Page(s): 402-404

Canyon Creek Christian Academy
75080, Richardson
See Ch. 4

Creative Preschool Co-op
75080, Richardson
Page(s): 108-110

Dallas Learning Center
75080, Richardson
Page(s): 266-268

Dallas North Montessori School, The
75080, Richardson
See Ch. 4

Discovery School at Canyon Creek
75080, Richardson
See Ch. 4

Epiphany Day School
75080, Richardson
Page(s): 172-174

Highland Academy
75080, Richardson
Page(s): 278-280

75080 continued

Richardson Adventist School
75080, Richardson
Page(s): 230-232

St. Paul the Apostle
75080, Richardson
Page(s): 226-228

75081

Alexander School, The
75081, Richardson
Page(s): 142-144

Early Learning Center at First Christian Church
75081, Richardson
See Ch. 4

75082

Peanut Gallery, The
75082, Richardson
See Ch. 4

Rainbow Connection Preschool and Kindergarten
75082, Richardson
See Ch. 4

ROCKWALL

75032

Country Day Montessori School
75032, Rockwall
Page(s): 338-340

Fulton Academy of Rockwall, The
75032, Rockwall
Page(s): 417-419

Holy Trinity Episcopal School
75032, Rockwall
Page(s): 175-177

ROWLETT

75088

Rowlett Christian Academy
75088, Rowlett
See Ch. 4

SHERMAN

75090

St. Mary's Catholic School
75090, Sherman
Page(s): 220-222

SOUTHLAKE

76092

Clariden School
76092, Southlake
Page(s): 185-187

Highland Meadow Montessori Academy
76092, Southlake
Page(s): 344-346

WAXAHACHIE

75165

First Christian Elementary and Preschool
75165, Waxahachie
Page(s): 414-416

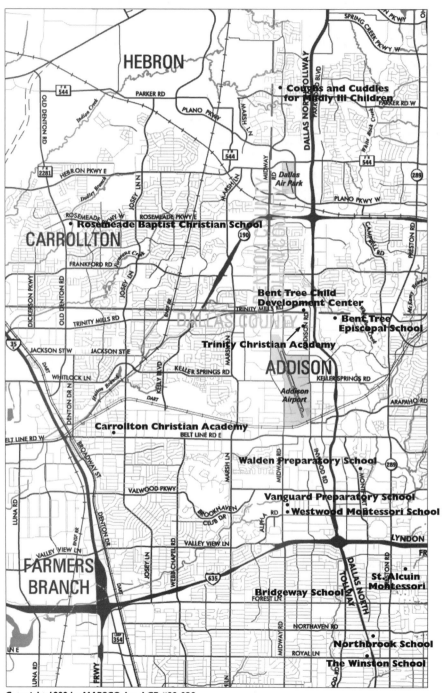

HEBRON

SPRING CREEK PKWY W

PARKER RD

PLANO PKWY

PARKER RD W

• Coughs and Cuddles
for Mildly Ill Children

Dallas
Air Park

PLANO PKWY W

ROSEMEADE PKWY W   ROSEMEADE PKWY E

• Rosemeade Baptist Christian School

CARROLLTON

FRANKFORD RD

TRINITY MILLS RD

TRINITY MILLS RD

DALLAS COUNTY

Bent Tree Child
Development Center

• Bent Tree
Episcopal School

Trinity Christian Academy

JACKSON ST W   JACKSON ST E

WHITLOCK LN

KELLER SPRINGS RD

ADDISON

KELLER SPRINGS RD

ARAPAHO RD

Addison
Airport

Carrollton Christian Academy

BELT LINE RD E

BELT LINE RD W

Walden Preparatory School

VALWOOD PKWY

Vanguard Preparatory School

BROOKHAVEN
CLUB DR

• Westwood Montessori School

VALLEY VIEW LN

VALLEY VIEW LN

LYNDON

FARMERS

St. Alcuin
Montessori

BRANCH

Bridgeway School

FOREST LN

NORTHAVEN RD

Northbrook School

ROYAL LN

The Winston School

482

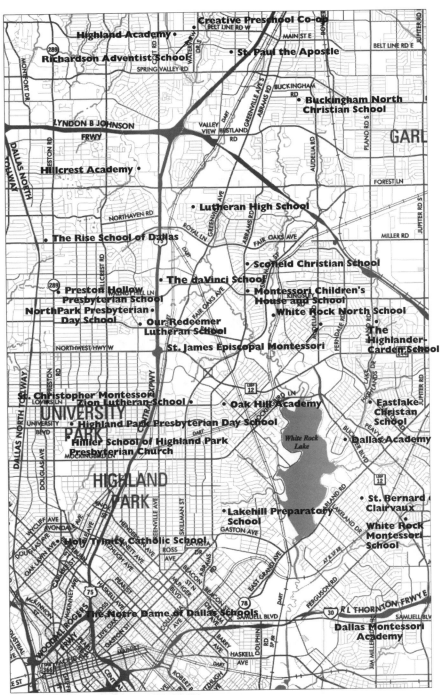

483

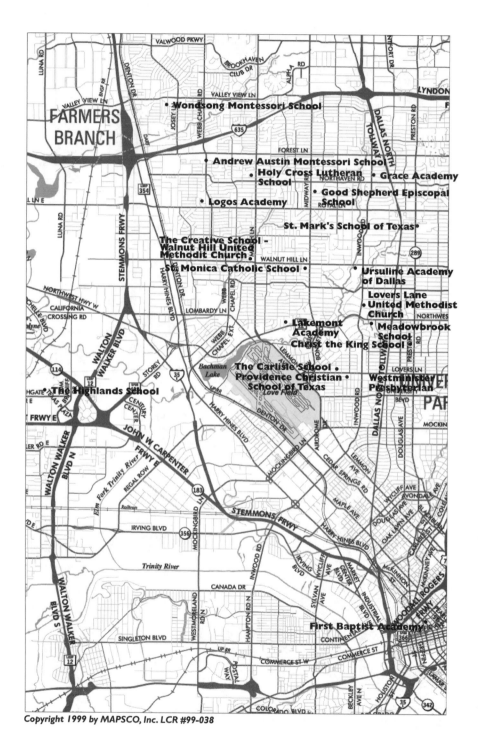

Copyright 1999 by MAPSCO, Inc. LCR #99-038

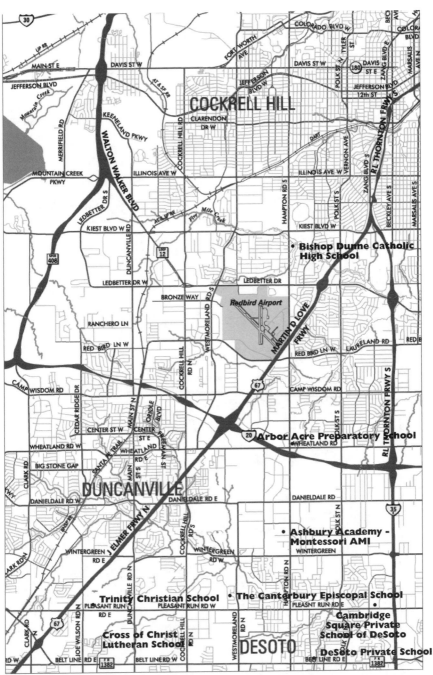

485

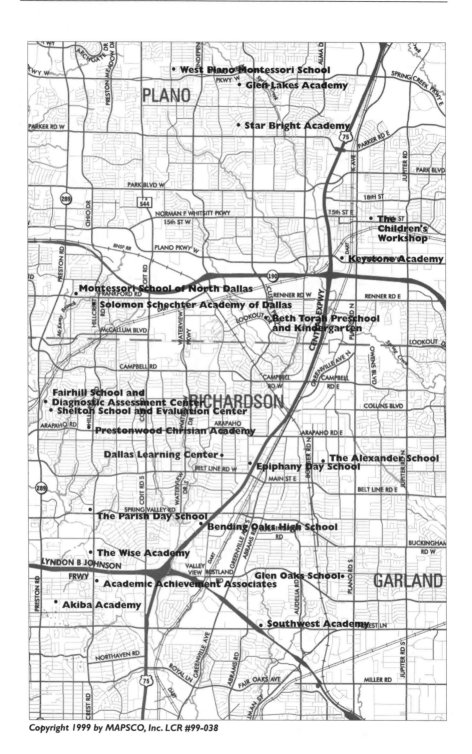

West Plano Montessori School

Glen Lakes Academy

PLANO

Star Bright Academy

The Children's Workshop

Keystone Academy

Montessori School of North Dallas

Solomon Schechter Academy of Dallas

Beth Torah Preschool and Kindergarten

Fairhill School and Diagnostic Assessment Center

RICHARDSON

Shelton School and Evaluation Center

Prestonwood Christian Academy

Dallas Learning Center

The Alexander School

Epiphany Day School

The Parish Day School

Bending Oaks High School

BUCKINGHAM

The Wise Academy

LYNDON B JOHNSON FRWY

Glen Oaks School

GARLAND

Academic Achievement Associates

Akiba Academy

Southwest Academy

486

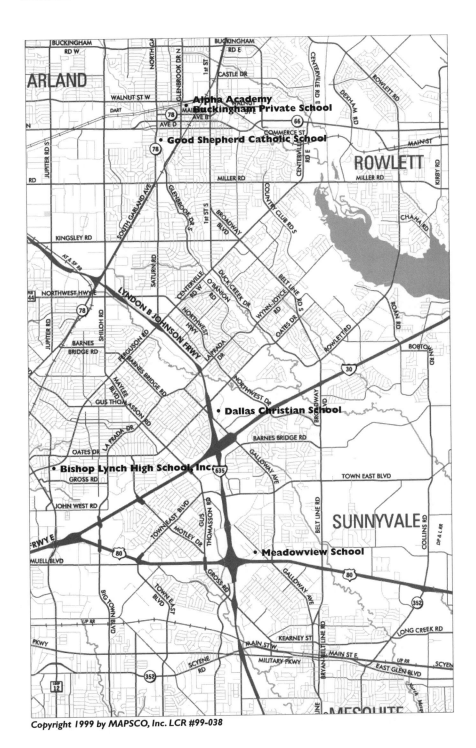

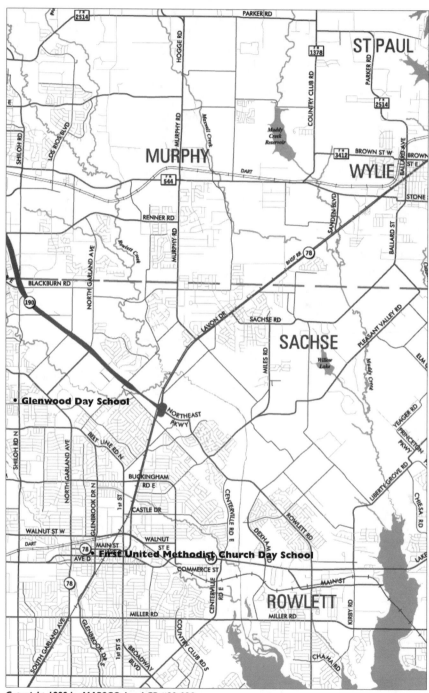

488

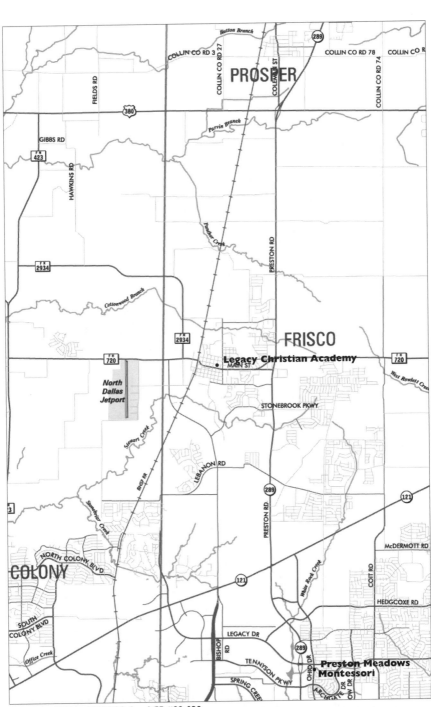

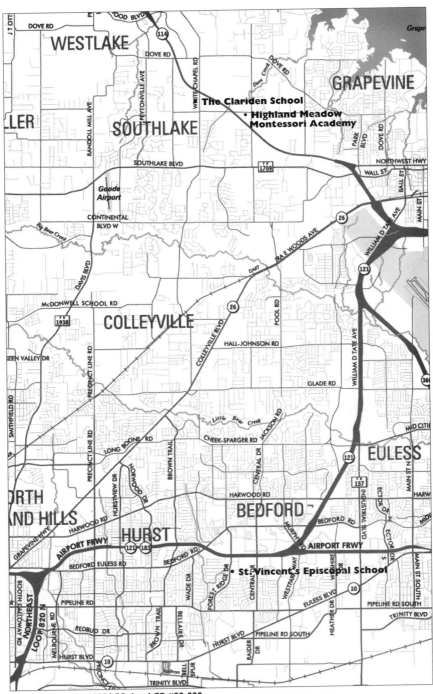

The Clariden School
• Highland Meadow
Montessori Academy

WESTLAKE

DOVE RD

GRAPEVINE

SOUTHLAKE

Goode
Airport

COLLEYVILLE

EULESS

BEDFORD

HURST

St. Vincent's Episcopal School

Copyright 1999 by MAPSCO, Inc. LCR #99-038

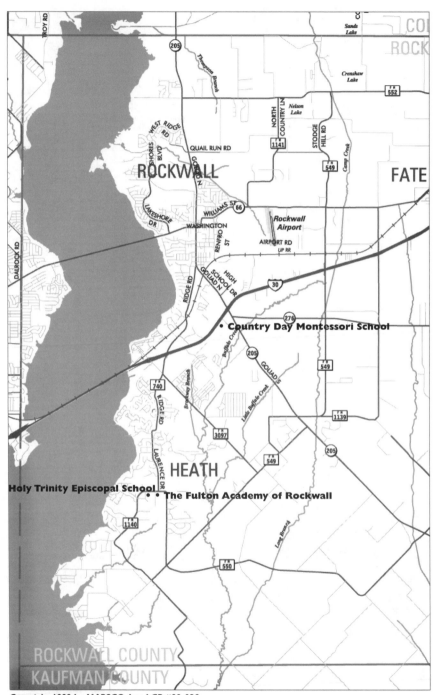

492

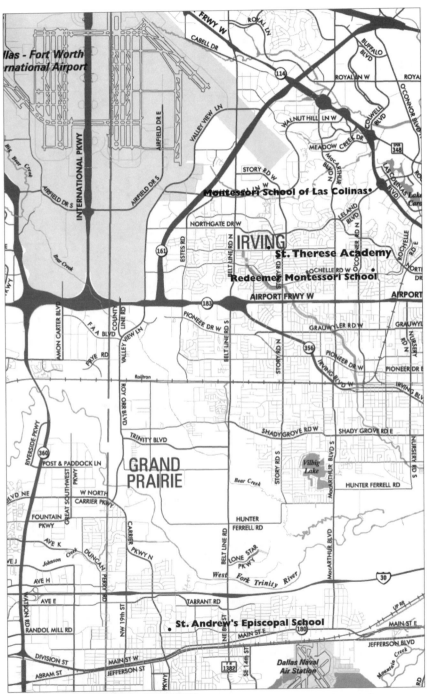

493

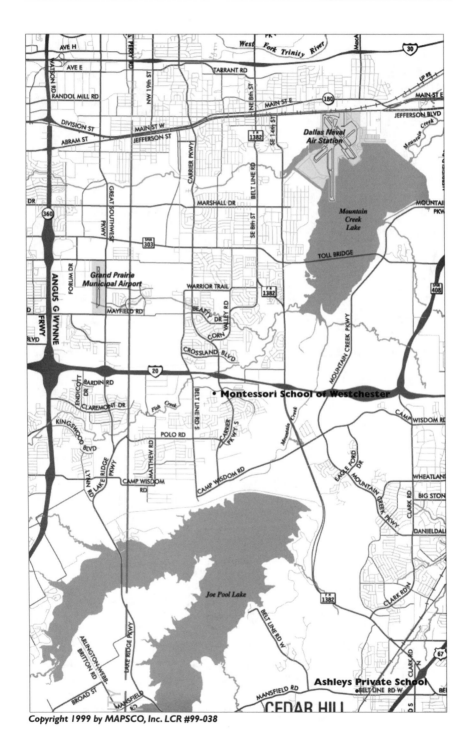

494

495

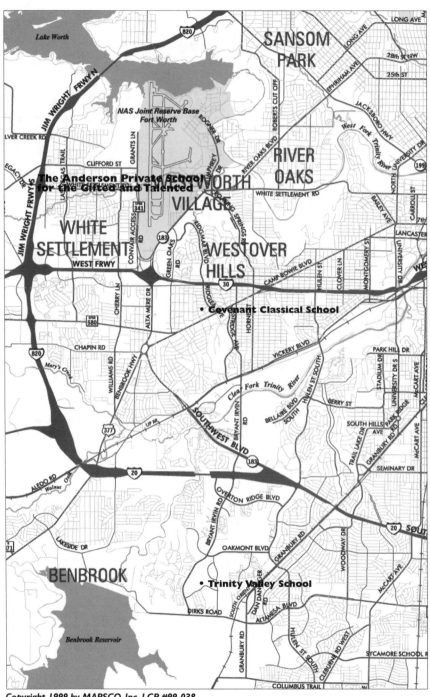

Copyright 1999 by MAPSCO, Inc. LCR #99-038

Chapter 4
Alphabetical Listing
of Schools

In this chapter, all the DFW schools are listed alphabetically to facilitate your search of the school listings.

This comprehensive chapter is also a newly added feature in *A Guide to DFW Private Schools*. When I began the 4th edition in the spring, I contacted each school included in this publication. As you can see from the acknowledgments, it was an enormous project to bring you up-to-date school data and involved many people. I hope that my tendency toward perfectionism — tough on my staff but good for my readers — resulted in more accurate and more thorough information.

We have provided you with an alphabetical listing of all educational facilities that we could locate. If any schools have been inadvertently omitted or recently opened, please contact us. Some of the schools listed did not provide detailed information for this publication, you can contact them directly for more information. If you would like to sponsor the publication of a school's information, please call our office for more details.

Academic Adventures
5720 LBJ freeway
Suite 180-A
Dallas, Texas 75244
Phone 972.702.9133
E-MAIL: info@dfwprivateschools.com
Web site: www.dfwprivateschools.com

FYI
(For Your Information)

Boys Only
Cistercian Preparatory School (see chapter 4)
Jesuit College Preparatory School (see chapter 4)
St. Mark's School of Texas (see ISAS)

Girls Only
The Hockaday School (see chapter 4)
Ursuline Academy of Dallas (see ISAS)

Schools Closed
Branch Schools
The Cornerstone School
Hearthstone Kindergarten
The Helen-Hardrick Christian School
Lexington Academy
Phoenix Academy
Sycamore School, Inc.
TreeTops International School
Williamson School
YouthCrossing Academy

Academic Achievement Associates

12820 Hillcrest Road, Suite 124 C
Dallas, TX 75230
Contact: Dorothy Baxter
Phone: (972) 490-6399
FAX: (972) 490-6416
Office Hours: 8:00 a.m. - 6:00 p.m. + evening tutoring/ counseling
E-MAIL: aaadot@yahoo.com Web Site: www.academicachievement.net
Accreditation: Additional Schools
Grades: Kindergarten - Adult
Page(s): 234-236

Akiba Academy

6210 Churchill Way
Dallas, TX 75230
Contact: Hanna Lambert
Phone: (972) 239-7248
FAX: (972) 239-6818
Office Hours: 7:45 a.m. - 5:30 p.m.
E-MAIL: Headmaster@akiba.dallas.tx.us Web Site: N/A
Accreditation: NAEYC/ SACS
Grades: 18 months - 8th grade
Page(s): 139-141

Alexander School, The

409 International Parkway
Richardson, TX 75081
Contact: David Bowlin, Director
Phone: (972) 690-9210
FAX: (972) 690-9284
Office Hours: 8:15 a.m. - 4:30 p.m. M-Th, 9:00 a.m. - 1:00 p.m. Fri.
E-MAIL: tas1@airmail.net Web Site: www.alexanderschool.com
Accreditation: SACS
Grades: 8th grade - 12th grade
Page(s): 142-144

Alpha Academy
701 State Street
Garland, TX 75040
Contact: Charles or Wilma York
Phone: (972) 272-2173
FAX: (972) 295-3263
Office Hours: 8:00 a.m. - 6:00 p.m.
E-MAIL: alphaacademy.org Web Site: N/A
Accreditation: ICAA/ NCSA
Grades: 2 years - 12th grade
Page(s): 52-54

All Saints Catholic School
5231 Meadowcreek
Dallas, TX 75247
Contact: Bobi White
Phone: (972) 778-0333
FAX: (972) 661-3963
Office Hours: 8:00 a.m. - 4:00 p.m.
E-MAIL: bwhite@allsaintsk8.org Web Site: www.homestead.com
flashallsaintscatholic
Accreditation: TCCED pending
Grades: Kindergarten - 8th grade

All Saints Episcopal School
8200 Tumbleweed Trail
Ft. Worth, TX 76108
Contact: Daniel Hernandez
Phone: (817) 246-2413
FAX: (817) 246-8320
Office Hours: 7:45 a.m. - 4:15 p.m.
E-MAIL: N/A Web Site: N/A
Accreditation: SAES
Grades: Kindergarten - 12th grade

Amberwood Montessori Academy
804 West Pioneer Drive
Irving, TX 75061
Contact: Mrs. Clinkenbeard
Phone: (972) 254-7112
FAX: N/A
Office Hours: 7:30 a.m. - 4:00 p.m.
E-MAIL: N/A   Web Site: N/A
Accreditation: Montessori
Grades: 2 1/2 years - 6th grade

Anderson Private School for the Gifted and Talented
14900 White Settlement Road
Fort Worth, TX. 76108
Contact: LeVonna Anderson
Phone: (817) 448-8484
FAX: N/A
Office Hours: 8:30 a.m. -4:30 p.m.
E-MAIL: N/A Web Site: N/A
Accreditation: TDPRS
Grades: Kindergarten - 12th grade
Page(s): 392-395

Andrew Austin Montessori School
10206 Webb Chapel Road
Dallas, TX 75229
Contact: Fran Bradshaw
Phone: (214) 350-3371
FAX: N/A
Office Hours: 8:30 a.m. - 4:30 p.m.
E-MAIL: Fbradshaw@andrewaustinschool.com
Web Site: www.andrewaustinschool.com
Accreditation: Montessori
Grades: 3 years - 9th grade
Page(s): 332-334

Arbor Acre Preparatory School
8000 South Hampton Road
Dallas, TX 75232
Contact: Mary Beth Cunningham
Phone: (972) 224-0511
FAX: (972) 224-0511 Call first
Office Hours: 8:00 a.m. - 4:30 p.m.
E-MAIL: N/A Web Site: N/A
Accreditation: SACS/ TACLD/ Alternative
Grades: 4 years - 8th grade
Page(s): 250-252

Ashbury Academy - Montessori AMI
219 Executive Way
DeSoto, TX 75115
Contact: Lakshmi Witharane
Phone: (972) 780-4700
FAX: (972) 780-4700
Office Hours: 8:30 a.m. - 4:00 p.m.
E-MAIL: sajiniw@aol.com Web Site: N/A
Accreditation: Montessori
Grades: 18 months - 6th grade
Page(s): 335-337

Ashleys Private School
310 W. Beltline Rd.
Cedar Hill, TX 75104
Contact: Sharon Ashley
Phone: (972) 291-1313
FAX: (972) 293-8056
Office Hours: 8:00 a.m. - 4:00 p.m.
E-MAIL: N/A Web Site: N/A
Accreditation: TDPRS
Grades: 4 years - 4th grade
Page(s): 396-398

Autistic Treatment Center

10503 Forest Lane, Suite 100
Dallas, TX 75243
Contact: Kristen N. Beard
Phone: (972) 644-2076 V/TDD
FAX: (972) 644-5650
Office Hours: 8:30 a.m.- 4:30 p.m. M-F
E-MAIL: www.autism-roundup.com Web Site: N/A
Accreditation: Alternative
Grades: Varies

Bending Oaks High School

11884 Greenville Avenue, Suite 120
Dallas, TX 75243
Contact: Brandy McNamara
Phone: (972) 669-0000
FAX: (972) 669-8149
Office Hours: 9:00 a.m. - 4:00 p.m.
E-MAIL: info@bohs.com Web Site: www.bohs.com
Accreditation: SACS/ Alternative
Grades: 9th grade - 12th grade
Page(s): 253-255

Bent Tree Child Development Center

17275 Addison Road
Addison, TX 75001
Contact: Charlotte Buchanan
Phone: (972) 931-0868
FAX: (972) 931-2103
Office Hours: 7:00 a.m - 6:30 p.m. M-F
E-MAIL: cbuchanan@benttreecdc.com Web Site: N/A
Accreditation: DAEYC/ NAEYC/ SECA/ TAEYC
Grades: Preschool - Kindergarten
Page(s): 102-104

Bent Tree Episcopal School
17405 Muirfield Dr.
Dallas, TX 75287
Contact: Gayla Jones
Phone: (972) 248-6575
FAX: (972) 248-6599
Office Hours: 8:30 a.m. - 2:30 p.m.
E-MAIL: N/A Web Site: N/A
Accreditation: TDPRS
Grades: 2 years - Kindergarten
Page(s): 399-401

Beth Torah Preschool & Kindergarten
720 Lookout Drive
Richardson, TX 75080
Contact: Ester Cohen
Phone: (972) 234-1549
FAX: (972) 783-1463
Office Hours: 8:30 am - 4:30 pm
E-MAIL: info@dfwprivateschools.com Web Site: N/A
Accreditation: TDPRS
Grades: Preschool - Kindergarten
Page(s): 402-404

Bethany Christian School
3300 W. Parker Road
Plano, TX 75075
Contact: Dr. Marvin Effa
Phone: (972) 596-5811
FAX: (972) 596-5814
Office Hours: 8:00 am - 4:00 pm
E-MAIL: N/A Web Site: N/A
Accreditation: ACSI
Grades: 4 years - 12th grade

Bishop Dunne Catholic High School

3900 Rugged Dr.
Dallas, TX 75224
Contact: Mario Root
Phone:(214) 339-6561 ext. 292
FAX: (214) 339-1438
Office Hours: 8:00 a.m. - 5:00 p.m. M-F
E-MAIL: mroot@bdhs.org Web Site: www.bdhs.org
Accreditation: TCCED
Grades: 7th grade - 12th grade
Page(s): 196-199

Bishop Lynch High School, Inc.

9750 Ferguson Road
Dallas, TX 75228
Contact: Terry May
Phone: (214) 324-3607 ext 127
FAX: (214) 324-3600
Office Hours: 7:30 a.m. - 3:30 p.m.
E-MAIL: willt@mail.bishoplynch.org Web Site: www.bishoplynch.org
Accreditation: SACS/ TCCED
Grades: 9th grade - 12th grade
Page(s): 200-202

Bridgeway School

7808 Clodus Fields Drive
Dallas, TX 75251
Contact: Tami Whitington or Margie English
Phone: (214) 991-9504 or (972) 770-0845
FAX: (214) 991-2417
Office Hours: 8:00 a.m. - 5:00 p.m.
E-MAIL: info@bridgewayschool.com Web Site: www.bridgewayschool.com
Accreditation: SACS/ Alternative
Grades: 7th grade - 12th grade
Page(s): 256-259

Buckingham North Christian School

801 West Buchingam
Garland, TX 75040
Contact: Veronica Marshall
Phone: (972) 495-0851
FAX: (972) 530-1315
Office Hours: 8:30 a.m. - 3:30 p.m.
E-MAIL: N/A Web Site: N/A
Accreditation: TACLD/ Alternative
Grades: 6 months - Kindergarten
Page(s): 260-262

Buckingham Private School

701 State Street
Garland, TX 75040
Contact: Charles or Wilma York
Phone: (972) 272-4638
FAX: (972) 295-3263
Office Hours: 8:30 a.m. - 6:00 p.m.
E-MAIL: alphaacademy.org Web Site: N/A
Accreditation: ICAA/ NCSA
Grades: 18 months - 12th grade
Page(s): 52-54

Burton Adventist Academy

4611 Kelly Elliott Road
Arlington, TX 76017
Contact: Annette Graves
Phone: (817) 561-4237
FAX: N/A
Office Hours: 7:45 a.m. - 4:00 p.m.
E-MAIL: N/A   Web Site: N/A
Accreditation: TDPRS
Grades: Kindergarten - 12th grade

Callier Child Development Preschool
1966 Inwood Road
Dallas, TX 75235
Contact: Gayle Wilson
Phone: (214) 905-3094
FAX: (214) 905-3022
Office Hours: 7:30 a.m. - 4:00 p.m.
E-MAIL: gwilson@callier.utdallas.edu
Web Site: www.dallasprivateschools.com/html/fea_schl.htm
Accreditation: DAEYC/ NAEYC/ TDPRS
Grades: 2 years - Kindergarten

Cambridge Square Private School of DeSoto
1121 East Pleasant Run Road
DeSoto, TX 75115
Contact: Mary Lowrey
Phone: (972) 224-5596
FAX: (972) 617-3074
Office Hours: 6:30 a.m. - 6:00 p.m.
E-MAIL: N/A Web Site: N/A
Accreditation: TAAPS pending/ TDPRS
Grades: 3 years - 8th grade
Page(s): 405-407

Canterbury Episcopal School, The
1708 North Westmoreland
DeSoto, TX 75115
Contact: Ron Ferguson, Headmaster
Phone: (972) 572-7200
FAX: (972) 572-7400
Office Hours: 7:45 am - 4:30 pm
E-MAIL: N/A Web Site: N/A
Accreditation: SAES
Grades: Kindergarten - 8th grade
Page(s): 169-171

Canyon Creek Academy
2800 Custer Parkway
Richardson, TX 75080
Contact: Reverend Jim Clark
Phone: (972) 231-4890
FAX: (972) 234-8414
Office Hours: N/A
E-MAIL: N/A Web Site: N/A
Accreditation: ACSI
Grades: 4 years - 12th grade

Carlisle School, The
4705 West Lovers Lane
Dallas, TX 75209
Contact: Dr. Richard Carlisle, Director
Phone: (214) 351-1833
FAX: N/A
Office Hours: 7:30 a.m. - 6:00 p.m.
E-MAIL: N/A Web Site: N/A
Accreditation: TDPRS/ Curriculum Alternative
Grades: 2 years - 6 years
Page(s): 237-239

Carrollton Christian Academy
1820 Pearl Street
Carrollton, TX 75006
Contact: Jan Foster
Phone: (972) 242-6688
FAX: (972) 245-0321
Office Hours: 7:30 a.m. - 4:00 p.m.
E-MAIL: jfoster@ccasaints.org Web Site: N/A
Accreditation: SACS
Grades: 3 years - 12th grade
Page(s): 145-147

Child's Garden Montessori School, A

1935 Old Denton Drive
Carrollton, TX 75006
Contact: Linda Landreth
Phone: (972) 446-2663
FAX: (972) 446-2662
Office Hours: 8:00 a.m. - 4:00 p.m.
E-MAIL: acgarden@juno.com   Web Site: N/A
Accreditation: Montessori
Grades: 2 years - 4th grade

Children's Center of First Community Church, The

6255 E. Mockingbird Lane
Dallas, TX 75214
Contact: Nancy Emerson, Director
Phone: (214) 823-2119
FAX: (214) 827-4113
Office Hours: 8:30 a.m. - 1:30 p.m.
E-MAIL: N/A Web Site: N/A
Accreditation: TDPRS
Grades: 2 1/2 years - 5 years

Children's Workshop, The

1409 14th Street
Plano, TX 75074
Contact: Jo M. Howser, Director
Phone: (972) 424-1932
FAX: (972) 424-8315
Office Hours: 8:30 a.m. - 4:30 p.m.
E-MAIL: N/A Web Site: N/A
Accreditation: NAEYC
Grades: 3 yrs - 5th grade
Page(s): 105-107

Children's World

3501 North Story Road
Irving, TX 75062
Contact: Tammy Webb, Asst. Director of Admissions
Phone: (972) 255-2134
FAX: (972) 659-6620
Office Hours: 7:00 a.m. - 6:00 p.m.
E-MAIL: N/A   Web Site: N/A
Accreditation: TDPRS
Grades: 18 months - 12 years

Christ Our Savior Lutheran School

140 South Heartz Road
Coppell, TX 75019
Contact: Tammy Rice
Phone: (972) 393-7074
FAX: (972) 462-0881
Office Hours: 7:30 a.m. - 4:30 p.m.
E-MAIL: N/A Web Site: N/A
Accreditation: LSAC/ TDPRS
Grades: 2 years - 5th grade

Christ The King School

4100 Colgate
Dallas, TX 75225
Contact: Gwyne Bohren, Registrar
Phone: (214) 365-1234
FAX: (214) 365-1236
Office Hours: 7:30 a.m. - 4:00 p.m.
E-MAIL: gbohren@cks.org Web Site: www.cks.org
Accreditation: TCCED
Grades: Kindergarten - 8th grade
Page(s): 203-205

Christian Childhood Development Center
9015 Plano Rd.
Dallas, TX 75238
Contact: Sally Fifer
Phone: (214) 349-4489
FAX: N/A
Office Hours: N/A
E-MAIL: N/A Web Site: N/A
Accreditation: TDPRS
Grades: 5 months - 4 years

ChristWay Academy
419 North Cedar Ridge
Duncanville, TX 75116
Contact: Charles Ooten
Phone: (972) 296-6525
FAX: (972) 780-7273
Office Hours: 8:30 a.m. - 4:00 p.m.
E-MAIL: N/A Web Site: N/A
Accreditation: ACSI
Grades: 1st grade - 12th grade

Cistercian Preparatory School
One Cistercian Road
Irving, TX 75014
Contact: Robert J. Haaser
Phone: (972) 273-2022
FAX: (972) 554-2294
Office Hours: 8:00 a.m. - 4:00 p.m.
E-MAIL: admissions@cistercian.org Web Site: www.cistercian.org
Accreditation: ISAS/ TCCED
Grades: 5th grade - 12th grade

Clariden School, The

1325 North White Chapel Blvd
Southlake, TX 76092
Contact: Charlane Baccus
Phone: (817) 481-7597
FAX: (817) 424-5561
Office Hours: 8:00 a.m. - 6:00 p.m.
E-MAIL: cbaccus@claridenschool.org Web Site: www.claridenschool.org
Accreditation: Montessori/ TAAPS pending
Grades: 3 yrs - 12th grade
Page(s): 185-187

Coughs and Cuddles for Mildly Ill Children

6100 W. Parker Road
Plano, TX 75093
Contact: Rose Marie Oliphant
Phone: (972) 608-8585
FAX: (972) 608-8587
Office Hours: 6:30 a.m. - 6:30 p.m.
E-MAIL: N/A Web Site: N/A
Accreditation: Curriculum Alternative
Grades: 6 weeks - 16 years
Page(s): 240-242

Country Day Montessori School

2305 Plaza Dr.
Rockwall, TX 75032
Contact: Margaret Lyman
Phone: (972) 771-6680
FAX: (972) 722-6680
Office Hours: 8:00 a.m. - 5:00 p.m. M-F
E-MAIL: CDMSchool@aol.com Web Site: cdmontessori.qpg.com
Accreditation: Montessori
Grades: 3 yrs - Kindergarten
Page(s): 338-340

Country Day School of Arlington

1100 Roosevelt Street
Arlington, TX 76011
Contact: Nick Stoneman, Headmaster
Phone: (817) 275-0851
FAX: (817) 275-0263
Office Hours: 7:45 a.m. - 4:00 p.m.
E-MAIL: admissions@country-day-school.com
Web Site: www.country-day-school.com
Accreditation: SACS
Grades: 2 years - 8th grade

Covenant Christian Academy

715 Cheek Sparger Lane
Colleyville, TX 76034
Contact: Director of Admissions
Phone: (817) 281-4333
FAX: (817) 281-4674
Office Hours: N/A
E-MAIL: N/A Web Site: N/A
Accreditation: ACSI
Grades: 4 yrs - 12th grade

Covenant Classical School

6401 Garland Ave
Fort Worth, TX 76116
Contact: Linda Shook
Phone: (817) 731-6447
FAX: (817) 731-6447
Office Hours: 8:00 a.m. - 2:00 p.m.
E-MAIL: ccsfw@flash.net Web Site: N/A
Accreditation: Curriculum Alternative
Grades: Kindergarten - 5th grade
Page(s): 314-316

Creative Preschool Co-op
1210 W. Beltline Road
Richardson, TX 75080
Contact: Kristie Carruthers, Director
Phone: (972) 234-4791
FAX: N/A
Office Hours: 8:30 a.m. - 12:30 p.m.
E-MAIL: N/A Web Site: N/A
Accreditation: NAEYC
Grades: 2 years - 4 years
Page(s): 108-110

Creative School, The - Walnut Hill United Methodist Church
10066 Marsh Lane
Dallas, TX 75229
Contact: Pam Douce, Director
Phone: (214) 352-0732
FAX: (214) 357-3753
Office Hours: 8:30 a.m. - 2:00 p.m.
E-MAIL: Creative@whumc.com   Web Site: www.whumc.com
Accreditation: DAEYC/ NAEYC
Grades: Preschool - Kindergarten
Page(s): 111-113

Cross of Christ Lutheran School
512 N. Cockrell Hill
DeSoto, TX 75115
Contact: Dennis Boldt, Principal
Phone: (972) 223-9586
FAX: (972) 223-8432
Office Hours: 8:15 a.m. - 3:15 p.m.
E-MAIL: dennisbl@airmail.net Web Site: N/A
Accreditation: LSAC
Grades: 3 years - 6th grade
Page(s): 85-87

daVinci School, The
5442 La Sierra Drive
Dallas, TX 75231
Contact: Mary Ann Greene, Director
Phone: (214) 373-9504
FAX: (214) 691-4603
Office Hours: 8:00 a.m. - 5:30 p.m.
E-MAIL: N/A Web Site: Davincischool.org
Accreditation: TDPRS
Grades: 18 months - K - Primer
Page(s): 408-410

Dallas Academy
950 Tiffany Way
Dallas, TX 75218
Contact: Jim Richardson, Director
Phone: (214) 324-1481
FAX: (214) 327-8537
Office Hours: 8:00 a.m. - 3:30 p.m.
E-MAIL: mail@dallas-academy.com
Web Site: WWW.DALLAS-ACADEMY.COM
Accreditation: SACS/ TAAPS/ Alternative
Grades: 7th grade - 12th grade
Page(s): 263-265

Dallas Christian School
1515 Republic Parkway
Mesquite, TX 75150
Contact: Ken Farris (elementary), Steve Woods (secondary)
Phone: (972) 270-5495
FAX: (972) 270-7581
Office Hours: 8:00 a.m. - 4:00 p.m.
E-MAIL: N/A Web Site: www.dallaschristian.com
Accreditation: NCSA/ SACS
Grades: 4 years - 12th grade
Page(s): 134-136

Dallas International School

6039 Churchill Way
Dallas, TX 75230
Contact: Robin Winkels-Kroeger
Phone: (972) 991-6379
FAX: (972) 991-6608
Office Hours: 8:30 a.m. - 5:00 p.m.
E-MAIL: rwkdis@metronet.com Web Site: N/A
Accreditation: Curriculum Alternative (French)
Grades: 3yrs - 12th grade

Dallas Learning Center

1021 Newberry Drive, Suite 1
Richardson, TX 75080
Contact: Kathleen Herrin-Kinard, Director
Phone: (972) 231-3723
FAX: (972) 231-8810 (call before faxing)
Office Hours: 9:00 a.m. - 3:00 p.m.
E-MAIL: N/A Web Site: N/A
Accreditation: NCACS, Alternative
Grades: 9th grade - 12th grade
Page(s): 266-268

Dallas Montessori Academy

5757 Samuell Blvd.
Dallas, TX 75228
Contact: James & Dina Paulik, President and Director
Phone: (214) 388-0091
FAX: (214) 388-3415
Office Hours: 8:00 a.m. -5:00 p.m.
E-MAIL: N/A Web Site: N/A
Accreditation: Montessori
Grades: 3 years - 8th grade
Page(s): 341-343

Dallas North Montessori School, The
1149 Rockingham Lane
Richardson, TX 75080
Contact: Jo Ann Moffat, Office Manager
Phone: (972) 669-3322
FAX: N/A
Office Hours: 8:00 a.m. - 5:00 p.m.
E-MAIL: N/A Web Site: N/A
Accreditation: Montessori, TDPRS
Grades: 3yrs - 3rd grade

DeSoto Private School
301 E. Beltline Road
DeSoto, TX 75115
Contact: Kenneth or Carolyn Larson, Owners
Phone: (972) 223-6450
FAX: (972) 230-0629
Office Hours: 6:30 a.m. - 6:00 p.m.
E-MAIL: N/A Web Site: N/A
Accreditation: TDPRS
Grades: 3 yrs - 6th grade
Page(s): 411-413

Discovery School at Canyon Creek Presbyterian Church
400 W. Campbell Road
Richardson, TX 75080
Contact: Marna Brown
Phone: (972) 669-9454
FAX: (972) 238-8214
Office Hours: 8:30 a.m. - 4:30 p.m.
E-MAIL: N/A Web Site: www.binion.com\discovery
Accreditation: SACS, TDPRS
Grades: 3 years - 6th grade

Early Learning Center at First Christian Church

601 E. Main St.
Richardson, TX 75081
Contact: Diana Miller
Phone: (972) 235-8233
FAX: (972) 234-2625 (attn: elc)
Office Hours: 8:15 a.m. - 12:15 p.m.
E-MAIL: N/A Web Site: N/A
Accreditation: NAEYC
Grades: 15 months - Preschool

East Dallas Community School

924 Wayne Street
Dallas, TX 75223
Contact: Mary Loew, Director
Phone: (214) 824-8950
FAX: (214) 827-7683
Office Hours: 8:00 a.m. - 4:00 p.m.
E-MAIL: N/A Web Site: N/A
Accreditation: Montessori/ NAEYC
Grades: 3yrs - 3rd grade

East Dallas Developmental Center

1926 Skillman
Dallas, TX 75206
Contact: Diane Evans, Director
Phone: (214) 821-7766
FAX: N/A
Office Hours: 7:30 a.m. - 6:00 p.m.
E-MAIL: N/A Web Site: N/A
Accreditation: TDPRS
Grades: Infant - Preschool

Eastlake Christian School
721 Easton
Dallas, TX 75218
Contact: Dr. Larry W. Wilson
Phone: (214) 349-4547
FAX: (214) 341- 6238
Office Hours: 8:00 a.m. - 4:00 p.m.
E-MAIL: info@ecsptf.org   Web Site: WWW.ECSPTF.ORG
Accreditation: ACSI/ ACTS
Grades: 4 years - 6th grade
Page(s): 28-30

Epiphany Day School
421 Custer Road
Richardson, TX 75080
Contact: Alexis Clayton, Ed.D
Phone: (972) 690-0275
FAX: (972) 644-8116
Office Hours: 9:00 am - 2:00 pm
E-MAIL: N/A Web Site: N/A
Accreditation: NAEYC/ SAES
Grades: 16 months - Kindergarten
Page(s): 172-174

Episcopal School of Dallas, The
4100 Merrell Road
Dallas, TX 75229
Contact: Ruth Burke, Director of Admissions
Phone: (214) 358-4368
FAX: (214) 353-5872
Office Hours: 8:00 a.m. - 4:00 p.m.; 24 hour voicemail
E-MAIL: burker@esdal.org   Web Site: esdallas.org/esd/
Accreditation: ISAS/ SAES
Grades: 3 years - 12th grade

Evangel Temple Christian School
300 West Pioneer Parkway
Grand Prairie, TX 75051
Contact: Cindy Collins
Phone: (972) 264-1303
FAX: (972) 264-1827
Office Hours: 7:30 a.m. - 4:30 p.m.
E-MAIL: N/A Web Site: N/A
Accreditation: ACSI
Grades: 2 yrs - 12th grade

Fair Oaks Day School
7825 Fair Oak Avenue
Dallas, TX 75231
Contact: Greg Stone
Phone: (214) 340-1121
FAX: (214) 340-8306
Office Hours: 7:00 a.m. - 6:30 p.m.
E-MAIL: N/A Web Site: N/A
Accreditation: TDPRS
Grades: 12 months - Kindergarten

Fairhill School and Diagnostic Assessment Center
16150 Preston Road
Dallas, TX 75248
Contact: Jane Sego, Executive Director
Phone: (972) 233-1026
FAX: (972) 233-8205
Office Hours: 8:00 a.m. - 4:30 p.m.
E-MAIL: fairhill@airmail.net   Web Site: http://web2.airmail.net/fairhill
Accreditation: SACS/ Alternative
Grades: 1st grade - 12th grade
Page(s): 269-271

Faith Lutheran School
1701 East Park Blvd.
Plano, TX 75074
Contact: School Office
Phone: (972) 423-7448
FAX: (972) 423-9618
Office Hours: 8:15 a.m. - 4:00 p.m.
E-MAIL: N/A Web Site: N/A
Accreditation: LSAC
Grades: 3 years - 8th grade

Fellowship Christian Academy
1808 W. Camp Wisdom Rd
Dallas, TX 75232
Contact: Shailendra Thomas, Principal
Phone: (214) 672-9123 opt.3
FAX: (972) 228-1329
Office Hours: 8:00 a.m. - 4:00 p.m.
E-MAIL: N/A Web Site: N/A
Accreditation: TDPRS
Grades: 18 months - 6th grade

First Baptist Academy
Box 868
Dallas, TX 75221
Contact: Admissions Office
Phone: (214) 969-2488
FAX: (214) 969-7797
Office Hours: 8:00 a.m. - 4:30 p.m.
E-MAIL: info@dallasprivateschools.com   Web Site: www.fbacademy.com
Accreditation: ACSI/ ACTABS/ SACS
Grades: Kindergarten - 12th grade
Page(s): 31-33

First Christian Elementary and Preschool
1109 Brown Street
Waxahachie, TX 75165
Contact: Joanne Bronson
Phone: (972) 937-1952
FAX: (972) 937-1997
Office Hours: 8:00 a.m. - 5:00 p.m.
E-MAIL: frstchrsch@aol.com   Web Site: N/A
Accreditation: TDPRS
Grades: Kindergarten - 5th grade
Page(s): 414-416

First United Methodist Church Day School
801 W. Ave. B at Glenbrook
Garland, TX 75040
Contact: Grace Ashley, Director
Phone: (972) 494-3096 or (972) 272-3471
FAX: (972) 272-3473
Office Hours: 8:30 a.m. - 4:30 p.m.
E-MAIL: fumcgar@airmail.net Web Site: www.shr.net/fumc
Accreditation: NAEYC
Grades: 3 years - Kindergarten, MDO
Page(s): 114-117

Fort Worth Christian School
7517 Bogart Drive
Ft. Worth, TX 76180
Contact: Brooks Kennedy
Phone: (817) 281-6504
FAX: (817) 281-7063
Office Hours: 8:00 a.m. - 4:30 p.m.
E-MAIL: info@fwc.org Web Site: www.fwc.org
Accreditation: SACS/ NCSA
Grades: 4 yrs - 12th grade

Fort Worth Country Day School

4200 Country Day Lane
Ft. Worth, TX 76109
Contact: Barbara Jiongo, Director of Admissions
Phone: (817) 732-7718
FAX: (817) 377-3425
Office Hours: 8:00 a.m. - 4:30 p.m.
E-MAIL: bjiongo@mail.fwcds.pvt.tenet.edu Web Site: N/A
Accreditation: ISAS
Grades: Kindergarten - 12th grade

Fulton Academy of Rockwall, The

1623 Laurence
Rockwall, TX 75032
Contact: Norma Morris
Phone: (972) 772-4445
FAX: (972) 772-9558
Office Hours: 8:00 a.m. - 5:00 p.m. M - F
 E-MAIL: N/A Web Site: N/A
Accreditation: TDPRS
Grades: 1st grade - 8th grade
Page(s): 417-419

Garland Christian Academy

1522 Lavon Drive
Garland, TX 75040
Contact: Mr. Grant Endicott
Phone: (972) 487-0043
FAX: (972) 487-1813
Office Hours: 7:30 a.m. - 3:30 p.m.
E-MAIL: N/A Web Site: N/A
Accreditation: ACSI
Grades: Kindergarten - 12th grade

Glen Lakes Academy

6000 Custer Road, Building 7
Plano, TX 75023
Contact: Cara Hill
Phone: (972) 517-7498
FAX: (972) 517-0133
Office Hours: 8:00 a.m. - 3:45 p.m.
E-MAIL: N/A Web Site: www.glenlakesacademy.com
Accreditation: SACS pending/ Alternative
Grades: 2nd grade - 9th grade
Page(s): 272-274

Glen Oaks School

12105 Plano Road
Dallas, TX 75243
Contact: Ashley Hutto, Director
Phone: (972) 231-3135
FAX: (972) 644-6373
Office Hours: 6:30 a.m. - 6:15 p.m.
E-MAIL: glenoaks@flash.net Web Site: N/A
Accreditation: NAEYC
Grades: 2 years - 4th grade
Page(s): 118-120

Glenview Christian School

4805 Northeast Loop 820
Ft. Worth, TX 76137
Contact: Sharon Neely, Principal
Phone: (817) 281-5155
FAX: (817) 514-0760
Office Hours: 8:00 a.m. - 4:15 p.m.
EMAIL: gcschool@flash.net Web Site: N/A
Accreditation: ACSI
Grades: 4 yrs - 7th grade

Glenwood Day School

2446 Apollo
Garland, TX 75044
Contact: Rhonda Corn-Kidd
Phone: (972) 530-4460
FAX: N/A
Office Hours: 7:30 a.m. - 5:30 p.m.
E-MAIL: glenwood@flash.net Web Site: N/A
Accreditation: CCMS/ NAEYC
Grades: 18 months - Kindergarten
Page(s): 121-123

Good Shepherd Catholic School

214 S. Garland Ave
Garland, TX 75040
Contact: David Ross, Principal
Phone: (972) 272-6533
FAX: (972) 272-0512
Office Hours: 7:30 a.m. - 4:00 p.m.
E-MAIL: goodsh@airmail.net Web Site: N/A
Accreditation: TCCED
Grades: 3 years - 8th grade
Page(s): 206-208

Good Shepherd Episcopal School

11122 Midway
Dallas, TX 75229
Contact: Nancy Lawrence, Director of Admissions
Phone: (214) 357-1610 ext 215
FAX: (214) 357-4105
Office Hours: 8:00 a.m. - 4:00 p.m., M - F
E-MAIL: NLawrence@GSES.org Web Site: www.gseschooldallas.org
Accreditation: ISAS/ SAES
Grades: 4 years - 8th grade
Page(s): 60-63

Good Shepherd Montessori School

7701 Virginia Parkway
McKinney, TX 75070
Contact: School Office
Phone: 1 (972) 547-4767
FAX: N/A
Office Hours: 8:45 a.m. - 3:15 p.m.
E-MAIL: N/A Web Site: N/A
Accreditation: AMI, Montessori
Grades: 18 months - 6th grade

Gospel Lighthouse Christian Academy

5525 West Illinois
Dallas, TX 75211
Contact: Paulette Bangert
Phone: (214) 339-2207
FAX: (214) 331-6695
Office Hours: 8:30 a.m. - 4:00 p.m.
E-MAIL: N/A Web Site: N/A
Accreditation: ACSI
Grades: 4 years - 12th grade

Grace Academy of Dallas

11306 A Inwood Road
Dallas, TX 75229
Contact: Letitia Brittain
Phone: (214) 696-5648
FAX: (214) 696-8713
Office Hours: 7:45 a.m. - 4:00 p.m.
E-MAIL: N/A Web Site: N/A
Accreditation: ACSI
Grades: 3 years - 6th grade
Page(s): 34-36

Greenhill School
4141 Spring Valley Road
Addison, TX 75001
Contact: Wendell M. Lee, Director of Admissions
Phone: (972) 661-1211
FAX: (972) 404-8217
Office Hours: 8:00 a.m. - 4:30 p.m.
E-MAIL: HOOGM@GREENHILL.ORG Web Site: N/A
Accreditation: ISAS
Grades: 3 1/2 years - 12th grade

Happy Hill Farm Academy/Home
HC51 - Box 56
Granbury, TX 76048
Contact: Todd L. Shipman, President/ CFO
Phone: (254) 897-4822
FAX: (254) 897-7650
Office Hours: 8:30 a.m. - 5:00 p.m.
E-MAIL: N/A Web Site: www.weblifepro.com/happyhill
Accreditation: SACS/ Alternative
Grades: Kindergarten - 12th grade
Page(s): 275-277

Harrington School, The
2638 Valley View
Farmers Branch, TX 75234
Contact: Robin Harrington
Phone: (972) 484-4215
FAX: N/A
Office Hours: 7:30 a.m. - 6:00 p.m.
E-MAIL: N/A Web Site: N/A
Accreditation: TDPRS
Grades: Preschool - Kindergarten

Highland Academy

1231 W. Beltline Road
Richardson, TX 75080
Contact: Lynda Handlogten
Phone: (972) 238-7567
FAX: (972) 238-7647
Office Hours: 8:00 a.m. - 3:00 p.m.
E-MAIL: highland@cyberramp.net Web Site: N/A
Accreditation: ASESA/ Alternative
Grades: Kindergarten - 8th grade
Page(s): 278-280

Highland Meadow Montessori Academy

1060 Highland Street
Southlake, TX 76092
Contact: Pat McCormick
Phone: (817) 488-2138
FAX: N/A
Office Hours: 8:30 a.m. - 3:00 p.m.
E-MAIL: N/A Web Site: N/A
Accreditation: Montessori
Grades: 2 years - 6th grade
Page(s): 344-346

Highland Park Presbyterian Day School

3821 University Blvd.
Dallas, TX 75205
Contact: Carrie H. Parsons, Director
Phone: (214) 559-5353
FAX: (214) 559-5357
Office Hours: 8:00 a.m. - 4:00 p.m.
E-MAIL: N/A Web Site: N/A
Accreditation: TAAPS
Grades: 3 years - 4th grade
Page(s): 188-190

Highland Park United Methodist Child Development
3300 Mockingbird Lane
Dallas, TX 75205
Contact: Lyn Vogeli, Director
Phone: (214) 521-2600
FAX: (214) 520-6451
Office Hours: 7:30 a.m. - 6:00 p.m.
E-MAIL: N/A   Web Site: N/A
Accreditation: NAEYC
Grades: Infants - Kindergarten

Highlander-Carden School, The
9120 Plano Road
Dallas, TX 75238
Contact: Dr. Betty Woodring, Director
Phone: (214) 348-3220
FAX: N/A
Office Hours: 8:00 a.m. - 4:00 p.m.
E-MAIL: N/A Web Site: N/A
Accreditation: Curriculum Alternative
Grades: 3 years - 6th grade
Page(s): 317-319

Highlands School, The
1451 East Northgate Drive
Irving, TX 75062
Contact: Susan Norton
Phone: (972) 554-1980
FAX: (972) 721-1691
Office Hours: 8:00 a.m. - 4:30 p.m.
E-MAIL: N/A Web Site: www.thehighlandsschool.org
Accreditation: TCCED
Grades: 3 years - 12th grade
Page(s): 209-212

Hillcrest Academy, The
12302 Park Central Drive
Dallas, TX 75251
Contact: Carrie Madden, Director of Admission
Phone: (972) 788-0292
FAX: (972) 788-1392
Hours: 8:00 a.m. - 5:00 p.m. M- F
E-MAIL: HCAcad1@aol.com Web Site: www.hillcrestacademy.org
Accreditation: SACS pending/ TDPRS
Grades: 3 years - 8th grade
Page(s): 148-151

Hillier School of Highland Park Presbyterian Church
3821 University Blvd.
Dallas, TX 75205
Contact: Larry Evans, Principal
Phone: (214) 559-5363
FAX: (214) 559-5377
Office Hours: 8:00 a.m. - 4:00 p.m.
E-MAIL: Evans@hppc.org Web Site: N/A
Accreditation: TAAPS/ Alternative
Grades: 1st grade - 8th grade
Page(s): 281-283

Hockaday School, The
11600 Welch Road
Dallas, TX 75229
Contact: Casey Hagerman Bobo
Phone: (214) 360-6532
FAX: (214) 363-0942
Office Hours: 8:30 a.m. - 5:00 p.m.
 E-MAIL: chagermanbobo@mail.hockaday.org Web Site: N/A
Accreditation: ISAS
Grades: 4 yrs - 12th grade

Holy Cross Lutheran School
11425 Marsh Lane
Dallas, TX 75229
Contact: Larry Hoffschneider, Principal
Phone: (214) 358-4396
FAX: (214) 358-4393
Office Hours: 8:15 a.m. - 4:45 p.m.
E-MAIL: N/A Web Site: N/A
Accreditation: LSAC
Grades: 3 years - 6th grade
Page(s): 88-90

Holy Family of Nazareth School
2323 Cheyenne
Irving, TX 75062
Contact: Micki McCutcheon
Phone: (972) 255-0205
FAX: (972) 252-0448
Office Hours: 7:30 a.m. - 4:00 p.m.
E-MAIL: N/A Web Site: N/A
Accreditation: TCCED
Grades: 4 yrs - 8th grade

Holy Trinity Catholic School
3815 Oak Lawn
Dallas, TX 75219
Contact: Ned Vanders, Principal
Phone: (214) 526-5113
FAX: (214) 526-4524
Office Hours: 8:00 a.m. - 4:30 p.m.
E-MAIL: N/A Web Site: N/A
Accreditation: TCCED
Grades: 3 years - 8th grade
Page(s): 213-215

Holy Trinity Episcopal School
1524 Smirl Drive
Heath, TX 75032
Contact: Dianna Fullerton, Interim Headmistress
Phone: (972) 772-6919
FAX: N/A
Office Hours: 8:30 a.m. - 4:30 p.m.
E-MAIL: judyhead@juno.com   Web Site: holytrinityepiscopal.org
Accreditation: SAES
Grades: 3 years - 3rd grade
Page(s): 175-177

Immaculate Conception School
400 N.E. 17th Street
Grand Prairie, TX 75050
Contact: Sister Mary Patrice Murray
Phone: (972) 264-8777
FAX: (972) 264-7742
Office Hours: 8:00 a.m. - 4:30 p.m.
E-MAIL: icsgp@swbell.net Web Site: N/A
Accreditation: TCCED
Grades: 3 years - 8th grade

J. Erik Jonsson Community School
106 East Tenth Street
Dallas, TX 75203
Contact: Paige Conley
Phone: (214) 915-1890
FAX: (214) 915-1863
Office Hours: 8:00 a.m. - 4:30 p.m.
E-MAIL: ralaniz@jonnsonschool.org Web Site: www.jonssonschool.org
Accreditation: SACS/ TAAPS
Grades: 4 years - 6th grade
Page(s): 191-193

Jesuit College Preparatory School

12345 Inwood
Dallas, TX 75244
Contact: Mike Earsing, Principal
Phone: (972) 387-8700
FAX: (972) 661-9349
Office Hours: 8:00 a.m. - 4:00 p.m.
E-MAIL: N/A Web Site www.jesuitcp.org
Accreditation: TCCED/ SACS
Grades: 9th grade - 12th grade

Jewish Community Center of Dallas

7900 Northaven
Dallas, TX 75230
Contact: Marcia Mauch, Director
Phone: (214) 739-0225
FAX: (214) 368-1709
Office Hours: 7:30 a.m. - 6:00 p.m.
E-MAIL: N/A Web Site: N/A
Accreditation: NAEYC
Grades: 16 months - Kindergarten

Keystone Academy

6506 Frankford Rd.
Dallas, TX 75252
Contact: Helen Werner, Director and Founder
Phone: (972) 250-4455
FAX: (972) 250-4960
Office Hours: 8:00 a.m. - 4:30 p.m.
E-MAIL: kacademy@juno.com   Web Site: http://gtesupersite.com/keystone
Accreditation: ACSI/ SACS/ Alternative
Grades: Kindergarten - 8th grade
Page(s): 284-286

Lakehill Preparatory School

2720 Hillside Drive
Dallas, TX 75214
Contact: Fran Holley
Phone: (214) 826-2931
FAX: (214) 826-4623
Office Hours: 7:45 a.m. - 4:30 p.m.
E-MAIL: N/A Web Site: N/A
Accreditation: ISAS/ SACS
Grades: Kindergarten - 12th grade
Page(s): 64-66

Lakemont Academy

3993 West Northwest Highway
Dallas, TX 75220
Contact: Edward Fidellow, Headmaster
Phone: (214) 351-6404
FAX: (214) 358-4510
Office Hours: 8:00 a.m. - 6:00 p.m.
E-MAIL: N/A Web Site: N/A
Accreditation: ACSI/ SACS/ Montessori
Grades: 18 months - 8th grade
Page(s): 152-154

Lakewood Presbyterian School

7020 Gaston Ave
Dallas, TX 75214
Contact: Arnie Roberstad
Phone: (214) 321-2864
FAX: N/A
Office Hours: 8:00 a.m. - 12:00 noon (Tuesday - Friday)
E-MAIL: N/A Web Site: N/A
Accreditation: TDPRS
Grades: 7th grade - 12th grade

Lakewood United Methodist Developmental Learning Center

2443 Abrams Road
Dallas, TX 75214
Contact: Judy Granger
Phone: (214) 824-1352
FAX: (214) 823-9213
Office Hours: 9:00 a.m. - 6:00 p.m.
E-MAIL: N/A Web Site: N/A
Accreditation: TDPRS
Grades: 6 weeks - 5 years

Lamplighter School, The

11611 Inwood Drive
Dallas, TX 75229
Contact: Dottie Blanchard
Phone: (214) 369-9201
FAX: (214) 369-5540
Office Hours: 8:00 a.m. - 4:00 p.m.
E-MAIL: lamplite@cyberramp.net Web Site: N/A
Accreditation: ISAS
Grades: 3 years - 4th grade

Legacy Christian Academy

7185 Main Street, Suite 201*
Frisco, TX 75034
Contact: Jody Capehart, Head of School
Phone: (972) 712-5777
FAX: (972) 712-8222
Office Hours: 8:00 a.m. - 4:00 p.m.
E-MAIL: legacychra@aol.com   Web Site: N/A
Accreditation: seeking ACSI and SACS
Grades: Kindergarten - 9th grade
Page(s): 37-39
* We are moving to a new campus and until the city names the street, we can say it
  is near "Preston and El Dorado" in Frisco.

Liberty Christian High School
10310 N. Central Expwy
Dallas, TX 75231
Contact: Holly Polson
Phone: (214) 361-5599
FAX: (214) 361-4901
Office Hours: 8:00 a.m. - 4:00 p.m.
E-MAIL: liberychristian@lch.net   Web Site: www.lch.net
Accreditation: ACTABS
Grades: 7th grade - 12th grade

Liberty Christian School
1500 S. Bonnie Brae
Denton, TX 76207
Contact: Brenda Fanara, Dean of Students
Phone: (940) 484-9733
FAX: (940) 381-2485
Office Hours: 8:00 a.m. - 4:00 p.m.
E-MAIL: Bfanara@liberyschool.org   Web Site: Libertyschool.org
Accreditation: SACS
Grades: Kindergarten - 12th grade

Little Red Schoolhouse
412 S. Bryan - Beltline
Mesquite, TX 75149
Contact: Marilyn Chappell
Phone: (972) 285-3962
FAX: N/A
Office Hours: 8:20 a.m. - 3:30 p.m.
E-MAIL: N/A Web Site: N/A
Accreditation: TDPRS
Grades: 3 yrs - 1st grade

Logos Academy
10919 Royal Haven
Dallas, TX 75229
Contact: Director of Admission
Phone: (214) 357-2995
FAX: (214) 357-0880
Office Hours: 8:00 a.m. - 3:30 p.m. M - F
E-MAIL: N/A Web Site: N/A
Accreditation: ACCS pending/ Additional Schools
Grades: 7th grade - 12th grade
Page(s): 243-245

Lovers Lane United Methodist Church
9200 Inwood Road
Dallas, TX 75220
Contact: Karla Perry
Phone: (214) 691-4721
FAX: (214) 692-0803
Office Hours: 8:30 a.m. - 2:00 p.m.
E-MAIL: linda@llumc.org Web Site: N/A
Accreditation: NAEYC
Grades: 6 months - 1st grade
Page(s): 124-126

Lutheran High School
8494 Stults Road
Dallas, TX 75243
Contact: Patricia Klekamp, Principal
Phone: (214) 349-8912
FAX: (214) 340-3095
Office Hours: 8:00 a.m. - 4:00 p.m
E-MAIL: donnafrieling@usa.net Web Site: www.lhsdfw.com
Accreditation: LSAC
Grades: 7th grade - 12th grade
Page(s): 91-93

Maryview/ Meritor Academy
115 W. Wintergreen
DeSoto, TX 75115
Contact: Rusty Freese
Phone: (972) 709-7991
FAX: (972) 709-8098
Office Hours: 8:00 a.m. - 3:30 p.m.
E-MAIL: N/A Web Site: N/A
Accreditation: TDPRS
Grades: 18 months - 4th grade

Meadowbrook School
5414 Northwest Highway
Dallas, TX 75220
Contact: Sharon L. Goldberg
Phone: (214) 369-4981
FAX: (214) 363-4981
Office Hours: 9:00 a.m. - 3:00 p.m.
E-MAIL: N/A Web Site: N/A
Accreditation: TDPRS/ Montessori
Grades: 3 years - Kindergarten
Page(s): 347-349

Meadowview School
2419 Franklin
Mesquite, TX 75150
Contact: Beverly Presley, Director
Phone: (972) 289-1831
FAX: (972) 289-8730
Office Hours: 8:00 a.m. - 4:00 p.m.
E-MAIL: mvschool@flash.net Web Site: www.flash.net/~mvschool
Accreditation: ASESA/ COPSES/ Alternative
Grades: 1st grade - 8th grade
Page(s): 287-289

Metropolitan Christian School
8501 Bruton Road
Dallas, TX 75217
Contact: Mr. Terry Carpenter, Headmaster
Phone: (214) 388-4426
FAX: (214) 381-2574
Office Hours: 8:00 a.m. - 5:00 p.m.
E-MAIL: mcs4426@aol.com Web Site: N/A
Accreditation: ACSI
Grades: 4 years - 12th grade

Montessori Children's House and School
7335 Abrams Road
Dallas, TX 75231
Contact: Kristina Geiser Wood
Phone: (214) 348-6276
FAX: (214) 348-6628
Office Hours: 8:00 a.m. - 3:00 p.m.
E-MAIL: N/A Web Site: N/A
Accreditation: Montessori
Grades: Preschool - Kindergarten
Page(s): 350-353

Montessori Episcopal School
602 North Old Orchard Lane
Lewisville, TX 75067
Contact: Eleanor Edwards
Phone: (972) 221-3533
FAX: (972) 221-3532
Office Hours: 8:00 a.m. - 4:00 p.m.
E-MAIL: N/A Web Site: N/A
Accreditation: Montessori
Grades: 2 years - 2nd grade

Montessori School of Las Colinas

4961 N. O'Connor Blvd.
Irving, TX 75062
Contact: Jo Harris, Director
Phone: (972) 717-0417
FAX: (972) 717-6737
Office Hours: 8:00 a.m. - 6:00 p.m.
E-MAIL: N/A Web Site: www.montessori.com
Accreditation: Montessori
Grades: 6 weeks - 1st grade
Page(s): 354-356

Montessori School of North Dallas

18303 Davenport
Dallas, TX 75252
Contact: Reena Khandpur, Director
Phone: (972) 985-8844
FAX: (972) 673-0118
Office Hours: 7:00 a.m. - 6:00 p.m.
E-MAIL: info@montessorischool.com Web Site: www.montessorischool.com
Accreditation: Montessori
Grades: 2 years - 1st grade
Page(s): 357-359

Montessori School of Park Cities

4011 Inwood Road
Dallas, TX 75209
Contact: Laura Powell
Phone: (214) 350-2503
FAX: N/A
Office Hours: 9:00 a.m. - 3:00 p.m.
E-MAIL: N/A Web Site: N/A
Accreditation: Montessori
Grades: 6 weeks - 5 years

Montessori School of Pleasant Grove

1655 Jim Miller Road
Dallas, TX 75217
Contact: Hazel Leffall
Phone: (214) 391-2176
FAX: N/A
Office Hours: 6:00 a.m. - 6:00 p.m.
E-MAIL: N/A Web Site: N/A
Accreditation: Montessori
Grades: Kindergarten

Montessori School of Westchester

290 E. Westchester Parkway
Grand Prairie, TX 75052
Contact: Amy Rose
Phone: (972) 262-1053
FAX: (972) 262-4123
Office Hours: 8:00 a.m. - 5:00 p.m.
E-MAIL: N/A Web Site: www.montessoriunlimited.com
Accreditation: Montessori
Grades: Preschool - Kindergarten
Page(s): 360-362

North Dallas Day School

9619 Greenville
Dallas, TX 75243
Contact: Barbara Coady
Phone: (214) 341-4366
FAX: (214) 341-4366 (call before faxing)
Office Hours: 6:45 a.m. - 6:00 p.m.
E-MAIL: N/A Web Site: N/A
Accreditation: TDPRS
Grades: 6 weeks - 2nd grade

North Garland Montessori School

1613 North Garland Avenue
Garland, TX 75040
Contact: Manooch Varasceh
Phone: (972) 494-9300
FAX: (972) 494-9300 (call before faxing)
Office Hours: 9:00 a.m. - 4:00 p.m.
E-MAIL: N/A   Web Site: N/A
Accreditation: Montessori
Grades: 3 years - 3rd grade

NorthPark Presbyterian Day School

9555 N. Central Expressway
Dallas, TX 75231
Contact: Claire Wood
Phone: (214) 361-8024
FAX: (214) 361-5398
Office Hours: 9:00 a.m. - 3:00 p.m.
E-MAIL: N/A Web Site: N/A
Accreditation: TDPRS
Grades: 1 year - Kindergarten
Page(s): 420-422

Northaven Co-operative Preschool & Kindergarten

11211 Preston Road
Dallas, TX 75230
Contact: Kathy Delsanter
Phone: (214) 691-7666
FAX: N/A
Office Hours: 9:00 a.m. - 3:00 p.m.
E-MAIL: N/A Web Site: N/A
Accreditation: NAEYC
Grades: 18 months - Kindergarten

Northbrook School
5608 Northaven Road
Dallas, TX 75230
Contact: Larry Goldman, Director
Phone: (214) 369-8330
FAX: (214) 369-8592
Office Hours: 6:45 a.m. - 6:00 p.m.
E-MAIL: LGOLD5608@aol.com Web Site: N/A
Accreditation: NAEYC/ TDPRS
Grades: 2 years - 4th grade
Page(s): 127-129

Notre Dame of Dallas Schools, The
2018 Allen Street
Dallas, TX 75204
Contact: Theresa Francis, Principal
Phone: (214) 720-3911
FAX: (214) 720-3913
Office Hours: 8:00 a.m. - 4:00 p.m.
E-MAIL: notredame.dallas@worldnet.att.net
Web Site: home.att.net/~notredame.dallas
Accreditation: TCCED/ Curriculum Alternative
Grades: 3 years - 21 years
Page(s): 320-322

Oak Hill Academy
6464 E. Lovers Lane
Dallas, TX 75214
Contact: Pam Quarterman, Director
Phone: (214) 368-0664
FAX: (214) 346-9866
Office Hours: 8:00 a.m. - 4:00 p.m.
E-MAIL: oakhillphq@aol.com Web Site: N/A
Accreditation: ASESA/ COPSES
Grades: 4 yrs - 8th grade
Page(s): 290-292

Oakridge School, The
5900 W. Pioneer Parkway
Arlington, TX 76013
Contact: Andy Broadus, Headmaster
Phone: (817) 451-4994
FAX: (817) 457-6681
Office Hours: 8:00 a.m. - 4:00 p.m.
E-MAIL: admiss@oakridge.pvt.k12.tx.us
Web Site: www.OAKRIDGE.PVT.K12.TX.US
Accreditation: ISAS/ SACS
Grades: 3 years - 12th grade
Page(s): 67-69

Our Redeemer Lutheran School
7611 Park Lane
Dallas, TX 75225
Contact: Dr. John R. Troutman
Phone: (214) 368-1465
FAX: (214) 368-1473
Office Hours: 8:00 a.m. - 5:00 p.m.
E-MAIL: cforc.com//cms/tx/dallas/our_redeemer Web Site: N/A
Accreditation: NLSAC/ LSAC
Grades: 3 years - 6th, MDO
Page(s): 94-96

Palisades Day School
505 Alma Road
Plano, TX 75075
Contact: Sheen Madni
Phone: (972) 423-5557
FAX: N/A
Office Hours: 7:30 a.m. - 5:30 p.m.
E-MAIL: N/A Web Site: N/A
Accreditation: TDPRS
Grades: 4 yrs - 5th grade

Parish Day School, The
14115 Hillcrest Road
Dallas, TX 75240
Contact: Marci McLean, Director of Admission
Phone: (972) 239-8011; (800) 909-9081
FAX: (972) 991-1237
Office Hours: 8:00 a.m.-4:00p.m.
E-MAIL: mmclean@mail.parishday.org Web Site: www.parishday.org
Accreditation: ISAS/ SAES/ NAEYC
Grades: 3 years - 6th grade
Page(s): 70-72

PATHfinders College Preparatory
2828 West Parker Road B106F
Plano, TX 75075
Contact:
Phone: (972) 943-1566
FAX: (972) 943-1567
Office Hours:
E-MAIL: pathfnd1@ix.netcom.com Web Site: N/A
Accreditation: TDPRS

Peanut Gallery, The
1855 Branch Hollow Drive
Carrollton, TX 75007
Contact: Tracy Mitnick
Phone: (972) 394-0613
FAX: N/A
Office Hours: 6:30 a.m. - 6:30 p.m.
E-MAIL: N/A Web Site: N/A
Accreditation: NAEYC
Grades: 6 weeks - 12 years

Peanut Gallery, The
13255 Noel Road
Dallas, TX 75240
Contact: Janet Puddicombe
Phone: (972) 702-9063
FAX: N/A
Office Hours: 6:30 a.m. - 6:30 p.m.
E-MAIL: N/A Web Site: N/A
Accreditation: TDPRS
Grades: 6 weeks - 2 years

Peanut Gallery, The
2151 Rosemeade Parkway
Carrollton, TX 75007
Contact: Lynn Keckonen
Phone: (972) 492-2448
FAX: N/A
Office Hours: 6:30 a.m. - 6:30 p.m.
E-MAIL: N/A Web Site: N/A
Accreditation: TDPRS
Grades: 6 weeks - 12 years

Peanut Gallery, The
5740 N. Colony Blvd.
Colony, TX 75056
Contact: Christie Adams
Phone: (972) 625-9867
FAX: N/A
Office Hours: 6:30 a.m. - 6:30 p.m.
E-MAIL: N/A Web Site: N/A
Accreditation: TDPRS
Grades: 6 weeks - 12 years

Peanut Gallery, The

8061 Walnut Hill
Dallas, TX 75231
Contact: Sylvia McMahon
Phone: (214) 696-2882
FAX: N/A
Office Hours: 6:30 a.m. - 6:30 p.m.
E-MAIL: N/A Web Site: N/A
Accreditation: TDPRS
Grades: 6 weeks - 5 years

Peanut Gallery, The

2100 N. Greenville Ave.
Richardson, TX 75082
Contact: Teresa Detrick, Director
Phone: (972) 907-9891
FAX: (972) 907-9895
Office Hours: 7:00 a.m. - 6:15 p.m.
E-MAIL: N/A Web Site: N/A
Accreditation: NAEYC
Grades: 6 weeks - 5 years

Preston Hollow Presbyterian School

9800 Preston Road
Dallas, TX 75230
Contact: Sheila Phaneuf, Director
Phone: (214) 368-3886
FAX: (214) 368-2255
Office Hours: 8:00 a.m. - 4:00 p.m.
E-MAIL: s.phaneuf@phps.org Web Site: www.phps.org
Accreditation: ASESA/ Alternative
Grades: 1st grade - 6th grade
Page(s): 293-295

Preston Meadows Montessori
6912 Ohio Drive
Plano, TX 75024
Contact: Sheila Sherwood
Phone: (972) 596-7094
FAX: (972) 596-8665
Office Hours: 8:00 a.m. - 5:00 p.m.
E-MAIL: N/A   Web Site: N/A
Accreditation: MEPI, Montessori
Grade: Preschool - Kindergarten
Page(s): 363-365

Preston-Royal Preschool
5600 Royal Lane
Dallas, TX 75229
Contact: Carol Stewart, Director
Phone: (214) 987-3446
FAX: (214) 369-8939
Office Hours: 8:30 a.m. - 2:00 p.m.
E-MAIL: N/A Web Site: N/A
Accreditation: NAEYC
Grades: 2 years - Preschool

Prestonwood Christian Academy
15720 Hillcrest
Dallas, TX 75248
Contact: Donna Mowrey, Principal
Phone: (972) 404-9796
FAX: 972-661-9886
Office Hours: 8:00 a.m. - 4:30 p.m.
E-MAIL: N/A Web Site: pwbc.org/pca.html
Accreditation: TDPRS
Grades: 4 yrs - 10th grade
Page(s): 423-425

Primrose School at Chase Oaks

6525 Chase Oaks
Plano, TX 75023
Contact: Rochelle Strandstra
Phone: (972) 517-1173
FAX: (972) 517-1173
Office Hours: 6:30 a.m. - 6:30 p.m.
E-MAIL: N/A Web Site: N/A
Accreditation: SACS/ TDPRS
Grades: Infant - 4 years

Prince of Peace Catholic School

5100 Plano Parkway West
Plano, TX 75093
Contact: Sandra Camillo
Phone: (972) 380-5505
FAX: (972) 380-5162
Office Hours: 7:30 a.m. - 4:00 p.m.
E-MAIL: scamillo@popschool.net Web Site: www.popschool.net
Accreditation: TCCED
Grades: Kindergarten - 8th grade

Prince of Peace Christian School

4000 N. Midway Road
Carrollton, TX 75007
Contact: Marilyn Hancock
Phone: (972) 447-9887 Ext. #460
FAX: (972) 447-0877
Office Hours: 7:30 a.m. - 5:00 p.m.
E-MAIL: mhancock@popcs.net Web Site: www.popcs.net
Accreditation: LSAC/ TDPRS
Grades: 3 years - 8th grade

Providence Christian School of Texas

5002 W. Lovers Lane
Dallas, TX 75209
Contact: James R. O'Dea
Phone: (214) 691-1030
FAX: (214) 691-9189
Office Hours: 7:30 a.m. - 4:00 p.m.
E-MAIL: jodea6654@aol.com Web Site: N/A
Accreditation: TDPRS
Grades: 4 years - 9th grade
Page(s): 426-428

Rainbow Connection Preschool & Kindergarten

1651 E. Campbell Road
Richardson, TX 75082
Contact: Naomi Hurst, Administrator; Phyllis Compton, Educational Director
Phone: (972) 644-0283
FAX: (972) 231-7093
Office Hours: 8:15 a.m. - 3:45 p.m.
E-MAIL: N/A Web Site: N/A
Accreditation: NAEYC
Grades: Preschool - Kindergarten

Redeemer Lutheran School

4513 Williams Road
Ft. Worth, TX 76116
Contact: James E. Wenzel, Principal
Phone: (817) 560-0032
FAX: (817) 560-0031
Office Hours: 8:00 a.m. - 4:00 p.m.
E-MAIL: wenzelje@flash.net Web Site: N/A
Accreditation: LSAC
Grades: 3 years - 9th grade

Redeemer Montessori School

120 E. Rochelle
Irving, TX 75062
Contact: Susan Story, Director
Phone: (972) 257-3517
FAX: (972) 255-4173
Office Hours: 8:00 a.m. - 4:00 p.m.
E-MAIL: N/A Web Site: N/A
Accreditation: Montessori
Grades: 2 1/2 years - 5th grade
Page(s): 366-368

Richardson Adventist School

1201 W. Beltline Road
Richardson, TX 75080
Contact: Stephan Gray
Phone: (972) 238-1183
FAX: (972) 644-3488
Office Hours: 7:30 a.m. - 5:00 p.m.
E-MAIL: ras1201@airmail.net Web Site: N/A
Accreditation: TSDA
Grades: Kindergarten - 10th grade
Page(s): 230-232

Rise School of Dallas, The

5923 Royal Lane
Dallas, TX 75230
Contact: Carol Kratville
Phone: (214) 373-4666
FAX: (214) 373-6545
Office Hours: 8:00 a.m. - 4:00 p.m.
E-MAIL: risedal@swbell.net Web Site: www.RISESCHOOL.com
Accreditation: Curriculum Alternative
Grades: Preschool
Page(s): 323-325

Rosemeade Baptist Christian School

1225 E. Rosemeade Pkwy
Carrollton, TX 75007
Contact: Sharon Potter, School Administrator
Phone: (972) 492-4253
FAX: (972) 394-7519
Office Hours: 7:45 a.m. - 4:00 p.m.
E-MAIL: dspotter@msn.com   Web Site: N/A
Accreditation: TDPRS
Grades: Kindergarten - 5th grade
Page(s): 429-431

Rowlett Christian Academy

8200 Schrade Rd.
Rowlett, TX. 75088
Contact: Terri Chaffin
Phone: (972) 412 - 7761
FAX: (972) 475-4403
Office Hours: 7:30 am -6:00 pm
E-MAIL: N/A Web Site: N/A
Accreditation: ACTS
Grades: 3 years - 12th grade

St. Alban's Episcopal School

911 S. Davis
Arlington, TX 76013
Contact: Kathy Bonds, Assistant Headmaster
Phone: (817) 460-6071
FAX: (817) 860-6816
Office Hours: 8:00 a.m. - 4:00 p.m.
E-MAIL: N/A Web Site: N/A
Accreditation: SAES
Grades: 3 years - 9th grade

St. Alcuin Montessori

6144 Churchill Way
Dallas, TX 75230
Contact: Peggy Larson, Director of Admission
Phone: (972) 239-1745
FAX: (972) 934-8727
Office Hours: 7:30 a.m. - 5:00 p.m.
E-MAIL: peg@saintalcuin.org Web Site: www.saintalcuin.org
Accreditation: AMI/ ISAS
Grades: 18 months - 8th grade
Page(s): 369-371

St. Andrew's Episcopal School

727 Hill Street
Grand Prairie, TX 75050
Contact: Betty Meek, Head of School
Phone: (972) 262-3817
FAX: (972) 264-3730
Office Hours: 9:00 a.m. - 4:00 p.m.
E-MAIL: N/A Web Site: N/A
Accreditation: SAES pending
Grades: 3 years - 5th grade
Page(s): 178-180

St. Bernard of Clairvaux

1420 Old Gate Lane
Dallas, TX 75218
Contact: Margaret Schmoeckel
Phone: (214) 321-2897
FAX: (214) 321-4060
Office Hours: 7:30 a.m. - 3:30 p.m.
E-MAIL: N/A Web Site: www.non-profits.org/stbernard
Accreditation: TCCED
Grades: Kindergarten - 8th grade
Page(s): 216-219

St. Christopher Montessori
7900 Lovers Lane
Dallas, TX 75225
Contact: Bettye or Becky Meyerson
Phone: (214) 363-9391
FAX: (214) 363-2795
Office Hours: 7:30 a.m. - 6:00 p.m.
E-MAIL: N/A   Web Site: N/A
Accreditation: AMS/ Montessori
Grades: 2 years - 3rd grade
Page(s): 372-374

St. Elizabeth of Hungary Catholic School
4019 South Hampton
Dallas, TX 75224
Contact: Patrick Magee, Principal
Phone: (214) 331-5139
FAX: (214) 467-4346
Office Hours: 7:30 a.m. - 4:00 p.m.
E-MAIL: N/A Web Sie: N/A
Accreditation: TCCED
Grades: 3 years - 8th grade

St. James Episcopal Montessori
9845 McCree
Dallas, TX 75238
Contact: Lisa Wilson, Adm. Assistant
Phone: (214) 348-1349
FAX: (214) 348-1368
Office Hours: 7:30 a.m. - 3:30 p.m.
E-MAIL: N/A Web Site: N/A
Accreditation: NAIS/ SAES/ Montessori
Grades: 2 years - 6th grade
Page(s): 375-377

St. John the Apostle Catholic School

7421 Glenview Drive
Ft. Worth, TX 76180
Contact: Erin Finn
Phone: (817) 284-2228
Fax: (817) 284-1800
Office Hours: 7:45 a.m. - 3:45 p.m.
E-MAIL: N/A   Web Site: www.stjs.org
Accreditation: TCCED
Grades: 3 years - 8th grade

St. John's Episcopal School

848 Harter Road
Dallas, TX 75218
Contact: Nancy Jacobs
Phone: (214) 328-9131
FAX: (214) 320-0205
Office Hours: 8:00 a.m. - 4:00 p.m.
E-MAIL: N/A Web Site: N/A
Accreditation: ISAS
Grades: 4 years - 8th grade

St. Mark's School of Texas

10600 Preston Road
Dallas, TX 75230-4000
Contact: Director of Admissions
Phone: (214) 346-8700
FAX: (214) 346-8701
Office Hours: 8:00 a.m. - 4:30 p.m.
E-MAIL: admission@smtexas.org Web Site: www.smtexas.org
Accreditation: ISAS
Grades: 1st grade - 12th grade
Page(s): 73

St. Mark's the Avangelist Catholic School
1201 Alma
Plano, TX 75075
Contact: Jo Arata
Phone: (972) 578-0610
FAX: (972) 423-3299
Office Hours: 7:45 a.m. - 4:00 p.m.
E-MAIL: N/A   Web Site: www.stmarkcatholicschool.com
Accreditation: TCCED
Grades: Kindergarten - 8th grade

St. Mary of Carmel
1716 Singleton Blvd
Dallas, TX 75212
Contact: Christina Clem
Phone: (214) 748-2934
FAX: (214) 760-9052
Office Hours: 8:00 a.m. - 3:00 p.m.
E-MAIL: N/A Web Site: N/A
Accreditation: TCCED
Grades: 4 years - 8th grade

St. Mary's Catholic School
713 S. Travis
Sherman, TX 75090
Contact: Francis Baird, Principal
Phone: (903) 893-2127
FAX: (903) 813-5489
Office Hours: 7:30 a.m. - 4:00 p.m.
E-MAIL: StMarysch@texoma.net Web Site: N/A
Accreditation: TCCED
Grades: 3 years - 6th grade
Page(s): 220-222

St. Monica Catholic School
4140 Walnut Hill Lane
Dallas, TX 75229
Contact: Roberta Allen, Secretary
Phone: (214) 351-5688
FAX: (214) 352-2608
Office Hours: 8:00 a.m. - 4:00 p.m.
E-MAIL: offsms@cathedral.org Web Site: www.stmonicaschool.org
Accreditation: TCCED
Grades: Kindergarten - 8th grade
Page(s): 223-225

St. Patrick School
9635 Ferndale Road
Dallas, TX 75238
Contact: Sister Bernarda Bludau
Phone: (214) 348-8070
FAX: (214) 503-7230
Office Hours: 7:30 a.m. - 4:00 p.m.
E-MAIL: saintpat@airmail.net Web Site: N/A
Accreditation: TCCED
Grades: 3 years - 8th grade

St. Paul Lutheran
1800 West Freeway
Ft. Worth, TX 76102
Contact: Janice Marut, Interim Principal
Phone: (817) 332-2281
FAX: (817) 332-2640
Office Hours: 8:00 a.m. - 5:00 p.m.
E-MAIL: stpaul@flash.net Web Site: N/A
Accreditation: LSAC
Grades: 4 years - 8th grade

St. Paul the Apostle

720 S. Floyd Road
Richardson, TX 75080
Contact: Mary C. Williams, Principal
Phone: (972) 235-3263
FAX: (972) 690-1542
Office Hours: 7:30 a.m. - 4:00 p.m.
E-MAIL: stpaul@airmail.net Web Site: N/A
Accreditation: TCCED
Grades: Kindergarten - 8th grade
Page(s): 226-228

St. Philip the Apostle Catholic School

8151 Military Parkway
Dallas, TX 75227
Contact: Mrs. Shirley Lange
Phone: (214) 381-4973
FAX: (214) 381-0466
Office Hours: 7:30 a.m. - 4:00 p.m.
E-MAIL: N/A Web Site: N/A
Accreditation: TCCED
Grades: Kindergarten - 8th grade

St. Philip's School

1600 Pennsylvania Avenue
Dallas, TX 75215
Contact: Michele Robinson
Phone: (214) 421-5221 ext. 14
FAX: (214) 428-5371
Office Hours: 8:00 a.m. - 5:30 p.m.
E-MAIL: michele.rochon@stphilips.com Web Site: N/A
Accreditation: ISAS
Grades: 3 years - 6th grade

St. Pius X Catholic School
3030 Gus Thomasson Road
Dallas, TX 75228
Contact: Church Office
Phone: (972) 279-2339 or (972) 279-6155
FAX: (972) 686-7510
Office Hours: N/A
E-MAIL: N/A Web Site: N/A
Accreditation: TCCED
Grades: Kindergarten - 8th grade

St. Rita School
12525 Inwood Road
Dallas, TX 75244
Contact: Pam Neville, Director of Admissions
Phone: (972) 239-3203
FAX: (972) 934-0657
Office Hours: 7:30 a.m. - 4:30 p.m.
E-MAIL: strita@airmail.net Web Site: www.strita.net
Accreditation: TCCED
Grades: Kindergarten - 8th grade

St. Therese Academy
2700 Finley Road
Irving, TX 75062
Contact: Mrs. Ellen Thomas, Headmaster
Phone: (972) 252-3000
FAX: (972) 570-1986
Office Hours: 8:00 a.m. - 4:00 p.m.
E-MAIL: N/A Web Site: N/A
Accreditation: NAPCIS pending
Grades: 4 years - 12th grade
Page(s): 246-248

St. Thomas Aquinas
3741 Abrams
Dallas, TX 75204
Contact: Dr. Carole Stabile
Phone: (214) 826-0566
FAX: (214) 826-0251
Office Hours: 7:30 a.m. - 4:00 p.m.
E-MAIL: cstabile.sta@esp.net Web Site: www.stthomasaquinas.org/prod01.htm
Accreditation: TCCED
Grades: 3 years - 8th grade

St. Vincent's Episcopal School
1300 Forest Ridge Drive
Bedford, TX 76022
Contact: Janet Blakeman, Headmaster
Phone: (817) 354-7979
FAX: (817) 354-5073
Office Hours: 8:00 a.m. - 4:00 p.m.
E-MAIL: sves@sves.org Web Site: www.sves.org
Accreditation: SAES/ TANS
Grades: 3 years - 6th grade
Page(s): 181-183

Schreiber Methodist Preschool
4525 Rickover Drive
Dallas, TX 75244
Contact: Marilyn Hodge
Phone: (972) 387-8191
FAX: (972) 387-0298
Office Hours: 8:30 a.m. - 12:30 p.m. (M); 8:30 a.m. - 2:30 p.m.
  (T-TH); 8:30 a.m. - 3:00 p.m. (F)
E-MAIL: N/A Web Site: N/A
Accreditation: NAEYC
Grades: Kindergarten, MDO

Scofield Christian School

7730 Abrams Road
Dallas, TX 75231
Contact: Ray Klodzinski, Principal
Phone: (214) 349-6843
FAX: (214) 342-2061
Office Hours: 8:00 a.m. - 4:00 p.m.
E-MAIL: SCSCH@Scofield.org Web Site: www.scofield.org
Accreditation: ACSI
Grades: 3 years - 6th grade
Page(s): 40-42

Selwyn School

3333 University Drive West
Denton, TX 76207
Contact: Director of Admission
Phone: (940) 382-6771
FAX: (940) 383-0704
Office Hours: 8:00 a.m. - 5:00 p.m.
E-MAIL: selwyn@iglobal.net Web Site: N/A
Accreditation: ISAS
Grades: 13 months - 8th grade
Page(s): 74-76

Shady Grove Christian Academy

1829 W. Shady Grove Rd
Grand Prairie, TX 75050
Contact: Frank Lugenheim
Phone: (972) 313-2431
FAX: (972) 313-2410
Office Hours: 8:00 a.m. - 4:00 p.m.
E-MAIL: N/A Web Site: web2.airmail.net/SGCA
Accreditation: ACSI
Grades: Kindergarten - 12th grade

Shelton School and Evaluation Center
15720 Hillcrest
Dallas, TX 75248
Contact: Diann Slaton, Admission Director
Phone: (972) 774-1772
FAX: (972) 991-3977
 Office Hours: 8:00 a.m. - 4:00 p.m.
E-MAIL: webmaster@shelton.org Web Site: www.shelton.org
Accreditation: SACS/ Alternative
Grades: 3 years - 12th grade
Page(s): 296-298

Sloan School
3131 N. O'Conner Road
Irving, TX 75062
Contact: Christy Sloan, Director
Phone: (972) 659-1199
FAX: (972) 855-6070
Office Hours: N/A
E-MAIL: N/A   Web Site: N/A
Accreditation: TDPRS
Grades: 2 1/2 years - 3rd grade

Smart Start Early Childhood Education Center
109 Natches Trace Drive
Coppell, TX 75019
Contact: Dee Jammal, Owner & Director
Phone: (972) 221-9774
FAX: N/A
Office Hours: 9:00 a.m. - 4:00 p.m.
E-MAIL: N/A   Web Site: N/A
Accreditation: TDPRS
Grades: 2 years - Preschool

Solomon Schechter Academy of Dallas

18011 Hillcrest Road
Dallas, TX 75252
Contact: Ms. Judi Glazer, Registrar
Phone: (972) 248-3032
FAX: (972) 248-0695
Office Hours: 7:30 a.m. - 6:00 p.m.
E-MAIL: N/A Web Site: N/A
Accreditation: SACS
Grades: 18 months - 8th grade
Page(s): 155-157

Southern Methodist University Study Skills Classes

P.O. Box 750384
Dallas, TX 75275
Contact: Nell Carvell, Director of Learning Therapy
Phone: (214) 768-2223
FAX: (214) 768-1071
Office Hours: 8:30 a.m. - 5:00 p.m.
E-MAIL: Learning.Therapy@smu.edu
Web Site: www.smu.edu/~dess/learning_therapy.html
Accreditation: SACS/ Alternative
Grades: 7th grade - 12th grade

Southwest Academy

600 S. Jupiter
Allen, TX 75002-4065
Contact: Beverly Dooley, Ph.D, Executive Director, Principal or Peggy Signall,
M.ED., Vice Principal
Phone: (972) 359-8291
FAX: (972) 340-6609
Office Hours: 8:00 a.m. - 4:00 p.m.
E-MAIL: swacad@buz.net Web Site: N/A
Accreditation: SACS/ TAAPS/ Alternative
Grades: 3 years - 8th grade
Page(s): 299-3020

Star Bright Academy
6000 Custer Road, Bldg. 5
Dallas, TX 75023
Contact: Karen Morrell
Phone: (972) 517-6730
FAX: (972) 379-7056
Office Hours: 10:00 a.m. - 9:00 p.m., Monday - Thursday
E-MAIL: star97bp.abigplanet.com Web Site: N/A
Accreditation: Curriculum Alternative
Grades: 1st grade - 12th grade
Page(s): 326-328

Temple Emanu-El Preschool
8500 Hillcrest
Dallas, TX 75225
Contact: Sheryl Feinberg
Phone: (214) 706-0020
FAX: (214) 706-0025
Office Hours: 9:00 a.m. - 5:00 p.m.
E-MAIL: N/A Web Site: N/A
Accreditation: NAEYC
Grades: 6 months - Kindergarten

Texas Christian Academy
915 WEB
Arlington, TX 76011
Contact: Tim Vanderveer
Phone: (817) 274-5201
FAX: (817) 265-5329
Office Hours: 8:00 a.m. - 4:30 p.m.
E-MAIL: TCA@Cyperramp.com Web Site: N/A
Accreditation: ACSI
Grades: 4 years - 12th grade
Page(s): 43-45

Trinity Christian Academy

17001 Addison Rd.
Addison, TX 75001
Contact: Mary Helen Noland
Phone: (972) 931-8325
FAX: (972) 931-8923
Office Hours: 8:00 a.m. - 3:30 p.m.
E-MAIL: N/A Web Site: www.trinitychristian.com
Accreditation: ACSI/ SACS/ TANS
Grades: Kindergarten - 12th grade
Page(s): 158-160

Trinity Christian School

1231 E. Pleasant Run Road
Cedar Hill, TX 75104
Contact: Chet Steele, Headmaster
Phone: (972) 291-2501
FAX: (972) 291-4739
Office Hours: 7:30 a.m. - 4:30 p.m.
E-MAIL: N/A Web Site: www.trinityministries.org
Accreditation: ICAA/ ACTS
Grades: 3 years - 12th grade
Page(s): 55-57

Trinity Episcopal Preschool

3401 Bellaire Drive South
Ft. Worth, TX 76109
Contact: Dainty Kostohryz
Phone: (817) 926-0750
FAX: N/A
Office Hours: 9:00 a.m. - 12:00 p.m.
E-MAIL: N/A Web Site: N/A
Accreditation: TDPRS/ Montessori
Grades: 2 years - 5 years

Trinity Lyceum
Permanent address:
305 South West
Arlington, TX 76010
Temporary address while remodeling:
2315 Crown Colony Drive
Arlington, TX 76011
Contact: Bernice Reid
Phone: (817) 469-6895
FAX: (817) 261-0925
Office Hours: 8:15 a.m. - 4:30 p.m.
E-MAIL: N/A Web Site: N/A
Accreditation: ACSI
Grades: 4 years - 12th grade
Page(s): 46-48

Trinity Valley School
7500 Dutch Branch Road
Ft. Worth, TX 76132
Contact: Judith Kinser
Phone: (817) 321-0100
FAX: (817) 321-0105
Office Hours: 8:00 a.m. - 4:00 p.m.
E-MAIL: tvs@ns.trinityvalleyschool.org Web Site: www.trinityvalleyschool.org
Accreditation: ISAS
Grades: Kindergarten - 12th grade
Page(s): 77-79

Tyler Street Christian Academy
927 West Tenth Street
Dallas, TX 75208
Contact: Karen J. Egger
Phone: (214) 941-9717
FAX: (214) 941-0324
Office Hours: 7:30 a.m. - 4:15 p.m.
E-MAIL: tsca@dallas.net Web Site: N/A
Accreditation: SACS
Grades: 3 years - 12th grade

Ursuline Academy of Dallas

4900 Walnut Hill Lane
Dallas, TX 75229
Contact: Tim Host
Phone: (214) 363-6551
FAX: (214) 363-5524
Office Hours: 10:00 a.m. - 4:00 p.m.
E-MAIL: thost@ursuline.pvt.k12.tx.us Web Site: N/A
Accreditation: ISAS/ TCCED/ SACS
Grades: 9th grade - 12th grade
Page(s): 80-82

Vanguard Preparatory School

4240 Omega
Dallas, TX 75244
Contact: Rosalind Funderburgh
Phone: (972) 404-1616
FAX: (972) 404-1641
Office Hours: 8:05 a.m. - 4:00 p.m.
E-MAIL: N/A Web Site: N/A
Accreditation: ASESA/ SACS/ Alternative
Grades: 4 years - 12th grade
Page(s): 303-305

Walden Preparatory School

14552 Monfort Drive
Dallas, TX 75240
Contact: Pamela Stone
Phone: (972) 233-6883
FAX: (972) 458-4553
Office Hours: 8:00 a.m. - 4:00 p.m.
E-MAIL: waldenprep@aol.com Web Site: N/A
Accreditation: SACS/ Alternative
Grades: 9th grade - 12th grade
Page(s): 306-308

West Plano Montessori School

3425 Ashington Lane
Plano, TX 75023
Contact: J. P. Khandpur, Director
Phone: (972) 618-8844
FAX: (972) 398-1798
Office Hours: 7:00 a.m. - 6:00 p.m.
E-MAIL: info@montessorischool.com Web Site: www.montessorischool.com
Accreditation: Montessori
Grades: 2 years - 1st grade
Page(s): 378-380

Westminster Presbyterian Preschool & Kindergarten

8200 Devonshire Drive
Dallas, TX 75209
Contact: Cristine L. Watson, M.S.
Phone: (214) 350-6155
FAX: (214) 351-0145
Office Hours: 8:30 a.m. - 1:00 p.m. (ext. hrs. TWTH - 2:30 p.m.)
E-MAIL: info@dfwprivateschools.com Web Site: N/A
Accreditation: NAEYC
Grades: Kindergarten, MDO
Page(s): 130-132

Westwood Montessori School

13618 Gamma Road
Dallas, TX 75244
Contact: Heather Lourcey
Phone: (972) 239-8598
FAX: (972) 239-1028
Office Hours: 8:30 a.m. - 3:30 p.m.
E-MAIL: wms1a@airmail.net Web Site: www.Westwoodschool.com
Accreditation: Montessori
Grades: 3 years - 8th grade
Page(s): 381-383

White Lake School, The
501 Oakland Blvd.
Ft. Worth, TX 76103
Contact: Jerry T. Johnson
Phone: (817) 457-6736
FAX: (817) 457-6766
Office Hours: N/A
E-MAIL: white.lake@worldnet.att.net Web Site: N/A
Accreditation: SACS
Grades: 4 years - 6th grade

White Rock Montessori School
1601 Oates Drive
Dallas, TX 75228
Contact: Sue Henry, Director
Phone: (214) 324-5580
FAX: (214) 324-5671
Office Hours: 8:30 a.m. - 5:00 p.m.
E-MAIL: WRMSCHOOL@aol.com Web Site: N/A
Accreditation: Montessori
Grades: 3 years - 8th grade
Page(s): 384-386

White Rock North School
9727 White Rock Trail
Dallas, TX 75238
Contact: Amy Adams, Head of School
Phone: (214) 348-7410
FAX: (214) 348-3109
Office Hours: 9:00 am - 6:00 pm Mon/Fri
E-MAIL: wrnsaaa@aol.com Web Site: N/A
Accreditation: SACS/ Montessori
Grades: 2 1/2 years - 8th grade
Page(s): 161-163

Windsong Montessori School
2825 Valley View #100
Farmers Branch, TX 75234
Contact: Julia "Jere" Albanesi
Phone: (972) 620-2466
FAX: (972) 620-2466
Office Hours: 7:30 a.m. - 6:00 p.m.
E-MAIL: N/A Web Site: N/A
Accreditation: Montessori
Grades: 2 1/2 years - 5th grade
Page(s): 387-389

Winston School, The
5707 Royal Lane
Dallas, TX 75229
Contact: Amy C. Smith
Phone: (214) 691-6950
FAX: (214) 691-1509
Office Hours: 8:00 a.m. -4:00 p.m.
E-MAIL: admissions@winston-school.org Web Site: www.winston-school.org
Accreditation: ISAS/ NAIS/ Alternative
Grades: 1st grade - 12th grade
Page(s): 309-312

Wise Academy, The
6930 Alpha Road
Dallas, TX 75240
Contact: Susan Horowitz, Head of School
Phone: (972) 789-1800
FAX: (972) 789-1801
Office Hours: 8:00 a.m. - 4:00 p.m.
E-MAIL: headwise@msn.com Web Site: N/A
Accreditation: SACS pending
Grades: 1st grade - 4th grade
Page(s): 164-166

Yavneh Academy of Dallas

9401 Douglas Avenue
Dallas, TX 75225
Contact: Rabbi Scott Steinman
Phone: (214) 363-7631
FAX: (214) 363-5684
Office Hours: 9:00 a.m. - 5:00 p.m.
E-MAIL: yavneh@why.net Web Site: N/A
Accreditation: TAAPS
Grades: 9th grade - 12th grade

Zion Lutheran School

6121 East Lovers Lane
Dallas, TX 75214
Contact: Douglas C. Molin, Principal
Phone: (214) 363-1630
FAX: (214) 361-2049
Office Hours: 8:00 a.m. - 5:00 p.m.
E-MAIL: dmolin@ziondallas.org Web Site: N/A
Accreditation: LSAC/ NLSA/ TANS
Grades: 3 years - 8th grade, MDO
Page(s): 97-99

NOTES